Rackets: Volume I

The Drug War:
A Trillion Dollar Con Game

Brian Saady

© 2017 by Brian Saady. All rights reserved.

Prerogative Publishing

Although every precaution has been taken to verify the accuracy of the information contained herein, the author and publisher assume no responsibility for any errors or omissions. No liability is assumed for damages that may result from the use of information contained within.

Book cover design by Daniel Ryves

Images for the cover art were derived from bigstockphoto.com

Printed in the U.S.A.

First Edition / April 2017

ISBN: 978-0-9987245-0-8

www.briansaady.com

CONTENTS

Introduction 1

1. Prison Industrial Complex 6
2. The Criminalization of Drugs 29
3. Marriage of Drug Cartels and "Too Big To Fail" Banks 53
4. Corporate Sponsored Drug War 68
5. The Economic Impact From Legal Marijuana 84
6. Medical Marijuana and Marijuana Myths 100
7. Lessons From the Prohibition of Alcohol and Harm Reduction 118
8. Hypocrisy 140
9. The Race Factor 161
10. The Cold War 2.0 183
11. The War on Terror, Civil Liberties, and Democracy 202
12. Government Protected Drug Trafficking Part I 224
13. Government Protected Drug Trafficking Part II 249

Names and Organizations 269

References and Notes 272

ACKNOWLEDGEMENTS

"That was so well-written, Brian. It was…it was…as though I had written it *myself*."

"Uncle Freddy"

Those words came from a friend of mine (my former boss) several years ago when reviewing some of my work. We've had a few good laughs about that comment since then. Nevertheless, he loved my writing and he gave me several editorial duties at work. I had dreamed of becoming an author for several years, but I hadn't taken any steps toward accomplishing that vision. However, those work assignments sparked something inside of me that prompted me to pursue my dream.

I'd like to thank all of my friends and family members who supported me along the way. In particular, I'd like to thank my friends, Brian Sharff and Dan Luby. You both provided me with the praise and constructive criticism that was necessary to complete an endeavor like this. Also, this project would never have materialized without the technical assistance from my friend, Cory Waters.

I'd also like to thank my wife, Zanilia. Your help was invaluable. Your critical analysis challenged me to push beyond my mental boundaries. You'll never know how highly I value your opinions. You not only assisted me with numerous tasks, but you also inspired me in so many other ways.

Lastly, I'd like to thank my mom, Marguerite Saady. None of this would have been possible without you. I could have never accomplished my dreams without your help. I can't stress enough the significance of your support. You've been my biggest supporter from the beginning to the end. I know that you spent countless hours refining these books in the pursuit of perfection. In fact, this book series would never have been published without your hard work, insight, eye for detail, corrections, revisions, among numerous other efforts.

Thank You!

INTRODUCTION

President-elect Barack Obama conducted a series of town hall meetings during his cross country "Mainstreet Tour." On December 4, 2009, there was a memorable moment in Allentown, PA. An audible buzz emerged from the crowd when it came time for questions from the audience. A large group of people eagerly pointed to one young man in hopes that Obama would call upon him. Obama said, "Whoa, whoa, whoa, whoa, whoa. Alright, I'll make you first just because everyone is very excited about this young man asking a question."

The young man was a sophomore at nearby Lehigh Carbon Community College and based on his studies of criminology he asked if the President had considered legalizing prostitution, gambling, drugs, and non-violent crime. The auditorium immediately filled with laughter. Obama handled it comically to the amusement of the audience by saying, "I appreciate the boldness of your question -- That will not be my job strategy." Again, the crowd laughed, but he then tried to save any embarrassment for the student by saying, "First of all, part of what you're supposed to do in college is question conventional wisdom. So you're doing exactly what you're supposed to be doing which is thinking in new ways about things." With that said, the President did genuinely react in a funny way, but the suggestion of legalizing drugs, prostitution, and gambling shouldn't elicit laughter in an auditorium full of adults.

It's easy to assume that someone with these libertarian or progressive ideals might yearn for a more debaucherous culture. However, that isn't an accurate presumption. These aren't frivolous issues. You can learn a great deal about a country solely based upon its policies regarding these three vices. Those policies alone are an immediate indicator of how much importance the country places on personal freedom, whether it is left-of-center or right-of-center, and if religion factors into governmental policies. Further examination of these issues gives tremendous insight into a country's history, culture, and its political, economic, and criminal justice systems, along with much more.

There is a common thread among these particular vice crimes-- the cure is worse than the disease. Our government has a profit incentive for maintaining those laws. Drugs, gambling, and prostitution are rackets in multiple senses of the word. First, these are illegal, underground activities. Secondly, the *prohibition* of drugs, gambling, and prostitution is a racket too, i.e. a dishonest and lucrative business scheme. Countless public officials have based their "law and order" reputations on suppressing these highly-visible, easily-investigated offenses while investigations for more serious crimes have been neglected.

The average person grasps that the real purpose behind police speed traps is raising revenue for the government, but many people are unfamiliar with the term "prison industrial complex." The rapid rise in the American prison population, as a result of the drug war, has created a vast bureaucracy, which now employs a massive voting bloc. They have a conflict of interest which opposes liberalizing our criminal justice system. Consequently, their strength in numbers has shaped our policies and thwarted common sense reforms in a similar manner that forced Eisenhower to warn about the military industrial complex.

By statute, we're all innocent until proven guilty, but, in reality, the scales of justice lean in the opposite direction. Much of that has to do with the fact that the drug war has put an undue burden on our courts. In fact, the police can literally take your money under the pretense of illegal drug activity, without making an arrest, thereby stripping your right to due process. In those cases of civil asset forfeiture, you must sue the government and prove your innocence to retrieve your property.

Likewise, the drug war is directly responsible for a system that has fundamentally corrupted the way law enforcement functions. Now, roughly half of the federal prison population is incarcerated for drug crimes. Every police department now has a direct financial incentive to crack down on illegal drugs, rather than pursue more urgent criminal cases. The result is a prison population that has nearly quintupled since the Reagan administration escalated the drug war. That explosive growth has even led the government to outsource our prisons to for-profit, publicly-traded corporations. These few companies now represent a multi-billion dollar industry and have perverted the political process, through campaign donations and lobbyists, to ensure there is an increasing prison population in the future.

In any event, drug addiction is a health issue, not one for the criminal justice system. Therefore, the most addictive drugs such as heroin, cocaine, and methamphetamine should be decriminalized after several harm reduction policies have been implemented, including needle exchange programs, heroin maintenance programs, among others. These ideas may initially seem revolutionary, but the lessons for harm reduction are not hypothetical. There are several noteworthy policies from around the world, although these social science experiments aren't well-known in the U.S.

Also, the health risks from marijuana have been severely exaggerated by the government, while research into marijuana's numerous medicinal benefits has been highly censored. Any independent person who looks into the scientific research should conclude that there is no practical reason for keeping it illegal. Marijuana needs to be legalized and regulated. Fortunately, we're finally at a tipping point when the majority of Americans support legalization, and that's primarily due to the substantial economic benefits. Hemp, marijuana's highly mischaracterized sister plant, has unbelievable economic potential as well. However, there still is an uphill battle to legalize both of these cash crops.

As you probably know, the term "con game" is short for a "confidence game" in which someone is ripped off by someone else preying upon his trust. In the same fashion, the government has ripped off the taxpayers to the tune of over $1 trillion dollars! The drug war is still being waged because the average American has been fed a full diet of propaganda. You've been lied to on so many fronts. For instance, the justification behind the first drug laws was based on openly racist fears. Legislators had some legitimate concern for the potential harm to society from drug addiction; however, their real fear was that minorities might have access to these drugs en masse. After all, minorities were viewed as less than human. That may seem like hyperbole, but the earliest drug legislation was drafted with language that openly targeted "uncivilized races." On the other hand, it is no longer socially acceptable for legislators to speak publicly in those terms. Drug laws are now officially colorblind by statute, but they are unofficially enforced differently. In fact, there is still a large contingent of society that isn't offended by the glaring statistical discrepancies for minorities imprisoned for drug crimes.

Nancy Reagan once said, "If you are a casual drug user, you're an accomplice to murder." She couldn't have been more wrong. The *prohibition* of drugs is responsible for an immeasurable level of violence between gangsters, traffickers, and drug cartels. With that said, it would be irresponsible to use inflammatory rhetoric to label drug war supporters as "accomplices to murder." However, it is imperative that we recognize the drug war for what it is -- a racket. The drug war exemplifies the extortion-related definition of "racketeering" in which an entity offers to solve a problem that wouldn't exist without its involvement.

It's obvious to anyone that the drug war is most profitable for the criminals in the drug cartels. What's much less obvious is that several major corporations also want to maintain the drug war to benefit their bottom line. In fact, the first federal marijuana law was seemingly drafted by a few powerful corporate interests and passed in a dubious fashion. This book examines that scandal in thorough detail. At a minimum, you will witness some examples demonstrating our nation's vulnerability to political corruption. Most likely, you will conclude that the initial basis behind our nation's first federal marijuana law was a complete fraud.

It's shocking how many seemingly innocuous names from the S&P 500 have been complicit with drug trafficking. In fact, most of the "too big to fail" banks have been caught laundering money for the major cartels, but they've only been slapped on the wrist. Big business fully supports the drug war with an army of highly compensated lobbyists and media stooges. In fact, big pharma funds the propaganda for the drug war. Nonetheless, the hypocrisy is lost on so many people because the most deadly drugs are legal and advertised on TV. Furthermore, our elected officials are even more hypocritical. Numerous diehard conservative drug warriors have suddenly become quite liberal when drug laws affected them personally. The Republicans always warn about the nanny state and want to cut government spending, all while wholeheartedly supporting tougher drug laws. Meanwhile, the Democrats, who are just as easily corrupted by corporate special interests, also ignore the lessons from the prohibition of alcohol.

There have been many lies involved with the war on drugs, but one aspect has been very direct; it's a war against American citizens. The drug war has been the justification for numerous laws that have sacrificed our constitutional rights. In an odd way, the drug war has intertwined with the Cold War and the War on Terror. Consequently, a potentially Orwellian technology surveillance state is in the making in reaction to our national security fears. However, draconian laws such as the PATRIOT Act are generally used to prosecute simple drug cases, not terrorism. The NSA's bulk data collection program received a lot of media attention after the Edward Snowden leaks. However, most people are unaware that the DEA developed a similar program that *preceded* and set the blueprint for the NSA's program.

The drug war has also served as a red herring behind our covert military efforts internationally. The U.S. funds "counternarcotics" operations in several countries. However, those programs, time and time again, serve as a stimulus package for the military industrial complex and enable various extreme right-wing groups. Thus, the drug war supports military coups and political repression throughout Latin America, a rising police state in Mexico, a developing "corporatocracy" in Honduras, and domestic terrorism in Colombia, among other atrocities.

The worst aspect of the drug war has been saved for last. Despite decades of "Just Say No" indoctrination, the U.S. government has surreptitiously been complicit with illegal drug trafficking for nearly a century. Our government has a long history with cherry picking their goals with the drug war in favor of geopolitics. In other words, our intelligence and military leaders have often prioritized our national security concerns over drug laws. In short, history has a way of repeating itself and our military allies have often been major drug traffickers, yet our top leaders have habitually looked the other way. That was the case in WWII, the Vietnam War, Iran-Contra, Afghanistan, among many other examples. To wrap up, what you've just read is filled with strong statements and may be shocking, but there is a litany of documentation to prove these assertions.

1

"We could be czars."

There are public service announcements that warn how a DUI will cost you about $10,000. Those costs include fines, court fees, legal fees, jail costs, bail bonds, probation services, etc. Those advertisements subtly illustrate how the "prison industrial complex" directly benefits from crime. That term refers to all of the sectors that benefit from a massive prison population, including law enforcement, prisons, and the entire legal system. This system employs millions of Americans as police officers, lawyers, judges, paralegals, parole officers, correctional officers, etc.

The prison industrial complex obviously has an incentive to keep drugs illegal. Their strength in numbers allows for a tremendous political influence from a large voting bloc with massive lobbying power. For example, *CNBC* found that nearly 800,000 Americans work for the prison industry, which is more than the U.S. auto industry.[1] That figure doesn't include all the other sectors associated with the prison industrial complex such as lawyers, police officers, etc. To be brief, the bureaucracy within the criminal justice system, like many other sectors of government, often acts out of self-interest to increase their funding.

The budget for the Drug Enforcement Administration (DEA) was initially $65 million with 2,775 employees in its first year of 1972. However, that budget has doubled each year on average to over $2.7 billion by 2013 with a staff of 11,053 employees.[2] Therefore, an organization with such a massive infrastructure and explosive growth requires its leaders to project a certain unbending image. As an illustration, the majority of Americans recognize that the drug war has been a failure, but the DEA refuses to acknowledge this fact. Consequently, Roger Warner, author of *Invisible Hand: The Marijuana Business*, had an interview with an official from the DEA and asked him the same question. Of course, the official said that they were winning the war on drugs. Instead of verbally disagreeing, Warner tossed a dime bag of marijuana ($10 worth) on the official's desk. To add insult to injury, that bag had been purchased hours before the interview in the park across the street from the DEA's office in Washington, DC.[3]

The DEA represents only a small portion of the war on drugs, but their track record demonstrates how bureaucratic motivation can dictate policies. For instance, marijuana is obviously a much less dangerous drug than cocaine, heroin, or methamphetamine. Nevertheless, Michele Leonhart, the former head of the DEA, stonewalled and refused to acknowledge this simple fact. She was asked by Congress to state "yes" or "no," if she agreed with this assertion. Instead, she repeatedly said, "I believe all illegal drugs are bad."[4] In a separate testimony, she even warned about the dangers of the legalization of marijuana leading to pets ingesting their owners' marijuana.[5]

Furthermore, the DEA, like many other law enforcement agencies, has unofficially prioritized marijuana arrests. In 2011, the DEA seized 571,189 kilograms of marijuana as opposed to 33,271 kilograms of cocaine, 1,067 kilograms of heroin, and 2,467 kilograms of methamphetamine.[6] In short, the DEA has prioritized marijuana over more dangerous drugs because marijuana is the most commonly used drug, making it "the lowest hanging fruit."

Police departments nationwide have a clear financial interest in keeping drugs illegal because their budgets would be significantly slashed if those laws were repealed. Also, our society generally oversimplifies how to evaluate law enforcement by focusing on the overall quantity of arrests, as opposed to the quality of arrests. Budgetary concerns systematically push police departments to prioritize resources into illegal drugs over other crimes because they're easier arrests.

That same statistic-minded bureaucracy has indirectly created incentives which can defy common sense at times. Stephen Downing, retired Los Angeles Deputy Chief of Police, insists that "federal anti-drug grants (prompt) police officers to abandon real crime victims in our communities in favor of ratcheting up their drug arrest stats."[7] In a surprising twist, the George W. Bush administration made significant cuts to those anti-drug federal grants. However, the Obama administration reversed those cuts by including $3 billion for anti-drug federal grants in the 2009 stimulus package.[8]

The drug war has pushed investigations for some of the most heinous crimes, including rape, to the background. One particular CNN report made in 2013 detailed a woman who had been raped in 1985. She followed up on her case over twenty years later and found out that her rape kit, the test for physical evidence in rape cases, hadn't even been submitted to the crime lab for testing.[9] The crime lab eventually processed her kit, but that was only because she was so persistent. As a result, they found a DNA match for her attacker. However, her attacker couldn't be prosecuted because the statute of limitations had expired. This wasn't an isolated incident as there are a staggering number of rape kits that are sitting in crime labs across the country that haven't been tested. *CBS News* conducted a five-month investigation in 2009 into untested rape kits and found that there were approximately 10,000 untested in Detroit, 5,191 in San Antonio, 3,846 in Houston, and 3,777 in Los Angeles just to name a few cities.[10]

One reason behind this backlog is that rape cases usually don't result in easy convictions, which makes some prosecutors reluctant to go forward with a case. We'd like to think that prosecutors are pursuing the appropriate cases. However, drug convictions are an easy way to pad a resume. Also, budgetary restrictions force rape kits (which cost about $1,500 each) to the back of the line behind drug testing which costs only a few dollars at a time.[11] Stephen Downing also added that the rape kit backlog has occurred partially due to the tremendous number of drug arrests; those court cases can't proceed until the lab test has been completed.[12]

There are clear conflicts of interest within the criminal justice system that jeopardize the right to a fair trial. After all, James Starrs, professor of law and forensic science at George Washington University, contends that crime lab technicians are often functioning, more or less, as "an arm of the prosecution."[13] Due to shows like CSI many people now consider forensic evidence, particularly from the FBI crime lab, to be "the gospel." However, the first FBI whistleblower, Frederic Whitehurst, exposed that some of their technicians had botched evidence and purposely mislead juries with their testimonies.[14]

It's now roughly 20 years later and the FBI has only reviewed 160 out of 2,600 convictions that involved their forensic laboratory. They found that there was flawed forensic testimony in almost every case they reviewed, including 32 instances in which the defendants had already been executed.[15] Furthermore, the FBI announced later that analysts had falsely testified to favor the prosecution in nearly every case involving forensic hair.[16]

There have been some other crime lab scandals, unrelated to the FBI, after Whitehurst went public in the 1990s. One of the most poignant examples came about in 2012 when a chemist from the Massachusetts crime lab, Annie Dookhan, pleaded guilty to producing fake drug test results in potentially thousands of cases. Dookhan wasn't coerced or bribed in any way; instead, she succumbed to systemic pressure. The prosecutors, police, and her supervisors had been thrilled with her efforts because she was two to three times more productive than her colleagues. Eventually, Dookhan was sentenced to three to five years in prison, but that means that she only served a fraction of the time compared to the numerous people she forced into mandatory minimum drug sentences from her falsified evidence.[17]

Another crime lab scandal was uncovered a few months prior in St. Paul, MN. Lauri Traub, the assistant public defender, was verifying results from a drug possession case when she discovered that the lab was run by a police sergeant who had no scientific background. Furthermore, the analysts were completely incompetent. Nevertheless, these officials presented themselves as experts in court on a daily basis.[18] They did so because the criminal justice system clearly values convictions more than acquittals.

Police also have an arrest and statistic oriented culture, but no police department will officially admit to having quotas. One NYPD officer told *The Nation* that the term "activity goals" is now the official term for their quotas.[19] Another NYPD officer offered a warning about quotas with an analogy; a fire department with quotas may need to "start setting fires" to meet their activity goals.[20] That example illustrates the definition of "racketeering" in which an organization offers to solve a problem that wouldn't exist without its involvement.

The pressure to meet quotas takes away an officer's ability to use discretion when appropriate. For example, Justin Hanners, a former police officer in Auburn, AL, described an incident for *Reason Magazine* in which he and his partner spotted an intoxicated man who had been quietly walking on the sidewalk. They questioned him and determined that it was safe to let him walk home without an arrest. However, Hanners' sergeant oversaw that incident and ordered his subordinate to arrest the man because he needed to boost his stats. Despite the direct order, Hanners refused.

Nonetheless, Hanners' partner, arrested the man for public intoxication.[21]

Quotas are the only imaginable explanation for some of the ends-justify-the-means tactics that occur in some drug cases. A disheartening version of *21 Jump Street* unfolded in Riverside, CA. An unsuspecting student suffering from autism, bipolar disorder, Tourette syndrome, and other nervous disorders, was caught in a trap. That young man's first and only friend in school turned out to be an undercover police officer who pressured him to buy marijuana. The undercover officer gave him $20 and claimed that he desperately needed the marijuana because he was dealing with a terrible family situation. Consequently, the young man tried to buy marijuana in school but couldn't find a seller. Ultimately, he resorted to buying half a joint from a homeless man. Regardless, the officer arrested him along with 21 other students, some of whom were also special needs students.[22]

Bureaucracies naturally tend to act out of self-preservation. Hence, police officers who try to reform the system are doing so at great peril. Adhyl Polanco was one of the NYPD officers who blew the whistle about the quota system. He provided audio evidence to the Internal Affairs office and later contacted *The Nation*. Thereupon, the NYPD reacted by arresting Polanco for writing false reports, the same reports that he gave to Internal Affairs.[23] Likewise, Justin Hanners was fired after he filed an official grievance with the Director of Public Safety.[24] For this reason, he insists that positive changes must come from outside of law enforcement because the pressures are too vast within the system.[25]

Police officers face the consequences for not making enough arrests, but they also have indirect financial incentives to make unnecessary arrests. Higher arrest numbers tend to lead to promotions. Also, they don't receive commissions from making an arrest, but police officers can earn overtime pay for working after their shift has ended, such as filling out paperwork and waiting to book an arrestee. Therefore, police can profit by making any arrest, whether necessary or frivolous, towards the end of their shift.[26] As a matter of fact, one officer told *The Nation* about how the police radio is often silent for periods of time until minutes before their shifts change. At that point, numerous petty arrests are heard over the scanners.[27]

Likewise, a report by the *Miami Herald* quoted a retired Metro-Dade Police Maj., Donald Matthews, who stated that his fellow officers flocked to the scene of a DUI "like it was sugar."[28] In some cases, as many as twelve officers were listed as witnesses for simple DUI busts when only one was necessary. Why? All witnesses will be subpoenaed to court, which leads to more overtime pay. Like DUIs, simple vice offenses (such as drugs, gambling, and prostitution) provide opportunities for corrupt cops to boost their salary. The most common term for these kinds of abusive practices is "collars for dollars."[29]

Not every police department abuses overtime pay, but it is seemingly visible in various cities. This may be surprising, but multiple local news broadcasts from cities such as Portland, Albuquerque, Philadelphia, and Houston, among others have reported that some police officers are earning over $100,000 per year.[30] To sum up, most police salaries are relatively modest, but if overtime pay is abused it can really add up.

Given these points, it is important to note that the information in this book isn't aimed at criticizing individual police officers or disparaging law enforcement. Instead, we need to address the systemic flaws of the criminal justice system. After all, improper incentives and consequences can prompt even the noblest officer to make unethical decisions. However, few politicians have been willing to reform any of these issues out of fear of being labeled "soft on crime." By the same token, that dreaded label has spawned some oversimplified choices for policy-making, including "3 strikes laws" and mandatory minimum sentences for drug offenses.

Politics often reigns supreme over sound decisions. Notably, the former U.S. Attorney General John N. Mitchell warned that mandatory minimum sentences were "counterproductive" and "irrational." Bear in mind, Mitchell was no bleeding-heart liberal; he served during the Nixon administration. In fact, he was sentenced to 19 months in prison for his leading role in the Watergate scandal.[31] Nonetheless, Mitchell was correct, and those laws are directly responsible for pushing violent felons out of prison and back into the population. To clarify, violent offenders frequently gain early release before non-violent drug offenders because many violent crimes don't have the same mandatory minimum sentences.[32] Simply put, anyone who supports the drug war, despite the rhetoric, isn't truly "tough on crime."

Simplistic policies like mandatory minimum sentences have taken away a judge's most important duty. Mandatory minimum sentences have shifted the power away from judges and into the hands of the prosecutors as they're the ones who choose which cases to bring to court. The U.S. Sentencing Commission is an independent agency within the judicial system and they detailed this unjust shift of power as early as 1991. In their report, they found that mandatory minimum sentences were condemned by every defense lawyer surveyed; even half of the prosecutors felt the same way.[33]

Mandatory minimum sentences are much harsher than the "tough on crime" crowd realizes. Hence, the drug war is artificially manufacturing an overpopulated prison system. Mark W. Bennett, a federal judge in Iowa, is more than knowledgeable on this subject. He once wrote an op-ed noting that drug cases take up 56% of his docket. He even serves in one of the most ultra-conservative areas of the country, yet he has *never* heard a juror recommend a sentence of a convicted drug offender on par with the mandatory minimum sentence. "(Their recommendations are) always far lower," wrote Bennett.[34]

TV and movies have crafted an unrealistic image of the criminal justice system. Our court system now has to operate with the speed of the fast food industry due to the overwhelming caseload. Over 90% of criminal cases result in plea agreements and federal drug cases result in plea deals at an even higher rate of 97%.[35] The average person pictures the spirited courtroom battles glamorized by the entertainment industry, but the main reason behind so many plea deals is that 80% of criminal defendants can't afford an attorney.[36] Instead, they are awarded a public defender who is drowning in cases.

The sheer number of arrests from the drug war is limiting our court system's ability to conduct a fair and speedy trial. For one thing, there were 1.8 million arrests for drug crimes in 2007, more than any other crime.[37] That piles onto a system that is crumbling. In that same year, there were about 15,000 public defenders who were forced to handle 5.6 million cases![38] It's impossible to adequately handle that kind of caseload.

Defendants often meet their public defender for the first time at their arraignment where they're almost always advised to take the plea agreement. If they don't agree to the plea deal, they face an implied "tax" with harsher penalties for taking their case to trial. We've become so accustomed to this system that we don't question it. However, if you were falsely arrested for a crime, would you think that it's fair to risk a more severe penalty for merely defending yourself? "I tell clients not to take those pleas, but, inside, I ask myself, 'God, what if they start listening to me?'" said one Baltimore public defender.[39]

Public defenders routinely aren't even present at initial bail and release hearings.[40] That's particularly troubling because the for-profit bail bond industry is responsible for a trend in which excessive bail amounts are assessed for non-violent misdemeanor offenses. That industry generates $2 billion a year in revenues and thus donates to like-minded candidates. In addition, most independent bail bond companies are backed by major insurance companies, which have an army of lobbyists at their disposal.[41] Consequently, these special interest groups have placed an undue burden upon the taxpayers.

Today, there are roughly 487,000 Americans in jail, awaiting trial, who are technically innocent until proven guilty.[42] Those prisoners alone cost the taxpayers $9 billion a year.[43] You would assume that those people are accused of violent crimes and represent a danger to society or a flight risk, however, that usually isn't the case. Most of them merely can't afford their bail. As a matter of fact, *Human Rights Watch* found that 87% of people in 2008 who were facing non-felony charges with bail set at $1,000 or less were incarcerated because they were unable to pay.[44] As a result, many people plead guilty because they can't afford bail.

You may wonder, "How much time do average defendants wait in jail before their trials?" Well, no one knows exactly because no federal government agency publishes those official statistics. That fact alone demonstrates how our federal government isn't particularly concerned with this issue. On the other hand, the *New York Daily News* found that accused felons in their state waited over two years on average for their trials.[45]

In contrast, the wait time for misdemeanors is much less. According to former U.S. Attorney General Eric Holder, the average stay is about two weeks for a simple misdemeanor.[46] That may not sound like much, but that wait time represents a punishment even if you're acquitted. You would have most likely lost your job, at a minimum, in that scenario. In some cases, the time spent waiting for trial is much more than the maximum penalty for the crime.

The New York Times demonstrated this by examining a small sample of low-level misdemeanor marijuana possession arrests. The maximum penalty for a first offense for minor possession is three months in jail in New York. However, *The New York Times* found that people who pled not-guilty were unofficially punished by the court system with several, lengthy rescheduling delays. It took 240 days on average before each trial was concluded.[47]

Debtors prisons have also been technically outlawed for most of American history. However, a ruling by the U.S. Supreme Court in 1983 reopened this possibility. At face value, *Bearden v. Georgia* outlawed debtors prisons by stating that people can't be jailed if they can't afford a criminal fine. But, no specific rules were issued for determining if a person can afford the fine.[48] In other words, it's difficult to determine whether someone is a deadbeat or is genuinely unable to pay the penalty.

As you know, the criminal justice system tends to error on the side of imprisonment and, as a result, an increasing number of people are serving time in jail because they have been unable pay the court-imposed fines. One of these instances made national news when a Pennsylvania woman died in jail in 2014. She was serving time because she couldn't pay $2,000 in fines (stemming from her child's truancy). A follow-up report by the *Associated Press* found that since 2000, from her county alone, 1,600 people had been jailed due specifically to truancy fines.[49] Again, there is no federal agency that tracks the exact extent of this issue.

Special interests have clearly had a large part in creating an overflowing prison population. Steve Bogira, author of *Courtroom 302*, noted that Nixon launched the drug war in 1973, the same year that the National Advisory Commission on Criminal Justice Standards and Goals asserted that prison wasn't a solution for reducing crime.[50] They recommended not building any more prisons. Despite the recommendation, 650 state and federal prisons were constructed in the 1980s and 1990s alone.[51]

Now nearly 1 in every 31 American adults (3.2%) is part of the criminal justice system.[52] That accounts for 7.3 million Americans who are either in prison, on parole, or on probation.[53] Consequently, the United States now has the dubious distinction of having the world's largest prison population. In fact, the United States has less than 5% of the world's population, but it has nearly 25% of the world's prisoners.⁵⁴ The leading reason behind this problem is the drug war.

In 1980, there were roughly 500,000 prisoners, 41,000 of whom were there for drug charges.⁵⁵ By 2010 the number of U.S. prisoners had grown to 2.4 million people, 507,000 of whom were there for drug charges.⁵⁶ To put it differently, the number of Americans in prison is higher than the population of New Mexico and the cost of incarcerating those individuals is over $60 billion a year.⁵⁷

The growth of the prison system has become so normalized that prison lobbyists have actually been able to convince some legislators that they can project the number of prisons that will be needed based upon the number of children that can read by the third grade. "That kind of cold-blooded analysis of problems that may have nothing to do with criminality is driving the discussion at the state legislative level," said Dr. L.C. Dorsey, Delta Research and Cultural Institute.⁵⁸ The prison system's growth has outpaced many private sector industries. In fact, many communities welcome the construction of new prisons because they're often built in rural areas that have been struggling economically.⁵⁹

The sheer size of the prison system lends itself to many layers of profiteering. As many as 90% of jails charge prisoners various fees during their incarceration.⁶⁰ These fees range from charges for medical care, booking, transportation -- even housing fees, among others. In fact, to pay for the fees assessed by the prison, the friends and family members that send money to prisoners have to pay exorbitant transaction charges, as high as 45%. Some of the largest banks, Bank of America and JPMorgan Chase, profit from this exploitive practice because they have a monopoly on money transfers to prisoners, which they obtained through no-bid government contracts.⁶¹

Corizon, America's largest prison healthcare contractor, earns about $1.4 billion in revenue annually. They're able to maximize their profits, in a predictable manner, by neglecting the services that are expected of them. Case in point, they refuse to treat Hepatitis C.⁶² There is also a $1.2 billion market for the few companies that contract for prison inmate phone calls. The charges for those calls are far above market prices, as much as $17 for a 15-minute call.⁶³

Plenty of corporations also profit from extremely cheap prison labor. Prison laborers are typically paid about $1 an hour. Many are paid nothing, but they can earn time off of their sentences.⁶⁴ There are obvious ethical questions involved with this practice, but the Supreme Court doesn't seem to find it offensive. In fact, former Justice Warren Burger loved the idea so much that he touted the idea of "factories with fences."[65] Consequently, some prisons have held labor strikes in hopes of gaining better living conditions and to create awareness of the issues involved with prison labor. However, most corporate media outlets have never covered this topic.[66] After all, it's the type of story which is sure to elicit very little sympathy from the public (without being informed of the profit motive behind prison labor). Then again, General Electric, the parent company of the "liberal" media giants NBC and MSNBC, has also financed the construction of privately operated prisons.[67]

There is a misconception that prison labor is only used for public works projects, such as highway cleanup. Furthermore, Americans have been misled with lies that prison labor won't compete with the free labor market; that simply isn't true. Honda once replaced United Auto Workers union workers in Ohio, making $20 an hour, with prison laborers. Furthermore, one advertisement by the state of Washington completely removed all of the pretenses. The ad said, "Are you experiencing high employee turnover? Worried about the cost of employee benefits? Getting hit by overseas competition? Having trouble motivating your workforce? Thinking about expansion space? Then the Washington State Department of Corrections Private Sector Partnerships is for you."[68]

PRIDE is a non-profit, government-run corporation that provides for-profit companies with cheap prison labor. They openly offer "a cost-effective way to occupy a portion of the ever-growing offender/inmate population." PRIDE has undercut the labor market in Florida so much so that it has become one of the largest printers in the state.[69] Likewise, a perfect storm for the private prison industry occurred in Alabama. Prison lobbyists helped create an immigration law similar to the infamous one in Arizona, S.B. 1070, which requires people to show identification without probable cause.[70] Subsequently, that law effectively pushed most of the immigrant labor out of the state. As a result, Alabama farmers have had difficulty finding laborers who are willing to work for the wages that they used to pay to illegal aliens. Many of those same farmers have since contracted with the state to get prisoners to work on their farms.[71]

You would probably be surprised by some of the corporate household names that have profited from prison labor, including Dell, Chevron, IBM, Motorola, Compaq, Texas Instruments, Microsoft, Victoria's Secret, Boeing, Nintendo, Starbucks, Toys R Us, and Costco.[72] These companies are enabled by a component of the Department of Justice, UNICOR. UNICOR provides various industries with prison labor services such as building military weapons, waste cleanup, electronics, and textiles.[73]

Michael Mansh is the owner-operator of a Pennsylvania manufacturer, Ashland Sales and Service, and he has first-hand experience with how this system undercuts small businesses. Mansh contracts with the U.S. Air Force and he has witnessed how this system removes taxpaying jobs from our economy. He also notes that corruption is often a part of our government's contracting system. In many cases, the taxpayers get ripped off by government officials who intentionally overpay for contracting services. In particular, his company competes directly with UNICOR by making the same products; yet, the Department of Defense rewards UNICOR with more lucrative contracts even though their business doesn't pay corporate taxes and their workers make roughly $1 an hour.[74]

Several major corporations profit from prison labor and there are now publicly-traded, for-profit companies that operate prisons. The staggering prison population has led the government to experiment with contracting to these companies. That development really embodies the most audacious form of prison profiteering, and these privately operated prisons are partnered with some of the most well-known financial giants. It costs an estimated $54,209 to build a single prison bed space and $31,286 a year to house a prisoner.[75] Therefore, private prisons often finance their construction projects with major banks. Thus, typical investment giants such as Goldman Sachs have never shied away from profiting this way as well as other controversial practices. In fact, it's appalling that companies convicted of money laundering, such as American Express, have financed private prisons full of drug offenders.[76]

Two companies dominate the private prison industry, the GEO Group (formerly Wackenhut) and Corrections Corporation of America (CCA). In 2009, those companies earned about $3.2 billion in revenue, employed over 24,000 people, operated 138 facilities, and held approximately 149,000 inmates in the United States.[77] The

GEO Group is a multinational corporation with locations in Canada, the United Kingdom, Australia, South Africa, and notably -- the Migrant Operations Center at Guantanamo Bay.[78]

The GEO Group made a public attempt at gaining mainstream recognition in 2013. Boca Raton, FL is the home of Florida Atlantic University (FAU) and the headquarters of the GEO Group. Hence, the GEO Group entered into a $6 million agreement for the official naming rights of Florida Atlantic University's football stadium. Why would a company pay for advertising when all of its income is derived from government contracts, and not consumers? The answer is simple. The concept of a corporation that profits from imprisoning people is jarring to most people. Therefore, it's a wise business decision to use public relations and marketing ventures that can subtly attach their brand with traditional sports like football. If they're able to do that, the concept of private prisons becomes more normalized and palatable to the public. However, this ploy backfired, and the company quickly backed out of the deal after the students protested in large numbers.[A][79]

The political argument in favor of privatizing prisons is that corporations are supposed to be more efficient with costs and services. In theory, private prisons *could* benefit the public if there were several companies competing and being held accountable. It would be a great option if private prisons actually competed based upon merit and were ranked according to which company had the safest prisons with the most opportunities for rehabilitation and education and the least recidivism. Unfortunately, the reality of the process for contracting with private prisons is that there is virtually *no* competition based on merit. It has to do more with political connections.

The "gladiator school" was the perfect example of this lack of accountability. That nickname referred to the Idaho Correctional Center, the most violent facility in the state, operated by Corrections Corporation of America (CCA). The *Associated Press* obtained a disturbing video that instantly demonstrated why that prison has a rate of violence over twice the statewide average. An inmate received brain damage due to a beating by another inmate, lasting

---

[A] George Zoley, the CEO of GEO Group, had been a long time executive faculty member of FAU. He was the chairman of the Board of Trustees, the Chair of the FAU Presidential Search Committee, and a member of the FAU Foundation board of directors.

several minutes, as the security guards stood by watching.[80] That wasn't an aberration as Stephen Pevar, a senior staff attorney for the ACLU, described the conditions in the Idaho Correctional Center as the most "disgraceful, revolting and inexcusable case of mass abuse and federal rights violations" that he's ever seen in his 39 years of experience.[81] A civil lawsuit found that CCA was not only negligent in their operation of the prison; they also later admitted to fraudulently covering up their neglect. CCA falsified documents that made it appear that key mandatory security positions were staffed, when in reality, those posts had been vacant for at least 4,800 hours.[82]

There are several shocking examples like this involving private prisons. The Inspector General (IG) of the Department of Justice issued a comprehensive review of the private prisons that house federal prisoners. The IG report concluded that private prisons don't offer significant savings to the taxpayers and there were more violent incidents in those facilities.[83] Hence, the Department of Justice announced in September of 2016 that all private prison contracts would eventually be phased out of the federal system.[84] That is progress, but it applies to only a small portion of the prison population. Most prisoners are housed in state facilities and we don't know if the Trump administration will uphold that directive.

The corruption with private prisons is part of a larger issue of government contracts. *The Project on Government Oversight* found that the federal government on average pays over twice as much to private contractors for comparable services.[85] That type of contracting isn't representative of free market capitalism; it's crony capitalism. Conversely, a study by the U.S. Government Accountability Office (GAO) found that the government does, at times, exercise strong fiscal discretion with contracts for a certain sector -- non-profit organizations. As a matter of fact, the federal government is so stingy with non-profit organizations that the revenues from those contracts are sometimes below their operating costs; meanwhile for-profit companies often game the system.[86] In one particular instance, lobbyists in Arizona for GEO Group were able to get an extra $900,000 in state funding for their client even though the Arizona Department of Corrections stated that those funds were unnecessary.[87]

It should be no surprise that the creation of the private prison industry had many of the familiar signs of crony capitalism.

Corrections Corporation of America (CCA) was founded in 1983 in Nashville, TN. Tom Beasley was the co-founder of the company while he was also the head of the Tennessee Republican Party.[88] Beasley also served as the campaign manager for the Governor, Lamar Alexander, who was crucial to the industry's formation. In fact, Alexander favored privatizing prisons so strongly that he supported a 99-year lease proposal for the entire state. Albeit, the state legislature refused that absurd proposition.[89] Nevertheless, Alexander went on to become a Tennessee Senator and his replacement for Governor was Ned McWerter, a significant shareholder of CCA.[90] McWerter naturally backed CCA and he stated in the company's 1995 Annual Report that "the federal government would be well served to privatize all of their corrections."[91]

The tremendous profits earned by the private prison industry have recycled into politics in the form of corruption, and the state of Florida offers an excellent case study on this matter. The GEO Group has given, since 2006, a total of $1.3 million in campaign contributions to Florida politicians.[92] The Governor, Rick Scott, received $25,000 from the GEO Group for his inaugural bash and $205,000 for his "Let's Get to Work" Committee. Also, the CEO of the GEO Group gave $20,000 to help refurbish the Governor's mansion, and a GEO Group lobbyist raised $3 million for his inaugural.[93] Furthermore, George Zoley, Geo Group's CEO, held a $10,000-a-plate fundraiser in his home for Rick Scott's campaign.[94]

The generous contributions from the GEO Group are a major red flag. That kind of money buys more than influence. In particular, Rick Scott attempted to privatize every prison in the state. Meanwhile, most states are liberalizing their marijuana laws, but the Florida legislature, on the other hand, passed a superficial law in 2013 to crack down on head shops. That law made it a felony, after a second offense, if a store owner is caught knowingly selling pipes, bongs, or hookahs for illegal drug usage.[B95]

[B] This bill was a pet issue for Florida State Rep. Darryl Rouson, Democrat. He was the primary force behind the creation of a Drug Paraphernalia Abatement Task Force in his county. He was also arrested for misdemeanor trespassing after a publicity stunt in which he entered a local head shop and asked for a pipe to smoke crack. The owner refused and told him to leave, but he refused and walked behind the counter and caused a scene. Rouson's moralist stunt was truly hypocritical because he had often defended drug dealers and users as

Mike Fasano, a Republican in the Florida state legislature, felt the wrath of the private prison industry after he merely questioned their cost saving potential. He committed the cardinal sin of asking for more research. After all, the GAO concluded that private prisons don't offer significant savings to taxpayers.[96] Be that as it may, Mike Haridopolos, a large recipient of GEO Group funding, reacted by stripping Fasano of his chairmanship of the subcommittee that oversees prison budgets.[97] In short, the cost benefits of private prisons are inconclusive because they vary from state to state. Private prisons have aided budgets in some states and added to the burden in others. Nonetheless, one study that was published after Fasano's dismissal vindicated his concerns. It found that Florida's private prisons cost $46.73 per prisoner per day compared to $42.36 per day for government-run prisons.[98]

The conflicts of interest with the private prison industry should be obvious to everyone, yet eight percent of American prisoners are now held in private prisons.[99] Those companies will certainly seek new ways to imprison people for as long as possible. Remarkably, CCA sent a proposal to 48 different state Governors with offers to purchase their state prisons in exchange for 20-year contracts.[100] Those contracts would have required the states to keep their prison populations at no less than 90% capacity, no matter what the crime rate. Thank goodness, every state rejected that outrageous proposition. Regardless, the prison lobbyists have still managed to win impressive victories for their clients.

The controversial immigration bill in Arizona, S.B. 1070, was one of the landmark victories for the private prison lobby. That law requires citizens to provide identification without probable cause. Mind you, parts of the law were written by a lobbying group, American Legislative Exchange Council (ALEC), which represents several industries, including private prisons.[101] In the end, that bill benefited the private prison industry by providing them with more illegal immigrants for their immigration detention facilities. Again, this is all paid for at the expense of the taxpayers.

This is a relatively new industry and it is startling to imagine how much power private prisons will have in another 30-40 years. They have already managed to manipulate the fourth amendment.

---

an attorney. In fact, he also had been a cocaine addict for 16 years who admittedly "should have 30 felonies (on his record)," but he was never arrested on a drug charge.

At this rate, your minor municipal violation might turn into an arrest record in the future. One possible sign of things to come happened with a Texas man, Jory Enck. He was thrown in jail for allegedly not returning a GED study guide to the public library.[102]

A non-profit public interest group, PR Watch, reported in 2012 about a foreboding incident in which CCA had participated in drug raids of an Arizona high school. The local police were provided with drug-sniffing dogs by CCA. Afterward, the school went into a prison style "lockdown" in which students were forced to line up against the wall and were not allowed to leave the building. This is part of a theme in which private prisons are specifically targeting adolescents to fill their juvenile facilities.[103]

This corruption was epitomized with a scandal labeled "cash for kids" by the media.[104] Two Pennsylvania judges had accepted approximately $2.6 million in bribes from private juvenile detention centers. In return, those judges increased the number of youths in their facilities by convicting teens for minor offenses that ordinarily would have been thrown out of court. One example was a 15-year-old with no prior indiscretions, who spent three months in a boot camp because she had created a MySpace page that mocked her high school's assistant principal. *She even included a disclosure on the page stating that it was a parody.*[105]

In 2010 the Department of Justice (DOJ) accused the city of Meridian, MS of similar crimes. According to the DOJ, the Meridian Police Department, Lauderdale County Youth Court, two youth court judges, and the Mississippi Department of Human Services were all part of a system that they described as "a school-to-prison pipeline."[106] Students were routinely incarcerated for minor school rule infractions. Police officers were referred to as a "taxi service" to prison with little to no questions asked by the police. Also, students were "incarcerated for days at a time without a probable cause hearing."[107] The situation in Meridian is an extreme example, but schools throughout the nation are increasingly coordinating with police to arrest youths for minor transgressions. A documentary by PBS's *Frontline*, "Locked Up in America," highlighted this issue after discovering that over 1,000 children in Kentucky are jailed annually for minor crimes such as skipping school.[108]

The case in Meridian led to another investigation, by the DOJ and *NPR News,* into the operations of the Walnut Grove Youth Correctional Facility, the nation's largest juvenile facility. The GEO

Group operated Walnut Grove, which is just 60 miles from Meridian, MS.[109] Obviously, prisons are rough places, but the investigators found that there was clear evidence of terrible negligence. The violence was so pervasive that the correctional officers were accused of setting up fights for entertainment purposes and taking bets on the action. Beatings were also customary from the guards, many of whom, were reportedly gang affiliated and condoned the possession of homemade weapons for certain inmates. In fact, investigators noted that the female staff had sex with male inmates at a rate that was "among the worst that we've seen in any facility anywhere in the nation."[110]

Despite the violent conditions, the GEO Group decreased the number of guards on staff, even though the number of prisoners increased. Therefore, this company clearly prioritizes profitability over security.[111] In the end, the conditions in the prison resulted in a federal court order in 2012 for sweeping reforms, but the GEO Group simply opted out of their contract one month after that order was issued. Nonetheless, that decision didn't hurt any future business with the government as the company continues to grow with more contracts.

You may be surprised to see the salaries for those at the top of the private prison business. *The Palm Beach Post* published the names of the highest-paid executives in Palm Beach County in 2009 and three from the GEO Group were in the top nine. The CEO earned $7,059,003, the COO earned $3,602,321, and the CFO earned $2,274,951.[112] There is only one way to earn those kinds of figures in that industry -- cutting costs. In an extreme example, one company even purchased land on a toxic waste dump in Pennsylvania for $1, hoping to build a facility there.[113] However, that plan wasn't approved by the government.

Correctional officer unions are in a constant battle against privatizing prisons because these facilities are typically understaffed with workers who often have no prior corrections experience.[114] According to some reports, private prison workers are often paid below the poverty line and in some cases are eligible for food stamps.[115] As a result of extreme cost cutting measures, the private prison industry has been unable to conclusively show better results at reducing violence in their facilities than the public sector. In fact, private prisons even get to "cherry pick" the safer prisoners for their institutions while leaving the more dangerous prisoners for the government to handle.[116]

Private prisons also get sweetheart tax deals. The GEO Group received approval to file as a real estate investment trust (REIT).[117] REIT's are a type of investment that trade like a stock and receive significant tax breaks but have to pay higher dividends. Those tax breaks add up to about $90-$110 million a year for the GEO Group.[118] CCA also converted to a REIT which saved the company roughly $70 million in taxes for 2013.[119] That is fantastic news for the select group of Wall Street moguls who gamble among themselves on America's prison population. It turns out that GEO Group has been a good gamble too. The GEO Group's stock price has increased over 2100% since its stock became public in 1994.

After their release, prisoners immediately enter into a debt system from the fees they incurred while in prison. Many states have even decided to privatize their probation and parole services. Chris Albin-Lackey, Senior Researcher for Human Rights Watch, has openly compared these private probation companies to "debt collectors."[120] Again, that's an easily predictable outcome as the bottom line is the top priority for any business. With that in mind, the GEO Group made a $415 million acquisition of Behavioral Interventions (the largest company that electronically monitors parolees and probationers) with a group of Wall Street firms, including Bank of America and JPMorgan, providing the financing.[121] It's absolutely absurd that the DOJ allowed that acquisition to take place as there is an unmistakable conflict of interest when the parent company profits from more prisoners.

Anyone can easily be thrown back in jail simply by getting behind on probation payments or failing a drug test. There are several other technical violations of probation which aren't even crimes such as missing a parole appointment, losing a job, keeping beer at home, staying out past curfew, etc. Two-thirds of parolees in the year 2000 were sent back to prison for technical violations, rather than actual crimes.[122] Considering all of these factors, it's easy to argue that this system pushes people, who had intended to turn their lives around, back into a life of crime. These kinds of "zero tolerance" policies with financial conflicts of interest are not only ineffective but are also wasteful to the taxpayers.

The drug war has highlighted some of the severely flawed policies within the criminal justice system and the root cause is often profit motive. Documents show that in 1989 the DOJ directed their attorneys to "divert personnel from other activities" if necessary to meet their commitment to "increase forfeiture production."[123] There is no crime that fills the government coffers like the drug war. As of 2008, the DOJ's forfeiture fund reached $3.1 billion, according to a study by the Cato Institute.[124] Eighty percent of those profits go directly back to the local police department that made the seizure.[C][125]

Some small towns rely heavily upon seizures to maintain their police departments. Albeit, it's not much different in larger cities with better budgets. Kurt Schmoke was the former Mayor of Baltimore and he said that when he served as a State's Attorney, "My office seized so many vehicles from drug dealers that many joked that I was the largest used car dealer in the city. In the war on drugs, this is how success is measured."[126] The former California Deputy Attorney General, Gary Schons says, "Much like a drug addict becomes addicted to drugs, law enforcement agencies have become dependent on asset forfeitures. They have to have it."[127]

The American government has had the right to confiscate criminal proceeds since its earliest days. Those laws were targeted at ship captains who tried to avoid paying tariffs.[128] However, asset forfeiture didn't reappear as a tool for law enforcement until roughly 200 years later. Surprisingly, it was the Department of Justice under the Nixon administration that warned against this system. The RICO Act (Racketeering Influenced and Corrupt Organizations) was passed in 1970 to target the mafia and it contained statutes enabling criminal forfeitures. However, at that time, DOJ officials warned Congress that asset forfeiture "would result in a large number of unintended consequences."[129]

Most Americans are aware that police departments confiscate the cash, cars, and homes of convicted drug dealers. However, those laws pertain to *criminal* asset forfeiture. On the other hand, a growing number of Americans are just now learning about *civil* asset forfeiture. Civil asset forfeiture became a tool for law enforcement during the Reagan administration with the Comprehensive Crime Control Act of 1984.[130] Under civil asset forfeiture, the police can

---

[C] In a unique example, police officers in Romulus, MI (a suburb of Detroit) were arrested in 2012 after using over $100,000 of their civil asset forfeitures fund to pay for marijuana, prostitutes, alcohol, and a hot tub.

confiscate your property based merely upon probable cause, the same burden of proof necessary to obtain a search warrant.

The government can confiscate your money or assets without even filing criminal charges, through civil asset forfeiture. "Unfortunately, I think I can say that our civil asset forfeiture laws are being used in terribly unjust ways, and are depriving innocent citizens of their property with nothing that can be called due process. This is wrong and it must be stopped," said former Rep. Henry Hyde (R-IL).[131] Mind you, those words came from one of the most conservative members of Congress and a long-time drug war advocate. The best evidence of this abuse of power is that 80% of these drug money confiscations don't result in criminal prosecutions.[132] That means that the police either didn't have enough evidence for a trial or they were motivated by financial interests.

It's difficult to retrieve your assets after a civil forfeiture. You first need to climb through a mountain of government red tape. Then, while facing the burden of proof, you have to prove your innocence with a civil lawsuit against the government.[133] Consequently, during routine traffic stops, numerous people have reported that police officers threatened them with arrest if they didn't willingly agree to hand over all of their cash via civil asset forfeiture. Some police departments even train their officers to immediately ask the driver if they're carrying any cash.[134]

Bobby Frederick, criminal defense attorney, is so accustomed to this abusive police practice that he refers to it as "highway robbery."[135] It's an apt term as the police confiscated more money via civil asset forfeiture in 2014 ($4.5 billion) than was collectively burglarized in the same year ($3.9 billion) by all of America's actual criminals![136] Many people don't know how to go through the process to retrieve their property and as Frederick points out, the legal fees involved make it pointless to contest the seizure unless it was for more than a few thousand dollars. In other words, it's essentially now illegal for you to travel anywhere with a sizeable amount of cash, for whatever reason. For instance, *The Washington Post* uncovered footage in which an officer seized cash during a traffic stop. The driver tried to tell his side of the story, but the officer ignored him. He said, "Good luck proving it. You'll burn it up in attorney fees before we give it back to you...I don't have to prove my case on the side of the road...I do this every single day."[137]

Reagan obviously didn't intend for this kind of government tyranny to unfold. He truly wanted to abolish drug addiction, but these asset forfeiture programs have incentivized the least efficient tactics of the drug war. To put it differently, the police have an incentive to chase the cash, not the actual drugs. After all, confiscated drugs are destroyed without a financial reward. Patrick Murphy, a former Police Commissioner of New York City, explained to Congress that his department had a financial incentive to place roadblocks on the southbound lane of I-95 which generally transports cash to make drug buys, rather than I-95 North which carries the drugs.[138] Likewise, *Channel 5 News* in Nashville, TN did an investigation into this practice. Drugs are more likely to enter Nashville, TN eastbound from Mexico on I-40 and the money travels westbound on I-40. Regardless, they found that there were ten times as many stops on the money side. In fact, the news crew even videotaped instances of near altercations between police officers from different departments in quasi-turf wars for the money side of the highway.[139]

A criminologist John Worral surveyed 770 police managers and executives and found that 40% believed that civil asset forfeiture is "necessary as a budget supplement."[140] Also, it's now common for prosecutors to drastically reduce the criminal penalties for major drug dealers if they agree to forfeit substantial money through civil asset forfeiture. To be exact, a Massachusetts investigation found that plea agreements to forfeit $10,000 or more bought the elimination or reduction of trafficking charges in almost 3/4 of such cases.[141] Conversely, low-level drug dealers who don't have many assets to offer, often serve full sentences while major traffickers can buy their way out of prison.[142]

The New York Times detailed one of these high-profile cases. A major drug kingpin, Claude Duboc, had amassed a fortune of 100 million dollars. He faced a mandatory life sentence, but his attorney negotiated a plea deal for only three to five years as long as he forfeited his entire estate. However, that deal fell through after investigators found out that his attorney, F. Lee Bailey (part of O.J. Simpson's "Dream Team"), had kept some of Duboc's money for himself.[143]

Russ Caswell, a motel owner in Tewksbury, MA, can personally describe the corrupt nature of our country's forfeiture laws. Caswell had never been accused of any crimes, but the federal government tried to seize his motel that was valued at $1.5-$1.8 million. Fifteen different drug-related incidents occurred on his property over a 14-year period, but Caswell was far from complicit in those crimes. In fact, he cooperated with the police in all of those cases. In some cases, he called the cops to report those incidents. Caswell was merely guilty of operating a motel located in a high crime area. Furthermore, there were more drug arrests at the Walmart on the same street over the same time period. Suffice it to say, the government chose to exploit Caswell because he was a much easier target. And, he would have lost his motel had not the Institute for Justice (a non-profit libertarian law firm) successfully defended him pro-bono.[144]

The city of Philadelphia has abused civil forfeiture more than any other city, over $6 million a year. Thus, the city's corrupt processes were the reason behind a federal class action lawsuit by the Institute for Justice. In some cases, people who hadn't been accused of a crime lost their homes. In these cases, a family member was typically convicted of a minor drug crime, but there was no evidence of consent or any involvement by the homeowner with drug activity.[145] Anyone with half a conscience would view these cases as terrible abuses of power, but some shameless bureaucrats look at Philadelphia as a blueprint for their city.

Harry S. Connelly, the city attorney for Las Cruces, NM, conducted a meeting touting the need for the city to take a more aggressive stance with civil forfeiture. In fact, he laughed about scenarios in which someone sells a dime bag of weed and the government confiscates the family's $300,000 home. "What a deal," he said. He later specifically praised Philadelphia's forfeiture program. "Just think what you could do as a legal department. We could be czars. We could own the city. We could be in the real estate business," said Connelly.[146]

Luckily, video from that conference became a national news story. Subsequently, the negative publicity led New Mexico lawmakers to pass a statewide ban on civil asset forfeiture.[147] Fortunately, nine other states have since banned asset forfeiture without a criminal conviction.[148] That shows that it is possible to affect positive policy changes with strong activism, but it is an uphill battle.

2

> "(Marijuana) can arouse in blacks and Hispanics a state of menacing fury or homicidal attack."

For most of American history, you could legally purchase the most dangerous and addictive drugs, such as cocaine and heroin, over the counter. Notable companies such as Merck and Parke-Davis manufactured cocaine; likewise, heroin was produced by Bayer.[1] Most cough syrups contained morphine. In fact, a Bordeaux wine laced with cocaine, known as "Vin Mariani" became quite popular beginning in the 1860s.[2] Cocaine and heroin were even available through mail order catalogs, including Sears and Roebuck.[3] Numerous magazine and newspaper ads featured "patent medicines" and "tonics" with morphine or cocaine as the primary ingredient. Despite their claims, those "medicines" were rarely patented and their users were often generally abusing them for recreational purposes.

Public education regarding these drugs was a rarity. Therefore, ignorance was one of the leading causes of drug addiction. Drug sales were completely unregulated and there wasn't much scientific research available regarding the side effects. Consequently, many people were duped into using these medicines because they were often advertised as cure-alls for nearly every imaginable ailment. Cocaine and heroin were marketed for toothaches, depression, insomnia, digestion, nervousness, as aphrodisiacs, etc. Some manufacturers, such as Bayer, even marketed their brand of cocaine or heroin as a remedy for morphine addiction. The first positive change occurred when Congress passed the Pure Food and Drug Act of 1906, which was the first law that required proper labeling of ingredients. As a result, sales of "patented medicines" dropped by one-third within one year after the law was passed. In fact, that's when all traces of cocaine were officially removed from Coca-Cola.[4]

At the present time, it's now evident that the drug war has caused more damage to society than the drugs themselves. America had a problem with drug addiction before the start of the drug war. However, despite full availability, there was not much crime associated with the sales of these drugs because the prices weren't inflated through the black market. Also, drug addiction was slightly less extensive than it is today. To be specific, the Public Health Service estimated in 1900 that there were 240,000 heroin and cocaine addicts. That meant that roughly 3 out of every 1,000 Americans were drug addicts.[5] In contrast, the National Survey on Drug Use and Health estimated in 2012 that there were nearly 1.6 million heroin and cocaine addicts. That accounts for a very similar number, roughly 5 out of every 1,000 Americans.[6] Obviously, those estimations can't be considered definitive, but the clear takeaway is that drug addiction hasn't diminished after a century of restrictive drug laws.

The first anti-drug law was passed in San Francisco in 1875.[7] That law banned commercial Chinese opium dens, but recreational use remained legal as long as it took place privately. Obviously, opiates such as heroin or morphine are potentially deadly and addictive drugs, but seemingly most of the motivation behind the opium law was based on racist fears. There was a tremendous amount of anti-Chinese sentiment due to a massive influx of Chinese workers who had immigrated to California during the gold rush.

Many local newspapers warned that Chinese men were luring white women into addiction and leading them into wanton sexuality with other races. As is the case with many generalizations, there was some sliver of truth. It was true that a disproportionately high percentage of middle-class white women were opium smokers.[8] However, that didn't happen due to a sinister plot by Chinese immigrants. Instead, some historians point to the fact that women weren't allowed to drink in saloons, which led many of them to smoke opium.[9] Nonetheless, women in Chinese opium dens were an uncomfortable sight for most white men. As an illustration, one San Francisco police report from 1881 openly mentioned "…white women and Chinamen side by side under the effects of this drug -- a humiliating sight to anyone with anything left of manhood."[10]

Certain ethnic groups were viewed as less than human and some lawmakers wanted to ban them from using drugs. To be exact, the U.S. Senate passed a bill in 1901 that prohibited the sale of opium and alcohol to "aboriginal tribes and uncivilized races." They later added provisions against sales to "Indians, Alaskans, the inhabitants of Hawaii, railroad workers, and immigrants at ports of entry."[11] In the end, that bill wasn't passed in the House.

Teddy Roosevelt publicly spoke out against racial discrimination. However, he also held openly racist, condescending views of minorities and felt they needed to be protected from themselves. During a speech honoring Abraham Lincoln, he pleaded with the crowd to show the "backward race" the path toward morality and prosperity. He warned that "vice and criminality of every kind are evils more potent for harm to the black race than all acts of oppression of white men put together."[12] Four years later, Roosevelt signed the first federal drug law, the Opium Exclusion Act of 1909. It banned the importation of opium for recreational use, but medical use remained legal.[13]

Some historians, on the other hand, believe that Teddy Roosevelt's support for the Opium Exclusion Act wasn't primarily motivated by fears of drug addiction. Instead, they suggest that he sought trade relations with China and made a symbolic gesture with a formal opium ban.[14] After all, opium was a hot button topic with the Chinese government, which had waged two Opium Wars decades earlier.

Shipments of opium, which was primarily grown in India, were tremendously profitable for the British Empire. Consequently, the British went to war with China for the right to sell opium within China's territory. China lost the first Opium War (1839–1842). Nonetheless, the Chinese government continued to try to implement their ban on opium. That led to the second Opium War (1856–1860) against the British and the French, but the Chinese lost again.[15]

In the 21st century, many people scoff at the idea that recreational drug use falls within the "inalienable rights" of "life, liberty, and the pursuit of happiness." However, drug use was considered a legal right until the early 20th century. The following remarks from a Congressional committee on opium in 1910 revealed that point of view. The former Speaker of the House, James Beaumont "Champ" Clark, said, "You cannot punish a man for doing a thing in his own home." During the same committee, he subsequently asked, "You are not going to try to make it a crime for a fellow to buy opium, are you?"[16] Oh, how the times have changed.

"For the first 140 years, our (country's laws) included the right to ingest whatever chemical you wished. Only in 1914 did that change and the change is probably the most radical public policy change in the history of the United States," said Joseph McNamara, research fellow for Stanford's Hoover Institution.[17] He was referring to the Harrison Narcotics Act, which was the first federal law to essentially ban the recreational use of opium and cocaine. However, it wasn't a direct prohibition. Instead, the medical use of opium and cocaine were limited through registration, taxation, regulation, and licensing.

Under the Harrison Act, drug users were required to get a prescription. In essence, it outlawed recreational use because doctors were forced to progressively decrease the dosage for drug addicts or face criminal penalties. As a result, roughly 25,000 doctors were arrested for violating this law by 1929.[18] The Harrison Act created a black market and marked the starting point of gangs dominating the distribution of contraband drugs.

Arnold Rothstein, known primarily as a gambling mogul of New York City who fixed the 1919 World Series, was one of the first and most notable criminals to profit from the illegal drug black market. Rothstein was one of the most truly organized criminals in history. His Jewish heritage restricted him from being a part of the Italian-American mafia, but he was the financier and mentor for mafiosos such as Lucky Luciano. Rothstein developed one of the largest illegal drug distribution networks through European companies where those drugs were still manufactured legally.[19]

Just like heroin legislation, the first cocaine laws were prompted by unfounded racial fears. Several newspapers printed violent tales of "cocaine-crazed negroes" during the early 20th century. Newspapers even published stories of black men who had become impervious to bullets. Mike Gray, author of *Drug Crazy: How We Got into This Mess and How We Can Get Out*, noted this irony: some southern black men were cocaine users, but they had often been supplied by white employers in hopes of more production.[20] Regardless, in some cases, cocaine possession was enough to justify a lynching in the South.[21] Cocaine became an easy scapegoat for local law enforcement officials. In fact, a report in 1910 by the State Department noted, "it has been authoritatively stated that cocaine is often the direct incentive to the crime of rape by the negroes of the South and other sections of the country."[22]

In that same year, Congress heard testimony asserting the same notion from the Vice President of the Pharmaceutical Examining Board of Pennsylvania, Dr. Christopher Koch. Dr. Koch warned about "Chinks" who kept white women as their "concubines" in their opium dens. He also said, "The colored people seem to have a weakness for it (cocaine)…It produces a kind of temporary insanity…and a great many of the Southern rape cases have been traced to cocaine." Whereas, just minutes later in his testimony, he rationalized that white professionals "take morphine to quiet them, and they take cocaine to brace them up."[23]

The first marijuana laws weren't explicitly directed at black people and Mexican-Americans by statute, but they were sponsored by law enforcement and became an extension of Jim Crow protocols. Historians Richard J. Bonnie and Charles H. Whitebread, authors of *The Marijuana Conviction: A History of Marijuana Prohibition in the United States*, documented a pervasive racial bias that motivated the formation of these laws. Only a few press clippings were necessary to drum up enough fear to pass those early marijuana laws. "All Mexicans are crazy, and this (marijuana) makes them crazy," was a quote from the floor of the Texas Senate in 1914.[24] That's where the first state marijuana law was passed and 27 states followed from 1915 to 1937.

Richard J. Bonnie and Charles Whitebread demonstrated that the first state marijuana laws weren't addressing an existing marijuana problem; instead, most states wanted to prevent a perceived *potential* threat.[25] Marijuana use was so uncommon that as of 1936 the Bureau of Narcotics had to show New York police officers what marijuana looked like.[26] Nonetheless, states passed marijuana laws with very little debate, nor any public backlash. Statements like this one from Montana on the floor of the statehouse during a marijuana vote in 1929 were typical. One man said, "Give one of these Mexican beet field workers a couple of puffs on a marijuana cigarette and he thinks he is in the bullring at Barcelona."[27]

Marijuana's existence dates as far back as 7000 BC, but it hasn't always been used as a recreational drug.[28] Cannabis has various plant species, one of which is hemp. The hemp plant looks very similar and produces virtually none of the psychoactive chemical, THC. Hemp produces a fiber substance that has historically been a very valuable commodity worldwide. Hemp was heavily ingrained in early American culture. George Washington and Thomas Jefferson grew hemp on their farms.[29] Jefferson wrote, "(Hemp) is of first necessity…to the wealth and protection of the country."[30] He even invented some machines and systems to process hemp. Also, John Quincy Adams traveled to Russia years before becoming President to report on their hemp manufacturing techniques.[31] By the same token, Ben Franklin owned a paper mill that processed hemp.³² In fact, the first and second drafts of the Declaration of Independence were written on hemp paper.³³ Even the first American flag made was from hemp fibers.³⁴

After the Civil War, hemp production declined slowly. There were a few factors involved. High protective tariffs, imposed by states, raised hemp prices to noncompetitive levels, but the strongest reason for the decline was that harvesting hemp was a very labor intensive process done by hand. There was no industrial equipment available that could efficiently remove the valuable hemp fiber from its stalk. As a result, most farmers chose other commodities and, by the 1930s, the industry had been almost entirely abandoned.³⁵

Despite the nation's high familiarity with hemp, most Americans were unaware that it was associated with the "illicit" drug described in the newspapers. Americans were convinced that marijuana turned black men into violent criminals targeting white people and this evil drug made Mexicans violent and crazy. Newspapers preyed upon fears that Mexicans would introduce their "killer weed" or "loco weed" to white children.³⁶

As a sign of the times, this type of reporting expanded newspaper circulation. Much of the hysteria surrounding marijuana can be tied to the newspaper magnate, William Randolph Hearst. Hearst held the largest circulation of newspapers in the country for many years. Then again, his newspapers were anything but cerebral. He didn't yearn for quality journalism. Instead, Hearst was strictly motivated by sales and power. Hearst's insistence upon style over substance helped to spawn the term "yellow journalism."[A]³⁷

"A Hearst newspaper is like a screaming woman running down the street with her throat cut," said one of his writers.³⁸ His newspapers featured tabloid-style headlines and dramatic stories that were often highly exaggerated or many times were entirely fictional. Vern Whaley, an editor for Hearst's *Herald-Examiner*, recalled one time when he discovered that they had the wrong

---

[A] Hearst's *New York Journal* was in a battle with Joseph Pulitzer's *New York World*. The Pulitzer name is now synonymous with credibility, but during the late 19th century Pulitzer's newspapers were just as sensational. In fact, it was Hearst who copied Pulitzer's style of journalism. *New York World* had a comic, "Hogan's Alley," which featured a comic with a character name the "yellow kid." Hearst later hired the artist of "Hogan's Alley" to stifle his competitor. However, Pulitzer simply created a new comic with a new "yellow kid" character and the term "yellow journalism" soon followed.

address in one of their stories. Whaley informed his editor that the address was a vacant lot. The copy chief, Vic Barnes, said, "Sit down, Vern. The whole story's a fake."[39] Furthermore, one Hearst reporter explained, "We do what the old man orders. One week he orders a campaign against rats. The next week he orders a campaign against dope peddlers. Pretty soon he's going to campaign against college professors. It's all bunk but orders are orders."[40]

Hearst habitually used his newspapers to skew public opinion in line with his personal issues. His legendary vindictive nature, narcissism, and his obsession with power resulted in a truly unique place in history as a political puppet master. When asked why he concentrated his business in the newspaper industry, instead of films, he replied, "I thought of it, but I decided against it. Because you can crush a man with journalism, and you can't with motion pictures."[41]

Orson Welles made a bold career decision to direct and star in *Citizen Kane*, a very unflattering film loosely based on Hearst's life. *Citizen Kane* is now considered by many to be the greatest film of all time, but it wasn't until decades after the movie's release that Welles received the recognition he was due. Hearst threatened Hollywood executives with bad publicity and many theaters dared not play the film. Hearst newspapers created a smear campaign of epic proportions. They alleged many things, including that Welles was a communist, and it resulted in investigations by the FBI.[42]

According to marijuana historian Jack Herer, author of *The Emperor Wears No Clothes*, Hearst's manufactured marijuana panic was part of a deeper conspiracy. Herer provided evidence suggesting that William Randolph Hearst, Andrew Mellon, and the DuPont family orchestrated the Marihuana Tax Act of 1937 as a means to suppress the hemp industry from competing with their business interests. Many researchers have added additional information to enhance Herer's accusations. The competition from a reinvigorated hemp industry would have cost them billions of dollars. Industrial hemp's benefits were common knowledge, but marijuana was a much easier target. All three of those possible conspirators had the means, motive, and character to pull off such a conspiracy. It's important to examine Herer's theory to learn the truth behind the prohibition of marijuana. Also, there were a few other related scandals during this time period which coincided with his theory.

These events demonstrated how easily top business tycoons were able to corrupt our political system.

Jack Herer found that marijuana and Mexicans became symbolic targets of Hearst after one particular incident in 1915 in which Pancho Villa captured Hearst's 1,625,000 acre Babicora Ranch in Chihuahua, Mexico in 1915.[43] In the process, they confiscated thousands of his horses for their cavalry. Adding insult to injury, the Babicora Ranch was used as their base of operations for two years.[44] Chris Conrad, author of *Hemp: Lifeline to the Future*, noted that the term "marihuana" had been virtually absent in the American press beforehand. (*American newspapers used that spelling, "marihuana," in the early 20th century.*) Hearst's newspapers then began using this foreign term extensively around this time and those reports created the marijuana panic.[45]

Hearst was incensed by the loss of his ranch in Mexico and used his newspapers to garner support for the capture of Pancho Villa. Such an aggressive stance contradicted his general political ideology because he had previously earned a reputation as a staunch isolationist, in line with most Americans at that time. However, Hearst often reversed his political opinions in accordance with his personal interests.[B46] Accordingly, Hearst's newspapers blasted Woodrow Wilson who had lightly defended the man called the "Robin Hood of Mexico" by the *New York Times*.[47] Hearst's papers chastised Wilson frequently with headlines such as "American Flag Only One Mexico Does not Respect."[48] Wilson later sent a 12,000 man army to capture Villa after they attacked American soil, but Hearst still wasn't satisfied. His writers mocked Gen. Pershing's battalion as a "perishing expedition" when they were ordered to leave Mexico to enter WWI.[49]

Hearst had financial incentives to misrepresent marijuana beyond boosting newspaper sales. A fully functional and industrialized hemp industry would have cost him a fortune as Hearst had a sunk cost (an investment in which the costs can't be recovered) because he owned thousands of acres of timberland. At that time, it had already been proven that hemp was a cheaper

---

[B] The Spanish-American War likely never would have occurred if not for the mass hysteria that his newspapers generated based on exaggerations and lies. One of his reporters in Cuba before the Spanish-American War said, "There is no trouble here. There will be no war." Hearst reportedly replied back, "You furnish the pictures, I'll furnish the war."

commercial alternative for paper. It grows in a fraction of the time with much less land needed. One report in 1916, USDA Bulletin No. 404, stated that 4.1 acres of timberland were necessary to produce the same amount of pulp for paper as that from 1 acre of hemp farmland, with four to seven times less pollution.[50] Had the hemp industry become industrialized and produced a cheaper form of paper with relatively limitless supply, it would have opened the door for much more competition in the newspaper business. That would have, in turn, ruined Hearst's life obsession with monopolizing his industry. It could have been similar to how the Internet leveled the playing field for more competition and revolutionized the newspaper business.

An invention, the decorticator, had the potential to revolutionize the hemp industry as the cotton gin revolutionized the production of cotton. George Schlichten invented the decorticator in 1916, but he was unable to get enough outside investment.[51] With that in mind, John D. Rockefeller tried to purchase the rights to the decorticator, but he was turned down.[52] No one knows Rockefeller's intentions, but he developed a reputation (with Standard Oil) for buying and subsequently, destroying his competition. Considering the financial threat that an industrialized hemp industry posed to Hearst, it's particularly notable that he personally recommended to Herbert Hoover that Harry Anslinger be appointed as the first commissioner of the Bureau of Narcotics.[53]

Harry Anslinger had been the Assistant Commissioner for the Bureau of Prohibition, the precursor to the Bureau of Narcotics. Anslinger was a very ambitious man who seemed primarily motivated by bureaucratic power. Notably, former U.S. Attorney Ramsey Clark pointed out that an unusually high number of agents within the Bureau were corrupt, yet Anslinger didn't address the issue. "The least you can make of it is that Anslinger was derelict in being so unaware of what was happening in his own agency. Apparently, he had decided as a matter of self-preservation not to address it," said Clark.[54]

Anslinger was appointed as the Commissioner of the Bureau of Narcotics in 1930. That was a time when government budgets weren't stable. That's seemingly why he did everything in his power to advance the Bureau's status while never letting facts get in the way of his agenda. Historian David Courtwright obtained some of Anslinger's internal memos, through Freedom of Information Act

(FOIA) requests, which exposed his lies. He published bogus addiction rate statistics that shined favorably upon the Bureau, but he acknowledged in his internal memos that the statistics were completely fictitious.[55]

The Bureau's initial stated purpose was to police heroin and cocaine. However, Anslinger made it his personal mission to see that marijuana became prohibited at the federal level. Bear in mind, the Bureau of Narcotics opposed potential federal marijuana laws before Anslinger took over. The Bureau lobbied against adding marijuana to the Harrison Act and the Narcotic Drugs Import and Export Act.[56] In fact, on January 25, 1929, A. L. Tennyson, chief counsel for the Bureau of Prohibition, wrote an official reply to Sen. Lawrence Phipps of Colorado who proposed the marijuana amendment to the Harrison Act:

> "(The) evils represented by the abuse of cannabis indica...do not appear to be nearly as widespread as those connected with the possession of opium, cocoa leaves or their derivatives...It is thought that this evil may more properly be met by state and municipal legislation, for which there is more ample fundamental authority."[57]

In fact, many people within the bureau recognized the misinformation within the sensationalized stories from the newspapers. The Bureau of Narcotics even made an official statement denouncing those reports. It read, "This publicity tends to magnify the extent of the evil and lends color to an inference that there is an alarming spread of the improper use of the drug, whereas the actual increase in such use may not have been inordinately large."[58]

The Bureau of Narcotic changed dramatically with Anslinger in charge. In his memoir, he acknowledged that the plan to establish federal marijuana laws was his own. He also noted that he used the media to connect this drug with violent crime. He wrote, "I reported on the growing list of crime, including rape and murder...I believe we did a thorough job."[59]

He understood the power of the media and made numerous public speeches along with radio appearances to warn the American public about the dangers of marijuana. There was no demagogue more visible than Anslinger with the subject of marijuana. He was a brilliant propagandist who was the ghost writer for various editorial pieces in Hearst newspapers. That included "Marihuana: Assassin of Youth" in Hearst's *American Magazine*. He once wrote, "If the hideous monster Frankenstein came face to face with the monster Marihuana, he would drop dead of fright."[60]

Anslinger recognized that, "If it bleeds, it leads," long before that media adage was born. There were several gruesome murders that he attributed to marijuana use even though his declarations were pure fiction. Anslinger pounced upon one such opportunity when a Tampa man, Victor Licata, killed his family in 1933 with an ax. Anslinger claimed that the man had been known by officers "as a sane, rather quiet young man" until he tried marijuana. However, records demonstrate that Anslinger's claims were false. Local police had sought to have Licata committed to a mental institution a year before the murder. Also, marijuana was never mentioned during his trial.[61] Regardless, cases like this helped Anslinger build the hysteria surrounding marijuana. He even forwarded informational packages, upon request, about marijuana for any defense attorneys who wanted to use "temporary insanity" plea for their clients.[62]

Anslinger was also an unapologetic racist. In fact, the Bureau needed a certain number of black agents to work in undercover operations, but Anslinger systematically made sure that they were never promoted. Black agents were regularly transferred so that they couldn't move into leadership positions.[63] Anslinger's racist tendencies made it easy for him to prey upon the nation's racial stereotypes. He claimed that marijuana "can arouse in blacks and Hispanics a state of menacing fury or homicidal attack. During this period, addicts have perpetrated some of the most bizarre and fantastic offenses and sex crimes known to police annals."[64] Once, without arousing any objection, he even testified that "coloreds with big lips lure white women with jazz and marijuana."[65]

Despite Anslinger's best efforts, this media campaign created a curiosity and new demand for the drug. Hence, a public relations nightmare ensued due to many famous entertainers, such as musicians, who openly smoked marijuana. Some jazz musicians even celebrated their marijuana use with songs such as "That Funny Reefer Man" by Cab Calloway, "Gimme a Reefer" by Bessie Smith, and "Muggles" by Louis Armstrong. Hence, Anslinger warned that there were "100,000 total marijuana smokers in the US, and most are Negroes, Hispanics, Filipinos, and entertainers. Their Satanic music, jazz, and swing, result from marijuana use. This marijuana causes white women to seek sexual relations with Negroes, entertainers, and any others."[66]

Much like J. Edgar Hoover who kept blackmail files on numerous Congressmen, Anslinger amassed personal files or "gore files" on many celebrities.[67] Those dossiers sparked investigations that led to the arrests of various stars, including Billie Holiday, Louis Armstrong, Dizzy Gillespie, Duke Ellington, and Robert Mitchum.[68] In fact, Hollywood directors had been coerced by Anslinger to such an extent that many of them submitted their scripts to the Federal Bureau of Narcotics for approval even though the Bureau didn't have the right to censor films.[69] In 1955 Frank Sinatra's *The Man with the Golden Arm* became the first film to defy movie censors by depicting a man who overcame drug addiction.[70]

Anslinger certainly had a bag of tricks, but, on the other hand, there were educated professionals who didn't fall for his con man tactics. Not everyone fell in line with his horror crusade. "Physicians in the United States knew the medicine as 'cannabis.' By using 'marihuana,' (Anslinger) sort of did an end run around the medical community," says Dr. Donald Abrams, professor of clinical medicine at the University of California, San Francisco (UCSF).[71] Marijuana, at that time, was available at pharmacies nationwide. After all, over 100 articles in various medical journals from 1840 to 1900 cited the benefits of cannabis. In fact, the American Pharmaceutical Association opposed the efforts "being made by sensationalist newspapers to enlarge upon the extended use of marihuana."[72]

Federal marijuana laws certainly weren't inspired by health authorities because the drug wasn't much of a concern. In fact, there were two major recreational drug studies during this era and neither study even mentioned marijuana, one by the Secretary of the Treasury in 1919 and one by the U.S. Public Health Service 1924.[73] Despite input from medical professionals, Anslinger's Machiavellian tactics were efficient and helped to subdue any concerns about the first federal marijuana law, the Marihuana Tax Act of 1937. That bill was written in secret over a two-year period in the Treasury Department.[74] It was later submitted to the House Ways and Means Committee. Marijuana historian Jack Herer pointed out that the committee's role was crucial to passing the bill because they could send it directly to the House of Representatives and bypass any other more appropriate committees. As a matter of fact, the Harrison Act was manufactured in the same way.[75]

The Ways and Means Committee gave the bill their rubber stamp and suppressed the medical community's qualified objections to the bill. The Ways and Means Committee heard testimony from Dr. William C. Woodward of the American Medical Association (AMA). Woodward vehemently disagreed with the bill and Anslinger's inflammatory claims. He pointed out that none of the appropriate government agencies, such as the Children's Bureau, had found evidence that children were using marijuana in large numbers.[76] Woodward also highlighted marijuana's medicinal qualities, objected to the criminal penalties, and openly questioned why the bill had been prepared secretly for so long. However, his testimony was received with condescending verbal pushback from the committee. They openly questioned Woodward's credibility by insisting that he didn't favor the bill because he wasn't involved in its drafting.[77]

All in all, Anslinger manufactured a moral panic surrounding marijuana. He also suppressed information about the industrial potential for hemp. He lied in his testimony before the Ways and Means Committee regarding his knowledge of the industry. He testified in 1937 that the new law would actually *protect* the legal hemp industry and further perjured himself by stating that he knew of only a few commercial uses for hemp such as cordage, hats, and bird seed.[78] Anslinger was in fact well versed in the hemp industry. Indeed, Minnesota House Representative Elmer Ryan contacted Anslinger directly on behalf of a group of hemp farmers who were in the process of using hemp to create plastic. (*The importance of that will be clarified later in this chapter.*) With that said, Anslinger assured him that no legitimate farmer needed to worry about the upcoming legislation.[79]

Anslinger was fully aware of the positive developments that were rapidly occurring in the hemp industry at that time. On September 29, 1936, he sent a supervisor to inspect the operation of H.W. Bellrose from World Fibre Corporation who had just been profiled days earlier by the *Chicago Tribune*.[80] Bellrose was sure that there would be an imminent resurgence of the hemp industry. In fact, records show that the Bureau of Narcotics had begun to monitor the commercial developments of the hemp industry in 1934.[81] Anslinger received glowing reports of the industry's potential for resurgence with specifics for most every major hemp producer, including their yields and specific methods. Many of the hemp producers had even acquired the rights to their own decorticator machinery. However, these machines hadn't been manufactured well and there were many breakdowns. Most of the hemp businesses were undercapitalized and poorly managed, yet still profitable.[82]

In the end, the Ways and Means Committee approved the Marihuana Tax Act, and the importance of that approval can't be understated because many Congressmen blindly accepted their recommendations. Otherwise, they were completely unfamiliar with marijuana. Furthermore, the bill was slated for a vote in the House on a late Friday session after many House members had already left for the weekend.[83] Hence, the remaining Congressmen had little interest in examining the merits of the bill. However, there was one member, Rep. Bertrand Snell (R-NY), who requested that the vote take place at another time. He added that it must be important because it came from the Ways and Means Committee.[84] This exchange followed:

> Rep. Rayburn: Mr. Speaker, if the gentleman will yield, I may say that the gentleman from North Carolina has stated to me that this bill has a unanimous report from the committee and that there is no controversy about it.
> Rep. Snell: What is the bill?
> Rep. Rayburn: It has something to do with something that is called marihuana. I believe it is a narcotic of some kind.
> Rep. Vinson (of the Ways and Means Committee): Marihuana is the same as hashish.
> Rep. Snell: Mr. Speaker, I am not going to object, but I think it is wrong to consider legislation of this character at this time of night.[85]

Nevertheless, very little debate followed and the bill passed easily. The only pertinent question was if the American Medical Association approved the bill. Rep. Vinson from Ways and Means blatantly lied about Dr. Woodward's testimony. He said that "Dr. Wharton" and the AMA fully supported the bill.[86]

The Marihuana Tax Act passed through the Senate just as easily. Senate leaders brushed off testimonies from hemp farmers who warned that the bill would end their businesses. These farmers lobbied for an exemption for hemp from the bill. One of those men, Matt Rens, grew quite frustrated with the proceedings as he could tell that the Senators weren't interested in hearing their perspective. He read between the lines and presumed that their ulterior motives were protecting corporate interests:

> Matt Rens: The real purpose of this bill is not to raise (tax) money, is it?
> Senator Brown: Well, we are sticking to the proposition that it is.
> Matt Rens: It will cost a million (jobs).
> Senator Brown: We thank you, Mr. Rens. (dismissed)[87]

The Marihuana Tax Act of 1937 didn't ban marijuana. Like the Harrison Act, it taxed marijuana into the shadows of the black market. Anyone who wanted to buy marijuana needed to travel to Washington D.C. to purchase a tax stamp. Thus, virtually no one was willing to do that. The Marijuana Tax Act of 1937 also taxed and regulated the hemp industry out of business. The Bureau of Narcotics enforced useless and completely unrealistic regulations, including a rule that a hemp farmer's crops must have no flowers or leaves. First of all, it's impossible to produce a hemp crop that has no flowers or leaves. Secondly, those flowers and leaves were worthless to a drug dealer.

The Bureau of Narcotics rarely granted hemp farming licenses. A group of Minnesota farmers who had successfully produced hemp for years before the Marijuana Tax Act applied for licenses unsuccessfully for several years after the Tax Act. In response, they contacted their Senator, Henrik Shipstead, to act on their behalf. However, Anslinger insinuated in a reply letter to Shipstead that those farmers had never applied for a license. He added that their applications probably would have been approved if they could produce hemp that was "substantially free of flowering tops and leaves."[88] That was the resulting situation for nearly everyone in the industry or they were buried in red tape. Albeit, the Bureau of Narcotics notably didn't harass one particular company, Matt Rens Hemp Company, because they provided supplies to the U.S. Navy.[89]

The Bureau of Narcotics knew that they were suppressing the potentially explosive growth of the hemp industry. They received many letters from the hemp industry requesting leniency. One letter, just months after the bill passed, from H.W. Bellrose on October 12, 1937, promised that a "re-birth" of the industry was imminent because of the capacity of his "World Fibre Corporation Mechanical

Decorticating machine."[90] Bellrose highlighted the numerous markets in which hemp was on the verge of entering full scale, including paper pulp. (*Again, remember that piece of information for later.*) "In the paper pulp industry alone, we are importing 80% of all paper as paper stock, and this industry runs well over one billion dollars per annum," he stated. Also, the Illinois Hemp Company provided correspondence from rope and paper manufacturers, along with Goodyear Tire & Rubber Company and the Ford Motor Company, who were interested in purchasing supplies from them.

Some members of the national media also reported about the potential rebirth of hemp. In February of 1938 *Mechanical Engineering Magazine* published an article "The Most Profitable and Desirable Crop That Can Be Grown" touting the economic potential of hemp. That same month, *Popular Mechanics* published a very similar article, "Hemp: The New Billion-Dollar Crop." It stated, "If federal regulations can be drawn to protect the public without preventing the legitimate culture of hemp, this new crop can add immeasurably to American agriculture and industry."[91]

Henry Ford was one of the business tycoons most adversely affected by hemp's new regulations. Ford aggressively experimented with developing cars that weren't fueled by alternatives to oil. In 1912 Ford began financing a project by Thomas Edison to improve upon batteries for electric automobiles, but that project ended two years later after an explosion in Edison's laboratory.[92] Ford's passion for agriculture seemed to have shaped his vision for cars that could be fueled by and manufactured from various crops. After all, his first car prototype in 1896 ran entirely on ethanol. Furthermore, in 1925, he told *The New York Times* that "ethanol was the fuel of the future."[93]

Ford was also a firm supporter of hemp. He asked, "Why use up the forests which were centuries in the making and the mines which required ages to lay down if we can get the equivalent of forest and mineral products in the annual growth of hemp fields?"[94] Ford began developing plans in 1929 for cars that were made from hemp, along with other plant materials. He continued those plans even after the 1937 Marihuana Tax Act. By 1941, he had created a prototype of his dream car. It was a plastic car and only the frame was made from steel. The plastic panels were a 70% blend of cellulose fibers from hemp, wheat straw, and sisal.[95] The car weighed about one-third less than traditional steel cars and was ten times as crash resistant. Henry Ford demonstrated for *Popular Mechanics* (December 1941 issue) the enhanced durability of his car by hitting it repeatedly with an ax. The ax didn't even leave a dent. Nonetheless, Ford was sarcastically asked in an interview in February of 1943 by *The Rotarian Magazine* if his plastic car would be mass produced within 50 years. Ford responded, "Fifty years from now! Tomorrow -- just as soon as this war is won. We're ready for it NOW!"[96] Unfortunately, that remarkable hemp car ended up remaining only a prototype as the regulations from hemp production diminished supplies to levels that weren't economically viable for mass production. Think about how many automobile accident casualties could have been prevented with this type of innovation!

Similar business interests and mutual necessity can make for strange bedfellows. Look no further than Hearst's relationship with one of the most controversial robber barons, Andrew Mellon. Before being associated with Mellon, Hearst's newspapers had been notably anti-big business and often focused on corruption. That changed, however, in his later years as his massive personal spending, which surpassed anyone throughout American history at the time, nearly led Hearst into bankruptcy in 1937.[97] That type of audacious spending is still on display with his castle, San Simeon. That property is almost half the size of Rhode Island![98] Consequently, by the 1920s, Hearst had begun to depend upon financing from big banks and no longer attacked them with his newspapers. Hearst and Mellon formed a cozy relationship in which Mellon used Hearst's papers to suppress scandals involving Mellon's business interests while Mellon indirectly financed Hearst.[99]

In an odd coincidence, Andrew Mellon was Harry Anslinger's uncle by marriage.[100] Mellon held vast fortunes in a variety of industries such as banking, steel, coal, and aluminum, but the aggressive tactics of his nephew-in-law ultimately benefitted his oil business by suppressing the hemp industry. If there was a conspiracy, it certainly wasn't out of character for Mellon as he had a long, well-documented history of corrupting politics for his personal benefit. For example, before entering office as the Secretary of the Treasury he actually had state divorce laws changed. That occurred just before his divorce and saved him a great deal of money. Mellon also maintained an active role with his bank,

Mellon National Bank, while serving as Secretary of the Treasury in violation of the Federal Reserve Act of 1913.

Congress unknowingly created a conflict of interest when the Federal Bureau of Narcotics was created within the Treasury Department in 1930 while Mellon was in charge. The Bureau of Prohibition (alcohol) had operated within the Treasury Department and it contained a Narcotics Division. However, Mellon managed to have the Bureau of Prohibition transferred from the Treasury Department to the Justice Department. He argued that it was "illogical" for the Treasury to be involved in law enforcement.[101] After all, Mellon was hardly an anti-vice activist. He had been a very public critic of the prohibition of alcohol and had owned distilleries before the Volstead Act. On the other hand, with Mellon's nephew at the helm, the Federal Bureau of Narcotics aggressively expanded the war against cannabis.

The separation between civil servant and private business interests apparently meant nothing to Mellon. One of Mellon's biographers, David Cannadine, noted several of Mellon's inconsistencies with his ideology. Mellon was passionately anti-tax, but he benefitted from protective tariffs on aluminum to gain a monopoly. He then pushed for all public buildings to be made from aluminum. Also, Mellon cited national security fears when he placed tariffs on Soviet-made products, but he didn't put tariffs on the Soviet manganese that his steel companies needed.[102] While in office, he openly lobbied on behalf of his companies, Gulf Oil and Alcoa. In fact, while serving as the ambassador to Great Britain, Mellon lobbied the U.S. State Department so persistently for aid in gaining Kuwaiti oil contracts for Gulf Oil, that one official warned "that he go easy on (that) question."[103] Mind you, Mellon was serving that ambassadorship in 1932 because he resigned from the Treasury to avoid the impeachment process that came about from his many scandals while in office.[104]

Mellon's interests aligned with the DuPont family which had been known primarily as a munitions manufacturer for over a century. For example, DuPont supplied 40% of the explosives for the Allies during WWI. DuPont then diversified into the auto industry with their takeover of General Motors in 1920. According to Jack Herer, that acquisition was partially financed by Mellon.[105] By the 1920s, DuPont was fully invested in a petroleum-based future because the company was the leading manufacturer of lead additives in fuel. Decades later, DuPont's numerous petroleum-based products continue to be sold in cars, including artificial leather, plastics, paints, etc.

To put it briefly, the DuPont family also had a massive financial interest in crushing competition from hemp. There were six different American patents issued from 1925 to 1935 for deriving cellulose from hemp. In fact, some of those patents were for processes for paper and plastics that directly competed with DuPont's core business model.[106] By the 1930s, DuPont was developing and patenting the rights to numerous petrochemical products that are still in use today. Notably, in 1937, DuPont patented processes for making plastics from coal and oil along with new techniques for making paper from wood pulp. Those processes accounted for 80% of their profits over the next 60 years, according to Jack Herer.[107]

Like most conspiracies, the case for the "hemp conspiracy" certainly lacks "smoking gun" evidence, but the circumstantial evidence is overwhelming. It's certainly well documented that the Marihuana Tax Act of 1937 was railroaded through Congress, but no one can know entirely all the motivations of the parties involved.[C108] To paraphrase Queen Elizabeth, no one has a window to men's souls.

For the modern reader, connecting names like DuPont to conspiracies is a challenge, but in the 1930s, the DuPont name was highly despised among the working class in America. They were viewed in a similar way to how companies such as Halliburton and

---

[C] Henry Ford never mentioned DuPont, Hearst, or Mellon as part of a conspiracy against him, but he had a very conspiratorial view of the world based on "international Jew bankers." He published hate-filled anti-Semitic newspapers and some of those articles were summarized in a book *The International Jew: The World's Foremost Problem*. Ford was an enigma. He wasn't anti-Semitic in his early life and it's believed that his hatred can be explained as manipulations from his closest adviser, Ernest Liebold, who was eventually exposed as a Nazi spy. Ford, like many other major corporations, including DuPont, generated huge profits from supplying the Nazis during WWII. Ford differed from those other companies as they were entirely motivated by profits and had supplied both sides of the war. On the other hand, Ford received the highest Medal of Honor by Adolf Hitler. He supplied the Nazis at the same time that he intentionally delayed supplies for the Allied Forces. Ford, a Holocaust denier, eventually died from a massive stroke, which reportedly occurred during an hour long presentation that happened to be his first visual evidence from the concentration camps.

Blackwater (which has changed its name two times due to bad publicity) are viewed today. DuPont acquired the moniker "merchants of death" from their war profiteering during WWI.[D109] Decades of public relations efforts have stripped away the memories of how they were guilty of the same type of corporate trust abuses synonymous with the Gilded Age. That included hiring members of a violent white supremacist organization that was an offshoot of the KKK, "the Black Legion," to murder and intimidate their labor union rivals.[110]

The DuPont family, along with other industrialists (J.P. Morgan), formed a political organization, the American Liberty League, that challenged the reforms of the New Deal era. History has proven that members of this group were the ringleaders of one of the most deplorable acts of corruption, not ordinary political lobbying. This was informally known as "the Business Plot," but few people know of this today.

Gen. Smedley Butler, author of *War is a Racket*, named members of the American Liberty League in his testimony before the McCormack-Dickstein Committee in 1934. Gen. Butler swore that he had been recruited by the nation's most powerful business leaders during the preliminary phase of plans to conduct a paramilitary coup in the U.S. According to Butler, he was offered money and a prominent political position. After all, he was a prime

---

[D] A similar conspiracy involving some of the same players began around the same time as the marijuana conspiracy. Starting in 1936, a group of companies, mainly General Motors, Standard Oil, Greyhound, and Firestone Tires, began systematically ending the electric streetcar throughout most major cities of the country. The plan was to the replace the electric car system with the city bus system. Those companies acquired National City Lines, which controlled the electric rail car system, and then cut off all money for maintaining the infrastructure. Naturally, that led to a decline in the quality of service by the electric system over time. Hence, most people supported scrapping the electric car system in favor of a gas and diesel powered bus system. The buses were built by General Motors, the fuel was supplied by Standard Oil, Firestone tires were on those buses, and Greyhound eventually converted many of those buses into their business of today. By 1947, a number of people in this scandal were charged by the FBI and convicted of conspiracy. However, there wasn't much of a clamor from the American public as they had grown to prefer their own cars over public transportation. Edwin Black's *Internal Combustion* provides a more thorough explanation and documentation of this particular scandal.

choice for those industrialists because he had the popular support of the troops after leading the "Bonus Marchers" protest after WWI.[111]

In the end, the McCormack-Dickstein Committee examined and confirmed Butler's accusations. They reported, "In the last few weeks of the committee's official life it received evidence showing that certain persons had made an attempt to establish a fascist organization in this country...There is no question that these attempts were discussed, were planned, and might have been placed in execution when and if the financial backers deemed it expedient."[112]

One notable reporter, Paul Comly French, backed up Butler's accusations and added that he had been told by one of the conspirators that the DuPont family planned to arm the coup through their company, Remington Arms Co.[113] Nonetheless, despite the conclusions of the McCormack-Dickstein Committee, Butler was widely mocked in the newspapers. The story has since faded from the public consciousness. It's not even a footnote in history textbooks even though a few authors have thoroughly documented this conspiracy. None of the conspirators were ever charged with any crimes because it would have been quite difficult to get a conviction due to their power and legal resources. Considering the challenge of convicting numerous business giants, some historians have speculated that FDR used the evidence from that investigation as leverage to get many of his New Deal reforms passed.[114]

Former New York Mayor Fiorello La Guardia (1934-1945) never mentioned a conspiracy involving the 1937 Marihuana Tax Act, but he had his doubts about the danger of the drug. He formed the La Guardia Committee in 1939, which was one of the first scientific and sociological studies conducted on marijuana. The conclusions of the study, after five years of research, firmly contradicted the propaganda circulating that marijuana is physically addictive and leads to violence.[115] This only angered Harry Anslinger who disputed the study and threatened to arrest anyone who conducted his own independent scientific research.[116]

Anslinger's credibility and public influence steadily increased over time. By the McCarthy era, Anslinger had transitioned drug war propaganda in line with the times. However, the relationship between Anslinger and McCarthy developed a major complication. Anslinger admitted in his memoir to secretly supplying heroin on a daily basis to "one of the most influential members of the Congress of the United States." His biographers firmly believed that it was Joseph McCarthy. Nonetheless, Anslinger never shied away from his assertions that "marijuana leads to pacifism and communist brainwashing."[117]

By the 1960s, public opinion about drugs, in particular, marijuana, had shifted after it had become commonplace on college campuses. Timothy Leary, an icon of 1960s counterculture, was labeled as the "most dangerous man in America" by Richard Nixon. He was a psychologist who advocated the benefits of psychedelic drugs based on his scientific experiments. Subsequently, he was arrested in 1966 with less than an ounce of marijuana and sentenced to 30 years in prison, along with a $30,000 fine. However, his lawyers successfully overturned his conviction through the appeals process and the U.S. Supreme Court ruled in 1969 that the 1937 Marihuana Tax Act was unconstitutional. In essence, they determined that the Marihuana Tax Act violated Leary's right to freedom from self-incrimination because he had to admit to breaking state law to pay the federal tax.[118] With that said, the Nixon administration quickly reestablished federal marijuana laws by signing the Controlled Substances Act of 1970, which is still in effect today.

Richard Nixon responded to the hippy movement of the 1960s by intensifying the drug war, calling it a "state of emergency." In fact, the term "drug war" was coined during his administration.[119] To subdue the growing public demand for legalization, Richard Nixon decided to form a commission on marijuana in 1970. However, this commission was all for show. Nixon even publicly stated, "I am against legalizing marijuana. Even if the commission does recommend that it be legalized, I will not follow that recommendation."[120] Furthermore, in private he demanded an "all-out war" that would fall in line with his view. Nixon said, "I want a goddamn strong statement on marijuana...one that just tears the ass out of them."[121]

It was the government's largest and most in-depth scientific study on marijuana at the time. Ray Shafer, the head of the commission for the study, was in line for a potential federal judgeship, pending Nixon's approval. Despite the political pressure, the Shafer Report was released in 1972 and the general conclusions were that marijuana's harm to the user is minimal and that it should be decriminalized. Needless to say, Shafer never received the federal judgeship that he desired, even though Nixon had previously stated in private that Shafer "had a damn good record. He's a good lawyer. He'd be a good judge, as good as anybody."[122] Shafer also testified before Congress stating, "Criminal law is too harsh a tool to apply to personal possession even in the effort to discourage use. It implies an overwhelming indictment of the behavior which we believe is not appropriate. The actual and potential harm of use of the drug is not great enough to justify intrusion by the criminal law into private behavior, a step which our society takes only 'with the greatest reluctance.'"[123]

Nixon had a conspiratorial view that support for drug legalization was part of a left-wing conspiracy. He said off the record that "every one of those bastards for legalizing marijuana is Jewish" and that "homosexuality, dope, immorality in general" were "the enemies of strong societies. That's why the Communists and the left-wingers are pushing the stuff, they're trying to destroy us."[124] Predictably, Nixon completely disregarded the Shafer commission's recommendations. He then signed for the formation of the Drug Enforcement Agency (DEA) in 1973, almost exactly one year to the day after Shafer's testimony. That decision merged all of the drug administrations into one agency with many more agents and a notably larger budget.

Edward Jay Epstein, author of *Agency of Fear: Opiates and Political Power in America*, documented that the drug war was the "perfect cover" for Nixon to abuse executive power, divert various federal agencies, and target his political enemies with illegal spying.[125] Epstein's book quoted a top Nixon administration official, Gene Rossides, who asked, "If not for Watergate, can you imagine what they would have done with the Drug Enforcement Agency?"[126] In that first year alone, an additional 128,000 Americans were arrested for marijuana.[127]

In contrast, Jimmy Carter was the first U.S. President to publicly campaign for ending the drug war. He wanted to decriminalize marijuana possession for up to one ounce. He felt that it was a states' rights issue and several states had already begun similar initiatives. "Penalties against possession of a drug should not be more damaging to an individual than the use of the drug itself..." said Carter.[128] Those were truly revolutionary words as no other U.S. President had addressed the drug issue in a humanitarian sense and as a public health problem, rather than as a moral or law & order issue.

Carter also appointed a controversial "drug czar," Dr. Peter G. Bourne, who represented a complete changing of the guard. All of his predecessors had fixated on enforcing the laws, whereas Bourne was more concerned with offering rehabilitation services. Bourne was quite candid and lacked the filter necessary for a career in politics. He openly considered the merits of decriminalizing heroin and cocaine.[129] In fact, he had written an article, "The Cocaine Myth," a few years earlier, which essentially suggested that recreational cocaine use didn't represent an ominous threat to public health.[130] There was some truth to what he had to say, but America's foremost authority on drugs would need to maintain a squeaky-clean reputation to carry on with such assertions credibly. Hence, Carter's bold choice blew up in his face after Bourne was caught in a scandal due to writing an illegal prescription for Quaaludes for one of his assistants.[131] Shortly afterward, Bourne resigned from his position, but not before some more public embarrassment unfolded. *The Washington Post* reported that Bourne had smoked pot and snorted cocaine while attending the Christmas party of NORML (the National Organization to Reform Marijuana Laws).[132]

All in all, these public embarrassments crushed Carter's resolve and all tangible reforms of our drug policies were put on the backburner. After all, his "drug czar" had reportedly partied with the drug-enthusiast and counterculture icon Hunter S. Thompson.[133] Ultimately, Middle America viewed him as a weak leader and his liberal drug policies were tossed to the wayside due to his plummeting approval ratings from a sputtering economy and the Iran hostage crisis. Thus, the direction of drug policy changed dramatically with Ronald Reagan's landslide victory. Nonetheless, the demand for illegal drugs surged during the "Just Say No" era. The Reagan administration responded by escalating the drug war and our federal budget has since exponentially increased, along with our prison population and black market crime. Likewise, no U.S. President has since responded to the drug issue as a public health problem and, as a result, we endure the absolute mess that is at hand right now.

3

> "Drug dealers aren't afraid to die. The death penalty doesn't mean anything unless you use it on people who are afraid to die...like the bankers who launder the drug money."
> George Carlin

George Carlin joked that "we wouldn't be able to buy drugs in schools and prisons anymore" if we executed "the white, middle-class Republican" money launderers.[1] The general public is beginning to realize how complicit the financial sector is with drug trafficking. However, there is an 800-pound gorilla in the room and it represents the vulnerability of our financial system without the cash flow of drug money. The banking industry, as a whole, was drowning in debt and strapped for cash during the last financial crisis. Drug money was one of the industry's primary safety outlets to pay collateral obligations and avoid bankruptcy. In fact, Antonio Maria Costa, the head of the UN Office on Drugs and Crime (the UN "drug czar"), stated that drug money literally saved the banks from an economic meltdown in 2008.[2]

The International Monetary Fund (IMF) estimates that money laundering represents 2-5% of all of the world's financial transactions: $500 Billion to $1.5 Trillion a year.[3] It's no wonder drug money laundering has become so pervasive when the Federal Reserve, the banking industry's most powerful regulatory body, has long neglected those duties. The Federal Reserve has acted more like a partner for the major banks in the face of rampant corporate crime. For instance, Miami has been one of the primary drug port cities in the U.S. since the 1970s and has hosted numerous community banks catering to that trade. Accordingly, Eric Schlosser, author of *Reefer Madness: Sex, Drugs, and Cheap Labor*, discovered one Miami bank that allowed a drug dealer to make cash deposits of $2 million per day.[4] That's why the Federal Reserve Bank of Miami reported in 1979 that its cash deposits were $5.5 billion higher than the deposits from all of the other twelve Federal Reserve Banks combined.[5]

The Federal Reserve has ignored evidence of widespread drug money laundering and demonstrated no willingness to punish this activity. Congress has lacked the political will to punish the bankers. That same Federal Reserve report led to a money laundering task force "Operation Greenback," which prosecuted some small community banks in Miami.[6] However, the Reagan administration cut back on the operation's funding. The IRS agent who headed the Operation Greenback task force, Mike McDonald, later expressed to *PBS Frontline* that money laundering investigations are more effective than drug task forces. He pointed out that a drug seizure doesn't damage a cartel as much as a money seizure. The costs to reproduce a shipment of drugs are quite low. On the other hand, a confiscation of drug money is a "dollar for dollar" loss for the cartel.[7]

Despite glaring red flags, the first consolidated drug money laundering laws weren't formed until 1986.[8] Those laws were sparked by the publicity from the "Pizza Connection" case, which was the longest federal trial in U.S. history. This case linked the Sicilian Mafia with numerous major banks, but only the smaller companies with far fewer lobbyists and less political clout faced criminal charges.[9]

Before 1986, banks were only responsible for reporting all transactions over $10,000 and suspicious activity. Congress has subsequently passed further laws, but the penalties for money laundering remain relatively soft. Consequently, the black market for money laundering is no longer centered primarily in Miami. It has expanded and several of the well-known financial giants have been caught or implicated, such as Bank of America, Citibank, Capital One, American Express, among many others.[10] Suffice it to say, it would be more difficult to name a major U.S. bank that *hasn't* been associated with money laundering.

Banks are, by law, obligated in their due diligence to verify the legitimacy of their clients' transactions, but clearly this isn't always the case. A 2001 Senate Finance Committee studied compliance from 20 of the largest banks. Senator Carl Levin (D-MI) found that almost every bank had accounts from suspicious offshore jurisdictions that were not properly monitored.[11]

Money laundering laws were established with the intent of punishing bankers if they're complicit in this activity. In other words, there needs to be some common sense deterrents for the banker not to look the other way when Scarface walks in the door with a duffel bag of cash. However, these laws have been implemented in a reverse fashion by not punishing the people who facilitate this vice. The government cherry-picks who to prosecute to the fullest extent of the law. Specifically, in 2014 a drug trafficker from Spain, Alvaro López Tardón, was sentenced in Miami to 150 years in prison. He was never accused of distributing drugs in the U.S. Instead, he transferred roughly $14 million to Miami where he purchased several condos, luxury cars, and pieces of jewelry.[12] To sum up, if Tardón had worked for an elite bank, he most likely would never have been indicted.

For large corporations, the rewards for laundering money far outweigh the risks. Take a recent example in what was one of the most significant money laundering cases on record with Wachovia (now Wells Fargo). Wachovia processed $373 billion in possible drug money transactions from 2004 to 2007. Federal regulators gave their company specific warnings about those transactions as early as 1996, but they continued the practice. Consequently, Wachovia received one of the largest penalties ever for this crime -- $160 million in fines and forfeitures.[13] A $160 million penalty gives the headline reader the impression of a firm punishment, but the fine pales in comparison to the profits. That is merely the cost of doing business in this black market. Also, none of the employees went to prison and, in an ironic twist, Wells Fargo had to agree to not use funds from their $25 billion bailout to pay the fines.[14]

HSBC, one of the world's largest financial institutions, received the highest fine to date for money laundering, $1.9 billion. That certainly generates headlines, but it doesn't appropriately punish the bank's criminal actions. After all, HSBC was the "preferred financial institution for drug cartels and money launderers," according to the U.S. Department of Justice (DOJ).[15] From 2006 to 2009, HSBC branches in the U.S. failed to monitor $670 billion in wire transfers and $9.4 billion in purchases of physical U.S. dollars from their offices in Mexico.[16] The activity was so brazen that Mexican drug traffickers learned the dimensions of the windows for the banks' tellers and, on a daily basis, they brought boxes of cash that could squeeze through those windows.[17]

HSBC also diversified their illegal money laundering operations by adding potential terrorist organizations as clients. They failed to monitor a total of $60 trillion in risky transactions worldwide and violated international treaties by conducting business with Iran, Cuba, Sudan, and Burma.[18] They also did business with Al Rajhi, Saudi Arabia's largest bank. That's particularly appalling because, according to a Senate report, some of the owners of Al Rajhi were linked to the 9/11 attacks. Hence, the American branch of HSBC, HBUS, discontinued business with Al Rajhi shortly after 9/11. But, they reestablished their business relationship in 2006 after Al Rajhi threatened HSBC with the possibility of losing all of their business worldwide.[19]

Nevertheless, HSBC avoided any appropriate penalties because of their economic power. Officials from the Treasury Department, along with regulators from the Federal Reserve and the Office of the Comptroller of the Currency, warned against penalizing HSBC too severely. They believed disastrous consequences might have resulted for the world's financial system.[20] The "too big to fail" theory is widely cited, but it needs to be addressed because it serves as a red herring that protects white collar criminals. Prosecuting *the employees* involved in money laundering will not hurt the economy in any way.

Former Attorney General, Eric Holder, testified in 2013 before Congress that the DOJ had been hesitant to prosecute some of the largest banks because they were considered too big to fail.[21] However, it was revealed in 2016 that Holder and other top officials of the DOJ overruled their staffers' recommendation to prosecute HSBC. This information came from a report issued by the House Committee on Financial Services' Republican staff. There were several other disturbing details in that story, including the fact that Holder "misled Congress" about the DOJ's reasons for not filing charges. In fact, HSBC was able to negotiate a more favorable plea deal *after* Holder had personally issued a "take-it-or-leave-it" deadline.[22] (Details about Eric Holder's conflicts of interest are covered more thoroughly in Chapter 8)

The government has the right to shut down a bank if the company is convicted of money laundering, but that rarely ever happens. The "too big to fail" banks are also considered too big to prosecute. To illustrate, law enforcement officials were still "bitterly divided about whether to indict Lehman Brothers" even after they caught the company red-handed, laundering millions of dollars of drug money for a high-level Mexican official, Mario Villanueva Madrid.[23] In fact, many of these "too big to fail" banks have been caught multiple times. Even in that scenario, no one goes to prison.

It's almost unprecedented for an executive to face criminal charges for these offenses; meanwhile, those people benefit the most from drug money profits in the form of gigantic bonuses. With those consequences and incentives in place, it's no wonder that this practice continues to thrive in the competitive world of Wall Street. Drug money obviously adds to a bank's balance sheet, but the cash flow can also function as short-term window dressing for investors.[24]

It has been over two decades since a notable bank received the "death penalty" for money laundering. It was the Bank of Credit and Commerce International (BCCI) which was "one of the most complex and secretive criminal organizations we have ever encountered," according to Robert Morgenthau, former Manhattan District Attorney. BCCI routinely laundered money for terrorist organizations, illegal arms dealers, and drug cartels. Robert Gates even referred to BCCI as the "Bank of Crooks and Criminals International" in an internal CIA report while he served as the agency's Deputy Director in the 1980s. The intelligence community overlooked the bank's flagrant criminal activities because they had also been prime customers of BCCI. The CIA, Britain's MI6, and Israel's Mossad often used BCCI for their secretive operations.[25]

Robert Mazur was the undercover agent responsible for shutting down BCCI in 1991 and the arrests of many Medellín Cartel members in the process. His book, *Infiltrator: My Secret Life Inside the Dirty Banks Behind Pablo Escobar's Medellín Cartel*, detailed the numerous bureaucratic obstacles which he faced. That book clearly demonstrated that drug money laundering often isn't a matter of drug dealers outsmarting bankers; instead high-level bankers are often completely aware of their clients' illegal means and they use every trick imaginable to cover the origin of their money.[26]

BCCI was the last case of its kind. The financial sector has successfully lobbied for less regulation and more privacy from these investigations. In many ways, the financial regulators' hands are tied. When Mazur discusses the tactics that he used with current agents he hears things like, "If I did that today, they'd put me in jail. We'll never get the chance to do that -- but we should."[27] In fact, the regulations in the U.S. are more lax than in Colombia, according to Alejandro Gaviria, Colombian economist and prominent researcher of money laundering. He said, "In Colombia, they ask questions of banks they'd never ask in the U.S. If they did, it would be against the laws of banking privacy."[28]

With that said, that doesn't mean that financial regulations don't exist as there are mountains of government red tape. However, these rules are the kinds which typically aren't effective and impact low-level employees. Wells Fargo once decided to fire a customer service representative, Richard Eggers, 68, rather than face a potential fine. Eggers wasn't a drug kingpin; instead, he had been arrested 49 years prior for placing a fake dime in a washing machine at a laundromat.[29]

The major banks have been severely negligent with their due diligence, but it's also unreasonable to expect banks to detect every case of suspicious activity by their customers. It's quite difficult to catch drug money launderers because skilled criminals use a complicated money trail. In one instance, authorities once arrested a man who transferred $36 million of cocaine funds from the U.S. to Colombia via Europe. That wasn't an easy case because he used roughly a hundred different accounts with 68 different banks in 9 different countries.[30]

However, bankers should be criminally prosecuted, not fined, when they *are involved* in criminal activity. Ramon Milian Rodriguez, a major money courier who laundered hundreds of millions of dollars for the Colombian cartels, testified before the Senate Subcommittee on Narcotics, Terrorism and International Operations. He mostly dealt with Citicorp (now Citibank) and Bank of America, but he said that many other major U.S. banks aggressively pursued him.[31] They had "special representatives" who recruited his services with entertainment, women, and cash.[32]

Years after Rodriguez's testimony, Citibank executives were accused of aiding Raúl Salinas, the brother of the former Mexican President Carlos Salinas, in money laundering. Raúl Salinas had a cushy government job that paid a salary of $192,000, yet he held Swiss bank accounts worth roughly $84 million.[33] He wasn't a trafficker, but he amassed such a fortune by accepting bribes from the Mexican and Colombian cartels. In fact, his greed earned him the nickname, "the bloodsucker."[34]

Even after Raúl's arrest was a matter of public record, Citibank employees reportedly instructed an operator to tell Raúl to give his account information to his brother who was waiting outside in a limousine.[35] In a similar fashion, one of Salinas's most notorious benefactors was the head of the Juárez cartel, Amado Carrillo Fuentes (aka "the Lord of the Skies"). Citibank helped transfer roughly $300 million for Carrillo Fuentes to a shell company with no corporate offices that posed as a bank in the Cayman Islands.[36]

This kind of brazen activity occurs because the systemic pressures against whistleblowers are evident for any industry. It's essentially career suicide. That's why Congress has passed various laws to protect them from prosecution, protect their jobs, and even include financial incentives for coming forward with information (up to 30% of the proceeds from the government's seizure). The federal government now pays a tremendous amount of money to criminal informants for drug cases. However, the government rarely incentivizes whistleblowers to implicate major financial institutions with money laundering.

Martin Woods discovered unrestrained criminal activity as the director of the Wachovia anti-money-laundering unit in London. In turn, he said that he was treated like a "business prevention officer" after he reported that information to Wachovia executives.[37] The executives ignored his pleas even though Woods' instincts were exactly right. They also told him to back off, issued a discipline letter, and scheduled a hearing for professional misconduct. Those kinds of aggravations led him to quit his job, but he received an undisclosed payment due to a lawsuit for harassment and detrimental treatment. Nonetheless, Woods noted that every Wachovia employee involved with this illegal activity has "either been promoted" or moved on "to a better job at other banks."[38]

Everett Stern, a former anti-money laundering compliance officer for HSBC, had similar experiences as a whistleblower. Stern discovered HSBC's criminal conduct within three weeks on the job.[39] He then immediately contacted the CIA, FBI, and other agencies. The fact that Stern was able to identify this criminal activity so quickly is particularly alarming because he, along with his colleagues, received virtually no training for detecting money laundering. Case in point, Stern checked out money laundering books from the library to gain the necessary knowledge for the job.[40]

According to Stern, HSBC was actively disguising the activities of known terrorist groups and drug cartels by changing their transaction codes (by adding a dot or a dash). "If I were to donate $1 to Hamas or Hezbollah I would go to jail for life...(for them) there's no consequence and they're still doing it," said Stern.[41]

HSBC's anti-money laundering compliance officers were offered financial incentives for quickly clearing transactions that had been flagged as suspicious. Also, compliance officers were chastised if they dared to go above and beyond the bare minimum standards by thoroughly examining those suspicious transactions.

Stern also asserted that the same type of money laundering practices are likely to continue at HSBC because they've only made superficial reforms. For instance, they fired a group of debt collectors and customer service reps from their credit card department and rehired them as anti-money laundering compliance officers. However, only a few of the new employees had experience with detecting money laundering. In other words, HSBC's money laundering department increased the number of staff members to give the appearance of greater compliance.[42]

One particular case demonstrated that the government is reluctant to protect whistleblowers and prosecute criminal bankers. Two years after resigning from his job at the Swiss banking giant UBS, Bradley Birkenfeld, voluntarily contacted U.S. federal authorities. He informed them that the bank was involved in a multi-billion dollar tax fraud scheme.[43] He opened the vault, so to speak, and revealed the secrets to their criminal enterprise. The information offered by Birkenfeld was the first of its kind. UBS wasn't merely a willfully ignorant company. No, their representatives traveled to the U.S. to recruit wealthy Americans to help them evade their taxes. In fact, UBS representatives were issued encrypted computers and trained in counter-surveillance to avoid being detected by the U.S. authorities.[44]

Doug Schulman, the IRS Commissioner, stated that Birkenfeld's information led to "an unprecedented amount of information on taxpayers who have evaded their tax obligation by hiding money offshore at UBS."[45] In short, Birkenfeld's information led to UBS's admission of hiding 19,000 American bank accounts, thus helping the U.S. Treasury collect billions of dollars in back taxes.[46] You would never guess Birkenfeld's reward for handing over this case on a silver platter? It was a 40-month sentence in a federal penitentiary.[47]

Typically criminal informants cooperate with the government to have their sentences reduced. However, Birkenfeld wasn't under investigation when he approached the federal authorities; it was of his own volition. Nevertheless, the DOJ charged him with conspiracy to commit tax fraud because he allegedly withheld information about one of his prior clients.[48] Not surprisingly, he received, by far, the harshest penalty for anyone involved. That type of precedent will certainly give future whistleblowers something to think about. Meanwhile, UBS was fined a portion of their proceeds, $780 million, but no one from the company faced any criminal charges.[49] Furthermore, UBS announced in 2015 that they were again under investigation by the DOJ for tax evasion with U.S. clients.[50]

Birkenfeld petitioned the Obama administration to get his sentence commuted, but that was unsuccessful.[51] In fact, three days after Birkenfeld's sentencing, Obama was seen playing golf in Martha's Vineyard with his close friend Robert Wolf, the president of UBS Americas.[52] That was certainly a controversial choice of golf partners at the time, but it's difficult to turn down one of your largest campaign donors.[A][53] That's also particularly alarming considering that the Obama campaign was adamant about the need for more transparency and more laws to protect whistleblowers.[B][54] In fact, it's part of a larger trend with the Obama administration that has prosecuted more whistleblowers than all other administrations combined.[55]

Birkenfeld would likely have never received a financial reward for his information if he had not been so open with the media. It was such a clearly symbolic story and it created enough political pressure for the U.S. government to grant him a portion of the reward that he was entitled to by law. After he served his sentence, he received a $104 million reward on September 11, 2012.[56] On a related note, just months prior, the Tax Justice Network released a study estimating that $21 trillion remains hidden in bank accounts worldwide by the world's wealthiest people.[57]

[A] UBS contributions totaled $534,166. Also, Obama's Attorney General, Eric Holder, had previously worked for them as an attorney, but he did recuse himself from the UBS investigation.

[B] Cause of Action, a transparency watchdog group, discovered an internal White House memo which showed that after only a few months in office, the Obama administration secretly took measures to block Freedom of Information Act requests that pertained to the White House. Nevertheless, Barack Obama was awarded a transparency award in 2011, despite his lousy record. He actually accepted the award in a secret meeting that didn't allow for any outside reporters.

Much of the general public is aware of the two-tiered justice system regarding the banks. (There will be much more detail in the next book, *Rackets Vol II: Dealing from the Bottom of the Deck: Hypocritical Gambling Laws Enrich Crooked Politicians, a Select-Few Casinos, and the Mob.*) As mentioned earlier, former Attorney General, Eric Holder, testified in 2013 before Congress that the DOJ had been hesitant to prosecute some of the largest banks because they were considered too big to fail.[58] There was a strong backlash from that statement and one year later Holder publicly backtracked stating, "No bank is too big to jail."[59]

Holder made that second statement after Credit Suisse, the second-largest Swiss bank, agreed to a felony plea bargain for also helping wealthy Americans avoid paying their federal taxes. Credit Suisse actively recruited more than 22,000 U.S. clients resulting in approximately $10 billion to $12 billion worth of deposits.[60] "A company's profitability or market share can never and will never be used as a shield from prosecution or penalty. And this action should put that misguided notion definitively to rest," said Holder.[61] Credit Suisse was the first major bank to plead guilty to a felony crime in the U.S. for over two decades.[62] But, the penalties were still quite minimal. They weren't even forced to reveal the identities of their criminal clientele and they were allowed to continue doing business in the U.S.[63]

Holder had previously stated that "no bank is too big to jail," but none of the executives faced any prison time. Credit Suisse was fined $2.6 billion, but critics have pointed out that the punishment was quite lenient, considering the extent and brazen nature of their crimes. Mark S. Henry, Senior Economist from Tax Justice Network, joked that "they're yodeling through the Alps over the light touch of Eric Holder."[64] In fact, their stock price rebounded significantly just one day after the announcement of their fine. The stock's rebound was enough to pay half the fine.[65] Credit Suisse's CEO even told shareholders that the penalty would have very little impact on their performance.[66]

It's ironic that Wall Street continues to enjoy free reign with laundering drug money. After all, the drug war's strongest supporters in the Republican Party typically favor trickle-down economics. The basic theory behind trickle-down economics, or supply-side economics, is that the largest businesses or suppliers should face the least burdens of regulation and taxing. Therefore, if the Republicans were truly committed to the drug war, then the same line of supply-side logic should apply to the drug war. However, the world's largest banks continue to get away with drug money laundering. Conversely, the companies that have faced harsh criminal penalties for money laundering aren't large enough to make a noticeable impact on the supply of drugs.

Low-level drug dealers don't have access to politically connected Wall Street firms. Instead, they usually launder their money through cash-heavy local businesses such as restaurants, night clubs, laundromats, car dealerships, jewelry stores, etc. And those small independent businesses are deemed by the government to be perfectly acceptable to fail. Consequently, these small-time criminals receive serious jail time and lose their businesses after they are caught laundering money.

Many notorious drug traffickers maintain very public profiles. In fact, some drug lords have made the Forbes Wealthiest Person rankings. The supply of drugs would be dramatically reduced if their white-collar enablers were punished similarly to street level drug dealers. Corporate criminals are more likely to snitch than drug dealers because they probably won't have the stomach for prison. There is also an honor code for not snitching in the criminal underworld or else they face deadly consequences.

Furthermore, someone who knowingly processes $1 million of drug money is just as guilty as someone who possesses $1 million of the product, yet there aren't any "3 strikes laws" or mandatory minimum sentences for corporate criminals. Thus, Ramon Milian Rodriguez pointed out that disparity during his Senate testimony. "First Boston (one of the several banks he did business with) paid a fine of $25,000 and I'm doing forty-two years."[67]

The federal government clearly doesn't have an interest in prosecuting white collar criminals. Very few law enforcement agents are assigned to follow the money trail of illegal drugs, compared to the physical product. There are nearly one million law enforcement agents nationwide and almost all of them are, in one way or another, dedicated to the drug war. But, less than 1% of them are solely focused on the money trail. As a matter of fact, the Financial Crimes Enforcement Network (FinCEN) is the primary governmental office dedicated to money laundering. Their entire staff consists of only 300 employees and they're responsible for all financial crimes, not just illegal drug money.[68] Furthermore, according to the latest information on the DEA's website, only 170 of their 5,233 special agents are dedicated to money laundering.^C There are also another 123 drug money laundering investigators from agencies outside of the DEA, such as IRS, ICE, FBI, National Guard, U.S. Postal Inspection Service, state and local police, etc.^{D69} That adds up to a total of 595 people specifically focused on money laundering. In sum, too much leeway is given to the banking sector if the government is truly dedicated to winning the drug war. Then again, what is the point when the federal government won't hold the worst offenders accountable?

There are limited resources dedicated to money laundering, but the federal government's response to money laundering is also often misdirected in a very disingenuous manner. Unfortunately, these money laundering statutes can be abused as an invasive tool overstepping our right to privacy. Some investigations are political in nature and don't target actual criminal activity. Case in point, the DOJ has a program, "Operation Chokepoint," which pressures banks to discontinue business with clients who are involved in a variety of legal, but controversial industries. As a result, several porn stars have publicly announced that their bank accounts were shut down because they were considered "high risk" clients.[70]

Also, small community banks, which service legal medical marijuana dispensaries, have been littered with so many federal regulations that several banks have found it easier to drop them as clients. Likewise, the IRS has in some cases prosecuted medical marijuana dispensaries for deducting their business expenses, such as wages and supplies. They cite an obscure law which bans deductions of any expense for any business "trafficking in controlled substances" that are prohibited by federal law.[71]

Dylan Donaldson, owner of a legal recreational marijuana dispensary in Colorado, notes the vast tax revenue his business has generated. Despite this fact, his business has "had 12 bank accounts

---

^C 159 special agents, 8 intelligence research analysts, and 3 DIs
^D IRS-Criminal Investigation: 12 full time and 4 part time Special Agents
ICE: 4 full time and 2 part time Special Agents
FBI: 1 full time Special Agent
U.S. Postal Inspection Service: 2 part time Postal Inspectors
National Guard: 3 full time Analysts
Financial Investigative Contractors: 24 full time and 5 part time
State & local Police Officers: 63 full time and 5 part time

over the last six years and, to date, they've all been shut down."[72] In fact, even the security companies that service these legal dispensaries can have trouble finding banking options too.[73] As a result, the government has created much more potential for violent crime because these dispensaries are forced to operate strictly in cash. And that has all been to project a *perception* of fighting the drug war.

Financial institutions aren't the only major corporations complicit with drug trafficking. We tend to think of front companies and shell corporations in regard to money laundering. However, in June of 2000, Attorney General Janet Reno held a private meeting with several executives from Fortune 500 companies, including Hewlett-Packard, Whirlpool, Ford, General Electric, and Sony, among others. The "Colombian Black Market Peso Exchange" was the focus of the meeting. At the time, officials estimated that as much as $5 billion a year was being laundered through this process that enables Colombian drug lords to purchase American goods from major corporations.[74]

It's a somewhat complicated scheme, but here's how it works. The Colombian cartels' funds are of no use to them if they can't spend the proceeds in their homeland. Therefore, the drug cartels contact currency brokers known as "peso brokers" who, for a hefty commission, convert their U.S. dollars to Colombian pesos. In turn, the "peso brokers" connect business people in Colombia with the distributors from major U.S. corporations. Those distributors obtain virtually anything that the cartels want to buy from major U.S. companies, everything from computers, appliances, cars, even helicopters.[75]

At first glance, it may sound as though the U.S. companies have no culpability in these transactions, but that isn't the case. They know the source of these funds as there are scorching red flags. After all, the peso brokers have couriers who deposit the cartel's dollars into numerous U.S. bank accounts in amounts below $10,000. Those deposits are then converted into non-cash funds such as personal checks, bank checks, money orders, traveler's checks, etc.[76] With a nudge and a wink, Colombian businessmen have paid these Fortune 500 companies with hundreds of those third-party checks at a time. All in all, that's actually more suspicious than if they offered duffel bags full of cash. Also, various U.S. companies have established back channels to conduct business with these unlicensed distributors because their goods are ultimately smuggled into Colombia. As a result, the Colombian government has been fleeced out of hundreds of millions of dollars in tax revenue. At one time, Colombian officials estimated that 45% of their imported consumer goods were purchased through the black market peso exchange.[77]

The meeting conducted by Janet Reno in 2000 wasn't the first of its kind. It was more of a final warning. There had, in fact, been a Congressional hearing solely focused on the black market peso exchange one year earlier. That hearing demonstrated how differently corporate criminals are treated. Sen. Chuck Grassley (R-IA) asked a Treasury official, Bonni Tischler, why only obscure small businesses had been prosecuted. She was fairly direct by explaining that it is much more difficult to prosecute major corporations, but she also evaded any confrontation by suggesting that "the object isn't to put our companies in jail. The object is to solve the problem."[78]

Again, there is a different set of rules for corporate America. One U.S. Customs official even claimed that the purpose of Janet Reno's meeting was to "educate these companies about how they are being victimized in the drug money laundering process."[79] To state the obvious, these corporate giants were anything but victims; these black market sales noticeably affected their bottom line. Specifically, General Electric's appliance sales in Latin America dropped by 20% when they took the appropriate steps to cut off their ties with the cartels.[80]

A wide range of Fortune 500 companies have been implicated in this black market, but the tobacco companies seem to be the worst offenders. After all, the black market peso exchange intersects with the underworld of contraband smuggling. The World Health Organization once estimated that 25% of the cigarettes sold worldwide have been smuggled across international borders to avoid taxes. The tobacco companies have facilitated this bootleg market to boost their bottom line. It's not a matter of ignorance on the part of these businesses as internal memos show that the company had specific backchannels for their "duty-free customers."[81]

The Colombian government responded in 2000 by suing Philip Morris (the maker of Marlboro) in federal court in Brooklyn, NY. The lawsuit sought $3 billion in damages and alleged that Philip Morris had knowingly dealt with smugglers, falsified documents to disguise that activity, and used Swiss bank accounts as a buffer with these transactions.[82] Furthermore, this underground commerce isn't limited to Colombia. The governments of Canada, Ecuador, and the European Union followed up with lawsuits in the U.S. courts against the top tobacco companies, Philip Morris and R.J. Reynolds. Both companies have been charged with racketeering, tax evasion, and money laundering.[83]

Philip Morris eventually settled with the European Union in 2004 for $1.25 billion.[84] On the other hand, the allegations against R.J. Reynolds have been much more serious and the company has battled their case for over a decade. According to the lawsuit, R.J. Reynolds conspired in a money laundering scheme involving mafia organizations around the world, including Colombia, Russia, and Italy. Also, their cigarettes served as a black market currency for these organized crime groups.[85] R.J. Reynolds has denied those allegations, but their primary defense has been that the U.S. courts don't have the jurisdiction because these alleged crimes (money laundering, racketeering, and tax evasion) took place in other countries. Ultimately, that was a wise decision by their company because the U.S. Supreme Court sided with R.J. Reynolds in 2016.[86] Who knows if Wall Street's finest will use this case as a defense in the future? In the end, these two companies were charged with the Racketeer Influenced and Corrupt Organizations Act (the RICO Act), but neither of them will be held accountable for criminal activity.

4

"The only difference between the Republican and Democratic parties is the velocities with which their knees hit the floor when corporations knock on their door."
Ralph Nader[1]

Neither of the major political parties has demonstrated any real commitment to ending the drug war. The Republican Party is the most ardent supporter of the drug war, yet this same support contradicts some of its main principles. In fact, it's difficult to name another political issue, other than the legalization of drugs, which would better accomplish the party's goals for reducing government spending while benefitting the private sector. Also, the Republican Party generally supports states' rights, except where states have legalized medical or recreational marijuana. The GOP has somehow successfully attached itself to the drug war while selling fears of "big government" and "the nanny state." Republican leaders tout the virtues of free markets, but apparently, they don't feel those same virtues apply to a free society. As Gore Vidal once stated, they prefer "laissez-faire" economics over "laissez-faire" values.[2]

Very few within the Democratic Party have displayed the political courage to challenge the drug war even though most of their political base would support them. In fact, many Democrats have used the drug war as a political bargaining chip. Some others have even used the drug war to try to "out-conservative" the conservatives. That was exactly the case with the Clinton administration. Many people assumed that Bill Clinton's infamous line, "I didn't inhale," was code meaning that he wouldn't support the drug war. However, marijuana arrests nearly doubled during his administration.[3]

Furthermore, the Democrats have kowtowed for decades to the special interests of the drug law enforcement community. Granted, that loyalty hasn't been reciprocated when push comes to shove. For example, during the 2006 congressional elections, the Office of National Drug Control Policy (ONDCP), an organization which is supposed to be politically independent, neglected Democrats while they made public appearances with 18 Congressional Republicans who were campaigning for re-election. The ONDCP also announced federal grants in some of those same congressional districts before the elections, which is a very common form of legal political kickbacks.[4]

The "hope" and "change" narrative from the Obama presidential campaign led many to assume that there would be a new drug policy. After all, during a 2004 Senatorial debate, Obama said, "I think the war on drugs has been a failure, and I think we need to rethink and decriminalize our marijuana laws but I'm not somebody who believes in legalization of marijuana."[5] He even mocked Bill Clinton during an interview in 2006 saying, "I inhaled frequently. That was the point."[6] However, he began to waffle on the issue once the presidency became a possibility. For instance, he hesitantly raised his hand in disagreement with Chris Dodd's suggestion of decriminalizing marijuana during a 2008 Democratic debate. However, Obama seemed to hedge by having one of his spokespersons say afterward that he misunderstood the question and that he supported decriminalization.[7]

After taking office, President Obama was less the statesman and more the politician. He conveyed an image sympathetic with liberal drug policies while acquiescing to conservative bureaucratic pressures. The vast majority of Americans want some liberal reforms. For example, seventy-four percent of Americans feel that federal authorities should no longer raid medical marijuana dispensaries that operate legally within state law.[8] Likewise, as a presidential hopeful, Obama promised, "What I'm not going to be doing is using Justice Department resources to try to circumvent state laws on this issue (medical marijuana) simply because I want folks to be investigating violent crimes and potential terrorism. We've got a lot of things for our law enforcement officers to deal with."[9]

It appeared that he would follow through with his promise when his administration even leaked a particular memo to the *Associated Press* early in the first term (October of 2009); it asserted that they would respect medical marijuana laws in states where it is legal.[10] Be that as it may, after some time it became apparent that the memo leak was nothing more than a political gesture. Medical marijuana dispensaries continued to face federal prosecutions from the Obama administration. In fact, the DEA raided twice as many medical marijuana dispensaries during Obama's first term than both of George W. Bush's terms combined.[A11]

Many people expected to see actual changes to drug policies when Obama appointed a liberal Drug Czar, Gil Kerlikowske, who had previously reduced drug arrests and focused more on harm reduction as the Chief of Police in Seattle, WA.[12] Kerlikowske has condemned the term "war on drugs" because "we're not at war with the people in this country."[13] He even told reporters that our financial crisis would eventually force a reevaluation of drug war policies.[14]

Despite the liberal rhetoric, the Obama administration has avoided making many bold changes to drug policy. In fact, Obama has contributed to the problem. After all, he nominated a well-known drug warrior, Michele Leonhart, to be the head of the DEA. As you may recall from the first chapter, she refused to admit that marijuana is less dangerous than heroin or cocaine. Obama also nominated her successor, Chuck Rosenberg, who claims that medical marijuana is "a joke."[15]

Obama's Attorney General, Eric Holder, promised during the midterm elections of 2010 to "vigorously enforce" federal marijuana laws regardless of California's voting results in a ballot to legalize recreational marijuana.[16] However, during Obama's re-election campaign in 2012, Eric Holder refused to comment as to how the Department of Justice would react if the same type of recreational marijuana law passed in a swing state such as Colorado.[17] Albeit, he eventually eased his stance, *after* Obama was re-elected. Thereupon, Holder established a "trust but verify approach" that essentially recognized states' rights where marijuana was legal.[18]

Obama has been unwilling to take any strong action at the executive level regarding the drug war. He has even mocked the idea publicly. For example, at a time when the economy was nosediving (663,000 Americans lost their jobs that month), the most popular issue from a Presidential town hall meeting on March 26, 2009 was whether the President believed that legalizing marijuana would have positive economic potential.[19] Obama chuckled at even considering the idea and stated, "I don't know what this says about the online

---

[A] These federal raids seem to have been selectively enforced for political purposes. There have been significantly more raids in California, a state which was never in doubt for Obama's re-election, compared to Colorado, a key swing state.

audience."[20] Likewise, most of the people in attendance mindlessly laughed along with him.

Obama has been questioned about marijuana several times during his presidency, but he has deftly managed to not take a real stance on the issue. He has stated lengthy, knowledgeable responses that demonstrate the damage that the drug war has caused to our country. However, he consistently spoke about this issue in a frustrated third-person type of narrative as though he were still a community organizer with no real power to affect change, not the President of the United States. Even in his final months as a lame duck, Obama was unwilling to say that he supported legalization in an interview with *Rolling Stone*, yet he stated that it should be treated like "cigarettes or alcohol."[21] In fact, he even mocked the way young people are very passionate about this issue during an interview with *Vice*.[22] In a patronizing way, he suggested that marijuana policy should be at the bottom of their political agenda. That's remarkably disappointing as there is arguably no other single domestic issue with more glaring flaws, but he willfully failed to take on a leadership role regarding the issue.

The two-party system is too entrenched with special interests to make significant short-term progress with drug policy. Drug policy, like most other political matters, has been corrupted by lobbyists and campaign donations. Most of the general public recognizes this fact and there has never been a time in recent history with such a high demand for a third party. A Gallup poll in 2013 found that 60% of Americans felt that a third political party was necessary. Meanwhile, only 26% of Americans felt that the two major parties adequately represent us.[23] In fact, Gallup found in 2015 that 43% of Americans self-identify as politically independent.[24] Consequently, that nonpartisan spirit had much to with the populist campaigns of Donald Trump and Bernie Sanders in 2016. Simply put, voters were refreshed to hear candidates who weren't beholden to corporate interests.

Due to his wealth, Trump was able to operate outside the traditional model of campaign financing. Americans want to vote more independently but don't do so because of systemic barriers. Ross Perot has been the most notable exception in recent history by breaking the barriers of the two-party system when he entered the presidential debates in 1992. The Commission on Presidential Debates, which is heavily financed by corporate donations, requires that a candidate's national poll numbers are at 15% before they are allowed to enter the debates.[25] Obviously, that policy blocks independent candidates because only someone who is very wealthy and willing to spend his or her own money to finance a campaign, like Perot, can participate.

It's not a coincidence that Barney Frank and Ron Paul were the most notable sponsors of the first federal proposal to end federal marijuana laws, H.R. 2306 or the "Ending Federal Marijuana Prohibition Act of 2011." Barney Frank introduced the bill and the only Republican, other than Ron Paul, to co-sponsor the bill was Dana Rohrabacher from California. Besides, only 18 of 255 House Democrats supported the bill.[26] Barney Frank is a Democrat and Ron Paul is a Republican but in name only. In reality, Frank is a Progressive and Paul is a Libertarian. Both men had long voting records that didn't match with the Democratic or Republican platforms as each voted his conscience. They remained registered as part of the two-party system because of tremendous campaign financing generated from those parties. Otherwise, it would have been impossible to be continually re-elected for decades as a third party candidate.

The Libertarians and Progressives are the only two parties that strongly support ending the drug war, but many voters are completely unfamiliar with their platforms. Legalizing marijuana is one of the most marketable issues for the Libertarian Party. Libertarians are very conservative economically and they strongly oppose government infringements upon personal freedoms and civil rights. "There is no reason in 21st century America that a fiscal conservative must be a social conservative as well," says Matt Welch, editor in chief of the libertarian *Reason Magazine*.[27] In fact, a poll by *Politico* in 2013 demonstrates that Republican voters are quietly shifting towards libertarianism, whether they realize it or not. Seventy-eight percent of the respondents who self-identified as fiscally conservative and socially moderate were Republicans and conservative independents.[28]

Some would even argue that Libertarians are a more authentic representation of conservative principles than Republicans; even the rhetoric of Ronald Reagan supports this theory. Reagan, who campaigned for Barry Goldwater, once concluded, "If you analyze it I believe the very heart and soul of conservatism is libertarianism."[29] Much of Reagan's rhetoric had a libertarian feel, but the record of his administration fell right in line with the contemporary Republican Party platform. However, he did appoint one of the most well-known free market libertarians and drug legalization advocates, Milton Friedman, as an economic advisor.

On the other hand, Progressives are economically and socially liberal. They can be generalized as the far left wing of the Democratic Party. There are a few parties within the umbrella of the Progressive Party; the most notable is the Green Party. Much like Libertarians, who represent real conservative principles better than the Republican Party, the Green Party and Progressives truly represent liberal principles better than the Democratic Party.

The Democratic Party has a history of spurning progressive candidates. As Gore Vidal asserted in an interview with *The Progressive*, there is only one major political party in this country. "It's the party of big corporations, the party of money. It has two right wings; one is Democrat and the other is Republican," said Vidal.[30] Take Ralph Nader for example. Nader, a consumer advocate who prompted auto manufacturers to add seat belts, is an icon for the far-left and Progressives. He ran for president with the Green Party in 2000 and has ruffled many feathers with the Democratic Party. In fact, he has been banned from entering the Democratic National Convention.[31]

A lesser known Progressive, Larry Agran (the former mayor of Irvine, CA), ran for the Democratic nomination in 1992, and he had a similar reception. Agran wanted to slash the military's budget in half and reinvest those funds for stimulative spending in America.[32] He even held the polling requirements to enter the Democratic debates, but he wasn't allowed to debate. Naturally, Agran protested from the crowd during one of the debates and yelled, "I request respectfully to be included in tonight's debate."[33] Moments later, he was ushered outside and arrested for disorderly conduct, resisting arrest, and trespassing. This is a reoccurring theme and in 2012 the Green Party candidate, Jill Stein, was also arrested after she tried to enter the presidential debate.[34]

It's almost impossible to win an election without the treasure chest that unions and corporations have at their disposal. The candidate who has raised the most money wins 93% of the time in the House of Representatives and it's 94% for Senate races.[35] Consequently, the costs for running a campaign have exploded over recent years. The average cost of a winning congressional campaign was $56,000 in 1974 and that figure rose to $1.1 million by 2008.[36]

The rising cost of campaign financing now forces politicians to raise thousands of dollars every day. Thus, Sen. Dick Durbin (D-IL) once described the amount of time politicians spend fundraising as "nothing short of amazing."[37] To be exact, former Rep Joe Walsh (R-IL) once estimated that he spent two to three hours per day fundraising "and that was on the low side (compared to other Congressmen.)"[38] Likewise, former Sen. George Voinovich (R-OH) estimated that his colleagues spend 20-25% of their work day raising money. In fact, he felt that he only truly carried out his duties as a Senator during his final two years in office, after serving two terms, because he decided not to run again. That was the only way that he could fully dedicate himself to the job.[39]

Tommy Boggs Jr., a top lobbyist and son of the former Democratic House majority leader, knows the dark truths behind how our political system actually operates. Hence, he describes our leaders to be more like "direct marketers and retail salesmen as opposed to legislators."[40] Not surprisingly, most politicians entertain any possible donor who will give them the time of day and dial for dollars just like any other telemarketer. Yes, both parties have call centers located blocks away from the Capitol. As a matter of fact, *The Huffington Post* obtained a PowerPoint presentation that the Democratic Congressional Campaign Committee showed to their party's new members of Congress in 2013. One particular slide suggested that they dedicate four hours a day for "call time," i.e. telemarketing.[41]

Calls from arthritic grandmothers dependent upon Social Security checks don't typically make it past the Congressman's secretary, but donors with enough money can rub elbows with these politicians. One single incident can demonstrate this imbalance and it took place in 1991 when the rapper Eazy-E attended an exclusive luncheon in which President Bush was the guest of honor. If you're not familiar with Eazy-E, he was essentially the founder of gangster rap. Eric Wright (Eazy-E), a former crack cocaine dealer, and his rap group, N.W.A., epitomized everything that the Republican Party hated. N.W.A.'s hit, "Fuck the Police," sparked riots in some cities and prompted the FBI to request censoring the album. Despite his reputation, Eric Wright received an invitation through the mail for this $2,000-a-plate luncheon with a group known as the Republican

Senatorial Inner Circle. The invitation was sent due to a clerical error, but he decided on a lark to pay to attend anyway.[42]

The arms race of campaign financing has escalated since then and it has a lot to do with a Supreme Court decision, *Citizens United v FEC*. Politicians have pandered to political action committees (PACs) dating back to the 1940s. PACs can donate to candidates who support their causes and these groups are funded by corporations, unions, and individuals. However, to level the playing field, there have always been limitations upon how much each donor can contribute. Those constraints became a moot point in 2010 with *Citizens United*. The U.S. Supreme Court ruled that corporations and unions have the same rights to freedom of speech as human beings. Therefore, there are no longer limitations on the amount of money that can be spent by corporations, unions, or individuals.

Citizens United didn't negate the contribution limitations for PACs, but it spawned newly formed committees informally known as "Super PACs." They differ from PACs in that they are not allowed to contribute to candidates directly, but Super PACs can accept unlimited money from corporations, unions, or individual people. In turn, the data from Super PACs demonstrates how the billionaire class can monopolize political debate. Super PACs raised over $567 million for the 2012 presidential election. Astoundingly, eighty percent of the Super PAC money was donated by 196 people or 0.000063% of the American public![43]

What's even more appalling is the anonymous nature in which the ultra-rich can alter elections. Super PACs are subject to transparency laws, but most donors skirt the law and hide their identities by contributing with various shell corporations. That's why most political attack ads are paid for by groups with nondescript names. For instance, Stephen Colbert satirically founded a Super Pac, "Americans for a Better Tomorrow, Tomorrow." You know these types of ads. "Don't vote for (insert name). He worships Satan and clubs baby seals on the weekends." Well, they're not quite that bad, but these ads certainly stretch the limits of defamation laws.

The lobbying system has, in essence, legalized corruption. With that said, there is nothing inherently wrong with lobbying. All citizens have the right to contact their elected officials. In fact, we all should be more active in that role. However, professional or registered lobbyists are quite different; their real power lies in raising money for candidates. They contribute vast sums of money directly to politicians. Also, they raise even more money by organizing fundraisers, such as the type of luncheon that Eazy-E once attended. That kind of indirect fundraising is known as "bundling." Consequently, it's clear why lobbyists can get sweetheart deals for their clients, such as removing specific regulations and gaining unique tax breaks.

There are now 24 active federal lobbyists for every member of Congress. Since the year 2000, the amount spent on lobbying has more than doubled to a figure of roughly $3.5 billion annually.[44] Our democracy has not only been trampled by corporations, but it is susceptible to foreign interests as approximately $1 out of every $8 spent lobbying comes from foreign governments.[45]

Lobbyists already have tremendous influence with lawmakers due to their fundraising capabilities, but they also know the ins and outs of politics. The main reason is that there is a revolving door with Capitol Hill and lobbyists. To put it differently, nearly 5,400 former congressional staffers have become federal lobbyists over the last ten years.[46] On the surface, that may seem like an innocuous connection, but the reality is quite different. Lobbyists are notorious for offering congressional staffers much more lucrative careers in lobbying after they leave office. It's a not a direct bribe, but the intent is implicit. One of the most infamous lobbyists, Jack Abramoff, explained in an interview with *60 Minutes* that "we owned them" after such an offer was accepted. The staffers would not only oblige every request by his firm but also come up with inventive ways to help his clients.[47]

One might assume that corrupting a staffer may be much ado about nothing, but the late Ted Kennedy estimated that "95% of the nitty-gritty work of drafting (bills) and negotiating (their final form) is now done by staff."[48] That's why, in some ways, the lobbyists are more powerful than the politicians. One indirect admission by former Rep. Tom DeLay (R-TX) demonstrates that shift of power. He said, "We know what we want to do and we find the people to help us do that. We go to the lobbyists and say, 'Help us get this in the appropriations bill.'"[49]

DeLay was referring to an unethical practice that is so common that it has a nickname, a "rider." A rider is an unrelated bill that is attached to "must pass" legislation such as appropriations bills which fund the government, otherwise the government has to shut down.

Many would assume that those kinds of backroom deals are only common in third world countries, but in the U.S. they are basically standard operating procedure. These deals are unethical, but they are also perfectly legal. Relatively anonymous congressional staffers aren't the only ones to cash in from becoming lobbyists. In theory, our elected officials should be less corruptible because they make more money and are subject to public scrutiny. However, many former Congressmen have become lobbyists as well. There are now 415 former Congressmen working as lobbyists and the trend is rapidly increasing. Only 3% of Congressmen became lobbyists after leaving office in 1974.[50] There is now so much more money to be made with the political process. Hence, sixty-five percent of the members of Congress who sought employment after leaving office in 2012 became lobbyists.[51]

When a former Congressman joins a lobbying firm it's a tremendous boost to the firm's profitability. They have basically unlimited access to any of their former colleagues and lobbying firms are willing to double their salaries once they leave office.[52] In fact, lobbyists who are former lawmakers sometimes have money remaining in their political action committee's fund. Consequently, they can donate the remaining balance to a current Congressman and that obviously enhances their chances to gain favorable legislation.[53]

Suffice it to say, special interests have corrupted the democratic process. Just ask one of the most well-respected marijuana scientific researchers Lester Grinspoon M.D., author of *Marihuana Reconsidered*. He began his research with the intention of demonstrating the danger of marijuana.[54] However, after years of research at Harvard Medical School, Grinspoon found that marijuana was hardly the threat that it had been made out to be. Instead, he concluded that marijuana was considerably less harmful than alcohol or tobacco and had medicinal benefits. In fact, Grinspoon discovered that marijuana was the best method for preventing the severe nausea that his son suffered during his fight with leukemia.[55] Grinspoon concluded that he "like so many other people in this country, had been brainwashed."[56] He was convinced that once the public was presented the scientific facts about marijuana that adult usage would be legalized within the decade. However, Grinspoon came to those conclusions over 40 years ago.[57]

Recent history has demonstrated that the American government treats drug policy in a thoroughly authoritarian manner. For example, a *CBS* poll from 1997 found that 62% of Americans approved of medical marijuana at a time when only one state, California, had legalized medical marijuana.[58] The marijuana lobby has almost no representation in comparison to the special interest groups that profit from the status quo. Regardless, some drug war advocates have the audacity to assert that the marijuana debate is being manipulated by a "powerful marijuana lobby." Dr. David Murray, the Chief Scientist with the Office of National Drug Control Policy, actually referred to medical marijuana lobbyists as "modern-day snake oil proponents" funded by millions of people "who want to legalize marijuana outright."[59] In reality, it is completely intellectually dishonest to insinuate that the marijuana lobby is the better-funded operation. Millions of Americans want marijuana to be legalized, but their combined fundraising efforts don't compare to the billions of dollars in special interests which help to maintain marijuana laws.

The most well-known non-profit organization fighting for legalized marijuana is the National Organization for the Reform of Marijuana Laws (NORML). NORML was formed in 1970 largely by a donation from Playboy's founder Hugh Hefner.[60] NORML generates public support for legalizing marijuana, lobbies politicians, and has created its own Political Action Committee (PAC). There are two other notable marijuana PACS, the Marijuana Policy Project and the Drug Policy Alliance. Those three groups combined have donated $651,862 lifetime to their supportive candidates, according to the Center for Responsive Politics.[61] That's an impressive number, but it's a drop in the bucket compared to the funds raised by the drug war's special interests.

The top five groups that have lobbied to keep marijuana laws in place are the police unions, private prison industry, alcohol companies, pharmaceutical industry, and prison guard unions.[62] In only one election year, 2012, the donations from the PACs of the pharmaceutical and healthcare product industry alone were $15.7 million.[63] That kind of money buys a lot of influence, to say the least. Remember, these major corporations are laser-focused on profitability and wouldn't spend that kind of money without a return on their investments. Any future federal legislation for the legalization of marijuana will have an army of well-connected lobbyists opposing it. There is strength in numbers. Hence, marijuana lobbyists would be outnumbered in a battle that would make the Alamo seem like a fair fight.

To be exact, the Marijuana Policy Project only has 18 full-time employees.[64] In contrast, the pharmaceutical industry spent over $236 million in 2012 for the services of 1,534 lobbyists.[65] That same year the alcohol industry spent $19.9 million for 266 lobbyists.[66] Likewise, law firms and commercial banks also spent $14.3 million in 2012 for 268 lobbyists and $61.9 million for 466 lobbyists respectively.[67] Is it fair to call this a rigged game? Considering the challenges, it's impressive that the marijuana lobby has been able to successfully lobby for reduced penalties nationwide and medical marijuana in 28 states and D.C.[68] Those results speak to the credibility of the movement.

Despite the strong case for legalizing marijuana, there is very little favorable press from the mainstream corporate media. Media companies make most of their money from advertising revenues and that results in a carefully crafted agenda dependent upon not offending their corporate sponsors. With that in mind, alcohol and pharmaceutical drugs are some of the media's heaviest advertisers and that creates an implied business partnership. In 2007 alone, drug companies spent $3.7 billion in direct-to-consumer advertising.[69] Consequently, the media must not bite the hand that feeds it, yet the popular notion of "liberal media bias" still exists. Yes, the majority of media outlets give favorable press for Democratic politicians, but the corporate media isn't hard hitting, grassroots, or very liberal, for that matter. After all, the United States ranks 46th in the World Press Freedom Index, behind Romania and ahead of Haiti.[70]

The television news industry is now primarily driven by Fortune 500 companies that are focused on profits, not independent journalism. That wasn't always the case as television news wasn't looked upon for driving profits in its pioneer days. It was considered a loss leader for the major networks. "The interests of the government, interests of the corporations, and the interests of the news media have kind of melded together," says Sharyl Attkisson, former *CBS* reporter.[71] The conflicts of interest with the major media companies now span over many industries. One study by a research team at Sonoma State University found that the ten major corporate media companies had 118 people serving on the board of directors. Those same 118 people were also board members of 288 different major corporations.[72] In other words, it's extremely difficult for any journalist working for those companies to operate in a truly independent manner.

Some news reports present a positive message associated with legalizing marijuana, but they're often watered-down. Those stories often feature bad puns like "Here's a story that is bound to end up in a cloud of smoke" or include obligatory video clips of Rastafarians or hippies playing with hacky sacks. The drug war serves as a ratings bonanza with an endless supply of stories which are sensational and easy to produce. CBS News aired "48 Hours on Crack Street" in 1986 to 15 million viewers, the highest ratings for a TV documentary in five and a half years.[73] Robert Stutman, former head of the DEA's office in New York City, once acknowledged how he "used the media." He said, "The media were only too willing to cooperate, because as far as New York media was concerned, crack was the hottest combat reporting story to come along since the end of the Vietnam War."[74] He even had an appearance on "48 Hours on Crack Street."

Seemingly everyone in the media was in competition to sensationalize crack cocaine. Tom Brokaw even claimed in 1986 that crack was America's "drug of choice" without triggering any real controversy.[75] In like fashion, it turns out that it was a hoax when President Bush gave a speech in 1989 in which he held up a large bag of crack cocaine for dramatic effect. Bush stated that the drugs had been purchased across the street from the White House. The cocaine was technically purchased there, but only because the DEA had to deliberately manipulate the dealer to the park across the street so that Bush's speech would have been "technically accurate" to drive home a stronger message.[76]

George H.W. Bush wasn't even the first President to use subtle drug war propaganda. For instance, Richard Nixon met with 48 different TV producers to pressure them to include anti-drug messages in their shows.[77] For those who doubt the power of covert propaganda, consider the example of Elvis Presley. Elvis was severely addicted to several powerful prescription drugs. He eventually died with several drugs in his system, yet he was thoroughly indoctrinated with this government disinformation.

Elvis wrote to Nixon praising the President's drug war efforts. In the letter, he mentioned reading about "drug abuse and Communist brainwashing" and he was concerned with "the drug culture, the hippie elements…Black Panthers, etc." He requested to operate secretly as a "federal agent at large." One of Nixon's top aides convinced the President to meet with him privately in December of 1970. Begrudgingly, he did. Nixon never gave Elvis any official power, but he suggested recording an album titled, "Getting High on Life" and issued him a badge as a "Special Assistant in the Bureau of Narcotics and Dangerous Drugs."[78]

As you know, history has a way of repeating itself. Now, the media is hyping a new drug, a highly potent synthetic stimulant, alpha-PVP. It is known as "flakka" and the sensational news reports imply everything short of an imminent zombie apocalypse. Many news agencies are playing the same video clips of erratic behavior on a loop and overstating the effects of this drug, including "superhuman strength." That's reminiscent of the times when newspapers claimed that cocaine made black men impervious to bullets. Flakka truly is a dangerous and addictive drug, but the coverage by the media has, once again, whittled away at our ability to think critically about a complex issue.

There has long existed a cozy connection between the press and the government. In the most extreme cases, the Government Accountability Office (GAO) has documented how our government violated covert propaganda laws to hype up the drug war. For example, the Office of National Drug Control Policy (ONDCP) produced drug-related video news broadcasts designed to appear just like regular newscasts. The ONDCP then distributed those videos to approximately 770 local news networks and those videos were seen in about 22 million homes. Also, there were no disclosures that the videos were made by the government, instead of the news organization.[79] Again, we have laws preventing propaganda for valid reasons, but no one has been held accountable.

The GAO also advocated, unsuccessfully, to discontinue funding the National Youth Anti-Drug Media Campaign, a $1.4 billion program which the GAO labeled as a failure in 2006.[80] Even the most well-known non-profit, anti-drug organization, The Partnership for a Drug-Free America (PDFA), has been littered with conflicts of interest from major corporations. The Partnership for a Drug-Free America actually accepted donations from the top tobacco and alcohol companies, and in fact, those companies used to be their largest contributors. Ultimately, public pressure eventually forced the PDFA to no longer accept their donations.[81]

That gesture was rather hollow as the PDFA continues to receive funding from corporations with clearly questionable motives. Case in point, most of their corporate partners for 2013-2014 (10 out of 16 companies) was from the pharmaceutical industry.[82] One of these, Mallinckrodt Pharmaceuticals, earns high profit margins from generic opioids. Two more of those partners, Endo Pharmaceuticals and Purdue Pharma, are the makers of Percocet and Oxycontin, which are commonly abused for recreational use. Another PDFA partner, Actavis, produced a particular type of codeine cough syrup that was frequently abused as well. That drug is known as "drank," "sizzurp," or "lean" and it has been prominently celebrated in rap music for many years. Consequently, that negative publicity led Actavis to take the drug off the market in 2014.[83]

The pharmaceutical companies are in the enviable position to be able to play both sides of the fence. They can portray a public image that condemns recreational drug usage with their tax-deductible donations to the Partnership for a Drug-Free America. Then again, a group of pharmaceutical companies hired lobbyists to block a requirement for a prescription to buy the over-the-counter medication that is the key ingredient in methamphetamine -- pseudoephedrine.[84]

Despite all of the drug war special interests, there is a clear trend expressed in public opinion polls that Americans are rapidly accepting the idea of legalized marijuana. In many ways, marijuana is a generational issue, because age is the most divisive factor associated with it, apart from party lines. Seventy-seven percent of people who are 18-34 years old favor legalization; only 45% of individuals aged 55 or older support legalization. Predictably, 67% of Democrats and 70% of independents prefer legalization compared to only 42% of Republicans.[85]

For the first time, a 2011 Gallup Poll found that 50% of Americans favored legalization![86] Gallup has been polling this issue for over four decades and there has been an explosive swing in public opinion. Approval for legal marijuana had remained stagnant at a range of 23% to 28% from the late 1970s to the late 1990s. Even in 2000, only 30% of Americans agreed with legalization.

The support for legalized marijuana has surged due to the success in the growing number of states that legalized medical marijuana. More importantly, the nation took notice in 2012 when both Colorado and Washington passed laws allowing recreational use of marijuana. In other words, the fact that this is now a realistic possibility has produced a level of credibility, thus chipping away at the stigma. As a matter of fact, a higher percentage of people in Colorado voted for legal marijuana in 2012 than for Obama.[87] Just six years earlier, Colorado had voted 59% against that same type of state ballot measure.[88] The results in Colorado and Washington were a game changer and support for legalization rose to 60% in October of 2016, three weeks before four more states (California, Massachusetts, Maine, and Nevada) voted for recreational marijuana.[89]

To wrap up, money in politics has an overwhelming influence. However, there is a realistic plan for ending the drug war and it starts with legalizing marijuana state by state. Decriminalizing the harder drugs would need to follow as the stigma would decline accordingly. What happened in Colorado and Washington didn't unfold because their state legislators suddenly developed a backbone. Instead, the voters decided for themselves with ballot measures. In fact, every state that legalized recreational marijuana (eight states and the District of Columbia) did so with ballot measures.

Sure, our elected officials are compromised by special interests, but we the people aren't. It takes grassroots efforts to change the inertia with this issue and that is exactly what has happened. At a minimum, the tax revenues from various state models with legalized marijuana will force the hand of the federal government. It's only a matter of time before marijuana is decriminalized at the federal level. Albeit, that likely won't happen quickly, despite the rising poll numbers.

5

"Industrial hemp? I'm not quite sure what industrialized hemp is."

Casual marijuana advocates often overstate the potential economic impact from legalization. Some even make a ludicrous suggestion that it would pay off the national debt. Legal marijuana, just like any other single solution, can't fix our $20 trillion national debt. Nevertheless, there clearly are no perfect forecasts for determining the potential economic impact of the legal marijuana industry in the future. However, according to the available data, approximately 1 in every 10 Americans smokes marijuana at least once a year. Among them, about 24 million Americans smoke marijuana on a regular basis.[1] CNBC offered a moderate estimate that a fully legal marijuana industry would generate $16-20 billion in taxes and $40 billion in sales annually.[2] Clearly, legal marijuana wouldn't be the economic miracle as some supporters expect it to be, but it still represents a mammoth economic impact. As the former Senator Everett Dirksen reportedly once said, "A billion here, a billion there, and pretty soon you're talking real money."[3]

Colorado's decision to legalize recreational and medical marijuana has added over $100 million to the state's budget annually. First, the state collected $76 million in taxes and fees from the legal marijuana industry.[4] Secondly, the state's criminal justice costs were reduced by up to $40 million annually, according to a conservative estimate by the Colorado Center on Law and Policy.[5] In addition, the legal marijuana industry in Colorado now employs roughly 10,000 people directly.[6]

On a national scale, the explosive growth of the medical marijuana industry has already surpassed the smartphone industry's growth, according to a report by Steve Berg, former managing director of Wells Fargo Bank.[7] Likewise, TheStreet.com estimated, as of 2014, there were already 175,000 people employed by the legal marijuana industry.[8] More importantly, that evaluation doesn't include the thousands of jobs that are created from unrelated industries as a result of a multiplier effect or "ripple effect." To clarify, whenever a job is created, that new source of wealth leads to more job creation. Granted, economists have more specific forecasts that gauge which sectors best advance the economy. Manufacturing is particularly stimulative and thus for every factory job that is created there is a multiplier effect that develops an additional 3.04 jobs. In addition, the wholesale & retail industry (another industry that would benefit from marijuana legalization) has a multiplier effect of 1.71.[9]

Some skeptics believe there would be little positive economic impact from legalization because marijuana is fairly easy to grow. Yes, a small percentage would grow their own marijuana, but the vast majority would not. There's no reason to believe that marijuana would be different from any other consumer good. We're a consumer-driven nation with a service economy. Americans can obviously cook their own meals, yet the restaurant industry recovered fairly well after the recession. In fact, SunTrust Banks published a study in 2015 which found that nearly a third of households making $75,000 or more annually were living paycheck to paycheck. Sixty-eight percent of those people blamed dining out as the main reason.[10] Likewise, many of the fruits and vegetables that we buy at the grocery store can also be easily grown in our backyards with very little effort, yet very few people decide to do so. Furthermore, cigarettes cost as much as $10 a pack in some states, but very few people have started rolling their own cigarettes. In that scenario, smokers only need to roll the tobacco, let alone grow it for significant savings; but, once again, most people don't do that.

The tobacco industry has lobbied in the past against marijuana to avoid competition, but they would also benefit from legalized marijuana. They already have a similar infrastructure in place with their distribution channels and manufacturing equipment for rolling cigarettes. They would also be able to mass produce marijuana at lower costs. Some even suggest that big tobacco will be able to monopolize production. However, that likely won't be the case as marijuana has a limitless number of different strains and is much less climate-sensitive than tobacco. Therefore, that opens the door to competition similar to how microbrewery beers or local wineries can compete with the largest alcoholic beverage companies. Microbrew beers or local wines can't compete in cost, but they can compete with their brand image and their own unique product.

There's no reason to believe that marijuana wouldn't create very similar entrepreneurial opportunities at the retail level as well.

For example, medical marijuana dispensaries in Denver, CO reportedly outnumber Starbucks locations.[11] Despite tremendous retail success, medical marijuana dispensaries have managed to avoid wide-scale franchising or consolidation. In addition, legal marijuana would spawn new specialized marijuana bars or lounges. There are thousands of bars, nightclubs, and liquor stores across America and most of them are small independently-owned businesses.

In short, it can't be overstated how important it is to stimulate small business opportunities. First, small businesses create more jobs than large corporations. Secondly, a higher percentage of profits are reinvested into the company with small businesses. Conversely, large corporations tend to distribute a disproportionate share of their profits to the executives and are quicker to lay off employees and outsource jobs.

Some Republican leaders like to speculate that the economy will decline if we end the drug war. They have successfully hijacked the debate with that oversimplified talking point by citing studies that estimate the economic harm from all illegal drugs. One such study by the White House's Office of National Drug Control Policy concluded that all illegal drugs resulted in $140.1 billion in economic costs in 1998.[A][12] It's an intellectually dishonest argument because over 70% of those costs ($99.3 billion) were from "productivity losses," primarily from incarceration.[13] Therefore, to state the obvious, ending the drug war would be a net cost savings and generate more economic activity.

There is also a false narrative that Americans will suddenly lose their ambition and lust for consumerism if we end the drug war. Remember, cocaine and heroin were sold over the counter for many decades, yet economists weren't the ones demanding to outlaw those drugs. In fact, in a similar vein, several prominent industrial titans led the movement to end the prohibition of alcohol. Many of them had mistakenly supported it in the beginning in hopes of more productivity.

The criminal justice system, in contrast, hurts the economy more than any "lazy stoner." It is difficult to quantify the indirect economic consequences of the drug war. Notwithstanding, there is a misconception that the punishment for illegal drugs, in particular,

---

[A] In that same year, the economic costs from alcohol were estimated at $184.6 billion.

marijuana, is no longer oppressive. Yes, most states no longer punish people with over twenty years in prison for simple marijuana possession. Presently, the penalty for simple possession, in most states, is generally less than a year in jail and/or a fine. That certainly represents a step in the right direction, but make no mistake about it; that is a harsh punishment for the average working class person with few contacts in the business world.[B][14] There are also fees associated with lawyers, court costs, probation, mandatory drug testing and drug treatment, etc. Undoubtedly, for people on the fringe of society, these types of consequences, in many cases, push them into a life of crime.

Reentering the workforce after a drug arrest can be quite difficult as we live in a digital world. Background checks are now fairly standard, even with minimum wage jobs. A drug conviction for many companies is an automatic disqualification, no matter how long ago the arrest took place. In like manner, a person can also be denied student loans or small business loans due to a drug conviction.[15] Furthermore, licenses can be denied for doctors, nurses, lawyers, teachers, or even barbers.[16] To sum up, all of these factors associated with drug arrests systematically result in creating fewer professionals.

The same factors also lead to underemployment which is different from unemployment. Underemployment occurs when someone is severely overqualified for his or her job. Surprisingly, many economists believe that underemployment is more damaging than unemployment. The reason being that it reduces a country's productivity as a whole when people don't realize their potential skill level. Underemployed workers are also taking away jobs from lower-skilled workers who would be a better fit for those positions. Consequently, it's next to impossible to put a price on the underemployment caused by millions of drug arrests.

The positive economic impact of legalizing marijuana and ending the drug war can't be denied. However, hemp is often neglected in this debate. It's criminal that our nation has been deprived of this incredible resource with environmental and economic benefits. Granted, the potential economic benefits that hemp has to offer may not be obvious to everyone as of right now and that's why it needs to be examined. There's no reason, other

---

[B] Seventeen states no longer punish a first-time marijuana possession arrest with jail time.

than legality, that hemp futures shouldn't be traded like wheat, corn, oil, or any other commodity. After all, hemp is arguably the most versatile raw material in the world that can produce thousands of different products.[17]

Hemp currently has an insignificant economic position, but that has little to do with its viability. Federal legislation killed this industry domestically and, consequently, research & development for hemp is 80 years behind the curve. Conversely, direct competitors to the hemp industry, such as petrochemical companies, have spent billions of dollars on research and development since the 1937 Marijuana Tax Act. For example, Dow Chemical spends more annually on research and development, over $1 billion, than the entire American domestic hemp industry generates in sales.

The hemp industry sadly isn't truly allowed to compete in the American market. As of today, U.S. farmers in nearly every state are not fully authorized to produce hemp for commercial purposes due to federal laws, despite the fact that America is the largest consumer for the hemp industry ($620 million annually) from foreign imports.[18] Limited legality and the controversial association with marijuana has destroyed nearly all potential corporate investment into hemp. Essentially, any manufacturer that considers using hemp as a raw material has to be a hemp aficionado. Whereas, there are limitless choices for other business opportunities without these hurdles.

Take Mitt Romney for example. He used to run an investment firm, Bain Capital, but he drew a blank when he was questioned about industrial hemp during his 2012 presidential run. He responded, "Industrial hemp? I'm not quite sure what industrialized hemp is."[19] Given these points, the byproducts and benefits of hemp are endless, but its value is almost entirely untapped without capital investment.

Hemp would be a godsend to most farmers as it is resistant to random weather patterns and grows quickly with little effort on their part. It also requires much less land and water than most crops. As Chris Conrad, author of *Hemp: Lifeline to the Future*, says it's also "self-seeding, self-fertilizing, and self-weeding."[20] In addition, hemp doesn't require the harmful chemicals that most commercial products need and it aerates the soil while improving soil conditions for other crop rotations. Hemp provides an ideal for free market capitalism with a diversity of products and a theoretically limitless supply. Nevertheless, ironically, hemp still has an extreme-left-wing-anti-capitalist connotation.

The U.S. has an ambiguous policy with hemp, and, as a result, there is a lot of understandable confusion surrounding its legal status. According to federal law, the Controlled Substances Act doesn't distinguish between hemp and marijuana; therefore, commercial hemp production is prohibited. For instance, the former Governor of California, Arnold Schwarzenegger, cited federal law after he vetoed an industrial hemp bill. "Unfortunately, I am very concerned that this bill would give legitimate growers a false sense of security and a belief that production of industrial hemp is somehow a legal activity under federal law," said Schwarzenegger.[21]

The bureaucracy of the drug war is the driving force behind our federal government's restrictions. After all, the international community isn't beholden to these stipulations. As of 1972, industrial hemp production has been permitted by the foremost anti-drug international treaty, the Single Convention on Narcotics Drugs. In addition, Bill Clinton in 1994 issued an Executive Order, 12919 the "National Defense Industrial Resources Preparedness," ordering that industrial hemp be stockpiled as a wartime precaution.[22]

On a positive note, Congress passed the Farm Bill of 2014 permitting hemp to be grown for research purposes as a pilot program. Subsequently, thirty-two states followed up with bills that fell within the limited parameters of the federal government.[23] Then again, that also means that it is still illegal to grow hemp in 18 states. Hemp also remains on the Controlled Substance list. Therefore, it is illegal to transport seeds and live plants across state lines. The Industrial Hemp Farming Act of 2015 was written to remove hemp from the Controlled Substance list and alleviate several other unnecessary regulations, but that bill never made it out of committee.

Licenses for hemp production must be approved by the DEA due to its listing as a Controlled Substance. And as you may have guessed, the DEA has often acted as a roadblock.[24] Prior to the Farm Bill of 2014, the DEA had, in some cases, taken more than three years to grant an approval.[25] In general, the DEA has eased some of their restrictive practices, but one incident shows that the agency is still committed to obstructionism. The DEA confiscated an approved shipment of hemp that the Kentucky Agriculture

Department was going to use for research. The agency eventually caved in after they were sued by the Kentucky Agriculture Department and Sen. Mitch McConnell (R-KY) had a personal meeting with the DEA Administrator.[26]

These kinds of incidents are clearly bureaucratic stonewalling because the regulatory needs for policing hemp are minimal. The federal government's regulations for hemp are completely unnecessary as it contains only trace amounts of THC (0.3% or less). Therefore, it's impossible to get "high" from it. Nevertheless, the DEA has insisted that the THC produced from hemp is "significant," but that couldn't be further from the truth.[27]

The DEA preys upon the general ignorance with this plant by suggesting that hemp farmers might mix marijuana plants among their crops. On the surface, that may sound like a valid concern for regulators, but it is pure fiction. The reason why is that hemp pollinates heavily, which is quite costly for marijuana growers. Pollination reduces the THC potency of a marijuana plant. Hence, marijuana growers separate the male plants, which pollinate, from the female plants. Remarkably, one male plant can virtually destroy the potency of an entire grow room. Therefore, any marijuana plant grown in a field of hemp would be absolutely worthless.[28]

Americans generally pride themselves on living in a capitalistic society, yet there are approximately 30 industrialized nations which produce hemp without these ridiculous regulations.[29] This policy adds another drain on the U.S. dollar and actually pushes legitimate industry outside our country. Companies within more socialist nations, in particular, Canada and England, have made significant innovations with hemp. Free to operate without obstacles, a Canadian company, Hempearth, is currently building and fueling the world's first airplane with hemp.[30] Also, the British sports and racing car manufacturer, Lotus, has already developed a prototype car, Eco Elise, which has a body and interior made largely of hemp. Furthermore, a Canadian company, Motive Industries, produces the Kestrel, which is an electric car with a body built from hemp. Just like Henry Ford's prototype car, the Kestrel plastic body pops back into its original shape after a powerful impact.[31]

A car body made from hemp is lighter and cheaper to produce. Consequently, both Ford and DaimlerChrysler have begun to import European hemp for door panels and various interior parts.[32] In fact, nearly every part of a car, notwithstanding the engine, can be made from hemp, including the windows, glass, interior, lubrication, paint, fuel, etc. In addition, the growing electric car market could further benefit from hemp. It appeared that graphene batteries were going to surpass lithium batteries. However, Dr. David Mitlin of Clarkson University found that hemp has the same energy storage capacity at only a fraction of the cost.[33]

Hemp can also replace most of the construction materials required for building a home. Home construction with hemp hasn't developed in the U.S. because of the high importation costs for shipping such bulky, heavy materials. However, this type of construction is a growing trend in Europe. "I look at the range of materials out there and I cannot find one to match hemp," says Kevin McCloud, host of the U.K. homebuilding project TV show, *Grand Designs*.[34]

Russ Martin, the former mayor of Ashville, North Carolina, owns the first American prototype of a home built predominantly from hemp. This was a deeply personal issue for the home designer, Anthony Brenner, as his daughter suffers from some extreme medical conditions that make her highly sensitive to various chemicals. Therefore, he needed the most environmentally sound materials. Hence, he chose a form of concrete that was a mixture of hemp, lime, and water, known as "hempcrete." Brenner describes the hempcrete as "a built-in air filter."[35] Traditional concrete needs chemicals such as formaldehyde, whereas hempcrete is non-toxic, chemical-free, and prevents mold and mildew damage.

Brenner adds, "The insulating factor and thermal capabilities are fantastic."[36] Consequently, the energy savings are incredible too. The homeowner, Russ Martin, told *CNN* that his energy bill is around $100 per month for a 3,400 square foot home.[37] The energy savings are part of why Brenner says that building hemp homes can be affordable, even with higher initial material costs from importation. Additionally, the skilled labor costs are drastically reduced with hempcrete because of its simplicity.

By the same token, building with a wood-like product known as "hemp board" is also simpler and saves on skilled labor versus traditional lumber. Numerous parts of a home can be built with hemp board, including the walls, doors, cabinets, flooring, and shelves. It's a fantastic product that is stronger than wood; therefore, fewer materials are needed. Also, it is resistant to fire and absorbs moisture, thereby reducing costly mold and mildew damage.

Altogether, the savings from hemp construction add up on the back-end when factoring in the maintenance and repair costs for a home.[38]

Full-scale industrial hemp production could also ease one of our nation's most notable issues, energy production. Energy is one of the nation's most pressing issues because it impacts several other issues, including foreign policy. With that said, hemp isn't a solution to the American energy problem as there simply isn't enough farmland available to supply our entire energy needs. Then again, *it isn't supposed to support our entire energy needs*. There shouldn't be a monopoly on any energy source, even clean, renewable sources. After all, consumers benefit with low prices and high quality from a diverse energy sector that has many competitors. Any commodity that can provide even a slight decrease in the demand for oil can lead to noticeable price reductions at the gas pump. Hemp, along with natural gas, hydrogen, solar, wind, coal, and oil will all be necessary for energy independence.

The Obama administration has promoted alternative energy sources much more than his predecessors, but the hemp industry has faced hostility from the Department of Justice under his administration. That is somewhat surprising considering that Obama twice voted for hemp legislation in the Illinois Senate.[39] However, on November 18, 2010, the DOJ issued a statement refusing even to meet with North Dakota state government officials to discuss hemp policy. They didn't want to "waste their time" and felt that a meeting was "not likely to be productive."[40]

That decision by the Obama administration was genuinely appalling. Keep in mind that workers were still cleaning up the damage from the BP oil spill at that time. Considering the circumstances, you would think that a green energy presidency would at least entertain a simple discussion. Unbeknownst to anyone, an interesting turn of historic events soon followed and highlighted the importance of energy policy, including the Fukushima nuclear disaster.

Obama reacted to the political pressure from the BP oil spill by restricting offshore drilling in the U.S. Astoundingly, he later decided to subsidize Brazilian offshore drilling for American consumption. He stated during a visit to Brazil on March 20, 2011, that he wanted Americans to be their "best customers."[41] The timing of that visit was significant as, one day prior, the President entered our military into the UN war in Libya (without Congressional approval). In fact, he didn't even have an official press conference until after the trip. Nevertheless, Obama stressed the importance of "humanitarian efforts" in Libya. Regardless, gaining further access to Libya's massive oil reserves was seemingly part of the motivation for that war.[42]

Another notable event occurred on December 7, 2010, just two weeks after the DOJ refused to discuss hemp policy. Dick Cheney was charged with bribery by the Nigerian government.[43] You may wonder, "How is that relevant?" That case illustrates the importance of developing energy sources domestically and just how desperate American energy companies are to find natural resources. The charge stemmed from the time Cheney was an executive with Halliburton. KBR, a former subsidiary of Halliburton, pleaded guilty in 2009 to bribing Nigerian officials with $180 million to obtain contracts for drilling natural gas in their country.[44] In all fairness, bribery is commonplace for many international business ventures, in particular, the energy sector.

Green energy critics like to point out that alternative energy sources generally need to be subsidized by the government before they can become competitive. Be that as it may, many of those same people often neglect to mention that the well-established oil and gas industry receives government subsidies that are considerably more generous. Doug Koplow of the energy consulting firm, Earth Track, estimates that the industry receives $41 billion annually at the behest of the taxpayers.[45] Consequently, the price that you pay at the gas pump is artificially low. That may be hard to believe for people living paycheck to paycheck and struggling to fill their gas tanks, but it is true.

The Milken Institute estimated that the true cost of a gallon of gasoline is about $14 a gallon.[46] Taxpayers are paying somewhere near that figure, in one way or another. There are a variety of factors, including the military budget allocated to defending oil distribution worldwide and the lives lost in the process, healthcare costs, and federal subsidies, among others. To be clear, the Defense Department spends anywhere from $55 billion to $96.3 billion annually to safeguard the oil supply and production worldwide.[47] That doesn't include the billions of dollars in foreign military aid to nations such as Egypt and Israel primarily to maintain the flow of oil in the region, nor the cost of the Iraq War that clearly had a great deal to do with access to oil reserves.

For obvious reasons, the Energy Policy Act was passed after the first Persian Gulf War and it required that 75% of the new vehicles purchased by federal agencies use alternative fuels.[48] However, that law has never been implemented. Meanwhile, hemp can produce one of the better choices for alternative fuels, cellulose ethanol. With that said, Americans tend to react negatively to the word ethanol. That is why it is necessary to examine America's experiment with corn-based ethanol.

Corn-based ethanol had been heavily subsidized up until 2011. At that point, the subsidies began to be phased out.[49] The subsidies lasted for several years for two primary reasons. The corn industry has a powerful lobbying group and Iowa is where the first presidential caucus is held. Hence, corn ethanol received up to a $0.45 per gallon government subsidy along with a $0.54 tariff on every gallon of Brazilian ethanol to protect American corn interests. Corn-based ethanol needed such drastic measures because it was totally inefficient. For every gallon of corn-based ethanol produced, 1.29 gallons of gas were necessary for its production.[50] In other words, *ethanol consumed more energy in production than it could generate!* Also, the increased demand for corn for ethanol production has resulted in higher food prices. With these facts in mind, there is a bright side. Over time, corn-based ethanol producers have become much more efficient and, as a result, their ethanol is now a net positive energy producer.[51] Nonetheless, there are better sources for ethanol.

Brazil, on the other hand, has had much more success with ethanol because they use sugar primarily, which is over two times more efficient than corn-based ethanol.[52] Unfortunately, sugar can only be grown in limited regions of the U.S. Anyhow, Brazil's ethanol investment created what is now a legitimate free market energy source. Brazilian consumers now have both fuels at their gas stations and it forces the two commodities to compete in pricing and efficiency. In turn, the development of sugarcane ethanol has helped Brazil to become energy independent. All in all, that has been crucial in Brazil's strong economic resurgence.

Brazil's model clearly influenced Congress to pass the Energy Independence and Security Act of 2007. That law required 16 billion gallons of ethanol to be produced by 2022; but, it must be cellulose based.[53] The reason behind the cellulose requirement is that cellulosic ethanol is the most efficient form of ethanol. It requires fewer natural resources for production, notably water. In addition, cellulosic ethanol produces fewer greenhouse gas emissions than sugar ethanol and 86% less than petroleum, according to a study cited by the U.S. Department of Energy.[54]

Cellulose is raw plant material and it is arguably the most abundant raw material on the planet. Therefore, the obvious question that follows is, "Why isn't cellulosic ethanol at every gas pump in the nation?" It is an issue that economists refer to as "economies of scale." In other words, no alternative energy company has been able to obtain a source for cellulose in quantities high enough to reduce the costs to a viable level for production. Consequently, the U.S. government has heavily subsidized switchgrass and corn for cellulosic ethanol production. Suffice it to say, that's an absurd choice because hemp has one of the highest yields for cellulose (64.8%), which is significantly better than corn (28% cellulose yield) and switchgrass (32.5% cellulose yield).[55] In addition, scientists have found that switchgrass requires significantly higher levels of water, levels that could potentially cause damage to the ecosystem.[56]

There are many other high-cellulose materials such as wood chips, sawdust, etc. But hemp clearly would be the most economical choice for farmers, absent any federal laws, because it has numerous other commercial uses. However, that is currently not a possibility due to our federal laws. An EPA report found that only one company has been able to produce cellulose at an economically viable rate; the costs of converting those materials are quite high. Many of the subsidized companies have gone bankrupt. To put it briefly, the cellulosic ethanol industry will either need to be continually subsidized or the U.S. will continue to import Brazilian sugarcane to meet the requirements of the Energy Independence and Security Act of 2007.[57]

The topics of energy and global warming usually lead to the butting of heads between the Republicans and Democrats. Both sides have legitimate concerns. The Republicans don't want to limit America's production and manufacturing capacity while China isn't restricted to the same environmental standards. On the other hand, the Democrats have valid environmental fears from global warming. Unfortunately, the issue of deforestation is often left out of the global warming debate and hemp has the potential to serve as an olive branch for both sides. Deforestation produces roughly 10-15% of the world's greenhouse gas emissions, on par with all of the world's automobiles.[58] Therefore, the U.S. could be a pioneer on this issue by letting hemp compete fairly in the marketplace against timberland for paper products. After all, hemp produces a better quality paper that can be recycled more often. The U.S. government could easily eliminate the $6.6 billion a year in special interest tax breaks that the U.S. paper industry receives.[59]

Industrial hemp production would also reduce our nation's dependence upon a crop with some very negative economic and environmental consequences, cotton. Hemp can produce a number of clothing materials which are considerably more durable and breathable than cotton. Albeit, many people envision something like a burlap sack when they hear about a hemp T-shirt. That isn't an accurate perception; hemp blends well with other materials and ultimately produces some very comfortable and durable clothing. Obviously, a certain number of consumers will always prefer cotton, but hemp offers an excellent alternative without the terrible health and environmental consequences. Hemp requires about half the water that cotton needs while cotton depletes soil conditions and is heavily reliant upon pesticides.[60] In fact, cotton only uses 2.4% of the world's farmable land, yet nearly 50% of the world's pesticides are used for cotton.[61] That's particularly concerning because pesticides are linked with many potential health problems, including autism, birth defects, diabetes, Alzheimer's, Parkinson's disease, and cancer.

In addition, the U.S. cotton industry receives $3 billion a year in subsidies. In fact, Brazil, a heavy cotton exporter, won a case against the United States through the World Trade Organization (WTO) because those subsidies violate international free trade agreements. Nonetheless, the U.S. government has never cut off the cotton industry's subsidies. Meanwhile, believe it or not, the U.S. government has even agreed to pay $147 million a year to Brazilian cotton farmers for the right to continue to subsidize the American cotton industry.[62] Yes, that's your tax dollars at work.

Hemp could also significantly reduce the tremendous number of low-dose toxins in our lives. There are various chemicals which, alone, won't kill us, but the accumulation of these pollutants certainly shortens our lifespans. Many of those toxins come from thousands of petroleum chemical products. Most people don't realize how our modern society would be unrecognizable without the thousands of plastic-based petroleum-chemical products of today.[63] They include obvious things such as plastic bottles, but there are also more subtle products such as shoes, clothing, cell phones, computers, beauty products, appliances, etc.

Petroleum or natural gas based products, such as plastic, can be replaced with hemp. That would have tremendous health and environmental ramifications because Americans generated 31 million tons of plastic waste in 2010 alone.[64] Furthermore, forty-five thousand tons of plastic are dumped into the ocean worldwide every year; the United Nations estimates there are 46,000 pieces of plastic in every square mile of ocean water. As a result, the numerous toxins from plastic enter our water supply, and even our food supply through a process called "bioaccumulation." This bioaccumulation occurs when people ingest toxins from ocean fish because fish eat the small pieces of plastic, mistaking plastic for food.[65] That process would be much less harmful to mankind's overall health if most plastics were made from hemp. After all, hemp contains none of the harmful chemicals found in most petroleum-based plastic. And amazingly, some forms of hemp plastic are even edible.

Conventional plastics are riddled with toxins, including a chemical additive known as Bisphenol A or BPA. This chemical is ubiquitous throughout modern American culture to a point where 93% of Americans have BPA in their urine, according to the Center for Disease Control. BPA is a chemical which mimics estrogen and disrupts the body's natural hormonal balance, which can lead to breast and prostate cancer.[66] Numerous independent studies link BPA with a variety of other conditions such as diabetes, obesity, reproductive failures, autism, and hyperactivity. In fact, Canada was the first nation to ban BPA in baby bottles and the FDA eventually followed suit after other nations such as China, Malaysia, and the European Union had passed similar measures.[67] Unfortunately, the replacement for BPA (Bisphenol S or BPS) also has estrogen mimicking qualities, but early research shows that it is less severe.[68]

There is one more monumental benefit to hemp plastic; it is biodegradable. The magnitude of biodegradable plastic is tremendous because plastic is altogether inefficient to recycle. According to the EPA, the overall recycling rate for plastic is only 9%.[69] That's in large part because many types of plastic can't be recycled; the plastic products that cannot be recycled are sent back to the dump. In the process, vast natural resources are wasted from transporting these materials back and forth. A professor from Clemson University, Dan Benjamin, has researched this process extensively and he has come to a conclusion that is contrary to what most people believe. Benjamin found that recycling plastic wastes more resources than it saves.[70]

As has been noted, hemp isn't a toxic substance. In fact, some experts believe that hemp is the most nutritionally complete food on the planet! It has every amino acid, including the nine essential amino acids that our bodies cannot produce, and is the richest known source of polyunsaturated essential fatty acids.[71] Many people take fish oil supplements to get the same nutrients found in hemp, but studies have found harmful substances (including traces of mercury) in some of those products.[72] Furthermore, hemp is a particularly popular health supplement, especially among vegans and vegetarians, because of its high protein content. This should be a relatively inexpensive food if it were mass produced, but it's fairly expensive with prices that fall in line with other more rare and exotic superfoods such as acai, chia seeds, and goji berries.

To sum up, the products and benefits from hemp are endless. The common thread between these products is that they're natural, much safer, and would create numerous business opportunities. The diverse environmental and health benefits also represent economic benefits, in the form of savings from fewer subsidies and reduced healthcare costs. Also, it is well documented that hemp and marijuana are two completely different products, yet the political establishment has dug in their heels to continue to restrict industrial hemp production.

The government displayed more flexibility with hemp policy seven decades ago. The federal hemp tax was put on hold during WWII in order to produce wartime supplies. The Department of Agriculture even produced the film *Hemp for Victory*, which explained the benefits of hemp, encouraged farmers to grow it, and how to process its various products. Despite the "reefer madness" government propaganda that was fresh in their memories, approximately 20,000 farmers cultivated 30,000 acres of hemp for the war effort.[73] Mind you, that was an era in which Americans were expected to band together and make sacrifices during times of war because it was understood that America needed to produce more than it consumed. In the context of today, there is a perpetual "War on Terror," yet no such measures have been taken. As a result, legislation that is guaranteed to develop new industries and production has been left on the back burner.

6

> "(Daily marijuana use) is the only thing that has (sustained) me (as) a contributing member of society for the last ten years."

The U.S. government has been discretely conducting medical marijuana research since 1968 on the campus of the University of Mississippi. The National Institute on Drug Abuse (NIDA) oversees this federal program that has uncovered several positive medical applications for marijuana, and yet medical marijuana remains illegal in 22 states. In fact, this program currently provides medical marijuana to a small number of patients through its Compassionate Use Investigational New Drug (IND) program. Every month, these patients receive over 300 joints grown from laboratories at the University of Mississippi.[1]

This unique program was developed in 1978 in response to a civil lawsuit against the government. Bob Randall had glaucoma and proved in court that he had a medical necessity for the drug. The Compassionate Use IND program later added more patients with various diseases and the program had a peak of 13 patients in 1991. However, the program stopped accepting new patients in the following year when Randall reached out to various AIDS groups and an onslaught of applicants tried to join. After all, this is a program that they wanted to remain secretive. Regardless, the current patients still receive their medicine, but today only four patients remain.[2]

Irvin Rosenfeld, the second person to enter the program, is one of the few surviving patients. He has a rare bone disorder called "multiple congenital cartilaginous exostoses." Since the age of 14, Rosenfeld had been prescribed hundreds of doses per month of various powerful pain drugs, including Dilaudid, Quaalude, Percocet, Darvon, and Valium. However, as of 1990, he no longer needs any of those medications, only marijuana. "That's why the pharmaceutical companies aren't happy with me," said Rosenfeld in an interview with *The Washington Post*.[3]

Rosenfeld also notes that the federal government has never published any reports in regard to the remarkable results marijuana has had on his health. Despite his severe medical condition,

Rosenfeld, at age 60, maintains a very active lifestyle and works full-time as a financial advisor. Rosenfeld is sure that marijuana has been the key to his remarkable turnaround. Otherwise, he adds, "I'd be a drain on society, not a productive member of society."[4]

"If marijuana were a new discovery rather than a well-known substance carrying cultural and political baggage, it would be hailed as a wonder drug," said Dr. Lester Grinspoon, the aforementioned professor at the Harvard Medical School.[5] Albeit, medical marijuana is hardly a new discovery. As early as 2737 BC, cannabis was a part of ancient Chinese medicine for a number of different ailments.[6] Furthermore, marijuana was first officially recognized for medicinal use in the U.S. in 1851.[7]

Glaucoma is probably the most recognized disease that can be directly treated by marijuana because it dramatically alleviates the pressure in the eye. Marijuana is also helpful with a range of conditions, including the common headache, migraines, menstrual cramps, insomnia, arthritis, and post-traumatic stress disorder.[A8] Although this may seem counterintuitive, marijuana can also benefit people with asthma.[9] Furthermore, inflammation, which is linked with most diseases, can be reduced with marijuana.[10]

Medical marijuana is primarily known for treating the symptoms of cancer and AIDS. It is commonly prescribed to reduce pain and alleviate nausea, particularly for patients who have to undergo chemotherapy. Marijuana has also proven to be very effective for reducing the debilitating spasms and seizures from some common nervous system diseases. These diseases include multiple sclerosis, epilepsy, Parkinson's disease, Lou Gehrig's disease, dystonia, and Tourette syndrome. For some of these patients, marijuana provides a new lease on life. Numerous news reports have profiled people whose seizures were nearly eliminated by marijuana use. Many of them had been suffering over 100 seizures per day.[11]

Medical marijuana is widely accepted by the vast majority of the population, even with age groups that are less supportive of recreational marijuana. An AARP poll, with people age 45 and over, once found that 72% of the respondents supported the legalization of medical marijuana.[12] That means that even the most passionate

---

[A] As of November 2015, Congress finally approved of Veterans Administration (VA) doctors prescribing marijuana for veterans suffering from PTSD in states where medical marijuana is legal.

drug war supporters understand the difference between recreational use and medical use. Then why is it that our politicians don't exhibit more compassion with this matter? After all, it takes a special kind of ego to deny the choice of medicine for a person in pain with a terminal disease.

Specific elements within the federal government are responsible for this kind of injustice, and they have ushered a disinformation crusade against medical marijuana. In particular, Dr. Robert DuPont, a pillar of the drug war establishment, has belittled this kind of research. Dr. DuPont served as the "Drug Czar" under Presidents Nixon and Ford. He was also the first director of the National Institute on Drug Abuse (NIDA). Hence, according to Dr. DuPont, "Those of the medical marijuana movement are putting on white coats and expressing concerns about the sick. But people need to see this for what it is...a fraud and a hoax."[13]

Dr. DuPont is well-known for his opposition to marijuana legalization, but he has an apparent conflict of interest. DuPont was also the co-founder of Bensinger, DuPont & Associates, which offers drug testing services. On the other hand, Dr. Mahmoud A. ElSohly served as a more independent judge. He was the head of research for NIDA's marijuana project with the University of Mississippi. His direct experience with scientific marijuana research led him to entirely different conclusions. As far back as 1995, Dr. ElSohly stated, "There is no question about the use of cannabis for certain conditions. It does have a history."[14]

In fact, there is a "publication bias" against medical marijuana, affirms Dr. Donald Abrams, a professor of Clinical Medicine at the University of California-San Francisco who conducts research at the Center for Medicinal Cannabis Research. Dr. Abrams says, "People are not particularly interested in publishing data suggesting that marijuana might have some benefits. All of those things, I think, sort of dampen anybody's enthusiasm to take on medical marijuana research."[15]

This disinformation campaign against medical marijuana surprisingly went into overdrive during the Clinton administration. With the support of Barry Goldwater, Arizona became the second state to legalize medical marijuana in 1998. The Clinton administration responded publicly by referring to the new state law as "dangerous heresy."[16] They didn't take this matter lightly and, in private, Bill Clinton's drug czar, Barry McCaffrey, organized a meeting in Washington with forty other anti-drug leaders. In attendance were officials from the DEA, Partnership for a Drug-Free America, the Office of National Drug Control Policy, among others. They were determined to "stop the spread of legalization to the (other) 48 states."[17]

Barry McCaffrey also commissioned a study in 1999 by the Institute of Medicine in hopes that it would discredit medical marijuana. However, much to McCaffrey's dismay, the study was highly supportive of medical marijuana.[18] Regardless, he and the rest of the drug war movement have never swayed in their commitment to fighting against medical marijuana.

The Controlled Substances Act established a hierarchy for the most dangerous drugs with five different levels, the highest level of danger labeled as "Schedule I." According to the guidelines, a drug should be classified as Schedule I if it has "high potential for abuse" and "no currently accepted medical use in treatment in the United States." On the other hand, Schedule II drugs also have "high potential for abuse," however those drugs do have "currently accepted medical use with severe restrictions."

Obviously, marijuana shouldn't be a Schedule I drug, but the DEA has insisted that it should remain that way. Keep in mind, that cocaine, various opiates, and methamphetamine are listed as Schedule II drugs! Not to mention, marijuana's Schedule I status blocks doctors from legally prescribing it to patients, even in states where medical marijuana is legal.

In 2009, the American Medical Association (AMA) suggested that marijuana should be rescheduled, yet it remains as a Schedule I drug today.[19] Marijuana clearly has its place in medicine, but the DEA has prolonged this dog and pony show for many years. Case in point, a report by the Drug Policy Alliance, "The DEA: Four Decades of Impeding and Rejecting Science," concisely illustrated the DEA's shameless strategy for obstructionism. The report stated, "The DEA took 16 years to issue a final decision to the first marijuana rescheduling petition, five years for the second, and nine years for the third."[20]

Despite intense organizational pressure, not everyone within the DEA has the followed the company line. The DEA's administrative law judge, Francis Young, ruled in 1988 that marijuana should be rescheduled. Young stated that "marijuana is one of the safest therapeutic substances known to man...capable of relieving the distress of great numbers of very ill people...It would be unreasonable, arbitrary, and capricious for the DEA to continue to stand between those sufferers and the benefits of this substance in light of the evidence."[21] Nonetheless, the DEA Administrator overruled his decision.[22] Again, in 2007, the DEA's administrative law judge, Mary Ellen Bittner, recommended that the government loosen its restrictions on marijuana research, yet nothing changed.[23]

The audacity of the federal witch-hunt against medical marijuana never ceases to amaze. For example, in 2007, the chief scientist for the Office of National Drug Control Policy, Dr. David Murray, testified before Congress. He claimed, "The medical marijuana movement is at best a mistake, at worst a deception. It has another victim involved here -- *the integrity of the drug approval process in America.*"[24] Well, contrary to Dr. Murray's beliefs, the drug approval process is quite flawed. In fact, it's a perfect example of the term "regulatory capture," in which the government protects the profits of the companies they regulate, rather than public interests. Much like how the revolving door with lobbyists and Capitol Hill corrodes the political system, there is an identical problem with the healthcare industry and its regulators.

A casual researcher could easily find several examples of corruption within the FDA. There may be no more jarring example than when nine scientists from the FDA's Center for Devices and Radiological Health officially contacted the Obama administration in 2009. They heard the "hope and change" rhetoric and seemingly expected the new administration to make good on its promises of whistleblower protection. This group explained that "an atmosphere does not exist at FDA where honest employees committed to integrity and the FDA mission can act without fear of reprisal."[25]

Those scientists revealed that three different medical devices had been recently approved by FDA administrators entirely due to outside political influences. In all three instances, the FDA approved these devices by overruling the scientists involved in the process. One of those decisions came about shortly after a phone call to the FDA from Rep. Christopher Shays (R-CT). As a result, the FDA approved a breast cancer screening device that exposed women to significantly higher levels of radiation.[26] This group of whistleblowers exposed broad-scale corruption, but as a result of their ethical conduct they were fired by the FDA. Furthermore, the FDA even placed spyware on their computers to hack into their personal email accounts after they went public with their information.[27]

The FDA has a bias against medical marijuana. The agency would relinquish much of its bureaucratic power if it acknowledged the medicinal benefits of marijuana. Simply put, a plant can't be patented, but the isolated compounds within it can be. Likewise, drug companies would obviously prefer a system in which consumers face potential jail time for marijuana use and are essentially coerced to pay sky high prices for prescription drugs that synthesize marijuana's chemicals.

The revolving door between employees of pharmaceutical companies and the FDA is well-documented, but there are other systemic conflicts of interest. Congress passed the Prescription Drug User Fee Act in 1992 enabling pharmaceutical companies to pay "user fees" to the FDA to speed up the approval process. In 2006 alone, those fees added up to $300 million.[28] In essence, that puts the FDA on the payroll of drug companies. As a result, the adverse side effects from various drugs are frequently repressed, even after they have been on the market.

Pharmacy retailers once sued Pfizer for allegedly conspiring with generic drug manufacturers to delay the launch of their cheaper generic drugs.[29] However, the FDA's "user fees" systematically generated similar results. Consumers were punished routinely with higher priced prescription drugs because generic drug companies couldn't pay "user fees" until 2012. In general, the approval process took twice as long.[30]

This cozy relationship between industry and regulators allows drug companies to influence the FDA's scientific standards for drug testing. Alarmingly, *The Washington Post* published a story exposing that drug companies paid hundreds of thousands of dollars to be included in meetings with the FDA's scientific panel when they decided upon testing and safety standards for painkiller medications.[31] That may have even been overkill as the FDA exercises very little oversight with clinical trials. Approximately 80% of clinical trials are performed overseas and only 0.7% of those trials are inspected by the FDA.[32] Furthermore, the FDA's efforts aren't much better within the U.S., as only 1.9% of trials are inspected.[33]

The FDA has established a rather laissez-faire environment for the major drug companies. The pharmaceutical companies can also thank the federal bureaucracy for stifling medical marijuana research. There is only one governmental agency, NIDA, with the authority to supply cannabis for scientific research. And, as you've probably guessed, NIDA has used their monopoly to block nearly all research of medical marijuana that doesn't represent pharmaceutical companies. One particular professor, Lyle Craker at the University of Massachusetts-Amherst, tried for almost ten years to get clearance for medical marijuana research before he finally gave up on the process.[34]

On the other hand, Dr. Sue Sisley from the University of Arizona's College of Medicine managed to get FDA approval for testing post-traumatic stress disorder with marijuana. As a psychiatrist with 15 years of experience treating veterans with PTSD, she was determined to test marijuana through a randomized, triple-blind study.[35] Sisley persevered and after a total of four years, she was granted full federal approval by NIDA. Unfortunately, she was abruptly fired from her three positions with the University of Arizona, just three months after gaining approval for her research. Sisley insists that she was fired for political reasons as she had received excellent job performance reviews and her employers provided her with no reason for her dismissal. "It'd be different if it was just one of the three positions," she said.[36] Afterward, she asserted that two influential Republican state legislators took issue with her advocacy and threatened university administrators with budgetary cutbacks.[37]

The FDA probably will never approve of smoking marijuana for medical purposes because of the carcinogens in the smoke. Currently, a pill with synthetic THC, Marinol, is the only FDA-approved form of medical marijuana. However, contrary to popular belief, there are advantages to using conventional marijuana. Case in point, swallowing a pill is horrible for someone suffering from nausea. Also, it's more difficult to get the proper dosage from a pill because its effects don't take place for about an hour. On the other hand, a marijuana smoker gets instant relief; therefore, the patient can immediately stop once they reach the appropriate comfort level. In fact, the former Surgeon General, Jocelyn Elders, noted that particular benefit to smoking marijuana versus Marinol.[38]

It's an outdated notion that smoking is a necessary part of being a medical marijuana patient because there have been tremendous breakthroughs, including edibles and topical solutions. Furthermore, there are now marijuana plants that contain virtually no THC, the psychoactive chemical. Those plants provide high levels of Cannabidiol (CBD), arguably marijuana's most medicinally relevant chemical that has anti-inflammatory and anti-spasmodic properties, without producing a high.[39] Notably, Marinol doesn't contain any CBD.

Sativex, made by GW Pharmaceuticals (based in the U.K.), differs from Marinol. It's an oral marijuana spray and it contains actual marijuana extracts of THC and CBD. Sativex was approved in Canada in 2005 and more recently throughout Europe. It still hasn't been approved by the FDA, but that is likely to happen soon. At that point, it will offer a decent compromise for those who need medical marijuana but are unwilling to take the legal risk associated with its use. After all, medical marijuana patients are violating federal law and the federal government indiscriminately enforces those laws. Consequently, that reinforces another issue. Pharmaceutical companies may be able to eventually offer a standardized form of medicine by isolating some of the 488 substances and 66 different cannabinoids contained within marijuana.[40] However, that doesn't mean that people should be denied access to conventional medical marijuana, thereby creating an effective monopoly for the pharmaceutical industry.

Medical marijuana patients, much to their surprise, often find that the intoxicating effect is rather mild in comparison to standard prescription pain drugs, many of which are legal opiates. The former talk show host Montel Williams explained that scenario, during an appearance on *The Doctor Oz Show*. Williams, who suffers from multiple sclerosis, was prescribed "7-8 Oxycontins a day" before he switched to medical marijuana. The opiates virtually incapacitated him and shut down his kidneys. He was no longer able to have a bowel movement before switching to marijuana. "(Daily marijuana use) is the only thing that has (sustained) me (as) a contributing member of society for the last ten years," says Montel Williams.[41]

Despite an arrest for medical marijuana, Williams has remained a very public figure for the medical marijuana movement. Also, his distinguished military career as a former corporal in the Marines and a lieutenant commander in the Navy should eliminate any doubts for skeptics. Suffice it to say, he isn't part of some "left-wing conspiracy."

It's well-documented that marijuana treats the symptoms of a variety of diseases. However, research shows that marijuana *can cure* several terminal diseases too. Dr. Robert Melamede, Professor of Biology at the University of Colorado, says, "Cannabinoids (marijuana) kill cancer cells, in many cases. People are not aware of that. They think cannabis -- anti-nausea. It's way beyond that."[42] Dr. Wai Liu, an oncologist at St. George's University of London, adds, "There's quite a lot of cancers that should respond quite nicely to these cannabis agents."[43] Dr. Liu notes that the drug companies are spending billions of dollars to produce drugs that mimic what cannabis does naturally.[44]

This may be hard to believe, but our bodies, along with most animals, naturally produce chemicals known as "endocannabinoids" that combat cancer. Don't be humbled if you're completely unfamiliar with that term because you're not alone. In fact, scientists weren't even aware that the endocannabinoid system (ECS) existed until the early 1990s. Consequently, related research is still very much in the preliminary stages. Nonetheless, the early findings are quite remarkable.

Endocannabinoids bind to various cells throughout the body, thereby regulating a variety of functions. Endocannabinoids act like a key that unlocks cells and provides them with orders. Here's where it gets more interesting. The chemicals in marijuana are remarkably similar to the endocannabinoids that our bodies naturally produce. "The only difference is that the endocannabinoids that we produce are in such small quantities. They're also rapidly degraded so that we're not high all the time," says Dr. Prakash Nagarkatti, a professor at the University of South Carolina.[45] Likewise, the cannabinoids from marijuana also bind with a variety of cells and regulate bodily functions, including cancer cells. Simply put, Dr. Nagarkatti explains that cannabinoids order "the cells to commit suicide and that's what they do."[46]

The American health industry is decades behind with this research because of the drug war. Israel, on the contrary, has far fewer repressive laws regarding marijuana research. Consequently, an Israeli chemist and professor at the Hebrew University of Jerusalem who began studying marijuana in 1963, Raphael Mechoulam, is known as "the father of medical marijuana." He says, "We have just scratched the surface and I greatly regret that I don't have another lifetime to devote to this field, for we may well discover that cannabinoids are involved in some way in all human diseases."[47]

The marijuana historian Jack Herer has alleged that the U.S. federal government has been aware of these kinds of discoveries and has censored the details. For instance, he cited a study in 1974 at the Medical College of Virginia led by Dr. Albert Munson. Those scientists originally intended to investigate possible damage to the immune system from marijuana use; but instead, they found that THC slowed the growth of cancer. *The Washington Post* on August 18, 1974 reported on it. The headline read, "Cancer Curb Is Studied," and included:

> The researchers found that THC slowed the growth of lung cancers, breast cancers, and a virus-induced leukemia in laboratory mice, and prolonged their lives by as much as 36 percent.[48]

Dr. Manuel Guzmán, Professor of Biochemistry & Molecular Biology at the University of Madrid (Spain), wanted to follow up on that same experiment but was unable to. He said, "In fact, I have attempted many times to obtain the journal article on the original investigation by these people, but it has proven impossible."[49] Nonetheless, Dr. Guzmán conducted similar cancer experiments in 2000 by injecting 45 lab rats with a cancer cell. Fifteen of them were the control group. Fifteen of the mice were injected with THC and the other fifteen were given a synthetic THC. Only three of the rats dosed with THC didn't benefit from the drug. The rest lived significantly longer and the tumors disappeared completely for three of them (15%).[50] The rats treated with the synthetic THC had similar results.

Dr. Prakash Nagarkatti conducted comparable experiments at the University of South Carolina. Dr. Nagarkatti found "that almost 25 to 30 percent of the mice completely rejected the tumor. They were completely cured." The remaining mice had a "significant reduction in the volume of the size of the tumors."[51] These types of animal-based experiments are obviously very promising, but Dr. Guzmán offered a warning. He says, "We do not know if this can be extrapolated to humans at all."[52] However, he is now conducting scientific experiments with humans in Leeds, England on behalf of GW Pharmaceuticals.

PBS NewsHour discovered that these kinds of tests are hardly isolated. Over the past few years, numerous American pharmaceutical companies have filed patents for synthetic marijuana drugs. Those patents claim to cure a number of maladies, including multiple sclerosis, Alzheimer's disease, Parkinson's disease, Tourette syndrome, rheumatoid arthritis, epilepsy, heart disease, various mental diseases, obesity, and a cure for cancer.[53] In fact, believe it or not, the U.S. government has a patent for cannabinoids, United States Patent 6630507. That was based on research from the National Institute of Health. The patent applies to treating strokes, trauma, Alzheimer's disease, Parkinson's disease, and HIV.[54] Again, this has all happened while marijuana remains classified as a Schedule I drug!

United States Patent 6630507 should eliminate any doubts for cynics. However, moderate critics of medical marijuana often acknowledge that medical marijuana has great potential, but they want the entire process to go through the FDA. Unfortunately, those currently suffering from terminal diseases and getting positive results from medical marijuana don't have time to wait for that process to come to fruition.

There is a real predicament unfolding within this gray area: recreational use of marijuana is illegal, while medical use is accepted. Some states allow doctors to prescribe marijuana for basically any ailment. Thus, many of those doctors are rebelling against our deeply flawed laws and knowingly prescribing marijuana for recreational use. In fact, the same type of situation occurred during the prohibition of alcohol. Today, many recreational marijuana users, particularly teenagers, have convinced themselves that using marijuana recreationally is good for their health.

Our country desperately needs to be presented the facts, both good and bad, about marijuana. The medicinal qualities of marijuana only add confusion to an already polarizing topic. Too many marijuana advocates choose to ignore the potential harm from abusing marijuana, but that is an understandable reaction to the misinformation that has been presented by the federal government. Again, early government-sponsored research, such as the La Guardia Committee and the Schafer report, was conducted in an independent manner and these projects concluded that marijuana was relatively benign. One of the tenets of scientific research is that the methodology should be transparent and peer-reviewed. However, that wasn't an option during Nixon's buildup to the drug war. After all, you need an ominous threat to pursue when you start throwing money at a problem. Thus, research was conducted with predetermined outcomes.

One such study conducted at Tulane University was released in 1974. It "proved" that marijuana could cause severe brain damage and death within three months of use. This was a useful propaganda tool, but Playboy and NORML called their bluff and demanded to see the government's research. After six years of formal requests and lawsuits, they found out that the government's "scientific" tests were nothing more than a cruel hoax intent upon swaying public opinion. These researchers used monkeys as test subjects and forced them to inhale the equivalent of 63 highly potent joints through a gas mask over a five minute period. As a result, the monkeys were suffocated to death; they didn't die from marijuana.[55]

The most controversial health aspect with marijuana is its effect on the brain. There is a consensus of scientific research that demonstrates how marijuana use for an adolescent or child will deteriorate the development of the brain. In turn, that slows the physical and mental maturation process.[56] On the other hand, there isn't a scientific consensus about the long-term effects for adults. For example, one study published in 2014 was heavily cited by the opposition to legalization. That study, "Long term effects of marijuana on the brain," concluded that there were changes to the brain for heavy users, however, the authors didn't find that those changes would necessarily lead to a reduction in IQ.[57] All in all, Americans have been inundated with propaganda, but several long-term studies have found that marijuana results in little to no damage to the brain.[58]

There are medical risks involved with marijuana, but those risks don't justify keeping it illegal. Consumers should be warned about the health consequences and allowed to make their own decisions. Then again, the side effects from marijuana pale in comparison to several of the prescription drugs advertised on TV. For one thing, marijuana suppresses the immune system, but the effect is minimal. Also, anyone with a mental disorder shouldn't self-medicate with marijuana because it can create feelings of panic and paranoia. The high from marijuana increases the heart rate, but there has never been a documented overdose from marijuana. With that said, anyone with hypertension or anyone at risk for stroke should consider avoiding it. Likewise, research into the long-term effects upon the cardiovascular system is still in the early stages. In fact, some French researchers have concluded that marijuana can lead to cardiovascular complications and they believe that those cases are underreported.[59]

To state the obvious, smoking any substance isn't good for your lungs. Consequently, the damage from marijuana smoke makes its users more likely to develop chronic bronchitis. More importantly, the issue of cancer needs to be addressed because all forms of smoke inherently contain carcinogens. Therefore, some scientists believe there is a *possibility* that smoking marijuana can lead to cancer and tumors. Dr. Donald Tashkin, head of the nation's cannabis pulmonary research program at UCLA, has been the leading researcher to test that hypothesis. He began conducting these experiments in the 1970s and, in fact, his early findings supported this theory. He determined that lesions in the lungs caused by marijuana were "pre-cancerous." That was based upon early-stage comparisons with patients who had cancer and tumors. However, Dr. Tashkin acknowledged that this kind of research needed to be conducted over many years. Nonetheless, many government sources were quick to celebrate and exhaustively cited Dr. Tashkin's research as definitive proof.[60]

However, as a follow-up, he conducted further research in a "largest of its kind" study that was released in 2006. Dr. Tashkin naturally assumed that the people who smoked marijuana heavily would have higher rates of lung cancer. Instead, much to his surprise, Dr. Tashkin found that marijuana smokers, even heavy smokers, had a slightly lower risk of lung cancer than non-smokers.[61] As a reminder, the endocannabinoid system (ECS) wasn't known to exist when Dr. Tashkin began his research four decades ago. Now, he points to the tumor-shrinking qualities of the ECS. Furthermore, he contends that the anti-inflammatory and autoimmune suppressing responses to marijuana are reasons why marijuana smokers are less likely than tobacco smokers to develop chronic obstructive pulmonary disease (COPD).[62]

Despite all of the scientific evidence, the Office of National Drug Control Policy (ONDCP) touted the hypothetical cancer risk from marijuana in their report, *Marijuana Myths and Facts: The Truth Behind 10 Popular Misconceptions*. Their Myth #3,

"Marijuana is not as harmful to your health as tobacco," asserts that marijuana is more detrimental to your health than cigarettes because there is a higher level of tar in marijuana smoke. Somehow, the ONDCP ignored that tobacco kills over 400,000 Americans a year, while there has never been a single documented death from marijuana. They also have chosen to omit any information about the anti-cancer effects of cannabinoids.

Arguably, the worst danger from marijuana, ironically, is its low toxicity. There is no hangover effect and that leads some users into overindulgence. However, that's not a medical risk. Real world observations suggest that frequent marijuana use leads to lethargy, but several long-term studies haven't been able to scientifically prove that moderate marijuana use causes unmotivated behavior.[63] One study in 2013, however, found that long-term marijuana users had lower dopamine levels, the chemical related with pleasure.[64]

Marijuana is also considerably less addictive than alcohol or tobacco. There are very slight physical withdrawal symptoms for heavy users, but most people don't find it difficult to quit marijuana. For casual users, any addiction is likely to be purely psychological. However, the government exaggerates the addictiveness of marijuana by citing the increasing number of patients in treatment for marijuana dependence. Most of those people didn't enter into treatment from their free will. In 2008, fifty-seven percent of the individuals in treatment for marijuana were there due to a referral from the legal system in hopes of reducing their criminal penalty. Only 15% of the people in treatment for marijuana were self-referred. Many of the rest were likely enrolled from parental pressure considering that 68% of the marijuana treatment cases were adolescents.[65]

On the bright side, the litany of readily available information about marijuana has forced the government to tone down its rhetoric. For example, Reagan's drug czar, Carlton Turner, once claimed that marijuana turned heterosexual men into homosexuals.[66] Obviously, that kind of soundbite in our current era would be mocked endlessly with wide-scale ridicule. With that said, numerous government officials still cite "the gateway theory" that marijuana leads to using more harmful drugs.

The best solution is to legalize marijuana and make a clear dividing line with the most harmful drugs. Prohibition forces marijuana smokers to develop connections with drug dealers and that makes it easier to try more dangerous illegal drugs. Also, marijuana users may falsely assume that the dangers of drugs, such as cocaine and heroin, have been exaggerated, as they have been with marijuana. In fact, the previously mentioned study by the Institute of Medicine (commissioned by Barry McCaffrey) found no evidence of marijuana causing people to experiment with harder drugs.[67] Even research from the RAND Corporation, which is closely aligned with the defense industry, disagrees with the gateway theory. In 2002, the RAND Drug Policy Research Center concluded that "policies aimed at reducing or eliminating marijuana availability are unlikely to make any dent in the hard drug problem."[68]

One of the government's last resorts has been to focus on the higher THC levels in today's marijuana. The DEA's Mark Trouville declared, "This ain't your grandfather's or your father's marijuana. This will hurt you. This will addict you. This will kill you."[69] That warning came about in 2007, but the death count has yet to begin. Yes, marijuana growers are now able to produce a more potent product, but that is directly related to prohibition. Drug traffickers have an incentive to transport the strongest product on the market because this is a bulky contraband material.

Besides, higher potency marijuana is actually a health benefit because people can inhale less smoke and get the same effect. Nonetheless, several government officials cite today's stronger marijuana as a scare tactic because it's effective with non-marijuana users who think of it like alcohol. Hard liquor poses more risk than beer if too much is consumed in a short period of time. However, that isn't an apples-to-apples comparison between marijuana and alcohol; there is no overdose risk with marijuana. You would have to perform an impossible task of smoking roughly 1,500 pounds of marijuana over 15 minutes for an overdose.[70]

Various government sources, including the ONDCP, continue to cite statistics linking higher rates of mental disorders, such as schizophrenia, and suicides with marijuana. However, these kinds of studies don't offer proof that marijuana is the *cause* of those problems. It's just as logical to conclude that people who committed suicide or were suffering from a mental illness made a poor decision to self-medicate with marijuana. That doesn't mean that marijuana *caused* the mental disorder or suicide. Regardless, that was the suggestion in Myth #1, "Marijuana is harmless," of the ONDCP's report *Marijuana Myths and Facts: The Truth Behind 10 Popular Misconceptions*.[71] Dr. Lester Grinspoon, whose expertise is in schizophrenia, has labeled those types of assertions as "absurd." He has cited that schizophrenia has consistently affected approximately 1% of the world's population for decades while an increasingly higher percentage of people use marijuana.[72]

Myth #4, "Marijuana makes you mellow," is similar. It cites statistics of higher rates of violence with marijuana users. Again, there's no scientific proof to show that marijuana is the *cause* of violent behavior. There are some other socioeconomic variables that lead to higher levels of violence that conveniently haven't been included by the ONDCP, such as income level, education, parental background, etc. Also, scientific tests, along with real world observations, connect marijuana with peaceful feelings, not violent actions. Meanwhile, we should look no further than America's drug of choice. Alcohol is involved in 40% of all violent crime in the U.S.[73]

The ONDCP even has the audacity to conflate the negative consequences of prohibition. Myth #7, "If I am buying marijuana, I'm not hurting anyone else," details the dangers of the drug trafficking cartels and the violence that takes place in the black market. Obviously, there is no more apparent solution to that problem than legalization. Myth #8, "My kids won't be exposed to marijuana," points out that marijuana is easily available to children. Again, this is another indictment of prohibition and the better policy for keeping drugs away from children would be to strictly enforce legalization for adult users. After all, it's difficult to find someone dealing alcohol or cigarette in schools.

Myth #10, "The government sends otherwise innocent people to prison for casual marijuana use," tries to minimize the punishment for marijuana possession. They point out that typically, first-time offenders usually aren't sent to prison. That is generally true depending upon the amount confiscated and where the arrest occurred. However, the general theme of the ONDCP's Myth # 10 is part of a widespread misperception that marijuana has become completely decriminalized. Every 42 seconds an American is arrested for marijuana, according to the FBI's statistics for 2011.[74] Eighty-seven percent of those marijuana arrests (over 750,000) were for possession alone.[75] Nonetheless, many in the drug law enforcement community like to downplay the penalties associated with a marijuana arrest. If that were truly the case, it would beg the question, "Why is there a need to make any of these arrests, in the first place?"

The last resort of drug war proponents is to claim there will be more car accidents if marijuana becomes legal. That sounds fairly logical considering that marijuana slows down your reaction time and limits your coordination. Nonetheless, numerous studies have found that driving while high on marijuana is much less dangerous than driving while drunk. Some studies have even documented better safety results from drivers high on marijuana than sober drivers.[76] However, that's an anomaly because no reasonable person would recommend driving while intoxicated by any substance.

A case study by Columbia University assigned a risk factor of 1.83 for driving while high on marijuana. That meant that driving 18.3 miles while high was equally dangerous to driving 10 miles while sober. That same study gave a risk factor of 4 for texting while driving and a risk factor of 12 for drunk driving.[77] Both alcohol and marijuana impair vision and slow down reflexes, but drunk drivers tend to drive more aggressively at higher speeds. On the other hand, marijuana smokers tend to be very conscious of their impairment and drive more conservatively to compensate. Likewise, a study by the U.S. Department of Transportation's National Highway Traffic Safety Administration concluded:

> "Drivers under the influence of marijuana retain insight in their performance and will compensate where they can, for example, by slowing down or increasing effort. As a consequence, THC's adverse effects on driving performance appear relatively small...Alcohol impaired driving performance according to the driving instructor but subjects did not perceive it; marijuana did not impair driving performance but the subjects themselves perceived their driving performance as such."[78]

Driving while high on marijuana is less dangerous than driving while drunk, however, no one wants an increase in the number of drivers using marijuana. Unfortunately, there will be tradeoffs when marijuana is legalized, but the existing evidence shows that legalization leads to a net decrease in traffic fatalities because there are less drunk drivers. After all, the alcohol industry has lobbied against marijuana for a reason; it cuts into their market share. In particular, one report documented that traffic fatalities declined in the states where medical marijuana was legalized, by a pair of economics professors, Daniel Rees (University of Colorado Denver) and D. Mark Anderson (Montana State University). They analyzed the data from the 13 states that legalized medical marijuana between 1990 and 2009 and concluded that alcohol consumption was reduced with drivers ages 20-29. Consequently, there were fewer overall traffic deaths.[79]

The takeaway is that, unfortunately, in a free society, there will always be a certain percentage of people who will drive while intoxicated. However, strictly from a perspective of practicality, driving overall would be safer if marijuana were the drug of choice. This aspect of the debate is no different from the overall trend. All in all, the danger from marijuana has been vastly exaggerated and the untapped medicinal qualities have been censored. Fortunately, the primary suspects behind this deception are staring us right in the face. It all comes down to money and power.

7

"We both think that we ought not to drink in the White House, but we feel that our own bedrooms are our house and we can do what we like here."
Warren G. Harding

The numerous parallels between the prohibition of alcohol and the current drug war are uncanny. The primary groups leading the prohibition movement were the Women's Christian Temperance Union (WCTU) and the Anti-Saloon League (ASL). Both groups represented large, religious non-partisan voting blocs that blamed alcohol for much of society's problems. They specialized in high-pressure tactics and effectively ousted politicians who didn't vote accordingly. In fact, the ASL's leader, Wayne Wheeler, proudly coined the term "pressure group."[1]

These groups were shameless and limitless propagandists. "Ethics be hanged," said William Eugene "Pussyfoot" Johnson, one of the most aggressive members of the ASL. Johnson literally bribed newspapers from across the nation to print articles under his pseudonym, "C.L. Trevitt, Literary Agent."[2] Likewise, Mary Hunt of the WCTU had her way with the nation's school boards. The WCTU's "Scientific Temperance Instruction" was inserted into public school textbooks nationwide and as many as 50% of public school textbooks needed an unofficial approval by Hunt.[3] The "Scientific Temperance Instruction" indoctrinated students with claims such as "when alcohol passes down the throat it burns off the skin, leaving it bare and burning."[4] By the same token, students read, "Nearly 3,000 infants are smothered yearly in bed by drunken parents."[5] Some textbooks even claimed that alcoholics could spontaneously combust.[6]

The prohibition movement began as a moral issue, but it transitioned into fuel for bigotry and racial hatred. A former Congressman from Alabama, Richmond Pearson Hobson, labeled prohibition as the "last stand of the great white race." He also introduced the first federal attempt at prohibition in 1914. Hobson warned that alcohol would send "a peaceable red man…back to the plane of the savage."[7] He added, "If a Negro takes up regular use of alcoholic beverage, in a short time he will degenerate to the level of the cannibal. No matter how high the stage of evolution, the result is the same."[8] The ASL clearly incentivized his open racism and he was the highest paid public speaker on behalf of their organization. Hobson drew large crowds and his rhetoric fell right in line with the Jim Crow aspirations of the Ku Klux Klan, which also publicly supported the prohibition movement.[9]

The open bigotry within the prohibition movement wasn't limited to the Deep South. Many in the north supported this propaganda and the timing coincided with a massive influx of immigrants of Italian, German, and Eastern European heritage. Some prohibition handouts stated that "Dagos, who drink excessively, live in a state of filth and use the knife on the slightest provocation."[10] In addition, Purley Baker of the ASL asserted that Germans "eat like gluttons and drink like swine."[11] That kind of anti-immigrant message, particularly anti-German claims, gained even more traction during World War I. Wayne Wheeler of the ASL called the Brewers Association the "enemy in the home camp" and their pamphlets warned of "treasonable liquor trade."[12] Wheeler, along with some politicians, publicly implored the government to investigate Anheuser-Busch and some other Milwaukee manufacturers because of their German background.[13]

Prohibition went into effect in 1920 with the 18th Amendment, the Volstead Act, but all didn't welcome it. The various ethnic groups that were denounced through propaganda tended to be the ones most targeted by the new law. In turn, New York City had protests in the streets with Irish, Germans, Italians, and African Americans together waving American flags and holding signs, such as "We're American Citizens, Not Inmates" and "We Prefer Brewers of Beer to Brewers of Bigotry."[14]

On the other hand, big business supported prohibition with hopes of better productivity from their workers. The Rockefellers, Carnegies, and Henry Ford were strong prohibitionists. Ford even enforced a "no drink, no saloon" rule. He believed, "Prohibition is a moral issue. For it is economically right. We now know that anything which is economically right is also morally right."[15] He went so far as to send inspectors into the homes of workers suspected of drinking alcohol.[16] He even suggested that the military should help enforce prohibition.[17]

The industrialists didn't foresee the rebellious response and cultural changes that ensued. Prohibition went into effect during a contradictory era when American individualism and the economy were advancing. The prohibitionists, or "drys," had promised that the country's moral compass would improve with prohibition; instead, it led to nationwide rebellion and disrespect for the law. The stigma associated with an arrest dissipated during prohibition. Notably, a San Francisco jury nullified a case against a bootlegger; in fact, they drank the evidence from the trial.[18] With that in mind, NASCAR originated during the prohibition period because many of the first race car drivers were bootleggers who souped up their cars to race away from prohibition agents.[19]

The forbidden fruit aspect of prohibition made drinking alcohol the "in" thing for many people. The whereabouts of speakeasies were anything but secret. Indeed, an estimated 35,000 speakeasies thrived at the peak of prohibition in New York City alone.[20] Many speakeasies employed youths to work as lookouts for their businesses, just like the drug gangs of today.[21] Moral reformers had hoped to curb rebellious behavior, but a reverse effect resulted from the semi-private nature of speakeasies. Saloons had been exclusively for men beforehand, but prohibition marked a new era and speakeasies were overflowing with women. The new generation of young cosmopolitan women, dubbed "flappers," brazenly flaunted their newfound social freedoms and sexuality. Most of the women dressed in a manner that was considered promiscuous for this time period, including sleeveless outfits and knee-high skirts.[22]

Alcohol consumption was rampant during prohibition even though people were putting their lives at risk. Obviously, there were no regulatory safeguards in place. Distilling liquor isn't a foolproof task and isn't meant for amateurs. During prohibition, drinkers faced unnecessary risks because several unscrupulous bootleggers used industrial alcohol or "wood alcohol." Consumers were at the mercy of bootleggers, some of whom paid scientists to remove as many of the toxins from industrial alcohol as possible.[23] Regardless, the wood alcohol taste and smell was nearly impossible to remove. As a matter of fact, many current cocktail recipes were developed during this time as a means for covering up the taste.[24]

Again, this underground market was littered with bootleggers who were either shameless or incompetent. By 1927, thousands of people were poisoned, resulting in blindness, paralysis, or death.[25] Obviously, a change needed to be made, but the Treasury made the wrong decision. In that same year, the Treasury Department *increased* the number of poisons added to industrial alcohol in hopes of further deterring Americans from drinking.[26] That reckless decision proved to be ineffective in curbing alcohol consumption and resulted in increased alcohol-related poisonings.[27]

As a result of prohibition, international smugglers were truly providing a public service; their contraband was the only safe option for American consumers. In fact, eighty percent of Canada's liquor was imported into the U.S. during prohibition.[28] Keep in mind, most Canadian provinces had imposed laws banning the sale of alcohol during this time. Albeit, the Canadian government recognized an opportunity and authorized the manufacturing of alcohol for foreign exports only. Consequently, the Detroit River became a prime port for smugglers.[29]

Conversely, the most famous rum runner, Bill McCoy, imported his supplies from the Caribbean. In fact, he was known for some of the finest quality liquor and that's how the phrase "the real McCoy" was popularized. Adding to his folklore, McCoy was one of the few in the bootleg business who didn't rely upon bribing American officials; he preferred to outwit his opposition. "Dealings of that sort would have killed the sport of the game for me," said McCoy.[30] He even developed "Rum Row," a flagrant demonstration of disrespect for American authorities. Rum Row was a group of large ships that stocked up on Caribbean liquor and operated as wholesalers for American smugglers. Those ships anchored just beyond U.S. jurisdiction, three miles offshore. Of course, the Coast Guard stationed boats next to Rum Row, but the smugglers usually owned sportier boats that could race away from the Coast Guard.[31]

Politics in the early 20th century often focused on the difference between the "haves" and "have-nots," and prohibition reinforced those images of a two-tiered society. The 18th Amendment banned the manufacture, sale, and distribution of alcohol; however, it didn't ban consumption. Therefore, the possession of alcohol in the home was legal, as long as it had been purchased before prohibition had been the implemented.[32] Hence, prohibition was merely a slight inconvenience for the wealthy. Anyone with a large enough estate never had any worries. However, the working class had to press its luck with the rotgut bathtub gin served at the local speakeasy.

Apparently, happy hour went on endlessly on Capitol Hill. "In my six years in Washington (1923-1929), I witnessed more drinking in the national capital than in New York," said New York

Congressman Emanuel Celler.[33] Mabel Willebrandt, Deputy Attorney General in charge of enforcing prohibition, admitted that "Senators and Congressmen appeared on the floor in a drunken condition" and "bootleggers infested the halls and corridors of Congress."[34] Even President Warren G. Harding was known to have an occasional drink. He was quoted as saying, "We both think that we ought not to drink in the White House, but we feel that our own bedrooms are our house and we can do what we like here."[35]

Congress's top bootlegger, George Cassiday, operated openly. In fact, his activity was so brazen that *The Washington Post* even published a series of articles about him, "The Man in the Green Hat." About 80% of the members of Congress relied upon his service, which he delivered from a large leather briefcase.[36] Cassiday even had his own office in the Cannon building of the House of Representatives until his arrest in 1925.[37] He received a light penalty, but he then decided to take his business to the Senate.[38] Operating just as freely, Cassiday occupied an office in the Russell building of the Senate until his arrest in 1930. At that point, Cassiday received an 18-month sentence. Conversely, the Senators from his client list merely had to deal with the embarrassment of having their names publicized.[39]

There were many contradictions with law enforcement during prohibition. Due to bribery, large percentages of local police forces were lax in their enforcement duties. However, every cop was *not* on the take. Obviously, many officers took their duty seriously despite the fact that few restrictions were in place to prevent abuses of power, such as illegal searches. Yes, law enforcement was clearly lax on Capitol Hill, but some of the more intrusive police tactics of today came about during prohibition, including the use of criminal forfeiture, undercover sting operations, and paid informants.[40]

Prohibition marked an era of new legal precedents and the courts usually sided with the government in favor of these aggressive tactics. For example, federal police openly conducted warrantless wiretaps to help convict a northwest booze baron, Roy Olmstead. Alarmingly, in 1928 the U.S. Supreme Court ruled in Olmstead v United States that the police didn't violate his 4th amendment rights.[41]

Before the onset of prohibition, New York Mayor Fiorello La Guardia warned that another 250,000 agents would be needed just to monitor the original 250,000 federal prohibition agents (his estimation for the necessary number of agents).⁴² He was prophetic; after all, there were 18,000 federal agents hired during the first eleven years of prohibition and 1,600 of them were eventually fired with 257 criminally prosecuted.⁴³

This era marked arguably the most widespread corruption in our nation's history. After all, Roy Olmstead, the "King of the Northwest Bootleggers," had been a Seattle cop. He was fired only a few weeks after prohibition went into effect. Even after leaving the force, his massive syndicate remained in the good graces of the local police for many years.⁴⁴ Olmstead's story was typical during this era as the tremendous profits from the black market of prohibition were simply irresistible to many civil servants.

George Remus, one of America's wealthiest bootleggers, estimated that half of his profits paid for the necessary bribes to maintain his operation.⁴⁵ "I tried to corner the graft market only to find out that there is not enough money in the world to buy up all the public officials who demand a share in the graft," said Remus.⁴⁶ Remus was a lawyer from Cincinnati, but he made his fortune by purchasing major whiskey distilleries before prohibition went into effect. He then acquired medicinal permits for manufacturing alcohol and flooded the black market with his supply. Consequently, he enjoyed an extravagant lifestyle and many believe that the main character from *The Great Gatsby* was loosely based upon George Remus.

Corruption was prevalent throughout police departments nationwide, but Chicago was probably the worst case scenario. The Chicago Police Chief admitted that sixty percent of his officers were "in the bootleg business."⁴⁷ In fact, even Chicago's Mayor, "Big" Bill Thompson was on Al Capone's payroll and he received a $260,000 campaign donation from Capone to boot.⁴⁸ In kind, Thompson unabashedly promised not to enforce the law during his campaign run of 1927. He said, "When I'm elected we will not only reopen places these people (the police) have closed, but we'll open ten thousand new ones...No copper (police officer) will invade your home and fan your mattress for a hip flask."⁴⁹ This was a rather chummy relationship as Al Capone had pictures of only three people on his wall -- George Washington, Abraham Lincoln, and "Big" Bill Thompson.

No one benefitted more from prohibition than organized crime. In recognition of the failure of prohibition, many people even sympathized with murderous organized criminals. Al Capone had been somewhat popular with the working class and was cheered in public.[50] After all, he supplied what many of the people wanted. However, that popularity dropped significantly after the much publicized "Saint Valentine's Day Massacre," a turf war with his rival Bugs Moran. That event became a tipping point in history and from that moment forward the media labeled Capone as "Public Enemy Number One." Consequently, the bloodshed from that day became a symbol and garnered tremendous popular support for ending prohibition.[51]

By the late 1920s, some industrial titans, such as John D. Rockefeller Jr., switched sides on the issue.[52] Pierre DuPont had also supported prohibition in its early days, but he later became a leading lobbyist for the Association Against the Prohibition Amendment (AAPA). The DuPont family gave tremendous funding to the AAPA. Albeit, their organization's credibility was damaged after violating the Federal Corrupt Practices Act of 1925. They had accepted significant donations (far more than the maximum contributions) from brewers and distillers.[53]

Pierre DuPont persevered and gained support among the wealthy after the economy crashed in 1929. These business leaders worried that future administrations would target them with significant tax increases. After all, the Treasury was in desperate need for tax revenues as a result of the Great Depression. In turn, the AAPA produced an influential brochure, "The Need of a New Source of Government Revenue," which touted the end of prohibition as the solution to the federal government's budget crisis.[54] DuPont suggested that duplicating the British liquor tax system would "permit the total abolition of the income tax, both personal and corporate."[55] Ending prohibition had also become very popular among the masses. Public polls showed that 73% of Americans supported the repeal of prohibition, which came about in 1933.[56] To sum up, job creation and the economic stimulus from alcohol overwhelmed any argument based on morality.

In the end, the prohibition movement was just as presumptuous then as it is today. In 1918, Wayne Wheeler of the ASL asserted that the Prohibition Unit would only need $5 million to eliminate the nation's problem with alcoholism. With that in mind, after nine years of prohibition, the sixth commissioner of the Prohibition Unit told Congress that $300 million wasn't enough funding. Without a doubt, the flow of alcohol was hardly suppressed during Prohibition, but there is some controversy as to what extent. Contrary to popular belief, several historians believe that there was an overall decrease in alcohol consumption. Be that as it may, the Presidential Wickersham Commission concluded differently in 1931. They found that alcohol consumption had, in fact, increased during prohibition.[57]

The drug war has been an even more obvious failure. By 1970, an estimated 4 million Americans had tried an illegal drug.[58] American taxpayers have spent over $1 trillion on the drug war since then and illegal drug usage has since skyrocketed even further.[59] Today, as many as 100 million Americans, about one-third of Americans, have tried marijuana at least once.[60] It should be obvious that it isn't realistic to put one-third of the population in jail. Keep in mind, those figures only apply to marijuana. Regardless of the results, our country continues to spend approximately $51 billion a year to fight the war on drugs.[61]

Prohibition was aptly termed the "Noble Experiment" and it resulted in an increased prison population, along with extensive black market crime. The homicide rate reached a record level in 1933 and it is no coincidence that the homicide rate didn't surpass that level until 1974 when Nixon intensified the drug war.[62] Also, roughly half of the prison population in 1930 was there for alcohol related offenses.[63] Likewise, roughly half of the inmates in federal prison are now serving drug sentences.[64] As a result, the court system is drowning with cases. But, once again, there is a precedent. Prohibition marked the first time in American history that the sheer number of cases forced judges to begin offering "plea bargains" to clear their backlog.[65]

People have now become accustomed to reports of drug-related violence. Remember, the Saint Valentine's Day Massacre of 1929 entailed the murder of seven people and sparked an organized outcry for change. Conversely, no singular event has prompted universal support to end the drug war. There are so many of these kinds of reports that we've become desensitized to the savagery. After all, it's not uncommon to hear of Mexican cartel mass burials or gang members chopping up their rivals' bodies and burning them in oil drums. In one case, they literally cut off the faces of their rivals, sewed them onto soccer balls, and then rolled the heads onto a nightclub dance floor as an intimidation tactic.[66]

What level of violence will it take to awaken the public to the realization that this second "Noble Experiment" went wrong? Many people have seemingly misinterpreted the cause of drug-related violence. They believe that drugs automatically turn all users into crazed maniacs, instead of realizing that the vast majority of drug-related violence has to do with controlling the black market distribution. Legalization would eliminate that violence.

Surprisingly, not everyone can connect the dots. Look no further than Bernard Kerik, former New York City Police Chief, who had a quick rise to fame due to a tough reputation. By all means, he is also a man who understands nuance. As the head of the Department of Corrections in New York City, he made several bold, progressive reforms of Rikers Island. Nonetheless, in 2001 he wrote in his memoir, *The Lost Son: A Life in Pursuit of Justice,* about a failed actress who sold marijuana to make ends meet. Before murdering her, two armed burglars stole all of her cash and drugs. They also shot four of her guests who happened to be in her apartment at the time of the robbery. Kerik wrote, "As I stood over them looking at the carnage, I couldn't help but think about the people in this country who continue to say that marijuana is a victimless crime. Tell it to the people lying there in a pool of blood."[67]

In a surprising twist, Kerik had a fall from grace and was later sentenced to nine years in prison for tax charges. He was seemingly the target of a political witch hunt, but that's neither here nor there. Anyhow, after leaving prison, he became even more vocal about the need for reforming the criminal justice system and proclaimed that several of his fellow inmates were sentenced needlessly for petty crimes. You would think that someone with his life perspective would recognize the harms of the drug war. Instead, he remained steadfast and told that same "victimless crime" anecdote, in 2014, during an interview with *Reason Magazine*.[68]

The drug war continues to provide appropriate comparisons to the prohibition era. For instance, the modern equivalent of "wood alcohol" is the synthetic marijuana sold as "herbal incense" or "potpourri" in head shops and convenience stores. This synthetic marijuana contains chemicals that are meant to closely mimic THC. Some users say that the high is somewhat comparable, but the side effects are indisputably much worse. It can cause agitation, hallucinations, seizures, vomiting and nausea, severe difficulty with breathing, and in some cases death. To be exact, there were 866 calls in 2010 into the American Association of Poison Control Centers for synthetic marijuana before the DEA placed a federal ban on the drug. Notwithstanding, those efforts are basically futile because the DEA has to play a game of whack a mole; the drug makers simply alter the chemical makeup slightly to skirt the banned substance list.[69]

Oddly enough, a research professor of organic chemistry at Clemson University, Dr. John W. Huffman, was the unwitting creator of this gray market of synthetic marijuana. Huffman developed various synthetic marijuana compounds for medical marijuana research. Regrettably, some people analyzed his research papers and were able to decipher his method of creation, a reverse engineering of sorts. Thus, an entirely new commercial market emerged. Naturally, he is frustrated with the series of events that unraveled and he warns about the dangers of synthetic marijuana, comparing it to playing Russian roulette. "You can't overdose on marijuana, but you might on these compounds," said Huffman. "These things are dangerous, and marijuana isn't, really."[70]

Another unintended consequence of the war on drugs has been a dramatic decrease in the rule of law. Gang culture has grown at such a rapid pace that there are now an estimated 900,000 current members involved in 20,000 different gangs in the U.S.[71] One cop explained, "Street gangs don't have to recruit; they're not running around looking under mattresses for recruits; kids want to join."[72] Consequently, legalizing drugs would cut off the main draw to gang activity, which is profit from the drug trade.

Police work is now more dangerous than ever, while the public increasingly perceives their efforts with more cynicism. The same kind of public backlash occurred during the Prohibition era from otherwise law abiding citizens. As a sign of the times, a prohibition administrator, Col. Ira L. Reeves, once lamented, "I do not know of a single agent on my force who was accepted by the community in which he lived as a welcome neighbor and citizen in whom people could place confidence."[73] Meanwhile, police officers, like a middle manager for a business, know the challenges involved with the drug war better than anyone. They don't have the power to make the necessary changes to drug policies.

Law enforcement officials are systematically censored from publicly airing any criticism of the drug war. In fact, some police officers have even been fired for merely questioning the merits of drug laws privately, in passing, among their peers.[74] That makes a non-profit organization such as Law Enforcement Action Partnership (LEAP) all the more credible. LEAP is comprised of current and retired police officers who openly want to end the drug war. Their organization was originally named Law Enforcement Against Prohibition. The group changed the name in January of 2017 to symbolize their expanded platform with a wider range of criminal justice reform issues, including police/community relations, harm reduction, mass incarceration, and more.

Peter Christ is the co-founder of LEAP and a former police captain with 20 years of experience. He says, "The legalization of drugs is not about the drugs. It is about the gangsters and terrorism that is supported by the illegal marketplace in this country."[75] It's a wise career decision to make such statements *after* retiring because some officers have even lost their jobs for just adding their names to some of LEAP's activism letters.[76]

The drug war wastes resources that could be used towards more serious crimes. Two economists from Florida State University, Bruce Benson and David Rasmussen, have been able to quantify that assertion. They found that every 1% increase in drug arrests leads to a 0.18% increase in serious crimes.[77] And it's not as though we don't have a serious issue with violent crime. Unfortunately, the majority of violent crime goes unpunished, in part due to how resources are diverted to the drug war. Precisely, in 2008, there were an estimated 1,382,012 violent crimes and the typical clearance rate for violent crimes is about 45%.[78] The likelihood of a murder being solved drops dramatically if the case isn't wrapped up within a few days. Most local police departments simply don't have the resources or staff to continue pursuing a cold case.

We need to reject the popular notion that the drug problem can be solved by law enforcement. Drug use hasn't been eliminated in tyrannical countries such as Iran, North Korea, and Saudi Arabia where dealing drugs is punishable by death. As a matter of fact, Iran has one of the highest rates of drug addiction in the world even though nine out of every ten executions are for drug charges.[79] Our culture must stop viewing drug addiction as a crime; instead, drug addiction must be recognized as a health problem. Drug addiction will never be eliminated with either the carrot or the stick; however, the carrot is a much better method for reducing this problem.

The more harmful and addictive drugs should be decriminalized, such as cocaine, heroin, and methamphetamine. Eventually, after a lengthy period of decriminalization, once the stigma has been reduced, a form of limited legalization for hardened addicts would be feasible. Once addictive drugs lose their outlaw image, they can be viewed for what they are -- debilitating, life-ruining habits.

Decriminalization will drastically reduce the black market price. Therefore, many addicts will not resort to crime to support what can be a $3,000 a month habit. It's not unreasonable for drug addicts to rationalize resorting to crime to support their habit when they already face prison time for simple possession. In comparison, alcoholics don't have to resort to robbery to support their addiction.

For some people, prison has served as the wake-up call to clean up. But for most, this is a horrible setting for breaking a drug addiction. Locking an addict into a prison cell surrounded by many other drug addicts and dangerous criminals is the worst scenario for overcoming addiction. The people will naturally be tempted to "escape" mentally with drugs, which are still widely available in prison.

A Canadian psychologist Bruce K. Alexander conducted a related study known as "Rat Park," that scientifically proved that prison is the worst setting for overcoming addiction. Alexander exposed a major flaw in drug addiction studies. These studies demonstrate that caged rats quickly become addicted to morphine when provided unlimited supplies of the drug. However, Alexander believed that the drugs were simply a coping mechanism because they were locked in a cage. Hence, Alexander created "Rat Park" to conduct the same types of experiments. Simply put, he wanted to create an environment in which the rats had space and freedom to pursue several pursuits of pleasure, including morphine. His subjects were provided with roughly 200 times more space than laboratory cages and they were able to mingle in a community with other rats. To be brief, the rats that were caged by themselves consumed almost 20 times as much morphine as the ones in Rat Park![80]

The best drug policy for America is simple. It should be much easier to go to rehab than to go to jail. As Baltimore's former Mayor Kurt Schmoke said, "The war on drugs...should be led by the Surgeon General, not the Attorney General."[81] Worst of all, our government squanders a prime opportunity to rehabilitate convicted drug offenders. According to the DEA, criminal recidivism rates drop from roughly 50% to 20% with treatment.[82] Then why do only one in five drug-addicted prisoners have access to drug rehab?[83] Unfortunately, it's not much different in the free world. A report from the Institute of Medicine found that 5.5 Million Americans clearly needed or probably needed drug therapy, but only 834,077 actually received treatment.[84]

There is limited access to drug addiction therapy, in large part, because the government doesn't provide much funding. In 2008, the federal government spent $13.7 billion on drug law enforcement as opposed to $3.2 million for drug treatment and research.[85] In other words, for every dollar spent treating drug addiction, we spent over $4,400 to enforce the laws. Each new presidential administration has promised to change that dynamic, but that has yet to happen. As a result, there are long waiting lists for government-subsidized treatment. Those people are waiting for months because drug addiction therapy is too expensive for the average person, particularly for a drug addict. Incidentally, comedian Sam Kinison joked that if you still had $13,000 for rehab, then you didn't have a problem, yet!!! At the present time, a typical rehab costs about $7,000 a month and $10,000 to $40,000 for the duration. The costs are so high that some rehab centers even have the same kind of 0% financing deals that are typically associated with auto dealerships.

America needs to follow a model of drug policy known as "harm reduction," which focuses on reducing society's negative impact from drug usage. Harm reduction policies aim for prevention and treatment, rather than incarceration. These policies are not only very cost effective, but the results are also more efficient overall. One example is needle exchange programs, which provide addicts with sterile needles so that they don't share them with other users and spread diseases, such as HIV and hepatitis. Many countries, in particular, European nations, began to successfully implement these programs in the 1980s. However, both major political parties in America generally oppose these programs. Hence, there are only 221 of those locations in our entire country.[86] In fact, federal funding for these programs has been prohibited in America since the 1980s. "Politically the country wasn't ready for it," said Bill Clinton, who regretted not changing the policy.[87] President Obama briefly lifted the federal ban, but it was reinstituted as part of a compromise on federal spending in 2011.[88] Fortunately, Congress officially ended the ban on funding these programs in January of 2016, but those funds can't pay for the actual needles.[89] That's politics for you.

There shouldn't be any controversy regarding these programs because there is no evidence that anyone will suddenly experiment with heroin because free needles are available. Imagine the response to this conversation starter, "Hey, honey! Let's get the kids and try some heroin!" These programs are for people with severe drug addictions. Various organizations, including the GAO, CDC, and World Health Organization, have universally recognized the effectiveness of needle exchange programs.[90] These programs reduce HIV rates by 33-40% among intravenous drug users.[91] The savings in healthcare costs are astounding and more than pay for the expense of these programs. To put it another way, the lifetime cost of medical care for each new person infected with HIV is $385,200. However, according to the Harm Reduction Coalition, investing that same amount of money into needle exchange programs prevents 30 future HIV infections![92]

You can thank Congress for some other crusades against practical harm reduction efforts. As the sponsor of the RAVE Act, "Reducing Americans' Vulnerability to Ecstasy Act," Joe Biden opposed the electronic music festivals (raves) where the drug, MDMA (ecstasy) is quite popular. With little fanfare, the RAVE Act generated scant support on its own and never made it out of committee. Nonetheless, Biden was able to get the RAVE Act passed without any formal debate by attaching it as a rider to an unrelated child abduction bill, the AMBER Alert Act of 2003.

The RAVE Act made it a crime if a venue holder "knowingly" allows illegal drug use at his facility, and it is punishable by up to 20 years in prison and a $250,000 fine.[93] That's overkill for combating a drug, ecstasy, which is fairly benign. In fact, MDMA used to be a legal drug that had been prescribed by therapists, particularly marriage counselors.[94] That changed in 1985 when the DEA labeled the drug to be a "serious health threat" after it had become popular for recreational use in the dance club party scene.[95]

The most valid risk for ecstasy users is overheating. That's why raves should have plenty of bottled water available and "chill rooms," but now business owners who offer those amenities are at risk for violating the law, all thanks to Joe Biden. After all, the language of the bill allows for incredibly broad interpretations.

That's why many concert promoters and club owners are now less willing to pay for emergency medical staff on the premises. The overdose risk from pure, pharmaceutical-grade MDMA is relatively low. However, the purity of this drug naturally declined once it entered the black market. These pills are now mixed with cheaper, sometimes toxic substances. Hence, some non-profit groups attend these festivals to test the purity of partygoers' pills. Then again, the RAVE ACT's broad stroke could determine that to be a complicit action. In fact, any venue that allows people to enter with glow sticks is at risk.[96]

It's absurd that politicians continue to obstruct common sense harm reduction efforts, but, then again, they've also been inundated with drug war propaganda. One notable politician, Kurt Schmoke, fought diligently to counter the conventional wisdom. In 1987, as Baltimore's first black mayor, he took a bold stance by advocating the decriminalization of drugs, along with the implementation of harm reduction policies. The progressive ideas of Kurt Schmoke, a former member of the Carter administration, were vilified nationally and his once promising political career flatlined.[97]

Think about the scene in *Pulp Fiction* in which Uma Thurman's character has a heroin overdose. John Travolta refused to take her to the hospital because he was afraid of going to prison. *Pulp Fiction* is only a movie, but that same scenario unfolds every day in America. Presently, only 22 states, along with the District of Columbia, have passed drug amnesty laws that protect anyone from criminal penalties who calls 911 to help someone who has overdosed.[98]

If you're not familiar with *Pulp Fiction*, Uma Thurman was stunningly saved from a heroin overdose with an injection of adrenaline (Epinephrine) to the heart. Again, this was only a fictional movie, but what if I told you that there is a real-life, injectable drug that can save people from dying of a heroin overdose? It's called naloxone (Narcan) and it's roughly 99% effective. This drug was approved by the FDA in 1971, but it has been strictly limited to emergency rooms and ambulances. The restrictions on naloxone are unreasonable because this drug doesn't produce a high. Therefore, there is no risk for abuse by recreational users. But, the "tough on crime" crowd has kept it that way for decades out of fears that more availability "might send the wrong message." The drug war is often posed as a moral issue, but our leaders are neglecting their moral obligation to save lives whenever possible.

Naloxone truly is a miracle drug, but it needs to be administered within a certain window of time. That's why it's imperative that naloxone is readily available over-the-counter for anyone who deems it necessary, be it friends/family of an addict, social workers, non-governmental organization (NGO) volunteers, etc. Luckily, nearly 30 years after Kurt Schmoke made a bold stand, some of his pioneering ideas are finally becoming less controversial. Now that the awareness of this drug is increasing, more and more states are allowing naloxone to be sold over-the-counter, even equipping police with it too.[99] Granted, there is still much progress to be made because there are still 23 states blocking access to this drug for anyone other than a healthcare professional.[100]

Some people swear by the success of their 12 step program, but there is still a high relapse rate. Even after receiving treatment, roughly 90% of heroin addicts relapse back into addiction.[101] That doesn't mean that all hope is lost. There are medication-assisted treatments to reduce an addict's cravings. These treatments are somewhat stigmatized, but that's an odd scenario in a country that overprescribes drugs for nearly every ailment. Nonetheless, naltrexone is a very safe and efficient drug, which works as a counter attack to heroin. This "opioid blocker" attaches to the receptors in the brain and takes away the pleasure of using heroin, thereby reducing the cravings.[A] There is one caveat: patients need to be free of heroin in their system for 7-10 days before taking naltrexone for it to be effective. This FDA-approved drug doesn't produce a high, nor is it addictive. Regrettably, our government hasn't made this drug more widely available.

There is a much more controversial treatment known as ibogaine. It is a hallucinogenic substance derived from the root of an African tree, iboba. Ibogaine, is illegal in the U.S., along with most other countries, but the ban is unnecessary because it is unlikely to be abused recreationally; the intense vomiting alone will ensure that. Nonetheless, V*ICE* aired a feature showing underground clubs in the U.S. that travel to Mexico for this drug.[102] It's oddly reminiscent of the film *Dallas Buyers Club*. Americans are willing to make such a trek because their past efforts have failed

---

[A] Naltrexone can also help alcoholics in the same manner, even pathological gamblers in some cases.

and anecdotal evidence shows that ibogaine reduces the cravings for heroin and it is effective with reducing relapses.

Still, an air of mystery surrounds this drug because there isn't much clinical information regarding ibogaine's medicinal qualities. It begs the question, "Why isn't there more scientific research on this treatment?" First, there is a patronizing view of this treatment due to its association with tribal rituals in South America and Africa. More importantly, an advocate of ibogaine, Dr. Ben Sessa (psychiatrist and addiction specialist), points out that there is no funding for research because it can't be patented; after all, it comes from a plant.[103]

Many Americans still oppose methadone treatments even though there is a substantial net positive impact. In comparison to incarceration, methadone saves the taxpayers tremendous resources by reducing crime and STDs associated with intravenous drug use. Albeit, methadone is more addictive than heroin and can be deadly too. It is horrible for your health, but it serves as a safer substitute to help the addict withdraw from opiates. Methadone has a longer lasting effect that allows patients to take only one dose a day (around $15 a day) without feeling intoxicated if the dosage is prescribed reasonably.[104] For those reasons, methadone users can maintain a more productive work life than heroin addicts who feel the need to use multiple times a day.

When methadone is administered correctly, the dosage is slowly reduced over time. Also, staffers counsel and refer patients for rehabilitation treatment in hopes of overcoming their addiction. Unfortunately, many of these clinics don't have the proper incentives because for-profit companies now run the majority of American methadone clinics. Clearly, it hurts their bottom line if these companies wean their clients off methadone. The industry's high-profit margins prompted Bain Capital, the venture capital firm founded by Mitt Romney, to acquire the largest company in the methadone industry, CRC Health Group, for $723 million in 2006.[105]

It doesn't take a genius to predict what followed. The company subsequently made several decisions in favor of profits over ethics, including employee cutbacks, resulting in more than a thousand regulatory citations since 2009. The remaining staff barely have time to assess the needs of the patient. Hence, they have to put their counseling responsibilities aside and function more like retail clerks.

Simply put, CRC doesn't have the controls in place to make sure that their patients aren't selling methadone in the black market, nor do they have an incentive to prevent that from happening.[106]

Methadone prescriptions are beneficial for many people, but it isn't the best course of action for all addicts. As many as 25% of people don't physically respond well to methadone.[107] In turn, there is a great deal of research professing that heroin prescriptions are a better option for that particular group. A study by the *New England Journal of Medicine* found that heroin addicts who were prescribed heroin, instead of methadone, were more likely to quit, stayed in treatment longer, and were much less likely to use the street version of the drug. After a year, 90% of the participants using heroin prescriptions were still in therapy, as opposed to only 54% of the methadone group.[108] In fact, a study published by the *Canadian Medical Association Journal* found that heroin prescriptions are also more cost-effective than methadone treatments and result in less crime and public healthcare costs.[109]

All in all, there are several innovative methods for treating addiction, but these revolutionary ideas won't be politically viable in America for quite a long time. In fact, methadone maintenance is still controversial in America and remains prohibited in many states. Keep in mind, methadone was strongly supported by Richard Nixon, of all people.[110] On the other hand, heroin prescriptions are much less controversial in many other countries that have these programs, including the Netherlands, Germany, Canada, Spain, Denmark, Norway, Luxembourg, and Australia.[111]

Switzerland was the first country to experiment with heroin prescriptions in 1994, along with specific injection facilities. Only long-term addicts participated in this experiment. The success of these studies has made heroin injection facilities a permanent part of the Swiss harm reduction model. These facilities are staffed with appropriate medical care professionals and addicts pay about 15 Swiss Francs a day (about $15 U.S.), much less than the street price. Consequently, injection facilities improve public safety by eliminating public, huddled masses of heroin addicts and their resulting crimes and needle sharing. Those facilities are also a non-confrontational way to subtly reintroduce addicts into mainstream culture and extend a lifeline in hopes of eventually getting them into treatment.

Ethan Nadelmann, executive director of the Drug Policy Alliance, summarized some of the conclusions of the Social Welfare Department in Zurich. He noted, "Heroin prescription is feasible...The health of the addicts in the program has clearly improved...Heroin per se causes very few, if any, problems when it is used in a controlled fashion and administered in hygienic conditions."[112] He added that the addicts didn't overdose, even with an unlimited supply available to them.[113] Over the years, seven other countries have developed their own heroin injection facilities. Nearly one hundred of these facilities exist throughout the world today, but here is the most remarkable fact. There has *never* been a single overdose death in one of these facilities.[114]

Switzerland's experiment with heroin injection facilities was a continuation of another experiment with harm reduction, the infamous "needle park" experiment which ended unsuccessfully in 1992. It was similar to the "Hamsterdam" episode of "The Wire." In 1987 Swiss authorities decided to gather all of their drug addicts into a park in Zurich, the Platzspitz. Police weren't allowed to make arrests in that park while social workers and healthcare workers passed out clean needles. Initially, there were about 200 addicts gathered in the park, but those numbers swelled to an estimated crowd of 20,000 within five years after the area had become a haven for addicts and dealers from other countries.[115] Creating an unsupervised drug-addict-red-light district, of sorts, led to an increase in the overall crime rate in the surrounding areas and the crowds became uncontrollable. However, the mob mentality problem from this experiment was virtually eliminated with supervised injection facilities. Also, there was a silver lining from the "needle park" experiment. The healthcare workers' efforts led to a decrease in AIDS rates.[116]

The Swiss later improved upon their first experiment. However, the Swiss "needle park experiment" is the example that drug war advocates like to cite when claiming that decriminalization isn't effective. Keep in mind that there isn't a cookie cutter method for harm reduction and decriminalization. In fact, one of the best-kept secrets in America is the success other countries have had from experimenting with different approaches to decriminalization. The rate of drug use in America is the highest in the world while many other countries have reduced their drug usage with a more laissez-faire approach.[117] Various countries have implemented different policies and that provides us with a vast array of possibilities to examine for a best-case model.

The Dutch are recognized for legalizing marijuana. Numerous other countries have decriminalized marijuana, but the Netherlands had been the only one to give it a de facto legal status until Ecuador followed suit in 2013. For all intents and purposes, the possession of a small amount of marijuana has been legal in the Netherlands since 1976.[118] Today, drug usage remains technically illegal, but the laws are simply not enforced and an estimated 1,200 to 1,500 "coffee houses" nationwide sell marijuana.[119] The Dutch have this ambiguous policy to avoid violating international treaties and opposition from the U.S government.

Ironically, Americans use marijuana at a considerably higher rate than the Dutch. Just how much more you may be thinking? Forty-two percent of Americans have tried marijuana compared to twenty-six percent in the Netherlands. In fact, the Netherlands has "the lowest rate of drug problem use in Europe," according to a study by the Open Society Global Drug Policy Program.[120]

The Dutch marijuana policy removed the rebellion factor for the youth and poked major holes in the theory that marijuana is a "gateway" to other drugs like cocaine and heroin. The best available statistics show that 14.7% of Americans have used cocaine and 1.5% have used heroin, while only 3.4% of the Dutch have used cocaine and 0.6% have tried heroin.[121] Why is there such a wide disparity? The most apparent conclusion is that the Dutch model has a clear separation between marijuana and harder drugs. Here's a point of interest. The average heroin addict's age was 25 in both the Netherlands and America during the 1970s, a time when both countries were changing their drug policies in opposite directions. By the late 1990s, the average age of a Dutch heroin addict was thirty-six. That meant that there were very few younger people trying the drug. Conversely, a flood of young Americans began experimenting with heroin as the drug war intensified and by the 1990s the average age for an American heroin addict was nineteen.[122] Our laws seem to have pushed people into experimenting with deadly drugs while the Netherlands has seen drug use drop with a laissez-faire approach.

In response to the success of the Dutch model, drug war advocates such as the former "Drug Czar" Barry McCaffrey have chosen to bash their policy. In 1998, McCaffrey actually asserted that the Dutch drug policy led to their murder rate doubling that of the United States. McCaffrey's claim was a brazen deception. Take a look at the facts. The murder rate in the Netherlands has ranged anywhere from one-fourth to one-half of that in America during the 1990s.[123] The Dutch murder rate has since remained at about one-fourth of that in America. In fact, the prison population in America has soared; whereas, the Netherlands shut down eight prisons in 2009 from a lack of demand.[124]

There are some very promising aspects of Portugal's harm reduction policy as well. In 2001, Portugal officially abolished criminal penalties for the possession of all illegal drugs. Drug traffickers are still prosecuted with strong penalties. Conversely, anyone caught possessing a small amount of a drug is sent to an addiction panel, instead of a criminal court. These panels consist of psychologists, addiction specialists, and social workers. Accordingly, they make recommendations for the drug user. But, here's the key to the success of the Portuguese model -- all treatment is voluntary. The drug user *can refuse* treatment without criminal punishment, but the specialists can grant an immediate entry into a drug rehab program. Mind you, the Portuguese can easily afford treatment solutions with the savings from incarceration. Regardless, these limited resources shouldn't be wasted on an unwilling recipient. After all, rehab is pointless if someone doesn't want the help. Consequently, the Portuguese model has led more people to voluntarily enter drug rehabilitation programs, as a result of decriminalization.[125]

There is one notable flaw with the Portuguese model. Marijuana should be legal and regulated just like alcohol and tobacco, but unlike the Dutch model, there isn't a de facto legalization of marijuana in Portugal. Nonetheless, the Portuguese have had tremendous harm reduction success with the more dangerous drugs. In fact, João Goulão, the President of the Institute of Drugs and Drug Addiction, held a press conference on the ten year anniversary of Portugal's policy change. He said, "There is no doubt that the phenomenon of addiction is in decline in Portugal."[126] He added that the number of "problematic" addicts was about 100,000 in the early 1990s, but that number had decreased to about 40,000.[127] Forty-four percent of criminal offenses in 1999 were committed under the influence of drugs and/or to fund drug consumption. However, that dropped to under 21% in 2012.[128] Also, the number of newly diagnosed drug-related AIDS cases dropped dramatically after decriminalization. There were 1,056 in 2001, as opposed to 56 in 2012! Finally, drug overdose deaths have significantly decreased as well; there were 80 in 2001, as opposed to 16 in 2012.[129] Given these points, you must be wondering, "How much longer do we have to wait until our country embraces this kind of outside-the-box thinking and takes action?"

8

American Deaths Per Year	
Tobacco	440,000
Alcohol (consumption only)	88,000
Car Accidents	38,000
Prescription Drug Overdose	20,044
Murder	16,442
Cocaine Overdose	5,100
Heroin Overdose	3,000
Marijuana Overdose	0

(various sources)[1]

Bill Maher once mocked the aggressive advertisements that direct you to tell your doctor that their company's drug is right for you. "Shouldn't your doctor tell you what drugs you need? When you tell your doctor isn't he just a dealer at that point," mused Bill Maher.[2] The American public generally trusts its government to protect them from the hidden dangers of prescription and over-the-counter drugs. However, that trust isn't fully warranted as the FDA has been featured in the GAO's annual report of "high risk" agencies that need drastic reforms.[3]

The FDA is in charge of regulating the shameless drug advertisements that inundate the airwaves. With that in mind, only one other developed nation in the world, New Zealand, allows prescription drugs to be advertised directly to consumers.[4] Then again, the American pharmaceutical industry used to abide by a term "ethical marketing," meaning that drug companies could only market to physicians. Granted, there are merits for direct-to-consumer drug advertisements as the flow of information and transparency are beneficial. However, there is an obvious need for checks and balances.

This experiment began with a print advertisement in 1981 in *Reader's Digest* and the first TV ad was aired in 1983.[5] At that time, the FDA had several rules in place requiring companies to offer a fair and balanced presentation. Generally speaking, this was a rather responsible era of advertising. Naturally, the nature of direct-to-consumer drug advertising changed in 1997 when the FDA significantly loosened the rules. As a result, pharmaceutical advertising skyrocketed from $700 million in 1996 to $4.5 billion by 2014.[6]

Facing this rising tide, Sen. Al Franken (D-MN) and Rep. Robert Berry (D-AR) introduced "the Protecting Americans from Drug Marketing Act." Their bill would have merely removed the tax break that drug companies receive for advertising, but it didn't benefit from much support from Congress. In effect, these advertisements have created an artificial demand with their marketing and branding. The U.S. now consumes roughly 40% of the world's pharmaceutical drugs, far exceeding the combined total from all of Europe, where most nations have universal healthcare.[7] Additionally, Americans have been imprinted with a false sense of security for these drugs. To be specific, a study by the *Journal of General Internal Medicine* found that advertisements had misleading or false claims 60% of the time with prescription drugs and 80% for over-the-counter drugs.[8]

In fairness, the FDA has an incredibly challenging and complicated job of regulating the drug industry. For example, federal regulators never envisioned this brave new world in which attractive celebrities would covertly advertise for pharmaceutical companies via social media. Notably, the FDA intervened after Kim Kardashian posted support for a morning sickness drug, Diclegis, via Instagram and Twitter. She reportedly received over $1 million for the endorsement, but the FDA forced her to subsequently add a disclosure that included the side effects of the drug.[9]

Unfortunately, there are many examples of special interests improperly influencing the agency. Hence, the legitimate health risks have been swept under the rug for some of the most seemingly innocuous drugs. For one thing, NutraSweet contains aspartame, which is the artificial sweetener used in many foods and diet drinks. Only a small percentage of consumers are aware that the FDA recognizes 92 symptoms associated with aspartame, including cancer, seizures, brain tumors, coma and even death.[10]

The circumstances surrounding the approval process of this drug are even more disturbing. G.D. Searle, Monsanto's predecessor, was the drug company that gained FDA approval of aspartame. They were successful despite providing the FDA with studies that were "incredibly sloppy science," according to the former FDA Commissioner, Alexander Schmidt. "What we discovered was reprehensible," said Schmidt.[11] As a result, he launched a task force investigation to verify the science behind aspartame. The FDA's lead investigator, Phillip Brodsky, later told Congress that the studies provided by G.D. Searle were the worst he had ever seen. Dr. Adrian Gross, another member of the FDA's task force member, added, "They (Searle) lied...(and) took great pains to camouflage these shortcomings of the study."[12]

The FDA's task force wasn't convinced that the actions by G.D. Searle were merely sloppy mistakes. Hence, they contacted the Department of Justice in 1976 to recommend a criminal investigation. The DOJ obliged and met with G.D. Searle's legal representatives from Sidley & Austin, a top Chicago law firm. Here's where the story becomes even murkier. An investigative journalist David Burnham noted a particularly suspicious development from those meetings. The head of that criminal investigation, Samuel K. Skinner III, was offered a position by Sidley & Austin. In turn, Skinner accepted their job offer and then recused himself from the investigation. At a minimum, Skinner's decision suspended the investigation for a period of time, thereby pushing investigative resources elsewhere. Worst of all, the delay may have protected G.D. Searle with the statute of limitations. In the end, the DOJ never pressed charges against G.D. Searle.[13]

One day after Reagan's inauguration, G.D. Searle reapplied to the FDA for approval. The timing was fortuitous as Donald Rumsfeld was then the company's CEO and he served on Reagan's transition team. Thereafter, Reagan appointed an ally of the pharmaceutical industry as the new FDA commissioner, Dr. Arthur Hall Hayes. This was a fortuitous turn of events for the executives of G.D. Searle. Hayes overruled the FDA's scientific panel to get aspartame approved. *And wouldn't you know it.* The favor was returned for Hayes after leaving the FDA. He later worked as a consultant for G.D. Searle's public relations firm. Likewise, some other FDA officials have subsequently been hired by the aspartame industry. That is just another example of the regulatory capture that can result from the revolving door between Washington and the private sector.[14]

Aspartame has now been on the market for many years and most people seemingly have had no adverse reactions. Or have they? Russell L. Blaylock, M.D. warns that many people don't take notice of the serious symptoms because "they're more resistant to the obvious toxic effects." Meanwhile, over the course of several years, the "subtle toxic effects (will eventually) produce obvious disease in those persons."[15] Then again, some people have had more direct, severe reactions. To be specific, FDA officials have estimated that only 1% of toxic reactions are likely to be reported and the agency received reports of 7,000 toxic reactions to aspartame from 1982 until 1995. In fact, there were likely more official reports of toxicity, but we can't be sure of the extent. After all, Congress found out in 1987 that the FDA had been transferring aspartame toxicity calls to the AIDS Hotline.[16]

Americans are generally unaware that some of the most frequently prescribed drugs are nearly identical to illegal street drugs. One such drug, Ritalin, or methylphenidate, is prescribed for Attention Deficit Hyperactive Disorder (ADHD). Ritalin, like Adderall, is a stimulant that produces virtually the same effects as amphetamines.[17] We should take pause because Americans consume approximately 90% of the world's Ritalin. Certainly, there are children who seem to benefit from these drugs, but there's clearly a profit motive that results in unnecessary prescriptions.[18] Some studies estimate that as many as 1,000,000 American children are misdiagnosed with ADHD.[19]

ADHD drugs are popular with adolescents for all night studying sessions. And that certainly doesn't sound like a dire situation, but with widespread distribution many young people are also abusing these drugs recreationally. Likewise, many adults were prescribed these drugs as children and now feel dependent upon the drug to stay productive at work. Hence, as of 2015, more American adults use ADHD drugs than children.[20] Despite their sanitized reputation, these prescription drugs, like amphetamines, can lead to high blood pressure, aggression, paranoia, cocaine cravings, heart attack, stroke, and suicide, among many other debilitating possibilities. That made this news from 2014 all the more disturbing when Shire Pharmaceuticals was fined $56.5 million for deceptive marketing with their drug Adderall XR. According to the DOJ, Shire made lofty claims that Adderall could prevent poor academic performance, loss of employment, criminal behavior, traffic accidents, and sexually transmitted disease.[21]

The manufacturers of ADHD drugs clearly benefitted from aggressive marketing, but that paled in comparison to the hoopla surrounding antidepressant drugs. Prozac was approved by the FDA in 1987 and the sales have since exploded.[22] Presently, one out of every five adults in America uses antidepressant medication![23] In fact, Prozac is ingrained in our culture to such an extent that there are even prescriptions available for dogs.[24] Again, some people are legitimately clinically depressed and respond favorably to these medicines; however, many people are just going through the normal phases in life and have been finessed by dynamic advertising.

So what's the danger with everyone taking "happy" pills? Antidepressant drugs, or S.S.R.I.s (selective serotonin reuptake inhibitors), essentially reduce the brain's ability to produce chemicals naturally. As a result, the user becomes quite dependent upon the drug.[25] Furthermore, many Americans are unfamiliar with the potential side effects of antidepressant drugs. Ironically, Prozac has some dire side effects, including depression, acne, loss of libido, insomnia, hallucinations, panic attacks, violence, and suicide.[26]

The suicide risks associated with antidepressants can be quite extreme, yet those risks are relatively undisclosed. For this reason, Dr. Peter R. Breggin M.D. testified before Congress in 2010 detailing how various manufacturers of antidepressants withheld research from the public demonstrating significantly higher rates of suicide attempts. He cited internal company documents from Ely Lilly (the manufacturer of Prozac) in which the company censored that information by labeling attempted suicides as "no drug effect." Likewise, they never disclosed that some clinical trials had a rate of suicide attempts that was 600% to 1,200% higher than placebos![27]

At this point, these kinds of stories probably aren't quite as shocking considering the deep pockets of drug companies, but that's where the government is supposed to intervene as an impartial regulator. Sadly, the FDA has abandoned that role. Here is another prime example of this regulatory capture. *The Washington Post* reported that a medical doctor from the FDA was scheduled to testify in 2004 before Congress about the suicide risks for children ingesting antidepressants. Remarkably, top FDA officials ordered that doctor to withhold specific documents that proved there were increased suicide risks.[28]

Isn't one of the tenets of the drug war to keep children off drugs? Yes, you've been inundated with that propaganda. Meanwhile, pharmaceutical companies make a fortune from doctors who overprescribe drugs to children. Alarmingly, ten million American children are given the top three antidepressants.[29] That's particularly dangerous due to the fact that the brains of children are still in a developmental stage.

Aggressive marketing has enabled some lazy parents to rationalize taking the easy way out by doping their children with prescription pills, rather than confronting problem behavior head on. We're all familiar with the image of staffers in mental institutions over-medicating inmates to keep them docile. It turns out that many foster parents are abusing this practice as well. Multiple reports have found that foster children have been prescribed antipsychotic or psychotropic drugs at alarming rates, sometimes for children as young as four.[30] In many cases, the side effects linger for many years after discontinuing the drug. Also, there are wide allegations of prison staffs abusing this power as well.[A31] Can something be done to prevent these kinds of abuses? Yes. The obvious first step would be to eliminate the financial conflicts of interest. Case in point, a statewide investigative report by the *Palm Beach Post* found that one out of every three doctors who had prescribed antipsychotic drugs to juvenile inmates had also received payments from major pharmaceutical companies.[32]

Many of these companies fraudulently market their drugs to children because they know that they're bulletproof. Their worst case scenario is a fine by the DOJ. Look no further than the pharmaceutical giant, GlaxoSmithKline. In 2012 they were issued the largest fine ever for a drug company, $3 billion. But, the actions by GlaxoSmithKline warranted criminal prosecutions beyond the fines imposed.[33] GlaxoSmithKline illegally marketed their antidepressant drug, Paxil, to children while excluding studies that demonstrated that Paxil *ineffectively* treated childhood depression.[34] In fact, the FDA never even approved Paxil for child prescriptions, but many doctors prescribed it anyway. Seemingly, those doctors were breaking the law, but that isn't the case; they are allowed to use their discretion. As a result of that loophole, it's estimated that about 15 percent of all drug sales in the U.S., as many as 10 million prescriptions annually, are not for their approved uses.[35]

On the other hand, the drug companies are not allowed to promote unapproved, or "off-label," uses for their drugs. Be that as it may, there is a multi-billion dollar "off-label" market that falls within the gray area of the law. Hence, the drug companies are going

---

[A] The U.S. Supreme Court has ruled that it's legal to force prisoners to take medication.

to stretch the limits of those laws. They can exploit this loophole by hiring a doctor as a spokesperson who *just so happens* to cite off-label benefits. That type of off-label promotion is legal as long as there isn't an explicit quid pro quo. Then again, any intelligent person understands that there is an implicit contract when you're accepting the kinds of speaking fees that these doctors receive.

The DOJ's investigation into GlaxoSmithKline revealed that the company had many doctors on their payroll, including the famous TV personality "Dr. Drew" Pinsky from *Celebrity Rehab* and *Loveline*. Dr. Drew received $275,000 in payments from GlaxoSmithKline in 1999. After receiving those payments, Dr. Drew publicly touted off-label benefits from their antidepressant drug, Wellbutrin, on his sex-advice show *Loveline*. Dr. Drew claimed that Wellbutrin "may enhance or at least not suppress sexual arousal" and insinuated that it could give women multiple orgasms. Those were particularly bold statements because most antidepressants lower libido; nevertheless, Dr. Drew can *legally* make those claims based on his clinical experience.[36]

Pharmaceutical companies are already toeing an ethical line without making payments to doctors. After all, doctors are routinely wined and dined with gourmet meals by their sales reps. You may be familiar with the expression that you will never meet an ugly pharma sales rep. If not, these companies are notorious for hiring gorgeous, young female sales reps to appeal to an industry of doctors who are mostly middle-aged or older males. That compounds some other ethical issues that emerge when drug companies pay doctors. To be fair, drug companies can't pay direct commissions for prescribing their drugs, but they can pay them to be "spokespersons." Specifically, GlaxoSmithKline can no longer pay doctors to promote their drugs, as a result of their scandal, but nearly all major drug companies still do so.[37]

Drug companies brazenly recruit doctors by paying for travel expenses to luxurious resorts and lavish them with free golf, massages, spa treatments, etc. In fact, one of the GlaxoSmithKline whistleblowers said that the speaking fees were so lucrative that some doctors actually quit their practices.[38] This may seem quite bleak for the future, but there is one glimmer of bright light. Congress actually passed a common sense regulation that now requires drug and medical device companies to publicly disclose their payments to doctors. Thankfully, you can now check to see if your doctor is on the take at the "Open Payments" page of the Centers for Medicare & Medicaid Services website.[39] Predictably, a report by *ProPublica* showed that drug companies decreased their payments to doctors after this transparency measure was put in place.[40] However, it is still an incredibly lucrative racket as doctors received $6.5 billion in 2014 from drug and medical device companies.[41]

Major pharmaceutical companies are "too big to jail," just like Wall Street. Anyone who sells illegal drugs to children, particularly in a drug-free school zone, faces a long prison sentence; whereas, the corporate drug dealers in tailored suits hardly ever face criminal charges. In the rare event of a pharmaceutical company executive facing criminal charges, the sentence is quite lenient. These laws apparently only apply to executives from companies with small profits and little political clout. One such individual, Marc S. Hermelin, was the CEO of an obscure company, KV Pharmaceuticals, which filed Chapter 11 in 2012. He was fined $1 million, had to forfeit $900,000, and received a sentence of 30 days in jail because his company sold jumbo tablets of morphine that were much stronger than the label specified.[42]

GlaxoSmithKline's $3 billion fine may seem like a strong punishment, but that is merely the cost of doing business, just as it is with drug money laundering. Plus, those costs are simply passed on to the consumer. Keep in mind, the government has a very strong deterrent at their disposal, other than prison, that could actually curb some of this criminal activity. These companies can be blocked from Medicare or Medicaid, which would cost them a fortune.[43] Our federal officials, unfortunately, rarely ever flex those muscles and that penalty is usually reserved for companies with much weaker balance sheets and few lobbyists.

Household names like Pfizer get to play by a different set of rules. In 2009 Pfizer was issued the second-largest fine for a drug company, $2.3 billion, but that dollar amount represented only three weeks of sales for their company.[44] Like GlaxoSmithKline, Pfizer was slapped on the wrist for marketing off-label uses of their drug, Bextra. As you may recall, Bextra was later taken off the market because millions of Americans were unknowingly risking their lives with that drug.[45] Regardless, fines clearly were never a real hindrance for Pfizer, a repeat offender. Back in 2004, Pfizer negotiated a settlement of $430 million for deceptively marketing their epilepsy drug Neurontin. They promoted a variety of off-label treatments, including those for bipolar disorder, migraines, and pain management. Again, the fine that their company was forced to pay was comparatively measly because the DOJ concluded that 94%, or $2.12 billion, of the revenue from Neurontin came from off-label use.[46] Obviously, that punishment was not a deterrent and Pfizer's "third strike" occurred in 2011 when the company settled with the DOJ for the off-label marketing of their drug Detrol.[47]

These corporate racketeers are callously putting people's lives at risk and there is a laundry list of similar cases with the same conclusions. The pharmaceutical industry has little fear of repercussions and the best example may be that OxyContin competes for sales with black market heroin. OxyContin is a synthetic opiate that is supposed to be prescribed strictly for severe pain, but the restrictions have loosened to the point where children as young as 11 years old can now be prescribed this drug under certain circumstances.[48] One particular advertisement during Super Bowl 2016 provided one of the more illustrative indicators of America's extensive prescription opiate use. "If you need an opioid to manage your chronic pain then you may be sooooo constipated. It feels like everyone can go, except you," stated the narrator. Apparently, so many Americans are taking prescription opioids that their kidneys are failing. Thus, Big Pharma introduced a new acronym into the vernacular, OIC (Opioid-Induced Constipation).

The FDA clearly hasn't learned its lesson from OxyContin. In 2014, FDA administrators overruled their advisory panel to approve Zohydro. This opioid is ten times more potent than OxyContin and it's crushable and dissolvable, which means that it can be snorted or injected.[49] As you probably remember, OxyContin used to be the drug of choice for Rush Limbaugh. Limbaugh's story clearly touches upon some of the hypocritical aspects of the drug war. Mind you, he was a fully functional drug addict who harmed no one but himself, like thousands and maybe millions of other Americans, and didn't need to be arrested. Nonetheless, in 2003 he criticized "liberal judges" and supported mandatory minimum sentences just months before he announced to his radio audience that he was temporarily leaving the airwaves to enter rehab.[50]

His audience wished him well upon his return to radio, yet most of them have remained committed to the drug war. This is a reoccurring theme with partisan politics. Loyal supporters can be selectively forgiving of their leaders but punitive with the rest of society. In Limbaugh's first day back at the job, he said, "Many people feel and think that when you go to a rehabilitation center for addictions or other things, that the people in there turn you into a linguini-spined liberal, and that's not true."[51] However, Limbaugh's rehab wasn't a success. And he should thank his lucky stars that some "linguini-spined liberals" allowed him to beat the rap.

In 2006, according to investigators, Limbaugh purchased roughly 2,000 pills over a six month period from four different doctors. Also, his former housekeeper alleged that she used to meet him a few miles from his mansion in the parking lot of a Denny's where she supplied him with even more pills.[52] Nonetheless, he was only sentenced to 18 months of probation. To state the obvious, that was an incredibly light sentence. Nearly anyone else who purchased thousands of pills would have automatically faced trafficking charges, which require stiff mandatory minimum sentences.

The companies that manufacture synthetic opiates aren't functioning in a harm reduction or non-profit capacity. Instead, they are trying to maximize their profits while knowing full and well that their drug is being abused. The executives of Purdue Pharma, the manufacturer of OxyContin, have demonstrated willful blindness as Florida doctors prescribed OxyContin at five times the national average. Their business was concentrated in Florida because the state didn't have a prescription drug monitoring program until 2010. In fact, the top 50 physicians who prescribed OxyContin were all in Florida. This activity was even more concentrated than you may imagine. Merely four pharmacy locations in Florida sold 12 million OxyContin pills over a three year period.[53]

Florida pharmacies essentially served as a wholesaler of black market OxyContin throughout the U.S. Likewise, addicts were able to "doctor shop" by traveling from clinic to clinic and purchase as many pills as legally possible in each location. OxyContin was distributed in Florida pain clinics, informally known as "pill mills," that often only accepted cash, didn't accept insurance, were equipped with security guards, and were in many cases owned by ex-convicts. One report mentioned that the lines were so long that employees could make $1,000 a week in tips by moving people to the front of the line.[54]

Obviously, for many users, OxyContin serves merely as a substitute for heroin, but many people with legitimate pain problems were duped into taking the drug. That was seemingly the case with Rush Limbaugh, who started taking the drug after back surgery. After all, most patients trust their doctor's word as the gospel and Purdue Pharma convinced doctors that it had "reduced addiction risk." In fact, Purdue Pharma's executives cited dubious studies to claim that opiates posed an addiction risk of "less than one percent."[55] Furthermore, their sales reps were indoctrinated with those assertions and thus they presented their drug to doctors as "virtually non-addictive."[56] Without a doubt, those were completely false marketing claims as OxyContin is just as addictive as heroin and provides virtually the same effects. It goes to show the effectiveness of marketing because there are people who still think that the addictive qualities from OxyContin were "removed."

Believe it or not, Purdue Pharma marketed its drug in a less honest manner than the average street dealer. Dope dealers don't pretend that heroin is anything than what it is. Furthermore, their business, oddly enough, tends to pick up after someone overdoses. The junkies in the area tend to flock to the same street corner where that deadly dose was sold; they assume that it must have been a strong batch. Keep in mind that they were most likely drawn into addiction by Big Pharma. Forget about marijuana as a gateway drug; four out of five heroin addicts started by abusing prescription drugs.[57]

There is a reason why OxyContin is the top brand name among legal narcotics and it has to do solely with the company's aggressive advertising. OxyContin hit the market in 1996, the same year in which California became the first state to legalize medical marijuana. Purdue Pharma convinced doctors that OxyContin, which is twice as strong as morphine, was a safer pain medication because the effects are spread over the course of hours. There is some truth to that theory because heroin addicts prefer a powerful, instant high. However, the safety label on OxyContin warned against the "rapid release" that would occur if the pills were crushed and snorted; it could also be dissolved in water and then injected for the same effect. In essence, the FDA's warning unintentionally served as a marketing tool to hardened drug addicts.[58]

Like many other prescription drugs, Purdue Pharma gained influence by providing thousands of healthcare professionals with all-expenses-paid informational junkets at exclusive resorts. They were then recruited to become paid spokespersons for the company.

In addition, Purdue Pharma compiled a database of every physician who already prescribed opiates for pain relief.[B59] Their sales reps then showered these doctors with an endless array of free branded promotional materials, an unprecedented approach for a Schedule II drug. Then again, the wheels had already been greased for these sales reps due to the advertisements that Purdue Pharma paid for in various medical journals. The claims in those ads downplayed the risks involved with their drug and thus the FDA cited their company twice for violations. Furthermore, Purdue Pharma provided an informational video for thousands of physicians even though the content hadn't been approved by the FDA, including the "less than one percent addictive" claim. All in all, this was a blitzkrieg of a marketing campaign and they knew the ins and outs of this racket.[60]

It pays to be a legal dope dealer and the Sackler family, the founders of Purdue Pharma, are now the 16th wealthiest family in America with $14 billion.[61] The patriarch of the family, Arthur Sackler, was truly the pioneer of modern pharmaceutical marketing, which led to his becoming one of the first inductees into the Medical Advertising Hall of Fame. (Yes, that's an actual organization.)

Beginning in the early 1950s, Sackler's medical advertising firm, William Douglas McAdams, completely remodeled how the drug industry operated. Picture Don Draper on steroids. He hired sales reps at a time when that wasn't customary and his chic, full-colored ads in medical journals essentially launched Pfizer into a superpower. These unorthodox approaches also led to making Valium the first $100 million drug.[62] Sackler even produced his own bogus medical journals to write favorable reports for his clients' drugs. Also, he established a shell company to serve as a public relations firm that flooded newspapers with sham stories to drum up artificial demand. These corrupt practices eventually resulted in a Congressional subpoena, but he managed to walk away scot-free.[63]

With all that said, Arthur Sackler always kept the circus act of his advertising business, William Douglas McAdams, separate from Purdue Pharma. In other words, you don't crap where you eat. In fact, Purdue Pharma ventured responsibly into the pain management sector in 1984 with MS Contin, morphine sulfate controlled-release tablets. However, the company took an ironic turn against his

---

[B] As of 2013, Purdue Pharma red-flagged 1,800 doctors nationally for irresponsible prescriptions, yet the company refused to release this information.

wishes, after his death in 1987, when MS Contin's patent was near expiration. Hence, Purdue Pharma hired William Douglas McAdams to promote OxyContin and we're all well aware of the destruction that followed.[64]

America now consumes 80% of the world's prescription opioids![65] OxyContin's sales growth was explosive. This one drug is the primary reason why pharmacy robberies have surged since its introduction to the market.[66] Consequently, several pharmacies have added bullet proof glass.[67] As the overdose death toll continued to mount, Purdue Pharma's executives maintained that their drug was virtually non-addictive. Naturally, the DEA and DOJ took notice, but Purdue Pharma managed to sidestep any real consequences thanks to the revolving door between business and government.

Purdue Pharma hired Rudy Giuliani's consulting firm, Giuliani Partners, in 2002 to handle damage control with the DEA. Giuliani reportedly received several million dollars for that contract.[68] Rudy Giuliani, i.e. "America's Mayor," was an ironic choice. His rise to fame came about decades earlier as the U.S. Attorney in Manhattan who prosecuted the mafia for heroin trafficking in the "Pizza Connection" cases. He further developed a zero-tolerance, anti-drug reputation as the mayor of New York City, so much so, he even opposed methadone treatments calling it "an Orwellian drug swap."[69]

Clearly, adding Giuliani was a public relations coup for Purdue Pharma, but he also had connections. Laura Nagel, formerly the DEA's chief investigator, added, "Rudy got them access to higher levels of government."[70] He was able to serve as an intermediary and conduct private meetings on their behalf with high-level officials from the DEA and DOJ.[71]

The Appalachian region seemed to be the area hardest hit by OxyContin, in particular, Kentucky and West Virginia. Consequently, the Attorney General of West Virginia, Darrell McGraw, filed a civil suit in 2001. Regardless, it was a tepid response to a number of allegations. Most notably, there was a charge that Purdue Pharma threatened pharmacies with legal action if they didn't fill every prescription, even in cases when they believed that the recipients were drug addicts. Ultimately, Purdue Pharma settled the case in 2004 for $10 million without having to admit to any criminal wrongdoing. That settlement enabled them to avoid airing their dirty laundry in court without entering any incriminating subpoenas into the public record.

Can you guess who strapped on his cape and saved the day for Purdue Pharma? It was Eric Holder, the former Deputy Attorney General under Clinton and future Attorney General for Obama. He arranged that plea bargain for Purdue Pharma in 2004 as a defense attorney with Covington & Burling.[72] That particular white shoe law office is arguably the preeminent defense team for Fortune 500 companies and their staff is inundated with a revolving door of former DOJ officials. (There are many more revelations regarding Eric Holder's role with the revolving door in the next book, *Rackets Vol II: Dealing from the Bottom of the Deck: Hypocritical Gambling Laws Enrich Crooked Politicians, a Select-Few Casinos, and the Mob*.)

That civil case didn't insulate Purdue Pharma from criminal prosecution and their company was later indicted in federal court by twenty-six states and the District of Columbia. Again, Rudy Giuliani acted on behalf of the defense. In addition, Purdue Pharma hired another white-shoe law firm, Debevoise & Plimpton, with Mary Jo White as the lead counsel.[73] She had previously developed a notable hard-nosed reputation while serving as the U.S. Attorney in Manhattan.

Ultimately, no one from their company went to prison. Purdue Pharma and three of their executives agreed to pay separate fines totaling $635 million.[74] Again, those penalties represent a small portion of the proceeds from their crimes as OxyContin accounted for roughly 90% of Purdue Pharma's profits and they sold $3.1 billion of OxyContin in 2010.[75] Mind you, that's far more money than most drug cartels generate.

This is the kind of case that demonstrates the power of the revolving door. As the adage goes, it's not what you know, but who you know. There was clearly enough evidence to send these executives to prison for many years, but that didn't happen. In fact, the lead prosecutor, John Brownlee (the U.S. attorney in Roanoke, VA) faced repercussions because his actions were considered to be unfair to Purdue Pharma.

Specifically, Brownlee insisted that Purdue Pharma must accept their plea bargain within a certain deadline. In response, Mary Jo White went over his head by contacting a senior DOJ official in hopes of an extension. That same official then called Brownlee to strong-arm him into an extension. Brownlee refused and enforced his deadline, but that choice landed him on the list of potential firings for U.S. attorneys. That was the same infamous list compiled by former Attorney General Alberto Gonzales who fired nine U.S. attorneys seemingly for political reasons.[76]

It would be unfair and inaccurate to single out Rudy Giuliani or these others as the only opportunistic political hypocrites in the drug war. Think about it. Drug testing is now a relatively standard requirement for most professions, yet lawmakers aren't forced to submit to a symbolic gesture like drug testing. There have been a few proposals for drug testing Congressmen, but those proposals have never made it to the floor of the U.S. Congress.[77]

In contrast, some states require welfare recipients to pass drug tests. Obviously, the issues of drug testing and welfare have some clear underlying connotations. Contrary to the "welfare queen" caricature, the results show that very few welfare recipients test positive for drugs, far below the national average. In fact, the average was well below 1% in most states. Consequently, the costs for operating these testing programs are higher than the savings.[78] Nonetheless, Oklahoma lawmakers drafted a bill in 2012 to drug test welfare recipients, including a provision with drug tests for lawmakers. Ultimately, the welfare drug testing bill passed, but the provision for testing politicians was removed before it passed.[79]

Many politicians have demonstrated no compassion with this issue because they were never arrested for their past drug use. It seems quite unlikely that Barack Obama would have become the first black President of the United States if he had been arrested for cocaine or marijuana, both of which he has admittedly used. In fact, Obama was reportedly such a weed aficionado that he mandated "Total Absorption" or "TA" when smoking among his group of close friends. According to David Maraniss, an Obama biographer, if his friend didn't fully absorb the hit off of a joint, he was "assessed a penalty" and his "turn was skipped the next time the joint came around."[80]

Former Indiana Governor, Mitch Daniels, assumed that his upcoming political career was wiped out after he was caught in 1970 with two shoeboxes full of marijuana, along with LSD and prescription drugs. He was then a financially privileged student at Princeton and the courts had tremendous mercy on him. He didn't even have to plead guilty to a drug charge; instead it was "maintaining a common nuisance" and he was only given a $350 fine. Remember, drug sentences were much more punitive in 1970.

For reference, Timothy Leary was arrested during this era with a much smaller quantity of marijuana and was sentenced to 30 years in prison! Nonetheless, at this present time in Indiana, Daniels would face six months to three years in prison with the same amount of marijuana, not including the LSD and prescription drugs. Regardless, several years later, Daniels told *The Daily Princetonian*, "Justice was served. I had used marijuana and I was fined for that, and that was appropriate."[81] Despite receiving favorable treatment from the criminal justice system, Daniels went on to support the drug war as president of the Hudson Institute, a conservative think tank, and as a senior political adviser for President Reagan.[82]

In fairness to Mitch Daniels, he did eventually gain some perspective and at one point endorsed alternative sentencing for nonviolent drug offenders as Indiana's Governor.[83] On the other hand, Bill Clinton and high-level members of his administration had smoked marijuana in their youth, yet the Clinton administration was one of the toughest in the war on drugs -- except when cases hit close to home. Clinton found time during "Pardongate" to pardon the drug charges of his brother.[84] Also, the son of Richard W. Riley, Clinton's Secretary of Education, faced federal charges of conspiring to sell cocaine and marijuana with a maximum penalty of life in prison and a $4 million fine. Remarkably, he was only sentenced to 6 months of house arrest.[85]

Al Gore, who admittedly smoked pot in the past, campaigned against medical marijuana in 2000 as a presidential candidate, even though his sister had been prescribed marijuana for her cancer. After that became a public source of contention, Gore pointed out that "it came in a prescription container with a label on it."[86] Even Donna Shalala, arguably the most liberal member of Clinton's cabinet and a former marijuana smoker, fell in line with the drug policy status quo. As the Secretary of Health and Human Services, she launched an aggressive campaign against legalizing marijuana, including an op-ed for *The Wall Street Journal*. She labeled marijuana as "a one-way ticket to dead-end hopes and dreams."[87]

Bill Clinton's famous line, "I didn't inhale," left many with an impression that he didn't support the drug war, even though marijuana arrests doubled during the Clinton administration. The public perception of Clinton being soft on the issue opened the door for numerous Republican leaders to criticize his commitment, including Newt Gingrich. Of all the detractors, Gingrich was an odd messenger who "doth protest too much." In regard to his past drug usage, Gingrich smugly referred to it as "a sign we were alive and in graduate school in that era."[88]

Newt touched upon a theme among some baby boomers who describe the drug culture of their youth in a permissive light, while every generation thereafter is somehow committing an eternal sin. With that said, he was at one time a maverick who broke outside of party lines to introduce a bill in 1981 that would have legalized medical marijuana.[89] However, over time, Gingrich compromised his values to fall in line with his party's platform. As Speaker of the House, he proposed the Drug Importer Death Penalty Act of 1997, which would have applied to anyone importing over two ounces of marijuana.[90]

Former Rep. Dan Burton (R-IN) also introduced legislation that would have imposed the death penalty for drug dealers. Luckily for Burton, his bill wasn't passed because his son was later arrested for transporting nearly eight pounds of marijuana. In fact, while awaiting trial, his son was arrested again for having a gun and 30 marijuana plants. Despite his father's strong stance against drug trafficking, he was afforded extremely preferential treatment. He faced mandatory minimum sentences of five and three years, but he walked away with only community service, probation, and house arrest.[91]

If we were to build a Congressional Hall of Fame for hypocrites, the first inductee would need to be former Rep. Randy "Duke" Cunningham (R-CA).[C] He also publicly scolded Clinton's supposed lack of commitment to the drug war. In September of 1996, he voted in favor of the death penalty for drug dealers. However, four months later, Cunningham's son was arrested for transporting 400 pounds of marijuana. While in custody, he admitted to being a member of a group that smuggled 30,000 pounds nationwide. Nonetheless, "Duke" Cunningham cried to the judge for mercy. Mind you, Duke was one of the most rabid conservatives of his era who once challenged a liberal Congressman to a fistfight on the floor of the House.[92] "My son has a good heart. He's never been in trouble

---

[C] There are many interesting details about Duke Cunningham's various scandals and his eventual prison sentence in *Rackets Vol III: Decriminalized Prostitution: The Common Sense Solution.*

before," he pleaded to the judge. In the end, his son wasn't prosecuted for the more serious trafficking offense that had a penalty of life in prison without parole. Instead, his son received only 2.5 years in prison and the sentence would have been even less severe if he had not tested positive for cocaine three times while out on bail.[93]

All of these examples illustrate that the criminal justice system selectively adopts a light touch for the privileged class. These examples could also be construed as the "compassionate conservatism" that George W. Bush championed. However, neither George W. Bush, nor his father, took actual steps to reduce the punitive nature of the drug war. With that in mind, George W. Bush, an admitted former alcoholic, was also rumored to have abused harder drugs in his past.

According to J.H. Hatfield, the author of *Fortunate Son: George W. Bush and the Making of an American President*, George W. Bush was arrested for cocaine possession in 1972, but the record was expunged due to his family's connections. Bush was reportedly only punished with community service.[94] Furthermore, Scott McClellan, Bush's former Press Secretary, wrote about an admission that the president once made in private. Bush didn't admit to illegal drug use per se, but his comments were actually even more revealing. Bush reportedly said, "You know, the truth is I honestly don't remember whether I tried (cocaine) or not. We had some pretty wild parties back in the day, and I just don't remember."[95]

George W. Bush likely used hard drugs in the past, but that can't be definitively proven. However, one of his dear family members, Noelle Bush, verifiably abused illegal drugs but never felt the wrath of the legal system. Noelle Bush's father, Jeb Bush, was the Governor of Florida in 2002. At the same time, her uncle, George W. Bush, was the President. Meanwhile, in January of 2002, she missed her first day of work at her new job because she was in jail for using a fake prescription to buy Xanax at a drive-through pharmacy. That crime is a felony with a maximum five-year sentence and $5,000 fine, but she was only forced to enter a rehabilitation program.[96] Despite the arrest, Noelle Bush was assured that she could start her new job. *That doesn't sound out of the ordinary, right*? "Due to personal circumstances, she was unable to begin her job. Infinity's job offer still stands and will be waiting when she is available to return to the workforce," said Infinity CEO Tom Lynch. "My thoughts and prayers are with the Bush family."[97]

Four months later, Noelle was forced to serve three days in jail after nurses accused her of stealing prescription pills from the drug treatment center. Police officers were called back again two months later to the same rehabilitation center where they found Noelle in possession of two grams of crack cocaine.[98] The judge warned Noelle that she could be charged with two felonies. However, after her third strike in a state where her father supported mandatory minimum sentences, the police dropped the charges against her. In the end, she only received 10 days in jail for contempt of court.[99]

These circumstances would have seemingly forced anyone to reevaluate their stance on the drug war, but that wasn't the case with Jeb Bush. For that reason, in 2015 during the Presidential campaign, Sen. Rand Paul (R-KY) publicly criticized Jeb Bush's "hypocrisy." Rand Paul pointed out that Jeb Bush openly smoked marijuana as a wealthy prep school student but continues to support the drug war.[100]

Arguably, the most passionate drug warrior from the George W. Bush administration was the former Attorney General, John Ashcroft. While serving as Missouri's Governor, he proposed a measure in 1992 that would have evicted entire families from public housing projects if any of their children were ever caught with marijuana.[101] Apparently, Ashcroft believed, in theory, that family members should be punished for the indiscretions of their relatives. However, earlier in that same year his nephews, Alex and Adam Ashcroft, were arrested in possession of 60 marijuana plants.[102]

Adam was never prosecuted, but Alex was convicted of felony possession with the intent to distribute. That number of plants would have qualified for a mandatory minimum sentence in the federal court. However, luckily for Alex, he was convicted in the state courts and walked away with only probation and community service. Alex even failed a drug test while on probation and still managed to stay out of jail.[103]

You would assume that John Ashcroft learned from that example and found that inflexible policies like mandatory minimum drug sentences have inherent flaws. No, instead, he was an adamant supporter of mandatory minimum sentences in his subsequent stint as a Senator. Furthermore, after entering the Bush administration, he was a ruthless tyrant for enforcing those laws. Ashcroft ordered all U.S. Attorneys to report any federal judge that didn't abide by mandatory minimum sentences.[104]

Tommy Chong, of Cheech and Chong, became one of Ashcroft's most prized targets. Tommy Chong wasn't a drug dealer; instead, he owned a company, Chong Glass, which sold bongs on the Internet. Tommy wasn't even involved with the company's operations; rather, he allowed his son to use his name to boost sales. Nonetheless, his company was the primary focus of "Operation Pipe Dreams," the largest undercover federal investigation into drug paraphernalia in U.S. history. It involved over 1,200 federal agents and resulted in the indictments of ten companies and fifty-five people, most notably Tommy Chong.[105]

Undercover federal agents traveled to Chong's headquarters in hopes that they would send a bong to a fictitious head shop. "It's typical Bush administration stuff. They couldn't get our company, these stoners, to ship them a bong to Beaver Falls, (PA)...It would be funny if it wasn't so sad," said Tommy Chong.[106] Initially, the employees of Chong Glass politely declined to make a shipment to Beaver Falls, PA with the understanding that it violated local laws. However, they eventually obliged the undercover officers after a lot of pleading for a one time exemption.[107]

Tommy Chong obviously didn't want to plead guilty, but he did so to placate the prosecutors who threatened to imprison his son and wife. Of the 55 people arrested, Tommy Chong was the only person to receive jail time. This was clearly a political witch hunt and the head prosecutor, Mary Beth Buchanan, even admitted that Tommy Chong's company "wasn't the biggest supplier."[108]

Chong's lawyers asked for probation, but the prosecution wanted to make an example of him. They pointed to Chong's resume of "trivializing law enforcement" and even asserted that bong sales fund terrorism. As a result, Tommy Chong was fined $20,000, lost $103,514 in federal forfeitures, and received a 9-month sentence on the most symbolic date of September 11, 2003.[109] Conversely, that case led to a promotion for Mary Beth Buchanan by John Ashcroft. Sadly enough, these kinds of bush-league cases build careers and, subsequently, she launched a run for the U.S. House of Representatives.

John McCain has never eased his strong drug war support, even though his wife had a serious drug problem. Cindy McCain, the multi-millionaire heiress from the beer industry, developed an addiction to prescription drugs, Percocet and Vicodin. This secret was exposed publicly, oddly enough, while she worked for her charitable organization, American Voluntary Medical Team, which benefits third world nations. The charity's medical director prescribed those two drugs for her under other employee names without their knowledge. Eventually, one of the employees found out and notified the DEA. Subsequently, they conducted an 11-month investigation and Cindy McCain faced federal charges of obtaining "a controlled substance by misrepresenting, fraud, forgery, deception or subterfuge." That crime could have resulted in a 20-year prison sentence, but her vast wealth and connections provided a shield. As part of her plea bargain, she only had to reimburse the DEA for their investigative costs, perform community service, and enter into drug addiction treatment.[110]

There are several more examples like this. However, the purpose of this chapter isn't to punish family members of influential politicians after the fact. We should all be so lucky to have those kinds of connections. Everyone should be able to benefit from a criminal justice system that assesses drug crimes with a level of compassion usually reserved for its own family members. In truth, we live in a class society and the same rules don't apply to everyone. The water on Capitol Hill must have a side effect that causes self-righteousness. It's obscene how our elected leaders pander to powerful corporations that conduct themselves just as gangsters do without any meaningful repercussions. You and I, on the other hand, would certainly be sent to prison for many years on conspiracy charges if we merely discussed breaking some of the laws that these companies violate on a regular basis.

9

"We disproportionately stop whites too much and minorities too little."
New York City Mayor Michael Bloomberg

In the aftermath of the Ferguson riots, FBI Director James Comey delivered a truly socially conscious speech, "The Hard Truths: Law Enforcement and Race." Comey said, "At many points in American history, law enforcement enforced the status quo, a status quo that was often brutally unfair to disfavored groups." He pointed out that police vans are still dubbed "paddy wagons," a direct and bigoted slight towards Irish Americans. "The Irish had tough times, but little compares to the experience on our soil of black Americans," added Comey.[1]

Comey keeps a reminder of this abuse of power on his desk; it's a shameless wiretap request by J. Edgar Hoover to monitor Martin Luther King. It's difficult to find someone with more noble goals than Martin Luther King, yet he was the target of some of the most invasive surveillance ever used by our federal government. The federal holiday dedicated to his birthday tends to whitewash the abuses committed by the federal government against him. The FBI compiled tens of thousands of documents on Martin Luther King. In particular, one internal memo was written just after his "I have a dream speech," in which King was labeled as the "most dangerous and effective Negro leader in the country."[2] The FBI was obsessed with "neutralizing" him and went to great lengths to do so including illegal break-ins to plant listening devices, public smears, threats, extortion, etc. Despite the great lengths of their investigations, the FBI was unable to launch a criminal case against King. Instead, they were able to capture audio tape from two of his sexual affairs and then sent a letter to him that threatened to leak that information to the press unless he killed himself.[3]

A similar memo by J Edgar Hoover mentioned, "Since the use of marijuana and other narcotics is widespread among members of the New Left, you should be alert to opportunities to have them arrested by local authorities on drug charges."[4] In like manner, a specific entry in the diary of H.R. Haldeman, one of Nixon's top advisors, encapsulated the President's biases and illustrated his devious means. They were discussing welfare reform when Nixon interjected that "the whole problem is really the blacks. The key is to devise a system that recognizes this while not appearing to."[5] Another top Nixon advisor, John Ehrlichman, was rather adamant during an interview, nearly 20 years after leaving office. He explained that Nixon's inner circle openly exploited the drug war to target anti-war protesters and black people. "Did we know we were lying about the drugs? Of course we did," deadpanned Ehrlichman.[6]

With the hindsight of history, these kinds of revelations aren't out of the blue. What's more disturbing is how the criminal justice system went about manifesting these goals and that the masses stood by watching it happen. At the present time, we'd like to think that our nation has completely evolved, but racial biases are still prevalent.

Look no further than a psychological study conducted in 2014 in one of the most liberal regions of the country. A pair of Stanford University researchers gathered two separate all-white groups to view a political video that opposed the state's "three strikes" laws. The video was identical for both groups, other than one variable in this experiment. The participants viewed several mug shots of various men of different races, but one of the groups viewed more black mug shots. After watching the video, they were offered a real-life petition for reducing sentencing laws. Suffice it to say, the mug shots of black men elicited less sympathy. Only 27% of the group who viewed more black faces supported reduced sentences; whereas, the petition was signed by 52% of the group who viewed fewer black faces.[7]

In many ways, the drug war is a socioeconomic class issue. After all, there are thousands of poor white people who have been rotting away for decades in maximum security prisons as well. Likewise, most Americans who support the drug war aren't consciously motivated by an inherently racist desire to suppress minorities. Nevertheless, the consequences of the drug war have done exactly that. Because of the drug war, the criminal justice system has impacted Americans in a very negative way, but the impact has been especially devastating to minorities. In 2010, black men were incarcerated at a rate of 3,074 per 100,000 residents.[8] That's nearly four times the rate for black men incarcerated by the end of apartheid in South Africa, which was 851 per 100,000 residents.[9] Hence, the NAACP has called for the end to the drug war.

These systemic problems are why the author Michelle Alexander, along with other social reform leaders, refers to the drug war as the "New Jim Crow."

The racial disparity associated with current profiteering from the prison industry has similarities to the debt peonage system. The 13th Amendment abolished slavery, but a loophole remained that established the debt peonage system throughout the South. This is an underreported aspect of American history, which was thoroughly documented in *Slavery by Another Name: The Re-Enslavement of Black Americans from the Civil War to World War II*, the 2009 Pulitzer Prize winner.

Black men were the exclusive source of labor for the peonage system in the South. Black "criminals" were charged with dubious crimes, such as changing employers without permission, curfew violations, vagrancy, loud talk in the presence of white women, or the ultimate taboo -- sex with white women. They were issued exorbitant fines that were in no way commensurate with the crime. As a result, very few could afford to pay and judges forced them to settle their debts by laboring for various private businesses. However, these repayment agreements were anything but forthright. The debt could last indefinitely as other fines could be assessed throughout the process. This was indentured servitude and the work conditions were often no different from slavery. Many of the laborers were shackled in chains, whipped, and/or simply worked to the point of death.[10]

Various laws were passed in the early 20th century to outlaw this practice, but they weren't widely enforced. In fact, in 1929, two Mississippi sheriffs reported making an extra $20,000 to $30,000 a year in bribes from local farmers by rounding up black men for "vagrancy" charges. Profiteers gathered at the local courthouse to bid on slave labor, including small businessmen and representatives from large corporations (notably US Steel). Alarmingly, the government as a whole didn't crack down on this practice until after WWII. Hence, these types of cases existed well into the 1950s. In total, there were an estimated 100,000 to 200,000 black men forced into this modern-day slavery.[11]

The severity of the Jim Crow era has obviously decreased tremendously, but many of these biases are subtly beneath the surface and are not exclusive to the Deep South. To paraphrase a Chris Rock joke, racism doesn't magically disappear north of the

Virginia state line. Drug usage is widely considered to be a black problem, but various studies have found that all races use drugs at roughly the same rates. Nonetheless, a 1995 issue of the *Journal of Alcohol and Drug Education* found that 95% of the people who were asked to describe a drug user pictured a black person.[12] Minorities are also stereotyped as drug dealers, but they're no more likely to deal drugs either. Even the former "drug czar" Barry McCaffrey acknowledged that most people buy their drugs from "their own race generally."[13]

The inner city is often targeted by law enforcement for drug arrests, while it's just as easy, if not easier, to find drugs on a college campus. With that said, it makes sense to put more police resources in high crime areas. As a matter of fact, a strong police presence would be welcomed by most of the residents in those areas *if* they were being protected in the true sense of the word. Instead, too many minorities have been wrapped up in this numbers game that the police are forced to play. They're routinely stopped for minor infractions to gain the legal right to conduct a search. This can be seen in the fact that black people accounted for 95% of all jaywalking arrests in Ferguson, MO, according to a study by the DOJ after the riots of 2014.[14] This kind of harassment takes place nationwide, to varying degrees, and it's the primary reason why 75% of the drug offenders in state prisons are black or Latino.[15]

How about we take an expert's word for it. Clarence Giarrusso, former head of the narcotics squad and the Police Chief of New Orleans, explained, "We made cases in black neighborhoods because it was easy. We didn't need a search warrant, it allowed us to meet our quotas, and it was ongoing."[16] There's no way to assess the collateral damage from this kind of selective enforcement. These communities need effective policing, not blanket racial profiling.

Drugs are considered a rite of passage in college. On the other hand, drug usage in the inner city is portrayed as urban blight. Law enforcement isn't nearly as aggressive with the college crowd for a few reasons. Those students' parents are much better connected than the average young black male and they also, as a whole, have more access to solid defense attorneys. Case in point, Matthew Fogg, a former U.S. Marshall and DEA special agent, openly questioned his supervisor as to why they were aggressively targeting the inner city while ignoring the wealthier suburbs. His supervisor told him, "They know judges. They know lawyers. They know politicians.

You start locking up their kids…and they're going to shut us down and there goes your overtime."[17]

Young white people are also much more likely to receive leniency after an arrest. Black juveniles were six times more likely to be sent to prison than whites for the identical crimes, according to one report in 2000 that focused on juveniles who had not yet been to prison.[18] Some believe bias isn't widespread in America because we elected Barack Obama, but there are still plenty of people with "Hope & Change" bumper stickers who lock their doors at the sight of a black man. Whether conscious or unconscious, there is an inherent bias in the criminal justice system. There aren't a high number of minorities in positions of power within the justice system. The positions that minorities usually hold within the justice system are at the lower levels of power, such as law enforcement or corrections, as opposed to lawyers, judges, or political officials.[19]

Many of the drug laws seem to be colorblind by statute, but in actuality, they're harshly directed towards minorities. Take the Anti-Drug Abuse Act of 1986 for example. That law made the mandatory minimum sentence for crack cocaine 100 times longer than the same amount of powder cocaine! Crack is falsely perceived as a more dangerous drug than powdered cocaine, but the two are the same drug. Powdered cocaine is perceived as having an air of exclusivity, while crack has a reputation as a drug of the ghetto. In actuality, the only difference is that crack is made by boiling cocaine powder with baking soda so that it can be easily smoked.

Obviously, there is a bias with the sentencing law, but many black leaders were the most vocal supporters of the Anti-Drug Abuse Act of 1986. Believe it or not, seventeen of the twenty-one members of the Congressional Black Caucus sponsored this inequitable legislation.[20] But keep in mind, that bill was signed during a time of duress when crack-related crime was surging. In hindsight, that decision was a mistake and that particular law has been heavily criticized over the years. Thus, in 2010, Barack Obama signed the Fair Sentencing Act and crack is now punishable with a minimum sentence that is 18 times longer than powdered cocaine. That is progress, but it's still far from fair as both are pharmacologically the same drug.[21]

Search and seizure laws are also subtly geared towards minorities. The case of Terry v Ohio (1968) in essence made it perfectly legal for police to frisk a black man without probable cause as long as he is walking in a rough neighborhood. An officer must have a "reasonable suspicion" to perform a frisk, but that is open to wide interpretation and the neighborhood in which the frisk takes place is the dominant factor. Peter Moskos, author of *Cop in the Hood: My Year Policing Baltimore's Eastern District*, notes that Terry v Ohio is race blind in theory, but officers frequently abuse "Terry frisks."[22] Also, police officers perform "consent searches" more often with minorities. Again, consent is often a very broadly interpreted term. For one thing, some officers claim that a person consented to a search after the officer yelled a command and that person simply complied.[23]

No police department officially endorses racial profiling, but it is certainly prevalent. One study took place on I-95 outside the Baltimore area. Twenty-one percent of the drivers on that stretch of road were minorities, yet they accounted for eighty percent of the people pulled over and searched.[24] In some circles that is informally referred to as "driving while black."

Albert W. Florence, a black man who works in finance, can certainly describe what that experience is like. In 2005, he was pulled over for speeding while driving with his family in his BMW. Florence had previously been issued a warrant for an unpaid fine stemming from a traffic offense. Albeit, he later paid the fine. And furthermore, he kept a document in the car that proved he had paid the fine. Anyhow, Florence showed the document to the officer to no avail and he was arrested. Ultimately, he was held in jail for eight days and strip searched twice.[25]

Norm Stamper, the former Police Chief of Seattle, WA, is now a member of Law Enforcement Action Partnership (LEAP). He has been quite candid that, as a young officer, he intentionally persecuted young black men on a routine basis. He baited young black men into altercations if they didn't cower to his authority, thereby granting him the authority to rough them up and choke them. Decades later, Stamper now clearly feels shame about his past and wants to reform the culture within various police departments. He found that some black officers felt pressure to discriminate against black people. One black officer tearfully explained, "You go along to get along. It's a white world. It's a white locker room."[26] All in all, Stamper acknowledges that progress has been made over time, but more progress is sorely needed.

"Working while black" can have other consequences as well. The *Miami Herald* reported about a black resident of Miami Gardens, Earl Sampson, who had been stopped by the local police 258 times over a four year period! That's not a misprint. Naturally, you would have to assume that Sampson has a lengthy rap sheet filled with violent crimes, but that isn't the case. Sampson isn't a danger to his community and his most serious arrest was for marijuana possession. He had been arrested 62 times for trespassing, often by the same officers; however, almost every one of those arrests took place at the convenience store where he works. In one instance, the store's video cameras captured footage of Sampson stocking the coolers just before he was handcuffed and arrested.[27]

The store's owner, Alex Saleh, had notified police on multiple occasions that Sampson was his employee and was not trespassing. He responded by installing security cameras to protect his staff and customers from *police harassment*, not to prevent shoplifting. One such encounter was captured on video in which a police officer opened a woman's purse to dump her belongings on the pavement. He simply walked away without saying a word after his search, i.e. rifling through her stuff with his foot, came up short of any contraband.[28]

These kinds of flippant confrontations magnified Saleh's regrets for his past participation in a "zero tolerance" program in which a sign was placed in his window. That sign granted the police broader authority for searches on the premises. After this continual harassment, Saleh took down the sign, but the police continued to badger his customers and employees. The police even put the sign back in his window against his wishes. Also, he said that officers became even more aggressive after he filed an official complaint.[29]

Too many Americans roll their eyes and question the motives of black activists whenever this subject is broached. That's why it's necessary for more people to hear activists like Bobby Constantino, a former Boston prosecutor. As a white youth from the suburbs, Constantino noted that he had always thought of the "police and the criminal justice system as their allies and friends."[30] Over time, he found throughout his career that minorities receive very different treatment from within the criminal justice system. A significant portion of his caseload involved drug crimes against minorities. Generally speaking, the remainder of his cases involved the kinds of petty crimes that police generally overlook in middle and upper-class suburban areas. Otherwise, Constantino felt that he only had a few cases every week that were truly important.[31]

Constantino decided to pull a publicity stunt/social experiment in which he walked through the Brownsville section of Brooklyn with a can of spray paint in an intentional and obvious attempt to get arrested. He was spotted by some officers but was not arrested before he vandalized City Hall. He detailed the incident with photographs in his blog. In fact, he returned to City Hall to turn himself in four times, to no avail, before he was arrested on his fifth visit. Constantino went into further detail for a story, "I Got Myself Arrested So I Could Look Inside the Justice System," for *The Atlantic*.[32]

There likely is no city with more systemic racial profiling than New York City. This stems from the 1980s when the crime rate surged and the average person was afraid to enter the subway or walk the streets at night. There was a need for a strong police presence, but racial profiling wasn't the answer. Presently, a selectively enforced "police state" is in the making. *Reuters* surveyed 25 black NYPD officers in 2014 and only one of them reported not being racially profiled or harassed while off-duty.[33]

NYPD officers are pressured to "stop and frisk" anyone suspected of a crime and fill out a "UF-250" form. The suspect's personal information is later entered into a massive database.[34] The stop and frisk program is officially aimed at getting guns off of the streets, but it has resulted in New York City having the highest number of marijuana arrests in America. Obviously, New York City is the largest city in America, but it had long been synonymous with a laissez-faire drug culture. But times have changed and in 2011 there were 50,684 arrests for misdemeanor possession of marijuana.[35]

In 2011, the NYPD officially performed 685,724 of these "stop and frisks." These encounters are often hostile and interchangeable with harassment as 36% of the "UF-250" reports didn't even list an appropriate "suspected crime."[36] This harassment is more often aimed at minorities, and one Hispanic teenager who had been routinely stopped and frisked recorded the audio with his cell phone. In fact, he had been stopped by the police during this same walk, just two blocks beforehand.

The Nation published that recording in which the teenager was told he was stopped because he had "his hood up" and "was looking at them." Only seconds later the officers threatened to slap him and arrest him. He asked what he would be charged with and the officer replied, "For being a fucking mutt." Then, while the officers had the young man's arm behind his back, they threatened him again. "Dude, I'm gonna break your fucking arm, then I'm gonna punch you in the fucking face." Once the officers decided to let the young man go he was shoved, threatened, and told to get lost.[37]

Eighty-five percent of people stopped and frisked are black or Latino.[38] That is out of proportion, as minorities make up roughly half of New York City's population. More importantly, the office of the public advocate for New York City reviewed the data and found that white people were the most likely to be carrying weapons. Weapons were found on white people one in every 49 stops, but 71 stops were needed to find weapons on Latinos and 93 stops were needed to find weapons on black people.[39]

Undoubtedly, those statistics demonstrate how many people inherently view minorities with more suspicion. Despite access to this information, Mayor Michael Bloomberg said that "we disproportionately stop whites too much and minorities too little." Astoundingly, Bloomberg didn't backtrack afterward from that statement. "The numbers don't lie," he said and asserted that 90% of murder suspects were identified as black or Latino.[40]

Well, the numbers do lie, according to Michael A. Wood Jr., a former Baltimore narcotics cop with 11 years of experience. He has become a whistleblower for reforming police misconduct and he'll be one of the first to tell you that stop and frisk statistics are "junk."[41] The reality of police harassment is much worse than the statistics indicate. Wood points out the fact that filling out paperwork is time-consuming. Therefore, most cops don't bother if a search is unsuccessful. This can be seen with the frisk that was recorded for *The Nation*.

In cases where police have been caught fabricating evidence, it seemingly most often victimizes minorities. For instance, the former police chief of both San Jose and Kansas City, Joseph McNamara, estimated that hundreds of thousands of police officers commit perjury with drug arrests. He said, "They don't feel lying under oath is wrong because politicians tell them they are engaged in a 'holy war' fighting evil...(These are generally) white cops (who) are testifying against poor blacks and Latinos."[42]

Two brothers, Jose and Maximo Colon, were awarded $300,000 in a settlement from a civil suit with the NYPD. Video evidence proved that NYPD narcotics detectives had falsely arrested them for selling cocaine.[43] One of the officers involved, Stephen Anderson, testified that falsifying evidence was common practice with drug cases to meet quotas. In fact, there is even a slang term for planting cocaine on a suspect called "flaking," and Anderson did it to protect his partner from being demoted. Also, he testified that "supervisors or undercovers and even investigators" were also guilty of this crime.[44] The federal judge who presided over the case, Jack Weinstein, agreed that the NYPD is plagued by "widespread falsification by arresting officers."[45] With that said, he believes that the vast majority of police aren't crooked, but there are enough so that it creates systematic corruption.

Even the early origins of drug education have a racist influence. Daryl Gates was one of the founders of DARE, the well-known anti-drug program.[A][46] Gates' extreme stance on drug use didn't belong anywhere in drug education. Indeed, he once told the Senate that casual drug use is "treason" and that casual drug users "ought to be taken out and shot."[47]

That's the same Daryl Gates who was the Chief of Police in Los Angeles whose comment was rehashed during the Rodney King riots. He stated that more black people may die from chokeholds because "the veins or arteries do not open up as fast as they do on normal people."[48] Daryl Gates is also widely credited with the creation of the first SWAT teams in 1966. The public was first introduced to the SWAT team with the well-publicized four-hour shootout between the LAPD and the Black Panther Party. Decades later in an interview with *NPR*, Gates reminisced about how the Black Panther shootout propelled SWAT teams into a standard nationwide. Gates said, "It was the first time we got to show off."[49]

For good reason, former Baltimore narcotics cop, Michael Wood Jr., has referred to his unit as an "occupying force."[50] Dr. Peter Kraska, Professor of Justice Studies at Eastern Kentucky

---

[A] The DARE program was developed and taught by police officers. One of the main lessons was for children to inform the police of anyone doing drugs, including their parents. Some kids did exactly as told and Nancy Reagan even used a 13-year old girl who did so to publicize the program. The girl turned her parents in and they were arrested for marijuana and cocaine. The family was broken apart and the parents were sent to prison.

University, has arguably been the foremost expert on the issue of militarized police departments and he asserts that police often use their civil asset forfeiture funds as a "slush fund" to continue the cycle of militarization.[51] Mind you, some police departments are even equipped with spy drone aircraft as though they're surveilling Fallujah.[52] Furthermore, a federal government program has distributed over $4.3 billion worth of surplus military equipment and supplies to various police departments nationwide since 1997.[53] To stem the tide, Obama made a slight reform in 2015 by restricting some of the items that can be issued, including armored vehicles and grenade launchers.[54] But, the cat is already out of the bag and police forces are armed to the teeth. When that type of armament is issued, it is going to be used whether necessary or not.

The militarization of the police force has led to an unnecessary reliance upon armed SWAT raids. The numbers have dramatically increased since police departments have become so well armed. Dr. Peter Kraska estimated that in 2014 there were 65,000 SWAT raids as opposed to about 3,000 per year in the early 1980s.[55] He said, "Remember these are not for terrorism, they're not for barricaded suspects, not for hostages. They are almost all…for low-level drug infractions."[56] If not for one journalist, Radley Balko (author of *Rise of the Warrior Cop* and *Overkill*), these kinds of revelations would have been buried within the minutia of academia. Balko has been a pioneering force who has persistently reported on this issue with the passion and focus of an activist.

SWAT teams routinely break into homes in pursuit of evidence of low-level crimes. Unfortunately, there isn't much definitive research available on this topic because the federal government doesn't publish SWAT raid statistics. Only one state, Utah, compiles this data and the findings aren't positive. In 2014, eighty-three percent of these encounters were for drug crimes and less than one percent were related to an active shooter scenario.[57] With a lack of transparency, there is a reliance on outside sources such as researchers like Kraska and Balko, along with news outlets to cover this issue.

An investigation in the Orlando area found the SWAT team's warrants were typically for crimes that were misdemeanors and usually only resulted in small fines or no charges at all. Another similar investigation by the *Palm Beach Post* found similar results with the area's SWAT teams. Most of the defendants were found guilty of minor crimes and were sentenced to less than six months in jail.[58] Likewise, the ACLU conducted a national investigation and found that only 7% of raids were for the actual situations that SWAT was originated to combat, i.e. hostage or active shooter scenarios.[59]

SWAT teams no longer even have to deal with the inconvenience of identifying themselves when they burst into a home. "No knock" warrants allow law enforcement officers to break into someone's house without knocking on the door to identify themselves, rather than waiting to see if the suspects will peacefully allow the search.[60] It should be no surprise that "no knock" raids were a product of the Nixon administration, in particular, the Watergate-stained former Attorney General John N. Mitchell. However, Mitchell preferred the term "quick entry" warrants for obvious public relations reasons.[61]

No knock warrants have steadily increased since the Nixon administration, but that type of warrant shouldn't be issued casually, for obvious reasons. It is particularly dangerous because the suspects don't know who is breaking into their home and may shoot at the officers, assuming that it's a home invasion. Unfortunately, the number of unnecessary raids will only increase in the future because police departments don't have the proper incentives and consequences in place. Police departments aren't liable for damages from raids and they face strong pressures to meet quotas.

After he led a raid into the wrong home of a 76-year-old woman, Cooper Landvatter, a Salt Lake City narcotics detective, told a judge that he was pressured with a quota from his supervisors to serve a search warrant every month. That woman luckily wasn't injured during the raid. An internal affairs investigation discovered that Landvatter had lied to the judge to justify the warrant. He said that he saw his informant buy drugs from the suspect's home, but Landvatter lost sight of him as the informant went up the steps. In the end, the review board report admitted that the quota Landvatter faced was "a very poor policy," but they felt that it didn't contribute significantly to raiding the incorrect home. Clearly, that was bureaucratic protectionism. Landvatter, and other officers who have made similar mistakes, most likely would not have cut corners had they not been faced with quotas. The systemic pressure is apparent because Landvatter's only punishment was a 20-hour suspension.[62]

Cheye Calvo and his family were the victims of one of these types of raids. Calvo's two pet dogs were shot and killed during a raid for a potential marijuana bust. Dog shootings as a result of police raids are now fairly common, so much so that Randal Lockwood of the American Society for the Prevention of Cruelty to Animals (ASPCA) follows these types of cases and estimates that 250-300 are reported with about 1,000 cases unreported every year.[63]

Many of these cases involve dogs that no reasonable person would consider dangerous, but officers are habitually cleared of any wrongdoing as long as they claim they were in danger. Lockwood estimates that 95% of the dog shootings are cleared by police departments.[64] In fact, in one case an officer was cleared after shooting a litter of 8-10 week old kittens.[65] The obvious takeaway is that many of these shootings are cases in which officers have a bloodlust and have found a way to get away with it.

The police didn't have a "no-knock" warrant to search Calvo's home, but they busted in without identifying themselves because Calvo's mother-in-law screamed when she saw the SWAT team. A box of marijuana had, in fact, been delivered to his address, but Calvo was exonerated almost immediately afterward. Drug traffickers used his address as part of a distribution scheme in which drugs were set to be delivered to various unknowing homeowners but the shipments were intercepted en route.[66] Nonetheless, this entire incident could have happened without any trauma or bloodshed if the local county police had done even the most basic due diligence concerning Calvo's background.

They were completely unaware that Cheye Calvo is the Mayor of Berwyn Heights, MD. The Berwyn Heights Police Department officials were not notified of the raid until afterward. Obviously, the Berwyn Heights Police Chief Patrick Murphy felt that this incident could have been easily prevented, without bloodshed, if he had been contacted first.[67] Even in situations like this, it is standard operating procedure for the police never to admit to any wrongdoing. County officials merely expressed "regret," but defended their deputies' actions. They said that "their guys did what they were supposed to do," "their deputies operated to the full extent of their capabilities," and even "offered a pat on the back for everyone involved."[68]

There certainly is a valid argument that, in some cases, no knock raids are appropriate if the suspect is a known violent felon; however, Calvo's case showcased how the modus operandi for SWAT raids is often to bust in and ask questions later. There have been some astonishing reports involving unnecessary force, including when the FDA conducted an armed raid to apprehend a Pennsylvania Amish dairy farmer who illegally sold raw milk.[69] Likewise, a group of Tibetan monks, who had come to this country on a worldwide peace mission, were rounded up at gunpoint by immigration officials after violating their visas.[70]

Cheye Calvo added, "What's extraordinary about my case is not that it happened; it's that actually people paid attention."[71] One can only imagine what happens in the poorest communities. An investigation by the ACLU confirmed those suspicions in their report, "War Comes Home: The Excessive Militarization of American Policing." The ACLU found "stark, often extreme, racial disparities in the use of SWAT."[72]

Worst of all, many of these raids are botched because the warrants are often based on tips from confidential criminal informants who have nothing to lose and everything to gain. These people have perverse incentives to get their criminal sentences reduced by any means necessary, the truth be damned. Unfortunately, the criminal informant system often functions conversely to how it was intended. Theoretically, nickel and dime drug dealers are supposed to snitch on more significant dealers. In reality, the traffickers at the highest levels have the most information to trade and often serve very little time in prison. This is similar to what was mentioned in the first chapter with civil asset forfeiture. The wealthiest dealers can buy their way out of prison with civil asset forfeiture, while the nickel and dime dealers are forced to serve their time. All in all, the criminal justice system often works down the food chain.

The dealers at the highest levels are also facing decades in prison or life. Therefore, they are further incentivized to exaggerate the stature of their underlings. Without a doubt, they will, in many cases, lie to implicate completely innocent people to produce more convictions for the prosecutors. As a result, it creates a chain reaction with more informants implicating other innocent people. There is no community that has been affected more by the informant system than the black community.

Some of these issues were brought to light by the DVD "Stop Snitching," which included a cameo from NBA star Carmelo Anthony. Unfortunately, the snitching controversy has a clear element of witness intimidation. The DVD's producer Rodney

Bethea claimed it was not about "the little old lady on the block." He said, "She is not considered a snitch. She's a civilian doing what she is supposed to do."[73] However, whether intentional or not, the stop snitching campaign has glamorized gangster culture and condoned witness intimidation, while many ignore the sociological consequences of the criminal informant system.

We're thoroughly accustomed to this informant system and don't question it. Then again, most people don't know how slim the burden of proof is with drug cases, particularly conspiracy drug cases. There is a difference between the letter of the law and what takes place in most criminal courts. Juries are notified about the incentives of criminal informants, but it's surprising how often a jury will convict someone based only on the word of a criminal informant. There is seemingly some innate human bias that assumes that the accused must be guilty of something otherwise the government would not have made its case.

A *PBS Frontline* documentary, "Snitch," brilliantly spotlighted a black community in Alabama where the median income is far below the poverty line. Uniontown, AL was supposedly the host of a distribution ring for 150 kilos of cocaine involving over 70 people; however, no actual drugs were seized. Gordon Armstrong III, defense attorney, explained that these convictions defied common sense. "Once you see what the evidence turned out to be, and you met the people involved, there's no way that that dollar figure and those amounts were possible," said Gordon.[74]

This conspiracy case was entirely a fabrication by a few criminal informants. One of the few actual drug dealers in this town of 2,000 people told the police that he would snitch on his own mother if it would help him. In the end, he kept his word by snitching on his own family members and several friends. Thus, a chain reaction ensued in which several other seemingly innocent people were framed and it netted over 70 arrests and the forfeiture of several modest homes. Again, there was no physical evidence and no drugs were confiscated, but several juries found the sole testimony of desperate criminal informants to be enough evidence to convict these people. One may wonder, "Would these juries have been as willing to convict a white person with the same level of proof?"

Many criminal informants have financial incentives, besides staying out of prison. They can receive a portion of proceeds from a drug bust, up to $500,000 or 25%, whichever is less, depending on the size of the seizure.[75] The potential financial rewards are enticing and, consequently, snitching has become a way of life for many people in poor communities. Remarkably, Alex White, an informant for the city of Atlanta, sued the city for wrongful termination when a high profile case blew his cover and ended his $30,000 a year career as a drug informant.[76] "I would say that the career path for a criminal informer is a lot more lucrative for that of an agent. Crime actually does pay," says Michael Levine, retired DEA agent.[77] It certainly seems that way as the DEA paid $26.2 million to criminal informants in 2013.[78]

Sometimes the use of criminal informants is contradictory and perplexing. The *Sun Sentinel* reported about a particularly effective and attractive female criminal informant in Sunrise, FL who earned $806,640 over a five-year period. To the surprise of many, Sunrise Police Department officials paid her exorbitant fees even though she was luring low-level cocaine dealers *from out of state into their town*.[79]

Consider the case of a Dallas criminal informant, Enrique Martinez-Alonso, who fell into his profession after he was arrested for selling one pound of cocaine to two Dallas undercover narcotics officers. Officers Mark Delapaz and Eddie Herrera offered him freedom in exchange for information resulting in two separate convictions. Martinez-Alonso did so and subsequently became the Dallas County Police Department's most prized informant, earning more than $210,000 over a two year period (2000 through 2001). He was paid on a commission basis, of sorts, and his information led to 35 high-profile drug arrests and the seizures of roughly a 1,000 pounds of cocaine and methamphetamine combined.[80]

The Dallas Police Department certainly reveled in his success, but there were a series of red flags involving all of Martinez-Alonso's cases. He never had to pay cash when making purchases for significant amounts of cocaine (anywhere from a few kilos to 50 kilos). The dealers always fronted him the drugs; it was always on credit. Also, officers Delapaz and Herrera never properly surveilled their informant. Therefore, they consistently lacked adequate corroborating evidence, such as video or audio recordings. Plus, all of Martinez-Alonso's traffickers were seemingly working-class Mexican-Americans, such as day laborers, construction workers, auto mechanics, etc. Furthermore, in every case the drugs were usually stashed in unlocked cars.[81]

All of these dealers claimed they were innocent, but one defense attorney, Cynthia Barbare, took her client, Jose Luis Vega, at his word. He claimed to be an honest auto mechanic and the dirt under his fingernails led her to believe him. She also found it odd that a reportedly wealthy drug trafficker lived in such a meager home. Her first line of defense was simply requesting that the drug lab test the veracity of the drugs. None of the prior dealers from Martinez-Alonso's cases had done so because the Dallas County court system unofficially penalized anyone who requested verification from the drug lab with a much lengthier sentence. The courts had only used the officers' field tests. Ultimately, Barbare's gutsy choice paid off and the lab results revealed that the drugs from Vega's case were counterfeit. Delapaz and Herrera had, in fact, confiscated 56 pounds of gypsum, a material for making drywall or pool cue chalk.[82]

This auto mechanic's case led to an inquiry and another conviction was overturned due to counterfeit drugs, again gypsum. In the months following 9/11, the media was notified about the second overturned case. In response, the Dallas Police Chief, Terrell Bolton, assumed the drug cartels were struggling to smuggle real drugs across the border. He publicly warned potential drug users, "Since September 11, you don't know what you're getting out there."[83] However, the chief's suspicions were completely misguided. The FBI investigated the other cases by Delapaz and Herrera and eventually 70 convictions were overturned due to counterfeit drugs![84]

This cunning snitch must have been a criminal mastermind to pull the wool over these officers' eyes, right? Wrong. It was all a fraud and, in fact, the officers kept much of the informant's reward money. Ultimately, four Dallas police officers, along with Martinez-Alonso, were later convicted of this perverse criminal conspiracy. To be brief, Delapaz served the longest sentence, two separate five-year sentences, yet his penalties pale in comparison to an actual drug trafficking charge. After all, these men targeted innocent Mexican-Americans by planting "drugs" in unlocked cars. In one instance, they hired a Mexican day-laborer and provided him with a car to drive to a job site. Upon arrival, the officers arrested him and seized the "drugs" from the trunk of the car.[85] That scenario was the blueprint for most of their busts.

You're probably asking yourself, "What could drive a person to commit such a heinous crime?" This may be the most extreme example of this particular type of corruption, but it demonstrates how the criminal informant process can be perverted with incentives. You can understand how a cop would be *tempted* to right some wrongs by framing known criminals. However, these Mexican-Americans weren't involved in any criminal activity. They were poor, working class immigrants, which made them easy cannon fodder. The police and their snitch knew that merely the testimony of an informant, without any other evidence, would be enough to convict these men.

The counterfeit drug scandal in Dallas began to unravel in 2001 simultaneously while another drug scandal with eerie similarities became national news. In Tulia, TX, a five-hour drive from Dallas, forty-six people were swept up in an early morning drug sting in July of 1999. Thirty-nine of the suspects were black, thus representing roughly 20% of the town's adult black population. The local newspaper in this tiny, predominantly white town labeled the 46 suspects as "garbage" and "scumbags."[86] Also, based upon a tip from the local authorities, reporters captured video footage of the perp walk as they were paraded to jail disheveled in their underwear.

The drug sting was the culmination of an 18-month undercover investigation by a narcotics agent, Tom Coleman. He was hired as part of a federal anti-drug program funded by the U.S. Department of Justice, specifically the Byrne grant.[B] As a result of such a high profile bust, Coleman was recognized as the Texas Lawman of the Year by the state's Attorney General in 1999.[87]

These cases resulted in a combined total of 750 years in prison, based entirely upon Coleman's testimony. Unlike the fake drug cases in Dallas, Coleman was only able to make several small cocaine purchases over the course of 18 months, none for more than five grams. Nevertheless, several of these defendants were labeled as "kingpins" during their trials. In fact, the police didn't even confiscate any drugs or weapons during their high-profile, 46-person raid. Albeit, those paltry amounts may have seemed like grand scale seizures in a town like Tulia, TX within a dry county with no legal alcohol.[88]

[B] As mentioned in the first chapter, the George W. Bush administration made significant cuts to this program. However, the Obama administration reversed those cuts and included $3 billion for anti-drug federal grants in the 2009 stimulus package.

It's not easy to infiltrate the drug dealing culture, particularly in a town of 5,000 people where everyone knows each other. However, Coleman was able to gain the confidence of an elderly black alcoholic, Eliga "Man" Kelly, by plying him with money and booze. In turn, Kelly essentially vouched for Coleman as he introduced him to various people to buy cocaine. However, most of the people he met weren't drug dealers; they were drug users. Also, several of the actual dealers refused to sell to Coleman.[89]

Understandably, the national media focused on the race and prejudicial aspects of the Tulia scandal. However, this scandal also exposed certain aspects of systemic incompetence. Most of these defendants couldn't afford private attorneys and depended upon public defenders. In one case, Joe Moore had two prior convictions and was facing a maximum 90-year sentence for selling three grams of cocaine.

However, Moore begged his public defender to call Eliga Kelly to stand in his defense. Moore claimed that Kelly witnessed him shoo Coleman off of his property. But, for whatever reasons, his public defender never bothered to call Kelly to the stand or even question him privately. As a result of that negligence, Joe Moore was sentenced to 90 years. Unlike most criminal informants, Eliga Kelly refused to lie under oath and in a subsequent trial for a different defendant, the prosecutor called Kelly to the stand. Kelly contradicted Coleman's testimony by naming several defendants, including Joe Moore, who refused to sell drugs to Coleman.[90]

The Tulia scandal wasn't quite as cut and dry as the media presented. Readers want the narrative to be simplified into a format of "good versus bad" or "innocent versus guilty." With this in mind, eight of these defendants admitted they sold drugs to Coleman; one even said that he smoked crack with him. "The people arrested were an easy target and the law enforcement knew no one would stand up for them," said one anonymous Tulia resident.[91] Although many of his clients had disfavored reputations, Jeff Blackburn (a private criminal defense attorney who helped get most of those cases overturned on appeal) was focused on preventing a miscarriage of justice. His clients were entitled to a fair trial based upon the facts of the case, not reputations.

Blackburn was candid that most of his clients were "in the (drug) life at some level" and many of them had prior arrests.[92] Billy Wafer was on probation for possession of marijuana at the time he was accused of selling cocaine to Coleman. "I ain't an angel, but I've never sold drugs," said Wafer.[93] Wafer, unlike most of the other defendants, had his charges dropped because he had a rock solid alibi with time cards from his job. Also, his supervisor testified verifying he was at work when Coleman claimed he sold him cocaine.[94]

Coleman never presented any physical evidence in any of his cases, such as drug money, recorded conversations, fingerprints, surveillance videos, etc. These cases relied merely on his testimony, which was shaky at best. In fact, he contradicted himself several times over the course of various trials. By all apparent indications, Coleman took shortcuts by being fast and loose with the facts. Again, financial incentives shaped this scandal and minorities appeared to be the easiest targets. Coleman apparently felt the pressure to generate some splashy headlines, the kind that keeps the federal grants rolling in.

Despite clear evidence that should have exonerated them, some defendants, such as Ramona Strickland, pled guilty fearing that they wouldn't receive a fair trial. In Strickland's case, Coleman's report noted that she was "about six months pregnant" even though she is a slim woman who wasn't pregnant at the time. Likewise, Cleveland Joe Henderson Jr. pled guilty with the same fears, even though his case file didn't actually name him. Instead, it named his father with a matching picture of his father.[95]

According to Jeff Blackburn's estimation, twelve of his clients weren't in any way involved with drugs.[96] One of those obvious cases was Tonya Michelle White who had no prior record, but her brother was a convicted drug dealer. In fact, her defense attorney found evidence proving that she wasn't even in the state of Texas on the date that Coleman claimed that she sold him drugs. Eventually, Tom Coleman's credibility was dismantled during the appeals process and his award for Texas Lawman of the Year became a national embarrassment. In the end, nearly every case was overturned and Texas Governor, Rick Perry, pardoned 35 individuals; that took place after many had served up to four years in prison.[97]

Coleman's background was riddled with red flags, but the Swisher County (Tulia) officials were seemingly desperate to hire anyone after they received their federal grant money. Coleman had never worked undercover before moving to Tulia. In fact, he had been fired from his prior law enforcement position. His previous supervisor warned Swisher County (Tulia) officials that he might have mental illnesses and was unfit for police work. Also, Coleman left town after racking up nearly $7,000 in debts from various local merchants. He was later arrested for abuse of power and for stealing gas. Those charges took place while he was undercover in Tulia, yet he wasn't suspended from the investigation. Nonetheless, the public defenders didn't present this information to the juries. In the end, Coleman was convicted of perjury and fired from a subsequent position at a different police department after having sex with his criminal informant, a drug-addicted prostitute.[98]

Coleman's credibility was paramount to gaining convictions, yet like the Dallas fake drug cases, there was evidence that he may have tampered with evidence as well. During the appeals process, the state's chemist corroborated a suspicion among some of the defense attorneys; the cocaine Coleman presented as evidence was far weaker than the drug market's basic standard. Therefore, those same attorneys theorized that Coleman was adding significant amounts of baking soda to the cocaine to manufacture more criminal cases and to pocket the police department's buy money in the process. They estimated that as much as $1,800 could have been pilfered by Coleman.[99]

Again, the Tulia scandal illustrated several of the inefficiencies of the criminal justice system and race was definitely a factor in some of these rulings. For instance, Freddie Brookins Jr. had no prior convictions, but he received the maximum penalty for the sale of three grams of cocaine, 20 years in prison. The prosecution seemingly influenced that decision by finding a way to slip into the record that his girlfriend was white.[100] Even though the injustices of these cases were well publicized, these people's reputations are still permanently ruined in the eyes of several locals. "'They made a mistake by letting us out.' You hear a lot of that," says Michelle Lee White, who works as a certified nursing assistant.[101]

Are there any other "Tulias" that haven't been uncovered? The evidence certainly suggests that it is to be very likely. In fact, according to Barbara Markham, a former undercover narcotics officer who is now blackballed due to her reform efforts, "There are whole task forces of Tom Colemans out there."[102]

To wrap up, the media has not provided enough coverage of the racial issues associated with law enforcement. Sure, the evening news shows video footage whenever a police officer shoots a black man, and that has led to some common sense reforms such as body cameras. However, most Americans are unaware of the full range of discrimination that minorities face as a result of the drug war, i.e. harassment, racial profiling, longer prison sentences, etc. Then again, there are many people who aren't necessarily racist, but they are apathetic about the civil rights of minorities because it hasn't directly affected their lives. However, if these people can't find compassion for others, these cynics should, at a minimum, realize that these consequences may eventually "come home to roost" because of the tremendous growing power of the prison industrial complex.

10

"Here in Buenaventura there are invisible borders and nobody crosses them. We've seen people who have crossed them and they haven't returned."

In many ways, the War on Terror and the drug war have merged. During the Reagan administration, drug war and terrorism rhetoric was nearly interchangeable with that of the McCarthy era. "We're in the middle of a major epidemic...Parents have a right to feel terror," said Donald Ian MacDonald, Reagan's top drug advisor.[1] He was referring to drugs. Marlin Fitzwater, Reagan's Press Secretary openly admitted that "everybody wants to out-drug each other in terms of political rhetoric."[2] Both sides of the political aisle engaged in this battle of hyperbole. Liberals like former Rep. Stephen Solarz (D-NY) compared the danger from the cartels to "intercontinental ballistic missiles" and wondered "why we treat (their) threat so lightly?"[3] Likewise, former Rep. Thomas F. Hartnett (R-SC) declared that drugs were a "national security threat...worse than any nuclear warfare or any chemical warfare waged on any battlefield."[4]

The Reagan administration used the term "narco-terrorism" as a propaganda tool. Those officials asserted that drug money from Latin America would be "a source of funds to support insurgencies and subversion."[5] This eased the way for amending the Posse Comitatus Act, which barred the military from domestic law enforcement, to allow military participation in counternarcotics operations.[6] Before then, the "drug war" had only been a war in a figurative sense.

The drug war has enabled the U.S. to unofficially resurrect the Cold War and subtly expand our military presence worldwide without declaring war. The typical American hears the term "foreign aid" and envisions something akin to bags of rice for the malnourished. However, the U.S. foreign aid budget serves as a means to assert our political agenda, and those funds often benefit wealthy countries in the form of military assistance.

One of our more notable "foreign aid" programs involves counternarcotics training for our international allies. That training has often served more subversive purposes. This is particularly evident in Latin America where the U.S. has a long history of supporting brutal dictators. Those dictators have often used military force while acting as puppets for U.S. corporate interests.

The School of the Americas (SOA) in Ft. Benning, GA hosts thousands of foreign military and police forces for counternarcotics training every year. Unfortunately, that's not the only kind of training offered at this school. This program has a particularly brutal reputation; their training manuals advocated the torture, extortion, kidnapping, and execution of civilian targets and their families. Those details were released by the Pentagon in 1996 due to political pressure, but the program remains intact. In a public relations gesture, the name of the School of the Americas was changed. It is now officially the Western Hemisphere Institute for Security Cooperation (WHINSEC).[7]

After leaving the program, these commandos are notorious for targeting liberal activists throughout Latin America. It's quite difficult to assess the amount of bloodshed and suffering at the hands of these men, but thousands of human rights violations can be attributed to various graduates of the program.[8] For example, several SOA graduates led Battalion 316, a CIA-supported death squad that kidnapped, tortured, and murdered hundreds of Hondurans during the 1980s.[9]

Obviously, the U.S. doesn't want to accept responsibility for any of these kinds of atrocities, but there have been eleven Latin American military dictators who graduated from the School of the Americas, including Manuel Noriega.[10] Consequently, many Latin Americans refer to the School of the Americas as the "escuela de golpes" or "school of coups."[11] On a related note, there is a clever adage in Latin America that suggests there has never been a coup in the U.S. because there isn't an American embassy on U.S. soil.[12] Likewise, it would be just as appropriate to say that there has never been a coup in the U.S. because there is no "School of the Latin Americas."

Our tax dollars support certain official causes, such as the drug war and spreading democracy, but those funds often finance underhanded missions. To illustrate, the U.S. government granted over $1 million to groups that were directly involved with the attempted military coup of Hugo Chávez in 2002. That included an organization closely linked to the CIA, the National Endowment for Democracy.[13] Hugo Chávez was labeled by some American media outlets as a dictator, but he was democratically re-elected in 2006 with 63% of the popular vote.[14] That's not to say that Chávez wasn't a tyrant, as he abused his power in numerous ways. But he was popular, especially among poor Venezuelans, for the same economic reasons that he was hated by the elite American business community.

If our government was truly committed to "spreading democracy," then we would have allowed the Venezuelan electorate to vote for their leaders without outside interference. After all, the socialist legacy of Chávez has made matters very clear. His country is now in shambles and crumbling under one of the worst rates of violent crime in the world. Despite controlling the most oil reserves in the world, Venezuela has one of the worst economies with record levels of inflation. Food shortages force Venezuelans to wait in lines that wrap around the block to buy basic goods.[15]

Anyhow, it should be no surprise that the Venezuelan military coup of 2002 was led by a group of SOA graduates.[16] Investigative journalist Greg Palast pointed out the curious timing of that coup, which took place just three days after Saddam Hussein suspended Iraqi oil exports as a form of protest against U.S. support for Israel.[17] Also, Iran and Libya threatened to do the same on the following day. Obviously, the Bush administration officially denied any involvement with the Venezuelan coup, but CIA documents have since been declassified proving that the Bush administration was, at a minimum, aware that the coup would take place.[18]

The Bush administration also admitted that they had met with the leaders of the coup beforehand on several occasions, including a powerful oil executive Pedro Carmona who was temporarily named President of Venezuela.[19] In fact, after Chávez was captured, this oil tycoon was greeted by the U.S. Ambassador and the Bush administration immediately recognized Carmona officially as the President.[A20] All in all, that turned out to be an embarrassing

---

[A] CNN's Otto Neustald, along with other journalists, claimed in the documentary *The War on Democracy* that the coup had been orchestrated through an elaborate ruse. The official version of the story is that Chávez ordered the military to shoot citizens during a protest march. However, Neustald said that he was contacted the night *before* the march and was told about the murders that would happen the next day. Neustald also said that he filmed a video on the evening *before* the coup in which various military leaders *reacted* to the murders and demanded that Chávez resign.

decision because the coup was nullified and Chávez was released after two days of mass protests.

Economic policy is the key factor in determining whether the U.S. government will support a Latin American nation. Many brutal regimes have been provided with financial support, via the drug war, as long as U.S. corporate interests in the region remained unhindered. We've been led to believe that the days of U.S. support for military coups ended with the Cold War, but that isn't the case. Four of the six generals who led the military coup in Honduras in 2009 had trained at the School of the Americas.[21] They ousted the liberal former President Manuel Zelaya, a Hugo Chávez ally.

The military coup was facilitated by the country's handful of ultra-wealthy families who control most of the nation's economy. Within hours after the coup took place, an infamous face from Honduras' past took to the airwaves in support of the coup. Billy Joya, a former leader of the death squad Battalion 316, served as an unofficial spokesman for the interim government.[22] Thousands of Hondurans protested the coup, but they were physically battered by the Honduran military.[23] Thereafter, a highly-questionable election took place months later; Amnesty International and the Center for Economic and Policy Research refused to recognize the authenticity of the election by documenting police violence and voter intimidation.[24]

The actions by the Honduran military were emblematic as the coup launched a dramatic shift towards fascism under the "Pepe" Lobo administration. Honduras had a serious problem with violence and corruption long before Lobo took over, but his response made the problems much worse by militarizing the police force. The former Police Commissioner María Luisa Borjas admitted, "It's scarier to meet up with five police officers on the streets than five gang members."[25] Bear in mind, Honduras has the highest murder rate in the world with gang violence so rampant that tens of thousands of Hondurans have fled to the U.S.[26]

Anyone who publicly opposed corruption, i.e. professors, journalists, and activists, became targets of the Honduran military and police.[27] Record numbers of reporters were murdered during the Lobo administration. Nonetheless, the administration downplayed the political nature of the numerous journalists' deaths and often found drug traffickers to be fine scapegoats for those murders.[28]

A Honduran nightly news broadcast captured the casual attitude of the Honduran elite in regard to murdering independent journalists. News cameras caught a verbal confrontation between a reporter and Adolfo Facussé, a member of Honduras' wealthiest family and a chief facilitator of the coup. After the verbal exchange, cameras filmed one of Facussé's goons asking him if he wanted the reporter killed. Fortunately, the reporter wasn't harmed, but this happened with absolutely no legal repercussions.[29]

The U.S. government certainly had a hand in the violence and chaos that ensued in Honduras. Hillary Clinton's State Department emails were the subject of much media attention during the Presidential campaign of 2016, but the Honduran coup was rarely mentioned. Regardless, her emails demonstrated in no uncertain terms that a military coup took place, yet the administration supported the coup through backchannels.[30] Under U.S. law, our government can't send foreign aid to any country whose leader took power via a military coup, but the administration tiptoed around the issue by never using that exact term. Hence, the U.S. government temporarily suspended those payments for a few months. However, the Obama administration increased their funding for Honduran counternarcotics operations by $85 million within Lobo's first two years.[31] In fact, Obama met with Pepe Lobo and praised his administration for "its commitment to democracy."[32]

Unfortunately, our drug war funding is indirectly empowering various crime bosses. According to the last Minister of Security, various Honduran officials serve as "air traffic controllers" for drug traffickers.[33] In fact, after leaving office in 2014, the former President's son, Fabio Lobo, was charged and later convicted in New York City for conspiring with a Honduran police official to smuggle a multi-ton shipment of cocaine into the U.S.[34]

Our government is aware of this contradiction, but, there are ulterior motives behind how our tax dollars are spent. U.S. embassy officials met with one of the chief facilitators of the Honduran coup, Miguel Facussé (the uncle of the former Honduran President Carlos Flores Facussé), while it was taking place. He was not only instrumental in organizing the coup, but his private jet was even used by Honduran military officials to forcibly transport former President Manuel Zelaya out of the country.[35] Miguel Facussé (now deceased) was one of the country's most powerful businessmen, but *WikiLeaks* released documents in 2011 with communications by

U.S. officials identifying him as a major drug trafficker as early as 2003.[36] Hence, by supporting the coup, the U.S. empowered this drug trafficker, along with others. After all, his private security forces had allegedly worked interchangeably with Honduran paramilitary forces. Numerous reports also linked those private forces with violent land grabs from poor farmers. That land has since been used to produce palm oil for Facussé's biofuel business, an industry notorious for money laundering in Latin America.[37]

The Honduran drug czar, Alfredo Landaverde Hernández, spoke with the *Miami Herald* in 2012 about the rampant corruption involving drug traffickers. He noted that all levels of law enforcement were "rotten to the core."[38] Those comments cost him dearly and two weeks later he was executed by a Honduran police death squad at the behest of a gang leader. As a matter of fact, the previous drug czar had been murdered in the same manner, also at the hands of the police.[39]

Obviously, reforms needed to be made, but the Pepe Lobo administration responded to this scandal, and others, by hiring a new national police chief, Juan Carlos "El Tigre" Bonilla (a former member of a Honduran police death squad and graduate of the School of the Americas). Naturally, the violence escalated with Bonilla at the helm. The *Associated Press* reported in 2013 that police death squads had murdered roughly 150 people in the capital city alone, and with more in the surrounding areas.[40] Unfortunately, most of the American media coverage has centered around the deaths of various gangs members, thereby leaving readers with the impression that the police are extremely "tough on crime." However, the police are working at the bidding of various gangs, i.e. snuffing out competition. In addition, this kind of coverage glosses over the politically motivated violence committed by the police against various activists.

The rule of law further disintegrated in Honduras when President Juan Orlando Hernández was controversially elected in 2013 after campaigning on a law and order ticket with a promise of "a soldier on every corner."[41] President Hernández essentially kept his promise by further militarizing the police force. Despite the atrocious human rights records under President Hernández, the Obama administration continued providing economic assistance to Honduras.

At this point, we have to ask, "Why are we throwing good money after bad?" All things considered, this is an obvious unspoken message to the rest of the world, particularly Latin America. The U.S. will support your regime as long as you're an economic and military ally. These kinds of foreign aid payments illustrate that our government is more concerned with maintaining military alliances than fighting the war on drugs. After all, Soto Cano Air Base in Honduras was a hub of operations during the Iran-Contra affair and it remains a key base for U.S. troops. Furthermore, three more military bases were built in Honduras after the coup.[42]

The President of the United States can't openly announce an initiative to relaunch the Cold War. That would certainly raise red flags internationally and Congress would be reluctant to authorize the spending. However, Congress has already essentially rubber-stamped this kind of program, albeit under the guise of the drug war. The U.S. has spent $20 billion over the last ten years for foreign military aid in Latin America, all specifically to combat illegal drugs. For this reason, there are now 4,000 U.S. troops stationed throughout Latin America.[43]

In an odd way, the drug war also contributes to the economic exploitation of third world nations that are committed by various international organizations, particularly the World Bank. The U.S. is the largest shareholder in the World Bank, which provides low-interest loans to major corporations in third world countries. These loans are supposed to spark economic development in impoverished nations, but, in reality, the World Bank's track record is abysmal. This organization is responsible for some truly corrupt eminent domain land grabs. There is a reoccurring theme with World Bank-funded projects in which the poorest citizens are displaced from their homes. In fact, a report by the *International Consortium of Investigative Journalists* concluded that 3.4 million people had been physically or economically displaced by World Bank-funded projects since 2004.[44]

Sometimes these evacuations are at gunpoint by the military or paramilitary forces that *our* tax dollars support indirectly through the drug war. For instance, the World Bank provided a $30 million loan to Miguel Facussé for his palm oil company, Corporacion Dinant. The World Bank also invested in a Honduran bank, Ficohsa, which had Corporacion Dinant as its third largest client. This all occurred despite widespread international reports of Facussé's alleged drug trafficking and the atrocities committed by his henchmen to obtain land for palm oil production.[45]

Bolivia was the host of a similar example involving the drug war, extreme corporate greed, and international banking organizations. Thousands of Bolivians took to the streets in April of 2000 to protest the privatization of their water supply to a U.S. based corporation, Bechtel. These people were outraged for good reason because Bechtel shamelessly exploited the citizens of one of the poorest countries in the world. Water prices doubled immediately and, in a symbolic gesture, Bolivians were actually expected to pay Bechtel for collecting their own rainwater![46]

The Bolivian government would have never made such a decision on their own, but they were pressured to privatize their water as part of a loan program with the World Bank and the International Monetary Fund (IMF). Under those circumstances, Bechtel received a no-bid, 40-year contract.[47] Unfortunately, this kind of crony capitalism is alive and well within the United States as well. Bechtel's vast political influence may be best demonstrated by the fact that their company made over $1 billion during the Iraq and Afghanistan wars, second only to Halliburton, largely from no-bid contracts.[48]

Even though the water privatization was clearly disastrous, the former Bolivian President Hugo Banzer ordered the police and military to clear the protestors from the streets, resulting in 6 fatalities and 175 people injured.[49] The international media covered the story but seemingly accepted a convenient excuse by President Banzer who blamed the violence from the protest on drug traffickers. The drug issue served as a red herring. Yes, some of the protesters were coca growers, including Evo Morales the future Bolivian president, but those growers don't produce cocaine. Instead, they sell coca leaves which are perfectly legal, healthy, used for tea or chewing, and a part of the local religious tradition. By the way, Coca-Cola still contains a non-narcotic extract from coca leaves.[50]

Unfortunately, the violence from this protest was mild in comparison to Hugo Banzer's reign of terror as a de facto leader. Banzer, another SOA graduate, ruled this country with an iron fist from 1971 to 1978.[51] Hundreds of protesters and suspected enemies of the state were falsely imprisoned, tortured, and murdered. In fact, universities were shut down and foreign nuns and priests with liberal leanings were deported.⁵²

Banzer was overthrown in 1978 and astoundingly elected President of Bolivia in 1997. Naturally, the violent protests of 2000 were predictable, but Banzer's public relations strategy was fairly effective with the international media. But, that shouldn't have been the case. Drug trafficking was an ironic scapegoat considering that Banzer had a regime that was quite cozy with Bolivian drug lords during his military dictatorship. In fact, he would likely have been indicted for many different charges had another military coup, "the cocaine coup," not taken place a few years later.⁵³ (*There will be far more details surrounding that coup in Chapter 12.*)

The American public takes the drug war at face value, thus allowing the U.S. to support key military alliances in Central and South America without much media attention. Again, every year billions of dollars are spent on U.S. military foreign aid throughout Latin America. This serves as an unofficial stimulus package for the military industrial complex. It's quite a racket. We're essentially buying our military and economic allies.

From 2005 to 2009, the government spent more than $3.1 billion on counternarcotics contracts in Latin America. The majority of that funding, $1.8 billion, went to only five contractors: DynCorp, Lockheed Martin, Raytheon, ITT, and ARINC. The top recipient, DynCorp, received $1.1 billion.⁵⁴ That should be no surprise as DynCorp has vast political connections, including former executives George Shultz and Caspar Weinberger who were cabinet members of the Reagan administration. Also, Bill Clinton's former drug czar, Gen. Barry McCaffrey, is one of DynCorp's board members.[B]⁵⁵

Mexico is one of the largest recipients of U.S. military aid for counternarcotics purposes. Since 2008, the U.S. has provided training and equipment through the Mérida Initiative. This is a substantial program that has equipped the Mexican government with $2.3 billion in military aid since 2008.⁵⁶ Again, this policy defies common sense as there is a long history of drug corruption in Mexico. Inserting the Mexican military into the equation only adds another layer of graft.

[B] McCaffrey has subtly influenced public opinion during hundreds of TV appearances as a "military analyst" for NBC News, yet his conflicts of interest have never been disclosed to the audience.

The Mexican government is responsible for thousands of drug arrests, but a study by *NPR* in 2010 demonstrated that the largest cartel, the Sinaloa cartel, had faced some of the lowest arrest figures.[57] It turns out that the American government has some explaining to do as well. Here's where it gets really interesting. An investigation by a Mexican newspaper, *El Universal*, published court documents in 2014 with testimony from a DEA agent and an official from the Department of Justice. Under oath, they verified that high-level U.S. government officials had arranged a deal with the Sinaloa cartel in which the cartel received protection in exchange for information about their rivals. That arrangement officially lasted from 2000 to 2012.[C58]

Suffice it to say, this was an absolute bombshell of a report, but that story was barely covered in the American press. Let's reflect upon that for a moment. The world's most powerful drug cartel cut a deal with the U.S. government and none of the major media outlets found that to be newsworthy?!? This story was also essentially whitewashed when the cartel's leader, Joaquin "El Chapo" Guzman was captured seven weeks later.

The capture of a major drug kingpin is always officially labeled as a "victory in the war on drugs," but business is still conducted behind bars in Mexico. In fact, El Chapo escaped prison in 2015 through a well-publicized dugout tunnel. His breakout wasn't unusual as prison escapes are fairly common for powerful drug traffickers in Mexico. El Chapo had even escaped a maximum security prison previously in 2001. Most reports say that he left in a laundry cart, but according to one of Mexico's most respected journalists Anabel Hernández, author of *Narcoland*, he was escorted out of the prison by government officials while dressed as a cop.[59]

El Chapo has been one of the most wanted fugitives in the world for over a decade, yet the Mexican government twice refused requests by the DEA to capture him. They officially objected to the DEA's requests because only U.S. officials would be allowed to conduct the raid. Nonetheless, the DEA provided Mexican authorities with Guzman's exact location twice, but on both occasions, he was able to successfully flee from attempts to capture

---

[C] Those documents came from the trial of "El Vincentillo" Jesus Vicente Zambada-Niebla, the son of the "logistics coordinator" of the cartel. El Vincentillo alleged that the ATF's scandal with "Operation Fast and Furious" was actually part of that same agreement.

him.[60] Occurrences like that are predictable as corruption has affected the highest levels of the Mexican military, police, and even past Presidents of Mexico.

Like clockwork, violence ensues after the arrest of a cartel leader as a result of a new struggle for power. Nonetheless, the bureaucrats in D.C. don't want to acknowledge that Mexico's drug war-related violence will never subside no matter how many "victories" are declared. Those "victories" don't affect the demand for illegal drugs. Furthermore, the inclusion of the Mexican military hasn't helped reduce the violence either; the death toll has steadily increased since that decision was made. The Mexican government conservatively estimated that there were 47,515 drug war related murders over the five-year period after the military was added to the counternarcotics effort.[61] In comparison, that is over six times the number of American soldiers who have died at war in Iraq and Afghanistan combined.[62] Believe it or not, but the crossfire is common enough that some schools in Mexico conduct "duck and cover" drills.[63]

This increased militarization has turned Mexico into what many would consider a police state. Mexico's National Human Rights Commission has pointed out that reports of human rights violations increased nearly ten-fold since 2006 when the military was introduced into the drug war in Mexico.[64] These violations range from illegal searches, kidnapping, extortion, rape, and murder. Nevertheless, some conservative critics, such as Bill O'Reilly, have claimed that the Mexican government hasn't been aggressive enough and needs to bring about martial law.[65]

Our funding of the drug war also amplifies the Mexican government's lengthy record of violently suppressing political dissidents. The international press detailed a recent example in 2014 in which 43 Mexican college students were killed after they were kidnapped by the local police. Those students were "arrested" but never made it to the local jail. Instead, they were delivered by the police to a drug gang, "Guerreros Unidos."[66] Ironically, those students from Iguala, a town of mostly indigenous groups known for anti-government protests, were en route to the capital city to commemorate Mexico's most infamous incident with political repression: the Tlatelolco massacre of 1968.

In the aftermath of these 43 deaths, the Mexican federal government launched an investigation, but various journalists have documented that Mexican officials clearly censored many details. In fact, in the process of investigating this crime, some other unrelated mass burials were discovered.[67] In addition, independent reporters have found that the Mexican military was in contact with the police force that captured the students. They were also tracking the movements of these students and didn't intervene to save them either.[68] Remember, that's the same government that we're funding in the war on drugs.

The Mexican government shares some enemies with the American government and our military foreign aid has indirectly supported violent attacks of indigenous groups with far-left-leaning ideals. One particular group, the Zapatistas, is a very left-wing group who rebelled against the NAFTA agreement. During that same year, a Mexican paramilitary group massacred 150 people in their region of Chiapas. A similar paramilitary raid in Chiapas followed in 1997 resulting in 45 indigenous people being killed. Most of them were women and children.[69]

To be brief, we know that our foreign military training will result in terrible collateral damage and human rights atrocities. However, it is difficult to name any U.S. government official who will acknowledge that these programs have been counterproductive. Based upon the law of averages, we're arming and training future drug cartel members. Case in point, look at the Zetas, which is arguably the most violent and formally militarized Mexican cartel. The modus operandi of the Zetas is to recruit individuals who have received military training. That includes various members of a right-wing paramilitary group in Guatemala, known as Kaibiles, who were trained at the School of the Americas.[70] As a matter of fact, the majority of the original members of the Zetas graduated from the School of the Americas as well. They were part of a Mexican Special Forces group, GAFE, known for torturing and killing left-wing groups (including the Zapatistas). Approximately 200 out of the 500 members of GAFE eventually transitioned into the Zetas.[71]

The militarization of the drug war in Mexico is a sequel to a policy, unofficially known as "Plan Colombia." With that said, it's important to understand the circumstances of the Colombian civil war before discussing Plan Colombia. Approximately 220,000 people have been killed over the course of this 52-year war. Roughly 80% of those victims were civilians who were caught in the middle of this power struggle between government soldiers, paramilitary groups, and communist rebel forces.[72] Thankfully, in late 2016 the Colombian government signed a peace agreement with their country's most powerful guerrilla organization, the Revolutionary Armed Forces of Colombia (FARC). The plan is for the remaining 7,000 members of the FARC to disarm and form a political party.[73]

As for Plan Colombia, it began in 2000 and it strengthened the Colombian military, which has a long history of corruption with drug trafficking.[74] Plan Colombia is the perfect example of the U.S. government using the pretense of the drug war to advance its economic and military interests. The primary target of Plan Colombia has been the FARC, which is an officially recognized terrorist organization that is responsible for an untold number of human rights violations. Their organization is a symbol for many far-left groups and their group had many ties with Hugo Chávez's regime in Venezuela.[75]

This communist rebel group was not a top Colombian drug trafficking organization when Plan Colombia was first implemented. Their primary source of income has always come from extortion; it's estimated that as many 40,000 people have been kidnapped and held for ransom by the FARC.[76] The FARC had been better-known for "taxing" the drug trade when Plan Colombia first went into effect. To be exact, the Colombian government estimated in 2001 that paramilitary groups controlled 40% of the cocaine exports; whereas, the FARC controlled only 2.5%, according to Peter Dale Scott (a professor at the University of California, Berkeley and author of several books on this topic).[77] However, as the war escalated, the FARC aggressively expanded into production by forcing Colombian farmers to grow cocaine.[78]

Economics and geopolitics were clearly the motivations behind Plan Colombia, not counternarcotics. Our government essentially turned a blind eye to the crimes against humanity committed by right-wing paramilitary groups (also official terrorist organizations), which were linked to the government. As mentioned earlier, Plan Colombia funded a government with numerous links to drug trafficking. Case in point, the Cali cartel operated smoothly like a corporation because of its vast network of bribes to politicians, police, and military officials. In other words, the Cali cartel was firmly entrenched within "the establishment." Thomas A. Constantine, the former DEA administrator, testified during their peak that the Cali cartel was "the most well-organized and well-financed crime organization in history."[79] By 1993, the cartel had roughly one-third of the police and military in Cali, Medellin, and Bogota on their payroll.[80] They even spent $6 million in campaign donations to get their favored presidential candidate, Ernesto Samper, elected in 1994.[81]

Suffice it to say, the counternarcotic goals of Plan Colombia were never achieved, but this initiative has been moderately successful in reducing the terror inflicted upon the country by the FARC. These communist terrorists often attacked corporate interests by bombing oil fields and targeted wealthy citizens for ransom, including a "peace tax" for anyone making over $1 million a year in Colombia.[82] Consequently, U.S. corporate interests in Colombia have benefitted from these anti-drug programs. BP, Exxon, and Occidental lobbied heavily for this program, but Occidental arguably benefited the most from the program.[D83] In 2003 and 2004, Congress set aside $98 million and $110 million respectively in federal funds for a brigade of U.S.-trained Colombian Special Forces to protect Occidental's Caño Limón pipeline.[84] The 480-mile Caño Limón pipeline had been a prime target for the FARC when Plan Colombia was implemented and those conditions remain today as there were 130 violent attacks on the pipeline committed by the FARC and ELN (second largest guerrilla fighting group) in 2014 alone.[85]

Occidental also tried to expand their drilling operations in a section of Colombian rainforests inhabited by a tribal group, the "U'wa." However, the tribe was so adamant in their opposition to the drilling that they threatened to commit mass suicide.[86] Four hundred U'wa tribesmen later held a peaceful demonstration on their land while surrounded by 5,000 Colombian troops.[87] Under normal circumstances, those tribesmen would have been slaughtered by the Colombian military, in conjunction with paramilitary groups. That didn't happen because the U'Wa tribe contacted the media and made their plight an international spectacle. The tribe even sent representatives to Washington, D.C. to lobby against Plan Colombia. They also sent representatives to meet with environmentally minded Al Gore, but despite Gore's reputation, he refused to speak with them.[88] After all, he had a conflict of interest

---

[D] Cigarette maker Philip Morris also heavily lobbied in favor of Plan Colombia. As mentioned in Chapter 3, Philip Morris profited tremendously from Colombian drug cartels.

because his father had been on the board of Occidental a few decades earlier. As a result, Al Gore held a significant position in the company as part of his inherited estate.[E][89]

A number of major international corporations, including BP and Coca-Cola, have been accused of paying Colombian paramilitary groups to terrorize and murder union leaders. The most publicized lawsuit involved Chiquita Banana (formerly United Fruit Company). Court documents showed that Chiquita paid $20,000 to $100,000 a month in extortion payments to the FARC after their factories had been bombed and several of their workers had been either kidnapped or murdered.[90] It's difficult to fault them for making those payments. But, on the other hand, court documents confirmed that $1.7 million was paid over a seven-year period to the main paramilitary group, the United Self-Defense Forces of Colombia (AUC).[91]

Again, Chiquita's representatives claimed that these payments to the AUC were strictly extortionary, but that doesn't stand to reason. Those funds ultimately paid for the murder and intimidation of key union organizers. Indeed, the AUC was responsible for the murder of 668 banana union workers, according to one estimate.[92] Court documents also proved that Chiquita provided access to their private port for arms and drug smuggling, along with arranging the delivery of 3,000 AK-47 assault rifles complete with 5 million rounds of ammunition.[93]

Needless to say, providing such support to a terrorist organization should have been severely punished, but the DOJ

[E] AL Gore also benefitted from a controversial deal in which Occidental acquired Elks Hills Naval Petroleum Reserve. For over a century, Elk Hills (near Bakersfield, CA) had been one of the most sought after properties for oil companies. In fact, the leasing rights to Elk Hills were the source of one of America's most infamous political bribery scandals, the Teapot Dome Scandal of the 1920s. Several oil companies continued lobbying the federal government to purchase Elks Hills Naval Petroleum Reserve for decades, but they were denied due to political pressure. However, Occidental purchased the rights to Elk Hills in 1998 in one of the largest privatizations in U.S. history. There appeared to be conflicts of interest as well. Al Gore's former campaign manager, Tony Coelho, served on the board of directors of ICF Kaiser International, which was in charge of determining the potential environmental damage from drilling in the area. The sale of Elks Hills tripled Occidental's oil reserves and their CEO later described it as their "crown jewel" "of domestic operations."

agreed to a plea bargain in which none of the employees went to prison and the company had to pay a $25 million penalty.[94] Furthermore, the DOJ essentially acted on behalf of the company with their press release by censoring details confirming that Chiquita wasn't merely the victim of extortion.[95] The AUC was doing the work of hitmen for Chiquita and some ex-paramilitary leaders have since come forward with corroborating statements.[96] Subsequently, the National Security Archive accessed a variety of private records via the Freedom of Information Act and published a damaging 5,500-page report, "The Chiquita Papers." The report demonstrated that there was also a quid pro quo agreement, including one internal company memo that mentioned that "we should continue making the payments; we can't get the same level of support from the military."[97]

With these details in the public record, a class action civil suit was filed against Chiquita on behalf of 4,000 victims of the AUC. Nonetheless, the U.S. Supreme Court dismissed the case stating that the court lacked the proper jurisdiction for crimes committed outside of the U.S.[98] By the same token, the Colombian Attorney General attempted to extradite eight Chiquita executives to stand trial within his jurisdiction, but that never happened.[99] Then again, it helps to have friends in high places. Chiquita was represented by none other than Eric Holder two years before he was appointed Attorney General by Barack Obama. As a defense attorney with Covington & Burling, Holder even went over the head of the lead prosecutor and contacted a senior DOJ official to help cement their lenient plea bargain.[F][100]

Keep in mind that the U.S. government went to great lengths to establish this extradition treaty as a means of fighting the drug war.

[F] This was another example of how the revolving door influences the judicial process. Chiquita executives conducted a private meeting in 2003 with Michael Chertoff, then Assistant Attorney General, and other DOJ officials, to notify them of the payments to the AUC. This meeting was arranged by Roderick Hills, a former colleague of Michael Chertoff. Chertoff made it clear that the payments were a crime, but he also suggested that the DOJ might not prosecute the company because they volunteered this information. Subsequently, Chiquita continued making payments to the AUC, but Chertoff never provided clear guidance for how the company should proceed with this matter. Ultimately, that was a critical component of Chiquita's defense. With that in mind, it should be noted that Chertoff was later hired by the law firm that defended Chiquita, Covington & Burling.

However, those officials never envisioned this reverse scenario in which top American businessmen would be complicit with narco-terrorists. Several other U.S. based companies are guilty of aiding and abetting these terrorists, but, fortunately for corporate America, the DOJ will never allow influential American executives to be held accountable for these crimes against humanity.

All in all, Plan Colombia further militarized a nation that has one of the highest rates of murder, kidnapping, and human rights violations. Right-wing paramilitary groups have served as an extension of the Colombian military, thereby giving the government even less accountability. Paramilitary leaders openly told the media that they coordinated with the Colombian military. Some of the founders of the AUC, including Carlos Castaño-Gil, were part of the group known as "Los Pepes" that was funded by the Cali cartel and worked with U.S. intelligence officials to kill Pablo Escobar.[101] Carlos Castaño-Gil, a notorious war criminal, was technically a fugitive at large; yet, he was an accessible, high-profile individual who made many media appearances.[102]

The atrocities committed by the AUC, were well-documented and well-known long before the U.S. started funding Plan Colombia. However, the U.S. waited until *after* Plan Colombia was approved to officially recognize the AUC as a "foreign terrorist organization" on September 10, 2001.[103] President Bush announced in the weeks after 9/11 in his declaration of the "War on Terror" that "any nation that continues to harbor or support terrorism will be regarded by the United States as a hostile regime."[104]

We dumped billions of dollars into Plan Colombia while Álvaro Uribe served as the President of Colombia. This is a very personal issue for Uribe because the FARC murdered his father and he has been linked with some paramilitary atrocities.[105] In fact, Uribe was named by one paramilitary leader as an "integral commander" of their group.[106] These associations between Colombian politicians and paramilitaries are extensive. Fifty-five members of the Colombian Congress have been convicted of criminal charges for their involvement with these paramilitary groups.[107]

The Colombian government has supported terrorism, plain and simple. Albeit, it's not the kind of terrorism that most Americans associate with that term, i.e. radical Muslim extremism. Instead, the Colombian government supports domestic terrorism against their citizens. And that's why it doesn't get much attention in the

American media. However, our tax dollars, in the name of the drug war, indirectly support this terrorism. This fact is exemplified in a report by *Human Rights Watch* in 2015 which concluded that Colombian soldiers executed hundreds and maybe thousands of innocent civilians as "false positives." Colombian soldiers had unofficial body count quotas to measure success in their fight with the FARC. Therefore, many of them murdered innocent people and labeled the victims as enemy combatants.[108] Although that report was released in 2015, documents from the National Security Archive demonstrate that the CIA and high-level U.S. diplomats were aware of these kinds of attacks as early as 1994.[109]

Additionally, our tax dollars have played a part in why there have been an estimated 6.7 million domestic refugees or internally displaced people in Colombia, thirteen percent of the population.[110] To clarify, Colombia has copious supplies of natural resources such as oil, gold, and silver, but there are millions of peasant farmers who live on these valuable plots of real estate. Hence, the paramilitaries are the primary villains behind this displacement. These armed forces, in particular, the AUC, have massacred entire towns and committed unspeakable crimes. They often chose victims at random to be raped or murdered as a terrorist threat. The remaining survivors were evacuated from their homes at gunpoint. Their towns have been bulldozed to make room for industrial production.[111]

A Dutch human rights group, Pax for Peace, issued a report "The Dark Side of Coal," which estimated that 59,000 people were displaced from the region of Cesar, Colombia. Accordingly, two particularly large international corporations, U.S. based Drummond and Swiss-based Glencore, were the two primary beneficiaries.[112] By the same token, many activists have labeled Colombian coltan, a mineral necessary for making cell phones, as "conflict minerals" due to how paramilitary groups control the trade of that resource.[113]

The AUC technically disbanded in 2006, but they split into different organizations that are still active. A leader of one of their splinter groups, Diego Vecino explained, "The AUC is finished as a registered trademark. But paramilitarism goes on."[114] The port city of Buenaventura is now dominated by gangs of former paramilitary members. As a result, approximately 20,000 people fled from the town in 2013 to avoid the threat of violence and extortion. A report by *Human Rights Watch* detailed the atrocities committed by these gangs in an attempt to control a valuable port city for transporting drugs. In fact, so many people have "disappeared" that the gangs built multiple "casas de pique" or "chop-up houses" where their victims were dismembered to hide the evidence.[115] "Many of us have a fear of going out of our own neighborhood. Here in Buenaventura there are invisible borders and nobody crosses them. We've seen people who have crossed them and they haven't returned," said Alvaro Valencia, Buenaventura resident.[116]

Such gruesome reports are barely visible in the U.S. media, which doesn't delve deeply into the indirect consequences of American drug policy. The drug war would have ended a long time ago if the network evening news broadcast covered these matters. Finding out the truth about the drug war can be a horrifying experience. U.S. foreign aid has indirectly supported widespread political chaos and human rights violations by various military and police forces, often suppressing political speech. Our government has a lot of blood on its hands, but most Americans are completely unaware of this fact.

11

"You know, we can milk this thing to 2015."

Unlike some other countries, American political activists don't face the threat of secret police squads that make subversives "disappear." However, political dissent certainly has unofficial penalties in the U.S., notably illegal surveillance by the federal government. In recent years, peaceful protests have been overwhelmed by increasingly militarized police forces, invoking fears of a repetition of the Kent State shootings. As mentioned in the prior chapter, that armament has been provided primarily for the drug war through an army surplus program. Likewise, the Department of Homeland Security (DHS) has a much more generous grant program that provides various police departments nationwide with military equipment to combat potential terrorist attacks. Consequently, those grants incentivize police officials to manufacture artificial terror threats.

Clearly, national security is a top concern for the federal government, but some local police departments want nothing more than their turn at the government teat. Case in point, the Missoula Police Department of Montana applied for a quarter million dollar grant from the DHS to purchase a mobile communications vehicle. They cited the potential threat from the nearby Rainbow Family Festival, a modern day imitation of Woodstock. The city eventually dropped that absurd request because the only danger to the public by this celebration was the threat of semi-nude hippies dancing in the woods. Nonetheless, the DHS has provided $34 billion of military equipment to police departments nationwide since 9/11 for anti-terrorism efforts.[1] In turn, many departments have monitored political activists in hopes of stifling domestic terrorism.

Some of the laws that have been labeled as anti-terrorism efforts have been primarily used for advancing the drug war. Conversely, some espionage programs were initiated as anti-drug initiatives, not for national security. Take for example the DEA's secretive bulk data collection program established in 1992. An investigative journalist, David Burnham (author of *Above the Law: Secret Deals, Political Fixes and Other Misadventures of the U.S. Department of Justice*), detailed this program at that time, but very few in the media showed any interest. Various federal agencies had collected information about targeted groups of American citizens beforehand, but this program was unprecedented by amassing information on a national scale. The DEA's warrantless database collected information on every American household, including marketing mailing lists, credit card information, voting records, income, occupation, etc.[2]

We've become desensitized to these kinds of invasions of privacy, but the DEA's program *preceded* the NSA's program and provided a blueprint that the NSA expanded. The DEA's program collected the data from every international phone call in the U.S. until 2013 when the program was shut down because of the backlash from the Edward Snowden leaks.[3] However, only a few Americans were even aware that the DEA's database existed until *USA Today* reported on this topic in 2015. Nevertheless, the program had no federal oversight and could be secretly reopened at any time.[4]

In the same context as the drug war, Americans have been led to believe this propaganda notion that we must sacrifice our freedoms to prevent another major terrorist attack. Several entertaining movies and TV series, such as "24," have perpetuated that myth. However, Americans have been sold a bill of goods because there were numerous warning signs of the impending terrorist attack, too many to list concisely. The 9/11 attacks didn't result from a lack of information. Instead, it revealed critical flaws within the strategies of our intelligence agencies. These agencies want sole credit for preventing a potential attack as it can lead to vast budget increases and prestige. Accordingly, the FBI and CIA have a well-known rivalry. They routinely withhold information from each other, even though they obviously have the same goals for national security.

There are several heartbreaking examples of how bureaucratic pissing matches resulted in different agencies hoarding information, thereby jeopardizing national security. For instance, two of the 9/11 hijackers, Khalid Almihdhar and Nawaf Alhazmi, were living with an FBI informant in San Diego before the attacks.[5] The CIA had tracked those two terrorists for years. Additionally, a former FBI agent, Mark Rossini, found out that those two known terrorists were on U.S. soil while he was working as part of a CIA-led task force, "the bin Laden Issue Station." Stunningly, the CIA refused to allow him to notify FBI headquarters.[6]

Even if America were to become a complete surveillance state with diminished rights against illegal search and seizure, it wouldn't prevent future terrorist attacks. The PATRIOT Act was presented as the solution to our security problems by making it easier for intelligence agencies to share information. But that is a moot point because these agencies have continued to constrain the flow of information to advance their agendas. Case in point, a Senate investigation report from 2012 found that post 9/11 intelligence information sharing programs have been a complete disaster.

The Department of Homeland Security set up "fusion centers" in every state for various agencies. These fusion centers have had very little oversight and have primarily focused their investigations into ordinary local crime such as drugs, not terrorism. "It's troubling that the very 'fusion' centers that were designed to share information in a post-9/11 world have become part of the problem. Instead of strengthening our counterterrorism efforts, they have too often wasted money and stepped on Americans' civil liberties," said Sen. Tom Coburn (R-OK) who initiated the investigation.[7] Despite their awful track record, these programs have been fairly popular in Congress. The reason being that it's another form of pork barrel spending in which they raise a lot of federal money for their constituents.

These misplaced priorities from counterterrorism authorities seem to have become more severe during the Obama administration. It's unimaginable the ways in which our tax dollars undermine the democratic process. Protesters from the Occupy Wall Street movement have faced absurd levels of surveillance, including undercover officers assigned to infiltrate their gatherings and to entrap them in illegal activities.

The government has set up fusion centers on the fringes of their protests in which multiple agencies, such as the FBI and Department of Homeland Security, team up with private companies to share information about the protestors. Considering the grand scale of this kind of intelligence sharing, it's astounding that the FBI once withheld information about a sniper who plotted to kill specific leaders of the Occupy Houston movement.[8] Kade Crockford of the ACLU astutely pointed out that if the situation were reversed, obviously the FBI would have warned Wall Street bankers if they had been the target of an assassination plot.[9]

The Partnership for Civil Justice Fund (PCJF) uncovered several documents through the Freedom of Information Act and found that the FBI persisted with their investigations even though their agents noted that the Occupy protestors were dedicated to peaceful political speech. The PCJF also published a report finding that the FBI had needlessly spied upon the group, School of the Americas Watch (SOA Watch), for ten years.[10]

SOA Watch was established by a Catholic priest, Father Roy Bourgeois, and is solely focused on peace and human rights. Father Bourgeois founded the group in 1990 after a few horrific, well-known massacres were committed by foreign troops trained at the School of the Americas. In 1980, four U.S. nuns were kidnapped, raped, tortured, and murdered by Salvadoran troops. Also, six Jesuit priests were murdered in 1989 by troops in El Salvador. In both cases, the assassination orders came from the Salvadoran military. In response, SOA Watch gathers every year in Fort Benning, GA in a vigil to honor those victims, among several others. Again, this group is entirely dedicated to ending the bloodshed, yet the FBI monitored this group with the pretext that it could be a terrorist group. Undercover FBI infiltrated their protests even though they reported that there was no threat of violent protest.[11]

Likewise, environmental activists have faced groundless scrutiny. In 2010 the FBI's Inspector General reported that members of Greenpeace had been investigated by the bureau for as many as five years "without adequate basis."[12] Similarly, an investigative journalist, Will Potter, who focuses on environmental and animal rights issues, was subjected to another baseless FBI investigation. He was even threatened with being placed on a domestic terrorist watch list if he refused to spy on various protest groups.[13] The list of these types of abuses goes on and on.[A14]

Using intelligence resources to monitor peaceful protestors, who no one would consider a national security threat, was a source of embarrassment for the FBI in the aftermath of the bombing at the Boston Marathon. The FBI was primarily focused on the Occupy

---

[A] An environmental activist, Eric McDavid, was released early in 2015 after nine years in prison. McDavid had been labeled an "eco-terrorist," but his supporters cleared his name by requesting several documents from his case through Freedom of Information Act requests. They discovered that the FBI not only seemingly entrapped him; the FBI also withheld thousands of documents that would have aided his defense.

protesters in Boston at that time. The FBI went to great lengths to share information about political protesters, yet didn't share information about the Boston Marathon bomber, Tamerlan Tsarnaev. Hindsight is obviously 20/20, but the Russian government had twice contacted the U.S. government to warn about Tsarnaev. The FBI investigated him and didn't believe that he was a threat. In fact, according to the defense attorneys of Dzokhar Tsarnaev, his brother was recruited by the FBI to be an informant. Nonetheless, the FBI didn't share their information with the local Boston police.[15]

The PATRIOT Act was supposed to prevent attacks like this one. In fact, the PATRIOT Act was sold to the public as a purely anti-terrorism measure that was critical to our national security. In actuality, it granted federal law enforcement extremely broad and sweeping powers for prosecuting many crimes that don't involve terrorism, in particular, drug trafficking. With this in mind, many of the provisions of the PATRIOT Act had been rejected by Congress *before* 9/11, but very few people, if anyone, actually read the PATRIOT Act because it had been changed in the middle of the night before voting.[16]

Our justice system is based on a simple constitutional tenet. The government must have a reasonable suspicion to obtain a warrant. In reality, the burden of proof necessary for "reasonable suspicion" is quite slim. After all, no judge in America is going to deny a warrant if there is even the slightest hint of a real security threat. So, in reality, the PATRIOT Act has negated that basic constitutional protection provided by the 4th Amendment. And if you want a clear picture of what the U.S. government prioritizes then look at what they investigate. Eighty-seven percent of the court-approved wiretaps in 2013 were for drug investigations.[17]

The PATRIOT Act included delayed notice, or "sneak and peek," search warrants, which allow federal authorities to enter your home and confiscate property without notifying you for a period of time. In other words, they legalized the "black bag operations" of the past. You would have to assume that burglars raided your home. Meanwhile, if the authorities are able to obtain probable cause evidence with a sneak and peek warrant, they can return with a traditional search warrant.[18] A report showed that 763 delayed notice search warrants were issued in 2008, along with 528 extensions of warrants. Less than 1% (5 out of 1,291) were issued for terrorism cases, whereas 65% (843 out of 1,291) were for drug cases.[19]

The PATRIOT Act created the legal justification for unprecedented surveillance of American citizens. The private records of American citizens (medical, employment, library, financial, telephone, and internet activity) are now available to federal authorities for investigation without reasonable cause.[20] The PATRIOT Act also made it easier for the government to access citizens' personal information through private third party companies. As a result, there are now 52 different federal agencies that purchase American citizens' private information from data mining companies, such as Acxiom and LexisNexis.[21]

We should all have a healthy fear of domestic surveillance because some of the most innocuous activities can be charged as crimes. There is a good reason for the adage "a prosecutor can indict a ham sandwich." A litany of obscure and inane laws exist which can trap even the most virtuous individual if every detail of his life is held up to a magnifying glass. It's naive to disregard intrusions upon civil rights because of the belief that "if you have nothing to hide, then you have nothing to worry about." The implication is that the *only* danger from illegal government surveillance is having your embarrassing details aired publicly.[B][22]

Nonetheless, the average person is willing to look the other way at civil liberties violations *if* law enforcement is disrupting legitimate threats to national security, but not petty crimes. It's a terrible precedent when the government's vast spying technology crosses over into routine law enforcement. We're all aware that, if unchecked, the federal government could establish a totalitarian state. The possibility of "Big Brother" is always presented as a hypothetical scenario whenever the subject of federal government domestic spying is broached. However, we are already beyond the

---

[B] The threat of public smearing is also a valid one as one of Edward Snowden's leaks documented that the NSA monitored the online pornography usage of specific Muslim public figures. The agency knew that those Muslims weren't involved in any kind of terrorist plots, but that information was obviously obtained for potentially smearing them in the future. Likewise, Juan Cole, a professor at the University of Michigan and public critic of the Iraq War, had become a major thorn in the side of the Bush administration. Glenn L. Carle, one former senior CIA officer, has alleged that the Bush White House had twice asked CIA officers to collect embarrassing information on Cole.

hypothetical stage and have entered into the preliminary stage of a technological police state.

That statement may appear to be outrageous, but consider the fact that the NSA is supposed to focus only on matters of national security, hence the name "National Security Agency." Nor is the agency allowed to spy on American citizens, but an investigative report by *Reuters* documented that the NSA has for decades been coordinating with U.S. law enforcement agencies to prosecute crimes that have nothing to do with national security. Time and time again, the drug war is the justification for implementing new law enforcement methods that stretch the limits of the Constitution and the investigation by *Reuters* found evidence of clear constitutional violations. The NSA shares information from their massive database with the Special Operations Division of the DEA and they distribute tips nationwide via a database that is available to thousands of federal, state, and local law enforcement officials.[23]

One federal official explained that the program provides police with a vehicle description, along with a time and place to pull over the suspect. The police simply need to find any reason to make a traffic stop and have a drug sniffing dog waiting nearby.[24] Prosecutors claim that they don't have to disclose the real reason for the traffic stop due to a process known as "parallel construction." To put it another way, this process allows law enforcement authorities to conceal when the investigation actually began.[25]

It wouldn't take a talented lawyer to prove that this procedure is unconstitutional in multiple instances, including the right to discovery of evidence and the illegal manner in which the NSA generally obtains their information. Nonetheless, the DEA stands behind the practice they've been using since the 1990s.[26] Sadly enough, the government still can't stop the flow of drugs into this country even with such heavy-handed programs in place.

The federal government eventually will have the technological capability to create a completely Orwellian police state. The question is whether the American public will allow the government to do so. That obviously hasn't happened yet; the government is only using NSA domestic spying programs for the drug war, as far as we know. However, parallel construction represents the first step towards a complete police state. Where does that slippery slope lead? What other law enforcement agencies will have access to the NSA's database? At what point is enough really enough? If more

Americans allow parallel construction to remain in place, it could easily serve as a precedent for a nightmarish scenario.

We need true leadership to make real changes and Barack Obama certainly campaigned on that promise. After all, Obama taught constitutional law courses at the University of Chicago and openly addressed some of these issues before entering the White House. In one of his speeches on the Senate floor in 2005, he criticized the PATRIOT Act as "legislation that puts our own Justice Department above the law. When National Security Letters are issued, they allow federal agents to conduct any search on any American, no matter how extensive or wide-ranging, without ever going before a judge to prove that the search is necessary. They simply need a sign-off from a local FBI official. That's all."[27]

Those words were quite prophetic. Two years later, the Inspector General of the Department of Justice (DOJ) issued a report stating that the FBI violated the law, as many as 3,000 times, with their use of "national security letters." Various companies received "national security letters" demanding the private information of American citizens and the Inspector General stated that up to 600 of those violations could have been "cases of serious misconduct."[28]

For whatever reasons, the constitutionalist rhetoric from Obama as a presidential candidate didn't transition into actions as President. Case in point, Obama did an about face in 2011 when he signed a four-year extension of the PATRIOT Act, a much longer extension than the proposal that had been put in place by the House Republicans.[29] That's particularly notable as some federal courts have ruled various provisions of the PATRIOT Act to be unconstitutional.

In recent years, technology has enabled federal authorities to gain unprecedented levels of private access; yet, very few checks and balances, along with proper oversight standards, have been established. In other words, there's no one watching the watchers. Plus, Congress has been asleep at the wheel. David M. Walker, the former head of the GAO, testified before Congress in 2008 that they don't use their office at the NSA because "we are not getting any requests (from Congress). So I do not want to have people sitting out there twiddling their thumbs."[30]

The Department of Justice has the unofficial duty to serve as a watchdog preventing federal abuses of power, but the DOJ hasn't even been able to monitor its own officials properly. The DOJ's

Inspector General issued a report in 2010 relating to allegations of civil liberties abuses by members of the DOJ. There were 1,997 complaints for the first half of the year, but only *one* had been fully investigated![31] In addition to owning that sketchy track record, the DOJ is also in the process of expanding upon a program that sparks obvious civil liberties concerns. The DOJ has a license plate data collection program that spans the nation. This program tracks license plates in real time and stores the data. It would be much less controversial if the program only tracked known fugitives at large, but it stores the records of everyone's traffic patterns. Again, this program likely would never have been implemented without justification from the drug war. It was originally a DEA program in states along the national border. However, the DOJ has expanded the program and uses the information to prosecute all sorts of crimes.[32]

Civil liberties violations aren't anything new as the history of abuses by American intelligence agencies spans many decades. LBJ initiated a CIA program in 1967, Operation CHAOS, which spied on American citizens in violation of the agency's mandate against domestic espionage. Tom Charles Huston, a Nixon administration official, later testified before Congress about the "mission creep" that occurs with these kinds of programs. Operation CHAOS eventually swelled to a database of 300,000 American citizens and organizations.[33]

Huston explained that these initiatives begin with honest intentions to focus on "the kid with a bomb." Naturally, these programs then proceed to surveil "the kid with a picket sign" and then "the kid with the bumper sticker of the opposing candidate. And you just keep moving down the line."[34] Anyhow, pressure within the agency eventually forced the former CIA Director, Richard Helms, to end the program, but in name only. Helms only changed the label of their targets from "political dissident" to "international terrorist."[35] Can you imagine if they had had the technology of today?

Former Sen. Frank Church (D-ID) conducted the most thoroughly documented investigation of the CIA, FBI, and NSA in 1975. The Church Committee exposed that the intelligence agencies had abused their power for decades by targeting law abiding American citizens who were generally activists for civil rights, women's rights, peace, free speech, Native Americans, political dissent, free press, labor, privacy, etc. One of those targets was Senator Church himself.[36] These agencies recklessly used methods such as illegal wiretaps, mail tampering, listening devices, break-ins, burglaries, manufacturing evidence, etc. All of those tactics and more were hallmarks of the FBI's infamous COINTELPRO program that was also detailed by the Church Committee.[37] As a result of the Church Committee's findings, Congress passed the Foreign Intelligence Surveillance Act (FISA) of 1978. This law established a secret independent court responsible for approving federal warrants to wiretap American citizens.[38]

The FISA court was supposed to nip abuses in the bud, but the problem has become much worse as technology has increased, thereby providing the government with more access to information. In fact, the FISA court serves as the federal government's rubber stamp; the number of applications for FISA increases every year and less than 1% are rejected.[39] Considering that lax oversight, it makes the actions by George W. Bush all the more appalling. He gave a secret presidential order in 2002, without Congressional approval, for the NSA to bypass the FISA courts to monitor American citizens illegally.[40] Under federal law, each warrantless wiretap is punishable as a felony offense with five years in prison and a $10,000 fine, but George Bush won't ever be donning a federal prison jumpsuit.[41]

The New York Times exposed that scandal in 2005 resulting in 30 lawsuits against all of the major telecommunications companies for cooperating with the NSA.[42] As a Senator, Barack Obama promised to filibuster an amendment to the FISA bill that granted immunity to the telecommunications companies. "There is no reason why telephone companies should be given blanket immunity to cover violations of the rights of the American people," he said.[43] However, after winning the Democratic Nomination in 2008 and with his eyes on the prize, Sen. Obama protected those companies by voting in favor of that same FISA amendment.[44]

None of the major communications companies have faced any criminal penalties for providing the NSA with full access to their customers' records without FISA approval. Remarkably, there was only one executive who refused to comply with the NSA's requests, Qwest's former CEO Joseph Nacchio. His decision to block the NSA was a bold one as Qwest had previously received a number of lucrative government contracts. What's particularly remarkable is that the only CEO to take a moral stand to protect American's right to privacy was someone whose name is far from synonymous with integrity. After all, the SEC charged Qwest with committing slightly over $4 billion worth of accounting fraud two years after Nacchio "resigned" from the company.[45] Nacchio was later convicted on charges of insider trading and has since claimed that his case was in retaliation for obstructing the NSA. He wasn't even allowed to mention his dispute with the NSA during his trial because that information was classified at that time.[46]

It is important to note that, contrary to popular opinion, the NSA's massive domestic data collection programs weren't in reaction to 9/11. Nacchio turned down the NSA's requests *before* 9/11.[47] These programs have since resulted in huge profits for the communications companies. To be exact, the NSA paid $278 million in 2013 to various communications companies.[48] The extent and endless array of abuses by NSA's programs are simply mind boggling.

Edward Snowden, as a former employee of Booz Allen Hamilton (a private contractor for the NSA), has been the primary whistleblower revealing classified information to the media. The first major revelation was about a program named PRISM in which the FISA court had ordered Verizon to hand over the daily phone logs for millions of their American customers. Rep. Loretta Sanchez (D-CA) and other lawmakers met with counterterrorism officials after the Verizon data collection was leaked to the media. She said, "I can't speak to what we learned in there…but I will tell you that I believe it's the tip of the iceberg."[49]

Snowden has been the source of numerous other classified leaks demonstrating that the NSA is collecting all imaginable electronic communications and designing entirely new invasive methods for domestic surveillance. Some examples defy the imagination when learning that the NSA literally developed programs to spy on Americans through their Xbox video game systems, along with other online video games such as World of Warcraft.[50]

Outrageous leaks of this kind will only continue to surface, yet most of the public wants to generalize these breaches along party lines. Several conservatives weren't bothered by the Bush administration's wiretaps, but they suddenly became vocal critics of NSA after Obama entered the White House. Conversely, many liberals were outraged with the NSA during the Bush administration, but they were the first to defend their tactics after Obama took office. Notably, Bill Maher said that he didn't have a problem with these programs as long as Obama was in office.[51]

Whether you approve of Snowden's actions or not, his leaks led Congress to make symbolic reforms of the bulk data collection programs. The rallies for reform were led by a memorable filibuster by Sen. Rand Paul (R-KY) and Sen. Ron Wyden (D-OR). The media overstated that Congress had allowed the PATRIOT ACT to expire. It was technically correct, but in its place Congress passed the USA Freedom Act, which was essentially the same program. The difference is that now the data from one of the NSA's numerous programs is stored by the telecommunications companies, not the NSA. And the NSA has full access to that information through the FISA court. Former NSA director Gen. Michael Hayden was admittedly surprised that Congress didn't make stronger reforms after two years of public relations battles due to the Snowden leaks. "This is it after two years? Cool," said Hayden during an interview with *The Wall Street Journal*. He then laughed and gave a thumbs up to the audience.[52]

"Spying on you won't help the government find a terrorist. It's a waste of resources, a waste of effort that also violates our rights," says Michael German, a former FBI agent with 16 years of total experience (12 with domestic terrorism).[53] Michael German has actual hands-on experience with preventing terrorist attacks. He twice infiltrated white supremacist militia groups and brought them to justice before they could harm anyone. Mike German points out that he was successful by using legal law enforcement methods and by following actual leads, rather than blanket surveillance. He should be a poster child for the FBI, but he resigned from his position in disgust with the bureau. According to German, in 2002 the FBI botched an opportunity to properly investigate a potential Islamic terrorist group and covered their tracks by falsifying documents afterward in a face-saving gesture.[54]

America is facing a verifiable terrorism threat, but our government has, at times, manipulated our fears for political and bureaucratic purposes. As an illustration, the former Secretary of Homeland Security, Tom Ridge, said that he was pressured by the Bush administration to raise terror alert levels to help Bush's re-election campaign in 2004.[55] Trevor Aaronson, author of *The Terror Factory: Inside the FBI's Manufactured War on Terrorism*, examined every alleged terrorist case that was tried in the ten years following 9/11. Out of 508 defendants, Aaronson determined that less than five of them involved actual terrorists posing an immediate danger.[56] That may seem unfathomable because there are constant news stories about how the FBI has foiled another terrorist plot, but those reports rarely mention that these "plots" were created by the federal government in the first place.

The FBI has embarked upon a new strategy for combating terrorism that generates electrifying headlines but falls short of actually preventing attacks. The FBI now conducts terrorism sting operations with a vast network of over 15,000 undercover informants on their payroll. The bureau's new model is a facsimile of the drug war's failed arrangement with criminal informants. Yes, criminal informants can generate a high number of convictions, but these aren't always the most reliable people. Remember, the example in Uniontown, AL with a 150-kilo conspiracy case that didn't retrieve any drugs?

The FBI's first terrorism case that was based primarily upon information from a criminal informant took place just six days after 9/11 with the "Detroit sleeper cell." The government's physical evidence was primarily a nondescript handwritten doodle and videos from a group of four Arab immigrants on vacation in Las Vegas and New York. The prosecution claimed those videos were evidence of "casing" a terror plot. The prosecution relied mainly upon a convicted scam artist/jailhouse snitch who agreed to testify that the group had planned a terrorist attack. However, the prosecution withheld evidence from the defense proving that the snitch openly bragged among his cellmates that he had fooled the FBI. Eventually, after serving three years in prison, the judge overturned their convictions for terrorism.[57]

The FBI's network of criminal informants typically have no connections to terrorism and many of them are drug snitches working undercover in exchange for the government waiving their sentences.[C] In some cases, the FBI has coerced these informants with threats of being placed on the government's no-fly list.[58] As with the drug war, these criminal informants have strong incentives to manufacture cases, the truth be damned. If not, they will be

---

[C] In one case, the FBI captured recordings of their informant shoplifting and purchasing heroin while he was working undercover. That informant had two prior convictions for drug trafficking along with robbery.

removed from the payroll and return to prison. Consequently, they typically entrap people who have no means or motives to commit an act of terrorism. These so-called "domestic terrorists" are often mentally ill or easily manipulated. Also, many of them agreed to participate in these "plots" because they had been offered substantial amounts of money. These "terrorists" rarely have any connections with actual terrorists, nor do they have the ability to commit a terrorist act.[59]

The "Liberty City Seven" case served as a prototype for these terrorism sting operations. There is always a vast divide between the information in the initial news reports and the final reports after the government discloses all of the details in court. As you may recall, the Liberty City Seven was a group of young black men from one of Miami's poorest areas, Liberty City. They were approached by an undercover FBI criminal informant, Abbas al-Saidi, who began his career as a drug snitch at the age of 16 and then transitioned into terrorism stings.[60]

He recruited the group to blow up the Sears Tower by offering to pay them $50,000, but there was no evidence to suggest that they would actually carry out "the plot." These young men had absolutely no affiliation with a terrorist organization nor did they have any weapons. All indications lead to the conclusion that this group was simply trying to hustle someone who turned out to be an undercover informant. The defendants were "homeless types" who "couldn't find their way down the end of the street," according to James J. Wedick, former FBI supervisory agent and consultant for the defense.[61]

Mike German has bravely acted as an FBI whistleblower and notes the importance of more protections for whistleblowers, particularly intelligence officers. After all, these federal agencies can overrule someone's rights from the Whistleblower Protection Act in cases of national security. Again, the Department of Justice is supposed to defend against constitutional abuses, but that hasn't been the case. Instead, the DOJ has prosecuted whistleblowers under the Espionage Act. The Espionage Act had historically only been reserved for actual traitors, but the Nixon administration changed the nature of the law and established a new precedent by targeting Daniel Ellsberg who released the "Pentagon Papers."[D][62]

[D] Nixon's operatives broke into the office of Ellsberg's therapist in hopes of finding embarrassing material. The burglars trashed the building in hopes of

Obama campaigned on a platform of reform and transparency, but his administration has treated credible whistleblowers with hostility. The Obama administration has prosecuted government whistleblowers (who leaked information to the press) with the Espionage Act eight times, more than every other administration combined throughout American history.[63]

The DOJ certainly values snitches within the criminal justice system, but it disdains them within the federal ranks. Some of these prosecutions have been blatant gestures to suppress dissent. Look no further than former CIA official John Kiriakou who was charged with violating the Espionage Act by revealing the identities of CIA operatives who led their secretive torture program. Those operatives also destroyed evidence of the program, but no one from the torture program was prosecuted. Instead, Kiriakou was sentenced to 30 months in prison.[64]

These prosecutions are indeed disingenuous considering that high-level government officials reveal sensitive information to the press on a daily basis. The difference is that the DOJ selectively prosecutes people who leak information that can be embarrassing to the government. Take David Petraeus, the former general and CIA director, for example. He was able to plead guilty to a simple misdemeanor charge after he provided his mistress/biographer with classified materials.[65] In contrast, the FBI investigated Michael Hastings for his "controversial reporting." Hastings had written many critical pieces about high-level military officials, including Petraeus, and the FBI's investigation continued even after Hastings' death.[66]

The federal government often muzzles whistleblowers even though every federal government worker has a legal obligation to abide by an oath to defend the Constitution. Typically, the formal process for reporting fraud, waste, or abuse is complicated and inept, so contacting the media has become a last resort. Case in point, a group of high-ranking NSA officials, Thomas Drake, Kirk Weibe, Bill Binney, and Ed Loomis went through the proper channels to report that the agency was illegally spying on Americans.[E] To no avail, they contacted Congress, the Chief Justice of the Supreme

---

making their entry appear like drug addicts barged in to steal prescription medications.

[E] Their group included a staff member of the House Intelligence Committee, Diane Roark.

Court, the Inspector General Office of the NSA, and the Department of Defense's Inspector General.[67]

Let's examine why these NSA officials needed to take such extreme measures. First of all, Bill Binney and Ed Loomis developed a program known as "Thin Thread" that was a perfect marriage of protecting national security and privacy. They developed an algorithm for pinpointing potential terrorist activity and their program was encrypted to keep everyone's personal information anonymous. No one could unlock that information unless the system detected suspicious activity. If so, the NSA still had to apply for a warrant. Otherwise, all unnecessary data was purged from the system after a short period of time. That eliminated clutter for security analysts by focusing solely on pertinent threats. Within a few months of Thin Thread's implementation, it helped the NSA track down key members of the Al Qaeda network.[68] To state the obvious, these officials should have been recognized as heroes, but the treatment they received afterward couldn't have been more to the contrary.

Thin Thread was fully operational by January of 2001 with a cost of only $3 million to develop, but the program was shut down by the former director of the NSA, Michael Hayden. Instead, Hayden lobbied Congress for a much bulkier program known as "Trailblazer," which removed all of the privacy protections. Trailblazer also needed much more time for completion and required a budget of $3-4 billion.

William Binney insists that NSA officials were concerned that the federal money spigot would be pulled if they supported Thin Thread. Greed was clearly one of the motivations and resulted in a disastrous decision from the agency. "Careers are built on projects and programs. The bigger, the better their career," added one of his fellow whistleblowers Thomas Drake during an interview with *60 Minutes*.[69] According to his fellow whistleblower Kirk Weibe, one of Trailblazer's project leaders said, "You know, we can milk this thing to 2015."[70]

Bill Binney, Kirk Weibe, and Ed Loomis resigned from the agency soon after 9/11 in disgust. "They traded the security of the people of the United States for money," says Binney.[71] Those three men were convinced that Thin Thread would have prevented the attacks. Thomas Drake quickly came to the same conclusion even though his first day of work at the NSA was coincidentally on

September 11, 2001. Although new to the job, he immediately observed systemic abuses of power that made "the Nixon administration and that whole era look like pikers."[72]

As stated earlier, this group of whistleblowers reported these issues through the proper channels. Ed Loomis said, "I didn't view it as whistleblowing when you filed a formal government-authorized complaint about government wrongdoing…That was following a government directive."[73] They were simply doing their patriotic duty by reporting this misconduct, yet the government used the PATRIOT Act in an attempt to pin a crime on them.[74] The FBI raided their homes in 2007, but no formal charges were filed. It was simply an intimidation tactic by the Bush administration.

Thomas Drake faced the worst consequences from his actions as a whistleblower because he leaked information to the press, unlike his colleagues. Mind you, some NSA whistleblowers had contacted the media during the Bush administration, but none of them faced the level of unprecedented retribution that occurred during the Obama administration. Drake never provided any classified information to the media, but he was charged in 2010 with violating the Espionage Act and faced 35 years in prison.

He refused to plead guilty and the government's case against him fell flat. After all, federal authorities claimed that the documents seized at Drake's home were classified, but those documents were unclassified and available in the public domain. In retribution, the government later reclassified those documents after they were seized from Drake. "It's like framing him, and 'We're going to frame you after the fact,'" said Bill Binney.[75] In a face-saving gesture, the prosecutors agreed to no prison time in exchange for Drake pleading guilty to the misdemeanor of misusing the agency's computer system.[76] Nonetheless, it was a "chilling message" to Drake and a clear warning to future whistleblowers.[77]

Edward Snowden received that message loud and clear. Thomas Drake, along with everyone else from his group of whistleblowers, asserts that the actions by Snowden were appropriate because the formal reporting process is grossly corrupt. On the other hand, George Ellard, the NSA's Inspector General, disagreed with that notion. "Snowden could've come to me," said Ellard in 2014. "In fact, he would have been given some protections."[78] Then again, Ellard was terminated two years later by the NSA for retaliating against another whistleblower.[79]

Russell Tice is another former NSA official who exhausted the formal reporting process and found it to be a farce. "Going to the Inspector General's office at NSA is a joke," says Tice. Russell Tice was one of the sources for *The New York Times* piece on the Bush administration's warrantless wiretaps, and he was fired as a result of his actions. "I went to the DODIG (Department of Defense's Inspector General). That was a joke."[80] He pointed out that going to Congress "was a joke" as well because they notified his superiors at the NSA while the agency was trying to build a criminal case against him.[81]

Tice never provided classified information to the media, unlike Snowden, but he has warned the public for many years about the "light police state" imposed by the NSA. "I sort of consider this a light police state because they're hiding the fact that it is a police state," says Tice.[82] He observed the NSA conduct illegal surveillance on a number of government officials, such as members of Congress. That included Barack Obama in the summer of 2004 before he became a U.S. Senator. In addition, former FISA court judges, U.S. Supreme Court justices, State Department officials, top military generals, among others were targeted, according to Tice.[83] It is easy to speculate that the individuals seeking that information hoped to find the kind of dirt for blackmail reminiscent of the J. Edgar Hoover era.

In contrast, the NSA, along with Barack Obama, has defended their programs, insisting that abuses are isolated incidents. "Nobody is listening to your calls...They are not looking at people's names, and they're not looking at content. But by sifting through this so-called metadata, they may identify potential leads with respect to folks who might engage in terrorism," says Obama.[84] In other words, the government insists that the NSA is limited to collecting all of the information about electronic communications, except the content of those messages.

Even if that were true, collecting and storing metadata alone is still terribly intrusive. In fact, the former head of NSA Michael Hayden admitted that metadata tells "everything" about someone. Essentially, the content of those communications is merely icing on the cake. "We kill people (terrorists) based on metadata. But that's not what we do with this metadata," said Hayden, in reference to domestic metadata collection.[85]

In contrast, top NSA whistleblowers insist that they're collecting much more than metadata. Russell Tice says that NSA "continues to lie about the full capability" of their programs. He added that their surveillance is at "the Orwellian scale...NSA is literally tapping every digital communication in this country. Content, not just the metadata, the content."[86] Bill Binney agrees that they're collecting much more than metadata. During an appearance on *Real Time with Bill Maher*, he noted that the entire world's metadata could be stored in the same amount of space used for that show's stage.[87] That makes one wonder just what the NSA has in store at their new, largest of its kind $2 billion data center in Bluffdale, UT. It's a one million square foot facility, roughly the size of 17 football fields.[88]

Bill Binney says "the intelligence community is bamboozling Congress...You can have both (civil liberties and national security)." He estimates that the data from "99.99% of all (domestic) communications" is useless to the NSA, should be erased, and is completely unrelated to terrorism.[89] The message from these whistleblowers carries tremendous credibility as they've sacrificed lucrative, prestigious careers, along with risking their reputations and freedom. On the other hand, the government has demonstrated that these top secret programs are untrustworthy. After all, senior NSA officials have lied under oath to Congress without any penalties. That's particularly disturbing and perplexing when, in comparison, the federal government found it necessary to charge Roger Clemens for lying about steroids to Congress. Likewise, Barry Bonds faced a ten-year investigation for allegedly perjuring himself regarding steroid use.[90]

In 2013, Sen. Ron Wyden (D-OR) asked a very straightforward question to the Director of National Intelligence, James Clapper. In fact, he disclosed the question to Clapper with two days' notice before he was due to testify before Congress. Wyden asked, "(Does) the NSA collect any type of data at all on millions of Americans." While under oath, Clapper replied, "No, not wittingly." That was a patently false claim and he later recanted in an interview. He thought Wyden asked a loaded question or a "when are you going to start/stop beating your wife kind of question...So I responded in what I thought was the most truthful, or least untruthful, manner by saying 'no.'"[91]

The NSA's Director Gen. Keith Alexander also lied to Congress stating that their telephone surveillance programs had prevented 54 terrorist plots. He later admitted those statistics weren't accurate after Sen. Patrick Leahy (D-VT) confronted him. Alexander then retreated by suggesting that one or maybe two had been thwarted through those programs.[92] Even that appears to be a lie as well. The NSA's bulk data collection programs haven't prevented *a single terrorist plot*, according to a group of thoroughly vetted Senators, Ron Wyden (D-OR), Mark Udall (D-CO), and Martin Heinrich (D-NM). Those three Senators are members of the Senate Intelligence Committee, meaning they have higher security clearances than nearly everyone in Congress. That group has extensively reviewed these programs and found "no evidence that the bulk collection of Americans' phone records has provided any intelligence of value that could not have been gathered through less intrusive means."[93]

Why is the intelligence community fighting tooth-and-nail to defend these programs that clearly violate the Constitution and are poor national defense strategies? It all comes down to money and power. Simply put, counterterrorism has become a racket. Remember, a colleague of NSA whistleblower Kirk Weibe wanted to "milk" the Trailblazer program until 2015. Likewise, Thomas Drake heard his supervisor refer to 9/11 as a "gift" to the NSA.[94] That was an accurate assessment as the U.S. government intelligence agencies' combined budgets have increased by 2150% since 9/11, for a total budget of $75 billion annually.[95] There are now over 4.2 million people with clearances for classified government information with over a million holding top secret clearances. A community with such size and powerful infrastructure will eat their young to justify their place in the bureaucracy.[96]

Intimidation tactics have kept the public in the dark as to the full extent of the NSA's surveillance. There is cause for concern even if the courts order the NSA to shut down specific programs. The U.S. participates in a much larger program, informally known as "the Five Eyes," in which Canada, Britain, Australia, and New Zealand share their intelligence information. Sharing intelligence sounds like a good idea, but there is a downside. It allows each nation to bypass its domestic surveillance laws and makes oversight a moot point. In other words, the U.S. can't spy on its citizens, but the governments of Canada, Britain, Australia, and New Zealand can spy on Americans. Accordingly, those agencies share that information with the U.S government and vice versa.

The size and scale of intelligence sharing program can't be understated. Mike Frost, a former intelligence agent at the CSE (the Canadian equivalent of the NSA), told *60 Minutes* in 2000 about a program, Echelon, which monitors every bit of electronic data across "every square inch" of the world. Frost told *60 Minutes* about an example in which a woman told her friend on the phone that her son had "really bombed last night" at his school play. The agent who monitored the data decided to err on the side of caution and placed her on a terrorist watch list.[97]

Examples like that partially explain how there were 875,000 people officially listed in the U.S. database of suspected terrorists in 2007. Then, the *Associated Press* reported in 2014 that another 1.5 million names had been added over the past five years.[98] There clearly cannot be a credible verification process in place because only one percent of the submitted names are eventually removed from the list. *CNN* reporter Drew Griffin's name was put on the No-Fly-List just two months after conducting an investigation of the TSA. That clearly appeared to be an act of retribution and Rep. Sheila Jackson Lee (D-TX) publicly called for an investigation. She also found that one of her colleagues, John Lewis (D-GA) was on the No-Fly-List and had been unable to get his name removed from it.[99]

We need to heed the warnings from the few within the intelligence community who have been brave enough to inform the public about the dangers of these programs. Suzanne Spaulding, former CIA Senior Attorney, offered some cautionary advice during an interview with *PBS Frontline*. She asserted that these programs inherently have flaws; therefore, you should be concerned even though you're not a terrorist. Spaulding warned that "it is inevitable that totally innocent Americans are going to be affected by these programs."[100] Harry Truman's words ring just as true now as they were in 1951. He said, "And when even one American--who has done nothing wrong--is forced by fear to shut his mind and close his mouth, then all Americans are in peril."[101]

To sum up, the drug war's far-reaching ramifications are unimaginable to the average person. Most Americans are completely unaware of how the drug war finances some of the most atrocious crimes against humanity, particularly in Latin America.

The U.S. government is complicit in these crimes, all for the sake of building our geopolitical and military alliances. Also, the drug war has eased the way for a number of other constitutional violations and establishing a technological surveillance state. With that said, there clearly is a bright note that leads us to a simple and positive solution. By ending the drug war, we can mitigate much of this damage.

12

"There is no question in my mind that people affiliated with, or on the payroll of, the CIA were involved in drug trafficking."
Sen. John Kerry

Outlawing vices like drugs, alcohol, gambling, or prostitution, by its nature, has bred police corruption in the past. And the situation is no different at the present time. After all, StopTheDrugWar.org publishes an article every week, "This Week's Corrupt Cops Stories." But that doesn't justify generalizing every police officer. The politicians are to blame because graft is a natural byproduct of prohibition policy. Bear in mind, people tend to envision a low-level beat cop when this topic is mentioned, but the drug war has been corrupted at the highest levels of government. In fact, the U.S. government has protected, armed, and paid some of the most powerful drug trafficking organizations in the world over the last 80 years as long as these criminals have been geopolitical allies.

It's ironic that Joe McCarthy convinced many Americans that communists were conspiring to flood America with illegal drugs. In actuality, the CIA has aligned itself with drug traffickers for decades in the name of fighting the spread of communism. By all outward appearances, organized crime and the CIA make for strange bedfellows, but they often share the same enemies. Typically, a communist or totalitarian regime is particularly brutal to crime syndicates because they pose a threat to the government's authority.

Criminals can be particularly handy with the CIA's cloak and dagger operations. The CIA-sponsored coup in Iran in 1953 was the first of its kind and provides an excellent example of this odd couple relationship. Kermit Roosevelt, the son of the former U.S. president Theodore Roosevelt, organized the CIA's mission, Operation Ajax. One of his first tasks was to pay the local Iranian crime bosses to cause havoc in the streets. These thugs-for-hire smashed storefront windows and vandalized mosques while screaming, "We love communism! We love Mossadegh!" This was a false flag, or staged event, intent upon leading Iranians to believe that the Prime Minister, Mohammad Mossadegh, had lost control of the country.[1]

You may wonder, "What was the catalyst for overthrowing a democratically elected leader such as Mossadegh, Time Magazine's

Man of the Year in 1951?" The Iranian Prime Minister didn't pose a national security threat, but he was a threat to international business interests. And the intelligence community has often conflated the two issues, thereby keeping liberal foreign leaders on a short leash. Mossadegh was elected on a promise of nationalizing the country's oil supply because Iran had been entangled in a drastically exploitive contract with the Anglo-Iranian Oil Company, i.e. present day British Petroleum (BP). The Anglo-Iranian Oil Company received 84% of the profits from Iran's oil supply and blocked all other companies, foreign or domestic, from drilling in the country.[2]

The British government appealed to the United Nations to enforce the contract and overrule Mossadegh's decision. However, Mossadegh traveled to New York and successfully presented his case to the U.N. Security Council. British officials later lobbied President Truman privately after the United Nations decided not to intervene in Iran. Albeit, they presented their plan to overthrow Mossadegh to no avail. Truman was outraged and refused.[3] On the other hand, the Eisenhower administration authorized the coup and thus our nation began enjoying the spoils of British colonialism. The coup placed the Shah of Iran (a Western-influenced dictator) into power and he, in turn, promptly handed over 40% of the nation's oil fields to U.S. based corporations.[4]

As detailed in Chapter 10, the military leaders of various U.S. supported coups received counternarcotics training at the School of the Americas. Military dictatorships are often havens for drug trafficking because that environment establishes a sense of lawlessness for the armed forces. In the process, many of these military coups have established brutal secretive police forces, including the SAVAK of Iran. Based upon the slightest suspicion, thousands of Iranians were murdered, tortured, and falsely imprisoned during the Shah's reign by his CIA-trained, secretive police force.

The Iranian coup also provided a framework for enlisting the services of the local gangsters and it has since become a staple within the CIA's playbook. Remarkably, by 1960, military manuals suggested the use of "smugglers" and "black market operators" to combat the spread of communism.[5] America's lengthy list of illegal foreign interventions has drastically enabled the power of organized crime worldwide. That may initially sound far-fetched, but reflect upon the experience of Dennis Dayle, a former high-level DEA agent stationed in Latin America. He once said that in his "30-year history in the Drug Enforcement Agency and related agencies, the major targets of (his) investigations almost invariably turned out to be working for the CIA."[6] Several other DEA agents have come upon this roadblock. That's why there is a strong rivalry between the DEA and the CIA. But there is a pecking order and the DEA customarily has to stand down.

The drug war has been a farce since its earliest days. Douglas Valentine, author of *The Strength of the Wolf: The Secret History of America's War on Drugs*, documented how the U.S. government began blocking high-level drug trafficking investigations before Harry Anslinger even took office with the Federal Bureau of Narcotics (FBN). Ralph Oyler, a top federal narcotics detective, traveled to China in 1926 to pursue a major heroin trafficking organization, but the U.S. War Department and State Department interfered with his investigation. They did so because his targets were closely connected with Chiang Kai-shek, a key geopolitical ally.[7]

Chiang Kai-shek was the political and military leader of the right-wing Chinese Nationalist Party (known as the Kuomintang or KMT). He removed the communist leaders from their party, including Mao Tse Tung, and led a revolution to take over the country. Chiang Kai-shek's regime was linked with Shanghai's most powerful criminal organization, the Green Gang, which controlled the opium supply. In fact, their organization had been hired by Chiang Kai-shek during the Shanghai Massacre of 1927, which killed thousands of communists or suspected communists.[8] Ultimately, the Chinese Nationalist Party (the KMT) won their civil war and controlled most of mainland China from 1928 to 1949.[9] Kai-shek returned the favor by appointing various members of the Green Gang as his government's top counternarcotics officials.[10]

Harry Anslinger's resume speaks for itself as he was a man who portrayed himself as a hardliner against drugs. However, Douglas Valentine discovered that "Anslinger fully knew about the ties between Chiang and opium dealers."[11] However, U.S. authorities didn't pursue Kai-shek because illegal drug money was necessary to fund their war efforts, thereby temporarily stifling the rise of Mao Tse Tung in China. Many people would agree with the decision to prioritize national security over the drug war, particularly in this instance. After all, Chairman Mao Tse Tung later gained power in 1949 and he was ultimately responsible for a staggering number of deaths. Forty-five million people were either starved, worked, or beaten to death during his regime![12] Nonetheless, when our government props up a thug, such as Chiang Kai-shek, it shatters the myth propagated by Anslinger and others that there is a "communist plot to poison Americans with drugs."

The United States government later escalated their complicity in the drug trade beyond merely turning a blind eye; federal agents began to actively collaborate with a known drug trafficker during WWII. The Office of Naval Intelligence (ONI) feared that the New York waterfront was susceptible to foreign attackers. Therefore, they contacted the organization that unofficially controlled the docks, the Italian-American mafia (La Cosa Nostra). According to Meyer Lansky, these ONI officers had been comically inept at infiltrating this blue-collar community on their own. He claimed that some ONI agents spoke out of the side of their mouths like the gangsters from the movies of the 1930s.[13]

Eventually, ONI officers met with Joey "Socks" Lanza, the mob boss of the Fulton Fish Market and United Seafood Workers Union. Lanza's power was reasonably limited, hence he referred them to the most powerful mafia boss, Charles "Lucky" Luciano, who was then in Dannemora prison (now Clinton Correctional).[14] In exchange for protection, Luciano was moved from Dannemora, then known as the "Siberia of prisons," to the more pleasant Great Meadows Prison where Luciano could more openly meet with various mafia leaders.[15]

Luciano was also an asset to the Office of Strategic Services (OSS), the CIA's predecessor, due to his connections with the Sicilian mafia. Otherwise, the agency had few intelligence sources in Italy during WWII. The Sicilian mafia certainly had the inclination to assist the war effort because their power dwindled during Mussolini's reign. Accordingly, several members of the Sicilian mafia fled to the U.S. during the 1920s.

Luciano communicated with Sicily's most dominant gangster in 1943 to help with the war effort, Don Calogero Vizzini, aka Don Calo. Don Calo, or the "Mayor" as Allied Forces nicknamed him, helped General Patton's Seventh Army gain safe landing in Sicily and a secure route through hundreds of miles of territory. Some historians disagree to what extent Don Calo helped the war effort, but he was named an honorary colonel by Allied Forces leaders.[16]

As a reward, U.S. intelligence officials convinced New York Governor Thomas Dewey to offer early parole to Luciano in 1946. He did so reluctantly. This was a personal issue for Dewey as he had successfully prosecuted Luciano ten years earlier. Dewey agreed to the parole on the condition that Luciano would be deported back to Italy. Consequently, many Americans were furious at the decision without knowing the background information and assumed that Dewey had been bribed. Over the years, several newspapers mentioned Luciano's "wartime services" without going into specifics. Hence, the New York Commissioner of Investigations, William Herlands, conducted an investigation in 1954 to verify Luciano's role in the war effort. Herlands released an internal report that confirmed Luciano's wartime services and cleared Dewey's name, but the details weren't released until 20 years later.[17]

Upon arrival in Italy in 1946, Luciano reinvigorated his crime family's heroin network. Albeit, his former underboss, Vito Genovese, had already laid the groundwork nearly a decade earlier. Genovese fled New York in 1937 to avoid a murder charge for killing a rival gangster. Oddly enough, Genovese was one of the few mobsters whom the dictator allowed to thrive. Heroin was legally purchased at that time through a pharmaceutical company in Milan, the Schiaparelli Company.[18] In return, Genovese made generous "donations" to Mussolini and his inner circle. He also arranged the murder of an anti-fascist writer in New York. For these reasons, Mussolini awarded him the highest civilian title, "Commendatore." Regardless, Genovese switched alliances when the Allied Forces invaded Sicily.[19] As a matter of fact, he was hired as an Army translator.[20]

The eventual removal of Mussolini from power provided the Sicilian mafia with newfound freedom, thus enabling them to corrupt Sicilian politics and return to business unscathed. However, the mafia's smooth business model found bumps in the road when the Italian government outlawed heroin in 1950. Lucky Luciano decided to find a new source for heroin production, the Corsican syndicate in France. The Corsicans dominated the heroin trade for decades because they controlled the port city of Marseilles. That city was crucial for commerce and, as a result, the Corsicans became an unlikely ally of the U.S. government. Both entities had a mutual fear of a communist takeover of France. The Corsicans were adamantly anti-communist. Notably, the Nazi Gestapo hired the Corsicans during WWII to spy on French communists.[21]

Similarly, the CIA supplied the Corsicans with money and arms to execute their anti-communist strategy, such as breaking up communist-led labor strikes. They paid for scab workers, ended labor strikes by starting riots, and killed key strike organizers.[22] In fact, during that same time period, Don Calo was performing similar tasks for the CIA by breaking strikes and rigging elections against communists in Italy.[23] The Corsicans' key allies enabled them to become one of the most politically connected syndicates whose organization prospered for over three decades. They later became known in the press as the "French Connection."[A][24]

While communism was suppressed in Europe, there was a regime change in China in 1949. America's ally, Chiang Kai-shek, had been a brutal dictator, but China was subjected to an exponentially more horrific reign of terror from this revolution. Chairman Mao Tse Tung's Communist Party took over and founded the present-day version of the People's Republic of China. The Chinese communists expelled the Nationalist Chinese (Kuomintang or KMT) who fled south to Burma (now Myanmar).

Alfred McCoy, author of *The Politics of Heroin in Southeast Asia*, noted that drug policies changed under the communist regime in China in the early 1950s. Opium laws were enforced more vigorously and farmers were forced to substitute opium for legal crops.[25] In contrast, the Nationalist Chinese (KMT) had no qualms with trafficking opium. As one KMT General Tuan Shi-wen said, "Here opium is money. And I need money."[26] The CIA seemingly accepted that sentiment as reality because the agency had limited funding to provide for the KMT, nor Congressional approval for their covert operation.

The Department of Defense and the CIA began financing the KMT's anti-communist mission in Burma as early as 1950. Consequently, the U.S. intelligence community clearly turned a blind eye to their smuggling efforts. Burmese opium production had increased to 300-400 tons annually by 1962, roughly a 1,000%

[A] The NYPD had confiscated $70 million worth of heroin by 1962, but ten years later the press reported that the heroin was missing. It had been stolen from police evidence--slowly--over the course of three years by various members of the NYPD. They replaced the heroin that they stole with flour.

increase over less than two decades.[27] This sparked a chain reaction with the formation of "the Golden Triangle," in reference to the geographic region of Burma, Thailand, and Laos in which the vast majority of the world's opium was produced for roughly three decades.

The KMT's troops were eventually forced out of Burma and fled to Thailand and Laos. Again, that didn't slow down opium production. The KMT had already established connections with some corrupt Thai authorities, many of whom were close allies of the CIA. One of the CIA's operatives in Thailand, Puttapron Khramkhruan, was captured by the DEA in Chicago with 59 pounds of opium in 1973. Nevertheless, an official from the DOJ explained that the charges against him were dropped because the CIA intervened as it may "prove embarrassing because of Mr. Khramkhruans's involvement with CIA activities in Thailand, Burma, and elsewhere."[28]

Intelligence officials were certainly aware that members of the KMT were major drug traffickers. In fact, the CIA's airline, Civil Air Transport (later Air America), often transported opium to various allied military leaders in Southeast Asia. Those planes were often loaded with opium after wartime supplies were delivered to the KMT.[29] The official narrative from the CIA is that their pilots never *knowingly* transported opium, but numerous pilots have said otherwise. One Air America pilot, Neal Hanson said, "Yes, I've seen the sticky bricks come on board, and no one challenged it."[30]

The opium culture was already rampant before the CIA began their secret war in Laos, but the agency also facilitated the trade. A correspondent for *Christian Science Monitor* reported in 1970 that the CIA "is cognizant of, if not a party to, the extensive movement of opium out of Laos." A pilot also told the reporter that "opium shipments get special CIA clearance and monitoring on their flights southward out of the country."[31] One former CIA agent stationed in Laos, Anthony Poshepny, went on the record many years later. He said, "It was all a contractual relationship, just like bankers and businessmen. A wonderful relationship. Just a mafia. A big organized mafia."[32]

The CIA's allies were essentially granted diplomatic immunity. The Laotian ambassador to France, Crown Prince Sopsaisana, had his luggage (filled with 60 kilos of heroin) confiscated at a Paris airport. The CIA intervened to help him avoid any charges. In fact, the CIA, along with the State Department, blocked various investigations by the Bureau of Narcotics citing that opium production was legal in Laos at that time.[33] The Laotian government did officially ban opium in 1971, but the ban had little effect on production.[34] In that same year, Laos produced 300 tons of opium, double the level of eleven years prior.[35]

Most people either scoffed or ignored the beatnik poet, Allen Ginsberg, who openly claimed in *Time Magazine*, February 9, 1959, that the CIA was involved in drug smuggling.[36] He later went into greater detail with his poem "CIA Dope Calypso." In fact, Ginsberg provided the University of Wisconsin-Madison professor, Alfred McCoy, with unpublished documents for his research into the CIA's involvement in the drug trade.[37] McCoy published *The Politics of Heroin in Southeast Asia* in 1972. It was a first-of-its-kind book that thoroughly detailed the CIA's role in drug smuggling. Various news reports had subtly touched upon this issue, but McCoy's work was the first to connect the dots in a meticulously well-documented manner. McCoy's efforts were rewarded with the following: his publisher was threatened with a national security lawsuit, McCoy's phone was tapped, and his taxes audited.[38] Rodney Campbell published *The Luciano Project: The Secret Wartime Collaboration of the Mafia and the U.S. Navy* in 1977 and like McCoy's book it was essentially censored by the major media outlets.

The media began to hint at the CIA's complicity in the region as U.S. troops entered the Vietnam War in large numbers. A CIA operative leaked a classified report to *The New York Times* about twenty-one Southeast Asian opium refineries. What wasn't mentioned was that most of those refineries were in areas controlled by U.S. allies.[39] Towards the end of the war, the media began to expose the high number of soldiers addicted to heroin. Likewise, two Congressmen, Robert Steele and Morgan Murphy, visited Vietnam and estimated there were 40,000 U.S. military heroin addicts. *The New York Times* believed it could have been as many as 80,000.[40]

Instead of attempting to resolve the problem, both the Pentagon and the Nixon administration were more concerned with self-preservation. The Pentagon estimated that only 100 to 200 U.S. soldiers were addicted to heroin.[41] Their methodology was based upon urine testing, even though the troops had ways around it, such as using another soldier's clean urine. Also, soldiers were informed of the date of the test in advance. If they failed the test they had to stay in Vietnam for more war duty. For this reason, soldiers had an extreme incentive to clean up temporarily.

The Nixon administration also swore that all of the troops who were addicted would be rehabilitated. Consequently, VA hospitals referred 12,000 U.S. soldiers returning from Vietnam for heroin addiction. Astoundingly, only 3 of the 12,000 referred were treated, according to a Congressional Subcommittee on Public Health.[42] Thus, thousands of U.S. soldiers returned home addicted to heroin and clearly expanded the demand for heroin in the U.S. In fact, massive amounts of heroin were transported into the U.S. in the body bags of dead soldiers. Their bodies had been gutted and stuffed with heroin. Michael Levine, then working with U.S. Customs and later with the DEA, said that he was thwarted from stopping those shipments by the CIA and the State Department a number of times because the suppliers were U.S. military allies.[43]

The Vietnam War was probably our most unpopular war and Zbigniew Brzezinski, Jimmy Carter's National Security Advisor, was determined to give the "USSR its own Vietnam War."[44] The plan was to draw them into a lengthy, expensive war effort and deplete their military resources while avoiding U.S. casualties. In 1979, Jimmy Carter authorized the CIA to fund the Mujahedeen rebels in Afghanistan against a Soviet invasion. Just like in the past, the U.S. allied with warlords who were openly funding their operations from opium production, most notably Gulbuddin Hekmatyar.[45]

White House advisor and drug war historian, Dr. David F. Musto, warned about the opium connection internally. He even wrote an op-ed in *The New York Times* predicting that our support would result in another Golden Triangle scenario.[46] Musto was prophetic and Afghan opium production tripled within three years. By 1982, 60% of the American and European heroin supply came from Afghanistan.[47]

The former Pakistani President, Muhammad Zia-ul-Haq, demanded that all CIA funding for the Mujahedeen fighters be funneled through Pakistan's version of the CIA, the Inter-Services Intelligence (ISI). As a result, Pakistan served its own interests and many top Pakistani government officials were clearly corrupted by Gulbuddin Hekmatyar's drug money. For instance, one of President Zia's associates held as much as $3 billion in a BCCI account, the notorious bank detailed in Chapter 4.[48] However, the ISI also served their national security interests by denying supplies to moderate, secular warlords. Instead, the ISI supported fundamental extremists, such as Hekmatyar, whose troops were known for shrieking chants of "Death to America!"[49]

The circumstances that encouraged pervasive opium trafficking in the Golden Triangle were much the same in Pakistan and Afghanistan. Heroin was exported from the same conduits that delivered supplies to the Mujahedeen.[50] Likewise, the top smugglers didn't have to worry about the U.S. authorities. *BBC* reporters briefly interviewed one of President Zia's associates, Mirza Iqbal Baig, whom Pakistani customs agents labeled "the most active dope dealer in the country."[51] Their meeting ended abruptly when Baig was questioned about drug trafficking and his henchmen savagely assaulted the reporters while local Pakistani police stood by. Baig was obviously a high-profile, internationally known drug smuggler, yet the DEA was obstructed from arresting him because it would have exposed the CIA's mission.[52]

Despite the free flow of millions of dollars of dope money, General Zia labeled the initial $400 million package authorized by Carter as "peanuts."[53] The Reagan administration seemingly concurred and $6 billion of military aid was provided to the Mujahedeen throughout the 1980s.[54] At any rate, the corruption within the Zia administration was well-documented, yet George H. W. Bush publicly praised Zia's efforts in the drug war and gave him an official visit in 1984.[55]

A year after the U.S. began funding the Mujahedeen, a "cocaine coup" took place in Bolivia in 1980, as mentioned in Chapter 10. The socialist administration of Hernán Siles Zuazo was about to take office before the Bolivian military took control of the government.[56] Unfortunately, military coups were quite customary in Bolivia. There have been 189 revolutions and coups in Bolivia since its independence in 1825![57] Again, these military dictatorships were often linked with drug traffickers, but what happened in 1980 was unprecedented.

The coup launched a new Bolivian regime run by General Luis Garcia Meza. Colonel Luis Arce Gomez, another SOA graduate, was installed as the Minister of the Interior even though he had earned the unflattering brand, the "Minister of Cocaine," in the international press.[58] After all, his cousin, Roberto Suarez Gomez, was the primary financier of the coup. You may not be familiar with the name Roberto Suarez, but you have likely seen a depiction of him. The character of the Bolivian cocaine kingpin, Alejandro Sosa, in the movie *Scarface* was based on Roberto Suarez.

The Brazilian government had named Roberto Suarez as their nation's leading supplier of cocaine one year *before* the coup took place.[59] The coup enabled Suarez to accumulate a level of wealth so vast that he offered to pay off the entire Bolivian government debt of $4.3 billion in 1983 in exchange for full immunity.[60] Suarez also benefited from the protection of top U.S. authorities despite such a notorious reputation internationally. According to the DEA's station chief in Argentina Michael Levine, Suarez's name wasn't even in the DEA database in 1980 even though that same database had "the names of every nickel-and-dime drug dealer from Bogota to Bangkok."[61] Levine was aware of Suarez's exploits and infiltrated his organization with an undercover operation. He caught several of the group's representatives red-handed, but the DEA's top brass stifled his investigation.[62]

The DEA even retaliated against Levine. In a very brave act, Levine risked his career by contacting the media about this corruption to no avail. No major media company was willing to print any of his revelations. Consequently, he wrote a book that documented our government's role in drug trafficking, *The Big White Lie: The Deep Cover Operation That Exposed the CIA Sabotage of the Drug War*. No DEA whistleblower has exposed so many details about the misperceptions of the drug war in such a public manner. Levine has made numerous media appearances since publishing *The Big White Lie*. He also established a podcast *Expert Witness Radio* that featured other whistleblowers who have exposed government corruption. All in all, Levine has made it very clear that the DEA plays second fiddle to the CIA.

Michael Levine shined a light on the fact that Klaus Barbie, a notorious Nazi war criminal nicknamed "the Butcher of Lyon," was one of the chief facilitators of the coup. Klaus Barbie's shipping company, Transmaritania, transported the drugs while his paramilitary group helped to consolidate the Bolivian cocaine market by targeting their rivals.[B63] About 140 different mid-level and small dealers were either tortured to death or jailed.[64]

[B] The co-owner of Transmaritania was another Nazi war criminal Friedrich Schwend.

U.S. intelligence agencies had protected Barbie from punishment for decades. In fact, he led a group of former Nazis for the U.S. Army's Counterintelligence Corps (CIC).[65] French officials had persistently pleaded for decades for Barbie's extradition to France to face trial, but he found safe haven in Bolivia until 1983, long after his role in the coup had been completed. With this in mind, it's necessary to explain that Barbie wasn't an isolated case. The U.S. military had an extensive program, Operation Paperclip, which recruited and harbored many Nazi war criminals and scientists after WWII in hopes of preventing them from aiding the Soviet Union. And the Soviet Union had its version of the program.[66]

The U.S. publicly denounced the coup by cutting off Bolivia's foreign aid in 1980.[67] However, the coup was unofficially sanctioned by the U.S. intelligence community because it fit their Cold War strategy. After all, Che Guevara viewed Bolivia as a viable destination for his revolutionary efforts. The "cocaine coup" resulted in the bombings, rapes, and murders of anyone who was merely suspected of being a communist sympathizer. Barbie's paramilitary group rounded up thousands and brought them to the La Paz soccer stadium and murdered them en masse.[68] Barbie's mercenaries, known as the "fiances of death," wore ski masks and swastika armbands. They were comprised of many neo-Nazis (including a few former Nazi SS officers) and drug traffickers who had been released from prison immediately following the coup.[69]

Several years later, Colonel Luis Arce Gomez, aka "the Minister of Cocaine," was captured and extradited to the U.S. In his heyday, he reportedly made $500 million a year, but he had been retired from the drug business for many years when he was captured.[70] In fact, Arce Gomez was an old man confined to a wheelchair and wasn't even in hiding. Make no mistake, he certainly needed to be brought to justice, but it was a decade too late. The capture of Arce Gomez happened two weeks before the U.S. invaded Panama in 1989, in Operation Just Cause.[71] Both of those events appear to be politically motivated as the U.S. media generally glossed over the fact that General Manuel Noriega had been a close ally of the CIA for decades.

Noriega began working for the CIA in 1967 as an operative, not an actual CIA agent. The CIA even helped him by pressuring prosecutors to drop a drug charge against him in 1971. By 1976, his salary was raised to $100,000 while George H.W. Bush was the CIA director. He even met with Bush in D.C. that same year.[72] However, Noriega's association with the CIA was discontinued during the Carter administration. Nonetheless, he was promptly put back on the payroll at the beginning of the Reagan administration.[73]

With the CIA's protection, along with other federal agencies, Noriega became a major player in the drug game. With that in mind, Richard Gregorie, formerly the Assistant U.S. Attorney in Miami, resigned from office in 1990. Various federal agencies had blocked him from prosecuting drug cases against foreign officials in the Caribbean and Latin America, including Noriega. Gregorie told *NBC Nightly News* that the U.S. government is "concerned that we are going to cause a problem in foreign policy areas and that is more important than stopping the dope problem."[74]

The U.S intelligence community began to cut the cord with Noriega after Seymour Hersh published a column about him in *The New York Times* on June 12, 1986. Coincidentally, Noriega was in Washington D.C. accepting a medal of honor from the Inter-American Defense Board when that article hit the newsstands.[75] Seymour Hersh's column quoted government sources who implicated Noriega in the drug trade, illegal arms, political assassination, and providing sensitive intelligence to Cuba.[76] Despite these revelations, the CIA still tried to protect Noriega, even after many in Congress began demanding investigations into the drug allegations. During a private phone call with former Sen. Jesse Helms (R-SC), CIA Director William Casey implored, "You don't understand! You are destroying our policy. There are some things you don't know about, things Noriega is doing for the United States."[77]

Likewise, Oliver North met with a representative for Noriega two months after the Hersh article. Noriega offered to "take care of the Sandinista leadership," i.e. political assassinations, if U.S. officials would agree to "help clean up his image" and lift the ban on arms sales to his Panamanian Defense Force. North suggested to his superior, Reagan's National Security Advisor John Poindexter, that the U.S. pay Noriega $1 million from funds raised by illegally selling arms to Iran. North pointed out that the plan was "sound" and offered "deniability."[78] The next day North arranged plans for a meeting between the CIA's Duane "Dewey" Clarridge and Noriega.[79] However, those plans were canceled after the press began to uncover aspects of the Iran-Contra Affair and the administration went into damage control mode.

"Clear and incontrovertible evidence was, at best, ignored, and at worst, hidden and denied by many different agencies and departments of the government of the United States in such a way as to provide cover and protection for (Noriega's) activities," said Norman Bailey, former National Security Council official.[80] Many U.S. officials had finally lost their patience with Noriega and that's when information about him was leaked to Seymour Hersh.[81] The reason was that Noriega often aided both sides of a conflict for his personal gain. As stated by the U.S. Senate Committee on Foreign Relations, "Noriega also understood the divided nature of the U.S. government and attempted to play each agency off against the others."[82] Reagan's Secretary of State George Shultz added, "You can't buy (Noriega), you can only rent him."[83]

Noriega drove U.S. intelligence officials to their wit's end when he forced a key ally, former Panamanian President Nicolás Ardito Barletta, out of office in 1985.[84] Barletta, an economics graduate of the University of Chicago and former World Bank Vice-President, helped establish the bank secrecy laws in Panama that enabled drug trafficking to flourish.[85] Furthermore, in an act of public defiance, Noriega welcomed the Sandinista leader, Daniel Ortega, to Panama after he was burned by the intelligence community.[86] Thereafter, Noriega nullified the election of another strong U.S. ally, President Guillermo Endara. That was one of the final straws for the U.S. government and it led to the invasion of Panama.

Nonetheless, the removal of Noriega had little impact on the drug trade, even though Operation Just Cause was declared a victory in the war on drugs. It was more a case of "meet the new boss, same as the old boss." In a symbolic moment, President Guillermo Endara was sworn in on a U.S. military base in 1989. His regime enforced a police state that incarcerated thousands of political prisoners without any criminal charges, according to *Human Rights Watch*.[87] Also, Panama's banking system increasingly became a haven for dirty money during Endara's administration. Panamanian bank deposits soared to $21 billion midway through 1991, a meteoric rise from $8.5 billion in 1989.[88]

The New York Times reported that the Endara administration resisted pressure from the U.S. State Department to improve their "inadequate" banking laws.[89] That was the tip of the iceberg as the article noted that Endara had been a director of a notorious Panamanian bank, Banco Interoceanico, linked with laundering money for both of the Colombian cartels. In a similar fashion, Vice President Guillermo Ford had been a part owner of the Dadeland Bank of Florida, which was also heavily involved in laundering money for the Medellín cartel. Not to mention, the Attorney General, Rogelio Cruz, had been the director of a Panamanian bank, the First Interamericas Bank, which was shut down due to its extensive money laundering on behalf of the Colombian cartels. The majority shareholder of the First Interamericas Bank was Gilberto Rodriguez, a leader of the Cali cartel![90]

Surprisingly, Noriega had been credited by the DEA in 1985 for aiding "Operation Pisces," which froze $14 million from 54 different bank accounts of major drug traffickers. However, it should be noted that most of those accounts were held by Noriega's rivals.[91] Noriega had a partnership with the Medellín cartel, in which he received a percentage of every shipment sent through their cocaine laboratory in the jungles of Darién, just beyond the Colombian border. A leopard can't change its spots and apparently Noriega couldn't resist double dealing, even with the likes of the Medellín cartel. He ordered his Panamanian Defense Forces to raid their lab in 1985 and soon regretted the decision as the cartel put a price on his head.[92]

Noriega was also a grand facilitator of the Iran-Contra scandal. To recap, in 1979 a group of Iranian students stormed the U.S. embassy in Iran and held 52 Americans hostage. The students were outraged by our government's support of the 1953 coup and the authoritarian regime of the Shah. During the hostage crisis, the Carter administration imposed an arms embargo on the Iranian government. The Reagan administration publicly supported the arms embargo, but its senior officials secretly arranged illegal arms sales to the Iranian government. The profits from those sales were used to support the Contras, which was a rebel group attempting to overthrow the Sandinistas, the socialist Nicaraguan regime. That's the official story in a nutshell, but the general public is unaware that significant portions of the Contras funding also came from illegal drug trafficking.

The first hint of this extensive conspiracy flew under the radar and it involved a high-profile drug bust that was dubbed the "Frogman case." Federal authorities seized over $100 million worth of cocaine from a Colombian freighter at a San Francisco pier.[C] That seizure led to some follow-up arrests of people involved in the drug ring. Included were two Nicaraguans who had raised money for the Contras, Julio Zavala and Carlos Cabezas. The FBI confiscated over $36,000 of Zavala's cash during his arrest. Internal CIA documents expressed concern that this drug bust had "the potential for disaster."[93] In response, the CIA intervened on behalf of Zavala, corroborating his claim that the money had been given to him by Contra leaders to purchase equipment in America. In the end, Zavala received a full refund from the U.S. government.[94]

The CIA's intervention in the "Frogman" case wasn't reported until years later, but reports by Robert Parry and Brian Barger of the *Associated Press* were much clearer and more direct. They reported on December 20, 1985 that "Nicaraguan rebels operating in northern Costa Rica have engaged in cocaine smuggling, using some of the profits to finance their war against Nicaragua's leftist government."[95] Such a story is journalistic gold, but Parry and Barger were pressured within the *AP* to move on to different stories. Parry quit his job at the *AP* due to their censoring of his Contra reports. In fact, his story only went public by fortuitous fate. His editors blocked the story for weeks before it was released by accident over the *AP's* Spanish language wire. As a result, it was then published in English.[96]

Many people suspected that the U.S. intelligence community was secretly arming the Nicaraguan rebels, in violation of a Congressional vote (the Boland Amendment). The physical evidence from the Iran-Contra scandal became undeniable when a U.S. aircraft carrying weapons for the Contras was shot down in Nicaragua in 1986. This was the beginning of a monumental scandal and there were more serious implications involving drug trafficking. Those weapons were transported by a CIA contractor into Nicaragua on a plane that was registered to Alder Berriman Seal, aka Barry Seal, one of the most experienced drug trafficking pilots of all time. Seal had smuggled roughly $3 to $5 billion worth of illegal drugs into America, according to estimates by the federal government. Seal had also performed other exercises for the CIA and DEA at different times.[97]

[C] The nickname for that case came about because some of the men aboard that ship were dressed in scuba gear.

Again, the drug trafficking aspect of the Iran-Contra scandal isn't common knowledge in part because the Reagan administration labeled the Sandinistas as drug traffickers who wanted "to poison our children."[98] Oddly enough, Barry Seal helped to create that myth. *The Washington Times* released an explosive story about an undercover DEA sting by Barry Seal in Nicaragua. Ronald Reagan later used the photos from that operation during a televised speech to gain support for the Contras. The CIA installed hidden cameras in his plane and captured images of Seal picking up a large shipment of cocaine from the Medellín cartel in a Nicaraguan airfield. In particular, the cameras snapped pictures of Pablo Escobar and someone whom the Reagan administration claimed was a high-level Sandinista official, Federico Vaughan.[99]

This was a perfectly executed public relations effort by the Reagan administration, but it was disingenuous to analogize the Sandinistas with drug trafficking. To clarify, Nicaragua was not a hub for drug trafficking. DEA officials confirmed that Seal's flight was their only evidence of drug dealing by the Sandinistas. Neither could the Justice Department, nor the State Department provide more evidence of drug trafficking by high-level Sandinistas.[100]

This DEA sting was brilliantly orchestrated by Barry Seal in exchange for leniency after being arrested in 1983 in possession of 200,000 quaaludes.[101] Decades after this incident, Jon Roberts, one of the "cocaine cowboys" or a top American associate of the Medellín cartel, said, "I never heard of flying cocaine out of Nicaragua. I never heard of Pablo (Escobar) personally loading one of our planes. But it's a fact Barry (Seal) got him to do this and took pictures of it."[102]

Otherwise, the transit points for Colombian cartels were usually in countries with friendlier U.S. relations, such as Panama, Costa Rica, or the Bahamas. But here's what happened. The leadership of the Medellín cartel briefly fled their home country. They bribed a high-level Sandinista for safe passage because the cartel had virtually declared war with the Colombian government in 1984 by assassinating the Colombian Minister of Justice, Rodrigo Lara Bonilla. Albeit, the Medellín cartel returned to Colombia and business as usual after a few months. But Barry Seal shrewdly seized upon that opportunity to capture images of them loading cocaine onto his plane in Nicaragua.[103]

Again, those photos were quite damning, but there was no evidence that the Nicaraguan man in the pictures, Federico Vaughan, was linked with the Sandinistas. In fact, Federico Vaughan was most likely an asset for U.S. intelligence officials because his phone number in Nicaragua had belonged to the U.S. embassy since 1981![104] Nicaraguan officials denied that Vaughan worked for the Interior Minister as claimed by the Reagan administration.[105]

Furthermore, Richard Gregorie, the head of the federal task force that supervised this case, admitted that federal prosecutors and drug enforcement couldn't verify anything regarding Vaughan's identity.[106] In case you're wondering, Richard Gregorie is the same Assistant U.S. Attorney in Miami who was mentioned earlier. He resigned because the U.S. government blocked his drug investigations of foreign officials. On the other hand, Gregorie was obviously given the green light for this investigation due to its political nature.

This DEA sting was part of an organized effort to sway the minds of American voters to finance the Contras. The Iran-Contra congressional committee and the GAO discovered that the Reagan administration had violated federal laws against domestic propaganda. They established the "Office of Public Diplomacy for Latin America and the Caribbean" under the guise of being a State Department program, but these officials reported directly to Oliver North of the National Security Council (NSC). This group consisted of CIA and Army experts of psychological warfare who manipulated American media coverage of Nicaragua.[107]

That kind of program is a staple of operations for the CIA and is perfectly legal for media coverage outside of the U.S. However, it is illegal for our intelligence agencies to manipulate media coverage *domestically*. They planted news stories and denigrated reporters who were critical of the Contras. In one such case, the head of this program, Otto Reich, alleged to *New York* magazine that the reporters covering the Contra drug trafficking story were bribed by the Sandinistas with prostitutes in return for negative press about the Contras.[108]

Oliver North served as the point man in this propaganda operation. He also hatched a plan with Manuel Noriega to make it appear that the Sandinistas were arming a communist rebel group in El Salvador. They planned a staged event that was meant to be a major media spectacle. A ship loaded with East German weapons, Pia Vesta, was supposed to be captured at sea by the Contras. They were supposed to "discover" the ship a few days before a Congressional vote for Contra funding. However, Noriega was blindsided by Seymour Hersh's report in *The New York Times*. Thus, two days later, he seized the Pia Vesta, refused to play along with the narrative that the Sandinistas were involved, and kept the weapons for himself.[109]

Oliver North also manipulated the "Pablo Escobar/Sandinista cocaine deal" in many ways. First of all, he requested that the Contras receive the $1.5 million proceeds from the Barry Seal/Medellín Cartel deal. Much to North's chagrin, the DEA denied that request.[110] Also, someone leaked the details of Seal's undercover operation to the press and Oliver North is the most likely suspect. After all, he had pressured the DEA to leak that information earlier to help pass a vote to fund the Contras. Albeit, North has officially denied leaking that information.[111]

If you're wondering about the importance of that press leak, consider that the report by *The Washington Times* prematurely blew Seal's cover. As a result, Barry Seal was murdered by the Medellín cartel, thereby killing the key witness in arguably the most high-profile drug case of all time. Many people are still perplexed as to why our nation's most valuable informant, Barry Seal, wasn't placed under federal witness protection while he had a $500,000 bounty on his head.[112]

In fact, a federal judge effectively gave him a death sentence by ordering Seal to stay in a halfway house. Additionally, Seal had to check in every day at the same time at a Salvation Army facility only a few miles from where he had regularly met with representatives from the Medellín cartel. "The government did everything but put a bull's eye on Barry's back," said Jon Roberts of the Medellín cartel.[113] The obvious conclusion is that Seal wasn't protected to cover up his role with trafficking guns and drugs for the Contras.

Oliver North was the government's fall guy for the Iran-Contra affair and, as a result, he is widely popular among conservatives with an unscathed image. He even had his show on *Fox News*, "War Stories." In a surreal moment, Oliver North made an advertisement for a video game, *Official Call of Duty: Black Ops 2*, which simulates covert military action. However, fans of Oliver North must be unaware of his involvement with drug trafficking by the

Contras. That's why two men held up a banner behind him, "Ask about the cocaine smuggling," during North's Iran-Contra testimony. The demonstrators were dragged out by police after shouting, "What about the cocaine dealing that the U.S. is paying for? Why don't you ask questions about the drug deliveries?"[114]

Oliver North's complicit role with drug trafficking is easily verifiable. The National Security Archive includes 15 separate entries from Oliver North's diary that clearly demonstrate his knowledge of Contra drug trafficking. According to Michael Levine of the DEA, who can recognize more subtle references, there were hundreds of more examples of Contra drug trafficking within North's diary.[115] One of the more obvious examples is an entry from August 9, 1985, which read, "Honduran DC-6 which is being used for runs out of New Orleans is probably being used for drug runs into U.S." That was about a plane flown by Mario Calero, the brother of Contra leader, Adolfo Calero.

Likewise, a diary entry on July 12, 1985, even included a direct accounting of drug profits as told to him by Maj. Gen. Richard Secord. It read, "$14M (million) to finance Supermarket (Contra arms warehouse in Honduras) came from drugs."[116] Investigators naturally questioned North about these kinds of entries, but he has denied any culpability. He claimed that he passed all relevant information to the DEA. However, there are no records to support his claims.

North also helped a Honduran general, José Bueso Rosa, receive a drastically reduced sentence after he was busted in 1984 by the FBI for a $40 million cocaine shipment. Rosa had been heavily involved with the Contras and he planned to use parts of the drug profits to assassinate the liberal Honduran President Roberto Suazo Córdoba. That plan was later described by the Justice Department as the "most significant case of narco-terrorism yet discovered."[117]

On the other hand, Oliver North submitted the name of Jack Terrell, a military trainer of the Contras, to the FBI as a potential terrorist after Terrell informed investigators about the drug shipments at John Hull's ranch.[118] John Hull, an American who owned a ranch in northern Costa Rica near the Nicaraguan border, wasn't a mere American expatriate pensioner. Instead, he received $10,000 a month from North's payroll as an intelligence operative.

Various sources corroborated that Hull's ranch was a primary transit point for arms shipments for Contra pilots/drug traffickers.[119]

The Costa Rican government didn't interfere with John Hull's ranch due to a secret warfare agreement with the Reagan administration. The Costa Rican President Luis Alberto Monge agreed to this compromise in 1982 in exchange for foreign aid payments.[120] The Contras' clandestine camps were given free rein in a country that is internationally renowned for neutrality and lacking a formal military. However, this arrangement was disbanded in 1986 with the election of Oscar Arias. He was even awarded the Nobel Peace Prize one year later for negotiating an agreement in which the Contras ceased fire and the Sandinistas democratized their nation.

The Arias administration investigated the drug and gun running activity on Hull's ranch. That decision represented a changing of the guard. After all, Costa Rican law enforcement officials later testified to the U.S. Senate Committee on Foreign Relations that they had been pressured to not investigate the Contra operations along the northern border.[121] As a result of this inquiry, John Hull was arrested in 1989 for drug trafficking and arms smuggling. Due to the findings from that investigation, Oscar Arias, banned Oliver North, along with other intelligence officials such as the CIA station chief in Costa Rica, from entering his country.[122]

A group of 19 U.S. Congressmen responded to the charges by pressuring the Costa Rican government to set Hull free. They warned that his trial would hurt "relations" between both countries, an indirect threat to cut off their foreign aid money. Ultimately, John Hull skipped bail and fled the country. He returned to the U.S. and our government refused Costa Rica's request for extradition. With that said, the circumstances regarding his escape are even more astonishing. A report by the Justice Department's Inspector General divulged that a DEA pilot transported Hull out of Costa Rica![123]

Keep in mind that Congress voted that the U.S. couldn't arm the Contra rebels, but an exemption was granted for providing "humanitarian aid." Hence, the State Department established a Nicaraguan Humanitarian Aid Office (NHAO). In spite of that intention, Oliver North was granted supervision of the program and the NHAO served as a cover for shipping weapons to the rebels.[124]

The NHAO contracted those services to various companies, many of which were fronts for drug traffickers. To be exact, the

NHAO contracted with six companies owned and operated by known or convicted drug traffickers.[125] Suffice it to say, they employed a veritable list of the who's who of the drug trafficking world. Take Ramon Milian Rodriguez for example. He was a top accountant for the Medellín cartel and was busted in 1983 carrying $5.4 million of the cartel's cash.[126] It was a high-profile case that was labeled as a victory in the war on drugs. In fact, Vice President Bush traveled to Florida for that photo opportunity.[127] Nonetheless, one of his companies, Frigorificos de Puntarenas, received a $237,000 NHAO contract to transport humanitarian aid while he was under indictment.[128]

The official line by the U.S. government is that this was an oversight or vetting issue. And we're supposed to believe that? Do you think that drug trafficking organizations ordinarily pursue government contracts? It would be naïve to believe that these lifelong smugglers were suddenly struck by patriotic fever and decided to back the Contras. Nevertheless, long after the fact, during a 2004 appearance on *Hannity & Colmes*, Oliver North emphatically stated that "nobody in the government of the United States...ever had anything to do with running drugs to support the Nicaraguan resistance...I will stand on that to my grave."[129] But that simply wasn't the case.

In particular, a Miami aviation company, Vortex, received over $300,000 through NHAO contracts beginning in 1985.[130] Vortex received its first contract while the company's executive Vice President, Michael Palmer, was under investigation by the FBI in three different jurisdictions. Simultaneously, prosecutors in Detroit were in the process of charging him with importing over 1,000 pounds of marijuana from Colombia.[131]

In fact, two years prior, Palmer had been briefly imprisoned in Colombia for drug trafficking, but he reportedly bribed his way to freedom.[132] He was charged again in 1989 for importing 300,000 pounds of marijuana. Nonetheless, both cases were dropped. Indeed, documents from the U.S. Customs Service showed that standard customs procedures were specifically expedited for Palmer at the request of an unnamed agency.[133] Furthermore, Vortex also employed a convicted drug smuggler from the Dominican Republic, Donaldo Frixone, who had been implicated in smuggling 19,000 pounds of marijuana just months before joining the company.[134]

There are several drug traffickers who were contracted to supply the Contras with humanitarian aid, but arguably the most notorious was a Honduran drug kingpin, Juan Matta Ballesteros aka "El Negro." The NHAO awarded a contract of $186,000 to SETCO Air, an airline known to be operated by Matta's associates. In fact, a report in 1983 by the U.S. Customs Service noted that Matta Ballesteros was a "class I DEA violator" and "SETCO aviation is a corporation formed by American businessmen who are dealing with Matta (Ballesteros) and are smuggling narcotics into the United States."[135] Despite the notorious reputation, SETCO received that contract a full year after Matta Ballesteros had been named as a top suspect in the high-profile murder of DEA agent Kiki Camarena.[136]

Matta Ballesteros rose to power in the prime transshipment point between Colombia and Mexico. He accumulated enough wealth that he, like Pablo Escobar and Roberto Suarez of Bolivia, offered to pay off the national debt of his home country.[137] He had maintained a very public profile in his homeland for years because the Honduran government provided him safe haven. After all, Matta Ballesteros helped finance a CIA-supported military coup in 1978.[138]

Ioan Grillo, author of *El Narco*, noted the suspicious timing of Matta Ballesteros's eventual capture. The U.S. government used extreme and illegal means to capture Matta Ballesteros, but the raid didn't take place until 12 days *after* the Contra/Sandinista ceasefire in 1988. In other words, Matta Ballesteros was no longer useful to the U.S. intelligence community at that point.

Honduras didn't have an extradition treaty with the U.S. Nonetheless, U.S. Marshals arranged for Honduran special force troops to illegally capture him and send him to the Dominican Republic where U.S. authorities were waiting for him. Unfortunately, his capture led to rioting, protests, and burning down the U.S. embassy because Matta Ballesteros was a Robin Hood of sorts and popular among poor Hondurans.[139]

One particular SETCO pilot was a longtime CIA contractor, Robert "Tosh" Plumlee. Plumlee later became a very public CIA whistleblower and he has estimated that SETCO pilots transported as much as 40 tons of cocaine![140] That estimate falls in line with assertions by the DEA's Michael Levine. According to Levine, one DEA agent in the Honduras office documented as much as 50 tons of cocaine (then about one-third of U.S. demand) was shipped by several Hondurans supporting the Contras. In an even more remarkable twist, that particular DEA office in Tegucigalpa, Honduras was shut down not long afterward.[141]

"Tosh" Plumlee has been very candid in media appearances about the CIA's role in drug trafficking. "I was flying sanctioned operations transporting cocaine out of Colombia and into the United States," Plumlee says.[142] During an interview with *FOX News* in 2013, he said, "Those entities (contractors) were cut outs financed and operated by the Central Intelligence Agency. Our operations were sanctioned by the federal government, controlled out of the Pentagon," said Plumlee.[143]

As early as 1983, Plumlee had informed authorities at the highest levels of government about the CIA drug trafficking. He met with former Sen. Gary Hart (D-CO) multiple times.[144] Gary Hart later documented Plumlee's efforts in a letter sent to John Kerry who was then leading a Senate subcommittee investigating the CIA's role in drug trafficking. Plumlee testified before the Kerry Committee in private, but his testimony was sealed and will remain classified until 2020.[145]

Another high-level whistleblower, Celerino "Cele" Castillo, came forward with information connecting the CIA with Contra drug trafficking. Castillo served as a DEA agent in El Salvador in the 1980s. He discovered that over two dozen pilots transporting Contra supplies were listed as known drug smugglers in the DEA database. They were all using airport hangars at Ilopango Air Force Base in El Salvador, owned by the CIA and the National Security Council. "(Oliver) North's people and the CIA were at the two hangars overseeing the operations at all times," Castillo said.[146]

The CIA operations at Ilopango were supervised by an infamous CIA agent, Félix Rodríguez.[147] He has a great deal of notoriety as a Bay of Pigs veteran and he was photographed next to Che Guevara's dead body.[148] Félix Rodríguez's deputy was another Cuban exile, Luis Posada.[149] Posada, also a Bay of Pigs veteran, was part of the CIA-supported, anti-Castro terrorist organization, CORU, which committed over 50 bombings, including a Cuban airliner killing 73 people.[150] In fact, the CIA was accused of bribing Venezuelan officials for Posada's escape from a Venezuelan prison, just before he started his Contra operations.[151]

The DEA's "Cele" Castillo acted as a whistleblower and reported his information through the proper channels of the DEA and FBI to no avail. Castillo was one of many whistleblowers who provided credible evidence for John Kerry's Senate subcommittee investigation, which thoroughly documented the CIA's role in drug trafficking with the Contras. Kerry concluded, "There is no question in my mind that people affiliated with, or on the payroll of, the CIA were involved in drug trafficking."[152]

You can't state it any more clearly than Senator Kerry. To wrap up, Manuel Noriega is usually the first person who people think of when this subject is broached. However, Noriega is only one in a long list of drug traffickers who have been enabled by the U.S. government as proxies in the Cold War. The next chapter (Government Protected Drug Trafficking Part II) demonstrates that these same scenarios continued to unfold even after the Cold War officially ended. The U.S. government has also frequently allied with some of the world's most powerful drug traffickers to win the War on Terror.

13

"If I'm guilty of all these things they say, then (the CIA is) guilty of them too."

Senator John Kerry's subcommittee heard from another whistleblower, Terry Reed, who had been a CIA operative before getting burned by the agency. In Reed's book, *Compromised: Clinton, Bush, and the CIA*, he detailed the agency's use of his front company, Maquinaria International, in Mexico to aid gunrunning and drug trafficking operations. Also, Reed trained pilots for the Contras in the rural town Mena, AR. That location also served as the base of operations for Barry Seal's drug and arms trafficking on behalf of the Contras.[1]

At this point, it's necessary to note this kind of corruption and complicity spans both sides of the political aisle. Several members of Bill Clinton's network of staff, lawyers, and campaign contributors were associated with the drug trafficking scandal in Mena, AR. There was a wealth of local media coverage surrounding drug activity in Mena, particularly by a TV reporter Theresa Dickie. While serving as the Governor of Arkansas, Clinton was presented with a petition with thousands of signatures by a citizen's group known as the "Arkansas Committee" demanding an investigation. Also, Charles Black, the local county prosecutor, specifically requested funds from the Governor's office for an investigation, but he never heard back from them.[2] Clinton dodged questions about Mena, AR while serving as the Governor stating that it was "a federal matter," but he was just as reluctant to investigate it once he was in the White House.[3]

What did Clinton stand to gain for covering up this covert operation? Obviously, it's not a wise choice politically to spurn the CIA as a presidential hopeful. Also, a percentage of the drug money made its way into the Clinton presidential campaign. A government program known as the Arkansas Development and Finance Authority (ADFA) laundered much of the drug money that was flowing through Mena, AR. The ADFA was originally developed to provide tax-free, low-interest loans for small businesses, but the program often ended up as a tool of crony capitalist handouts, according to Larry Nichols, the former Marketing Director for the ADFA. "I was literally working, sitting in the middle of Bill Clinton's political machine," said Nichols.[4]

The ADFA provided loans to CIA shell companies, many of which were building untraceable weapons for the Contras. In return, those companies funneled campaign contributions to Bill Clinton. Dan Lasater, a close friend and significant campaign contributor to Bill Clinton, was in charge of how the ADFA's funds were dispersed.[A] Governor Clinton signed off on a $664 million bond contract for Lasater's firm as the underwriter, i.e. the bond seller. As a result, Lasater's firm earned $1.6 million in commissions.[5]

Mind you, Lasater was under investigation for cocaine trafficking at the time that he received the contract. A report by the FBI stated that Lasater "was the main supplier of cocaine to the investment banking and bond community in the United States outside of New York City."[6] Lasater was later convicted and while serving his sentence, Patsy Thomasson, was appointed as the CEO of Lasater's company. Nonetheless, Clinton subsequently pardoned Lasater in 1990 as the Arkansas Governor. And, despite a clear appearance of corruption, he appointed Patsy Thomasson as the Director of White House Office of Administration.[7]

A former IRS agent, William Duncan, was assigned to investigate the Mena, AR allegations and followed the drug money trail through the Arkansas Bond market. However, he later resigned from his position due to the extensive obstruction he faced by the federal government. "I've always thought it was a wonderful thing to be able to serve your country as a federal law enforcement agent, and for 15 years I did not encounter anything like the corruption which I encountered after the Mena investigations began," said Duncan.[8] Duncan was a very credible whistleblower. He testified to Congress, "The United States Attorney, Western Judicial District of Arkansas, assured us that there were no national security or other issues involved which would impede investigation and prosecution of criminal violations in Arkansas, however, he refused to issue

---

[A] As a favor, Lasater hired Bill Clinton's brother, Roger, to work at his office.

subpoenas for critical witnesses, interfered in the investigations, apparently misled grand juries about evidence and availability of witnesses, refused to allow investigators to present evidence to the grand jury, and in general made a mockery of the entire investigative and judicial process."[9]

Duncan contacted various national media outlets but became frustrated with the process. Bill Plante of *CBS News* investigated the story but ran into numerous roadblocks. He said, "Mena is a perplexing and difficult story. There is a trail-- tens of millions of dollars in cocaine profits, and we don't know where it leads. It is a trail that has been blocked by the National Security Council. The FAA, FBI, Customs, CIA, Justice, DEA, and the IRS were all involved in Mena."[10]

None of the parties involved in the Mena, Arkansas scandal were held accountable. And that story slowly faded from the public's consciousness. However, an investigative journalist with the San Jose Mercury News, Gary Webb, later resurrected mainstream attention to the CIA's links with drug trafficking. Webb wrote a three-part series titled "Dark Alliance" in 1996 that revealed an aspect of Iran-Contra that had been widely neglected by the press for years. Remarkably, Webb came upon this story indirectly after listening to testimony from a paid DEA informant, Oscar Danilo Blandon, in a California drug case. Blandon testified that he had sold cocaine for the benefit of the Contras in Nicaragua.[11]

Oscar Danilo Blandon wasn't any ordinary drug dealer. He had been a wealthy Nicaraguan entrenched within the Somoza regime before he was exiled by the Sandinistas. He and his business partner, Norwin Meneses, began raising money for the Contras from cocaine proceeds in 1982. Meneses was another exiled Nicaraguan who had a well-documented trafficking record before his actions with the Contras. After all, he was known as "el Rey de las Drogas" or "the king of drugs" in the Nicaraguan newspapers. Thus, Blandon's connections seemingly enabled him to sell pure cocaine at prices that were reportedly far below the market price. According to his testimony, by 1986 he was supplying four to five different dealers with approximately 100 kilos of cocaine per week.[12]

Gary Webb wrote about this link between drug trafficking and the Contras in the *San Jose Mercury News*, and his reports quickly gained a national audience. There was an explosive reaction when people learned that Blandon was the supplier to a Los Angeles crack kingpin, "Freeway" Rick Ross, who was instrumental in the rise of crack cocaine. Webb never claimed that Rick Ross invented crack cocaine; instead, Webb insisted that the demand for crack cocaine was increasing on its own and Ross merely was a grand facilitator.

Some people inferred that the resulting crack cocaine explosion in the African-American community was an intentional act of suppression by the CIA. However, that was never implied by Webb, nor did he provide any evidence to back up that kind of interpretation. He believed that it was a "chain reaction" and a "horrible accident of history."[13] Nonetheless, some media critics used that as a straw man argument to discredit Webb. Gary Webb's work was thoroughly criticized by many media outlets, most notably *The New York Times*, *The Washington Post*, and the *Los Angeles Times*. Very few newspapers decided to dig deeper into the CIA's role with drug traffickers and instead many personally attacked Webb's reputation. In fact, the *Los Angeles Times* even had an unofficial "Get Gary Webb Team," of 17 writers focused upon discrediting his work.[14]

One can only speculate as to the motivations behind the media war that attacked Webb's credibility. Several researchers/writers have detailed the CIA's role in drug trafficking and most have received undeserved criticism, but nothing like the condemnation Webb faced. The safer career decision in journalism is to write critical op-eds that label someone as a "conspiracy theorist," rather than conducting an arduous investigation that requires many resources, much time, and an enormous burden of proof when confronting organizations such as the CIA.

The CIA often uses operatives for their rogue missions, thereby adding degrees of separation and providing plausible deniability. Instead of truly investigating, many "establishment reporters" function more like defense attorneys after this type of scandal. They often downplay the extent of the agency's knowledge about their operatives' drug activity. Be that as it may, it would be more disturbing if the Central Intelligence Agency were *truly* unaware of their operatives' drug trafficking. They are not Keystone Cops; they are, after all, the Central Intelligence Agency.

Howard Kurtz, dubbed by many as the top media critic, was a reporter at *The Washington Post* when Webb's story broke. He took the easy route by mocking Webb stating, "Oliver Stone, check your voicemail."[15] On the other hand, Robert Parry pointed out the "double standard" with how "Webb was held to the strictest standards of journalism" while Kurtz can "make judgments based on ignorance. Kurtz would face no repercussions for ridiculing a fellow journalist who was factually correct."[16] As you may remember, Robert Parry, an award-winning journalist, was one of the *Associated Press* reporters who first broke the story of Contra cocaine trafficking in 1985. Parry has faced this kind of criticism, albeit on a much smaller scale because his story didn't receive as much attention via the Internet.[B]

Robert Parry noted that the Executive Editor of the *San Jose Mercury News*, Jerry Ceppos, received an award for ethics from the Society of Professional Journalists *after* he acquiesced to outside pressure by retracting the story.[17] Webb's career was ruined by all of the controversy surrounding this one story, yet Kurtz's career ascended later with a career in television at *Fox News*. Bear in mind, Kurtz took that job after his credibility took some hits. He left his position as the host of CNN's "Reliable Sources," ironically after making a number of highly visible factual errors.[18] But, Kurtz never faced a hailstorm of criticism like that of Webb because he hasn't been an adversary to the establishment.

There is an institutional bias within the media for supporting the power structure. Lawrence Zuckerman from *Time Magazine* also investigated the drug trafficking allegations surrounding the Contras, but his work wasn't published. His editor told him, "*Time* is institutionally behind the Contras. If this story was about the Sandinistas and drugs you'd have no trouble getting it in the magazine."[19] Prolific news organizations often receive information firsthand from government sources, therefore they aren't likely to burn bridges. Consequently, they're more likely to act as gatekeepers.

An article, "Managing a Nightmare: CIA Public Affairs and the Drug Conspiracy Story," was declassified from the CIA's internal

---

[B] Parry is one of the earliest founders of independent online journalism, *Consortium News*.

journal. It was written shortly after Webb's series was published and it further demonstrated the agency's connections within the media.[20] The article delighted in the manner in which the mainstream press protected the agency. The CIA has some unofficial partnerships within the press, notably *The Washington Post*. Katharine Graham, the former publisher of *The Washington Post*, once essentially pledged her allegiance during a speech at CIA headquarters in 1988. She said, "We live in a dirty and dangerous world. There are some things the general public does not need to know and shouldn't. I believe democracy flourishes when the government can take legitimate steps to keep its secrets and when the press can decide whether to print what it knows."[21]

There obviously is an argument for government secrecy and the press using discretion when appropriate, but there also has to be a line drawn to prevent blatant conflicts of interest. Case in point, the leading reporter from *The Washington Post* challenging Gary Webb's story, Walter Pincus, had admittedly worked for the CIA during his college days.[22] *The Washington Post* featured Pincus's dismissal of Webb on the front page. Meanwhile, the research from their paper's investigative journalist, Doug Farah, overall supported Webb's reports. Nevertheless, Farah's article was considerably condensed and printed at the back of the paper.[23]

The CIA has had their tentacles in the media for many years and their powers have extended well past "conflicts of interest." Dating back to the 1970s, the Church Committee found that over 400 reporters from over 25 media outlets had carried out specific assignments on behalf of the agency through a propaganda program known as "Operation Mockingbird."[24] Not to mention, an internal memo from 1991 was declassified and it expressed specifics regarding the involvement of the CIA's Public Affairs Office (PAO) with the media:

> PAO now has relationships with reporters from every major wire service, newspaper, news weekly, and television network in the nation. This has helped us turn some "intelligence failure" stories into "intelligence success" stories, and it has contributed to the accuracy of countless others. In many instances, we have persuaded reporters to postpone, change, hold, or even scrap stories that could have adversely affected national security interests or jeopardized sources and methods.[25]

It's unknown to what extent the CIA is currently entangled with the media as that type of information would require a brand new Congressional investigation. However, in a separate and more modern investigation by *The Intercept*, their news outlet processed several Freedom of Information Act requests and found many current reporters with questionable relationships connected to the CIA. *The Intercept* discovered that Ken Dilanian routinely sent his unpublished work to the agency before publishing it with the *Los Angeles Times*. He even once asked in an email, "You wouldn't put out disinformation on this, would you?"[26]

A separate investigation by *Judicial Watch* found that a *New York Times* reporter, Mark Mazzetti, literally forwarded the unpublished work of a fellow *Times* reporter, Maureen Dowd, to a CIA spokeswoman. The CIA was worried that Dowd's report would be unflattering to the agency, but Mazzetti reassured the CIA spokesperson by writing, "See, nothing to worry about."[27]

The corporate media lambasted Gary Webb, but they were unable to completely censor his findings. With Sen. Barbara Boxer (D-CA) and Rep. Maxine Waters (D-CA) demanding a formal investigation, the CIA, in an unusual move, actually made a public relations gesture.[28] The CIA Director, John Deutch, conducted a town hall meeting in front of an angry Los Angeles audience. One man, Michael Ruppert, publicly confronted the director. "I am a former Los Angeles police narcotics detective and I worked South Central Los Angeles. I will tell you emphatically Director Deutsch as a former Los Angeles police narcotics detective that the agency has dealt drugs throughout this country for a long time." The crowd immediately gasped and loudly applauded.

Ruppert continued, "Director Deutch, I will refer you to three specific agency operations known as Amadeus, Pegasus, and Watchtower. I have Watchtower documents heavily redacted by the agency. I was personally exposed to CIA operations and recruited by CIA personnel in the late 70s to become involved in protecting agency drug operations in this country. I've been trying to get this out for 18 years and I have the evidence."[29]

Webb also published a follow-up book to his three-part newspaper series, *Dark Alliance: The CIA, the Contras, and the*

Crack Cocaine Explosion, which featured a great deal of convincing evidence from a litany of government documents and highly credible government witnesses. Webb's efforts created enough controversy to force the CIA to form an internal investigation by the Inspector General, Frederick Hitz.

Hitz functioned like a spokesman for the agency by telling the media that the CIA wasn't complicit in drug trafficking. In some cases, the denials in the report were downright comical. The Hitz report acknowledged that the CIA intervened with the U.S. Attorney's office in San Francisco with the "Frogman Case," in which a Nicaraguan received a $36,000 refund from the government. However, the report stated that "CIA personnel reached the erroneous conclusion that one of the two individuals…was a former CIA asset."[30]

The CIA wisely guessed that very few people would bother to read the report. As Michael Ruppert pointed out, the report was released on October 8, 1998, which was a great day to bury a story. The House of Representatives voted to begin the impeachment process against Bill Clinton.[31] Despite public assurances by Hitz that downplayed the role of the CIA, the devil is in the details. The report named over 50 major drug traffickers connected with the Contras, including Eulalio Francisco Castro Paz (Frank Castro).[C32]

Frank Castro was a Cuban exile, a Bay of Pigs veteran, and the founder of the anti-Fidel Castro terrorist organization CORU. He didn't take part in Contra missions, but Frank Castro helped finance them. Robert Owen, Oliver North's top aid, stated that he had heard from several sources that Frank Castro was contributing $200,000 a month to the Contras. Castro had been charged in Texas in 1983 for trafficking 425,000 pounds of marijuana. He then provided the

---

[c] Webb's career was ruined after "Dark Alliance." His reputation was considered "discredited" by the increasingly soundbite driven culture and echo chamber journalism. No large budget newspaper was willing to hire him and in 2004 he was found dead at home from *two* gun shots to the head. It was ruled a suicide. Considering Webb's list of enemies and the circumstances, it understandably left many people suspecting foul play. However, Nick Schou, the author of *Kill the Messenger* which honored Gary Webb, backed up the suicide story. He pointed out that the first bullet hit his cheek, likely from pulling away at the last moment. The second bullet nicked an artery and he ultimately bled to death.

Contras with substantial funding, including multiple aircraft. Consequently, the drug charge against Castro was dropped and the CIA withheld information from the Kerry committee.[33]

There were many other damning admissions proving that the CIA was aware of their operatives' drug dealing and withheld information from the appropriate authorities. A 1982 letter between the CIA's director, William Casey, and the U.S. Attorney General, William French Smith, established a loophole allowing CIA agents to give their operatives carte blanche. That letter established that CIA agents were not required to report offenses of drug trafficking by their operatives, even though numerous other crimes were required to be reported. Both sides had to agree on reporting procedures via this "Memorandum of Understanding," which essentially allowed the CIA to cover up whatever they wanted.[34] The CIA's Inspector General Hitz later conceded that the agreement was a "mixed message."[D][35]

Gary Webb faced the worst onslaught of criticism, more than any other journalist covering the CIA's association with drug trafficking, likely because his story gained the most attention. It was the first of its kind during the Internet era. Coincidentally, a different high-profile case of CIA-related drug trafficking was in the news less than two weeks after Donald Deutsch's town hall meeting on November 15, 1996. A Venezuelan General, Ramon Guillén Dávila, working in conjunction with the CIA, was indicted for importing cocaine into the U.S. In that case, the CIA had met with the head of the DEA requesting permission to allow the Venezuelan general to ship one ton of pure cocaine into Miami. The CIA claimed that their goal was to boost the general's credibility so that he could eventually infiltrate the Colombian cartels. The DEA refused to allow that shipment, but General Guillén Dávila made the delivery anyway.

[D] George H.W. Bush faced the same kind of scrutiny from former Congresswoman Bella Abzug at the House Subcommittee on Government Information and Individual Rights when he was the Director of the CIA. Bush explained that the agency had the right to protect their agents in the name of national security. The Abzug Committee stated, "It was ironic that the CIA should be given responsibility of narcotic intelligence, particularly since they are supporting the prime movers."

Ultimately, the CIA didn't infiltrate the Colombian cartels and didn't even intercept the drug shipment.[36]

A CIA spokesman referred to this operation as a "most regrettable incident."[37] On the other hand, Robert Bonner, the former head of the DEA at that time, told *60 Minutes*, "It's called drug trafficking. It's called drug smuggling."[E38] Likewise, Annabelle Grimm, the top DEA agent in Venezuela, told *60 Minutes* that it was very unlikely that Guillén Dávila was acting without CIA consent. She said, "General Guillén and his officers didn't go to the bathroom without telling Mark McFarlin or the CIA what they were doing."[39] Mark McFarlin, Guillén's handler at the CIA, resigned afterward without facing any charges.

The timing of that story by *60 Minutes* was interesting because one week earlier *The New York Times* published an article, "CIA Formed Haitian Unit Later Tied to Narcotics Trade." The leaders of a CIA-supported military coup, the National Intelligence Service (SIN), were this nation's leading drug traffickers.[40] Haiti's first democratically elected President, Jean-Bertrand Aristide, was overthrown and exiled from the island in 1991 by a group of former SOA graduates, just months after his election.[41]

The U.S. government officially denounced the coup by issuing a trade embargo, but Aristide publicly declared that the few Haitians who weren't suffering from that decision were the corrupt military leaders who made millions from the drug trade. In fact, a top DEA official in Haiti, Tony Greco, had to leave the country in fear for his life after he busted a high-level Haitian counternarcotics official. Greco received a death threat over his confidential phone line that was only known by two people, the leaders of the coup, Gen. Raoul

---

[E] That decision by the CIA has similarities to a situation with a government informant for the U.S. Customs Service. Rodney Matthews began his career as a paid criminal informant after his arrest in 1984 with 564 pounds of marijuana. The U.S. government paid him more than $200,000 for information that led to four separate convictions, however his government handlers never made any attempts to curtail his illegal activities. Matthews upgraded his status by acting as a courier for the top cocaine kingpins. On New Year's Eve 1988, Texas authorities arrested him with 1,800 pounds of cocaine, but he was set free by the U.S. Customs Service. Matthews's partner, Jimmie Ellard, estimated afterward that they actually moved about $6 billion worth of drugs over a five-year period, during an interview with ABC News *Primetime*.

Cedras and the Police Chief Joseph-Michel Francois.[42] These de facto leaders controlled the country until 1994. Afterward, several of those military commanders were arrested by the DEA. However, that was after they were no longer of use to the intelligence community. In particular, Joseph-Michel Francois was arrested for exporting a whopping 33 tons of cocaine and heroin![43]

Obviously, the U.S. government publicly denounced the coup, but its actions were to the contrary. From 1991 to 1994, the CIA secretly funded the leadership of Haiti's most brutal paramilitary group, FRAPH, responsible for the murders of thousands of Haitians.[44] FRAPH's founder, Emmanuel "Toto" Constant, later fled to the U.S. in 1995. And as you would expect, Haitian authorities pleaded for him to be extradited back to his homeland to stand trial for war crimes.

In response, Constant took aggressive action on his behalf by suing the U.S. government for wrongful imprisonment, citing the CIA's complicity in his crimes. During an appearance on *60 Minutes*, he memorably asserted, "If I'm guilty of all these things they say, then they are guilty of them too."[45] Mind you, any Haitian even suspected of privately making such kinds of anti-government speech would have been summarily executed by his paramilitary forces. Nonetheless, the U.S. government released him from prison and provided him political asylum. Yes, a bona fide war criminal was granted safe haven by the U.S. government.

Emmanuel "Toto" Constant lived freely in New York City working as a real estate agent for many years. He would have never been brought to justice if he had not committed the most unforgivable sin in American society; he scammed bankers out of money. Constant was a member of a $1 million mortgage fraud scheme and in 2008 he was sentenced to a maximum of 15 years in prison.[46] That one example tells you primarily everything that you need to know about the American power structure. The federal government protected a war criminal who was responsible for the murder, rape, and torture of thousands of innocent Haitians, but all bets were off after he defrauded U.S. banks.

At this point, it's time to reassert the obvious; the CIA operates far beyond congressional oversight. Well, hold onto your hat because it gets worse. It made worldwide news when a DEA agent in Mexico, Enrique "Kiki" Camarena, was kidnapped, sadistically tortured for three days, and murdered in 1985.[F47] Camarena's death was seemingly in retribution for successfully raiding some marijuana plantations owned by the Guadalajara cartel, the precursor to the Sinaloa cartel. His death garnered more support for the drug war and he became a martyr. Conversely, details from that murder came to light years later and exposed that the CIA was also in bed with major drug traffickers in Mexico. Unfortunately, the general public is completely unaware of these details.

Remember, Juan Matta Ballesteros, "El Negro"? He's the Honduran drug lord whose company, SETCO, had been contracted to supply humanitarian aid. He was also one of the co-conspirators convicted for Camarena's murder. Juan Matta Ballesteros was the primary middleman between Colombia and the Guadalajara cartel. One of the leaders of the Guadalajara cartel, Miguel Ángel Félix Gallardo aka El Padrino "The Godfather," was also convicted for Camarena's murder. During his trial, one of his pilots testified that Félix Gallardo felt that his operation would remain safe because he supplied arms to the Contras.[48] After all, the DEA contacted the CIA in 1982 for help with a money laundering investigation, but they refused. The DEA later found that El Padrino had laundered as much as $20 million a month through a single Bank of America account.[49]

The Guadalajara cartel received protection from the highest levels of the Mexican government, in particular, Mexico's former version of the CIA, Federal Security Directorate (DFS). This corruption was no more evident than when DEA officials attempted to capture Rafael Caro Quintero, another Guadalajara cartel leader, for the murder of Camarena. DEA agents were thwarted by over 50 armed DFS agents who shielded him before making a getaway flight. Caro Quintero laughed at the DEA agents from the doorway of his plane with a bottle of champagne saying, "My children, next time, bring more guns," according to Hector Berrellez, the lead DEA investigator of Camarena's death.[50] Such an egregious act, among many more, led to the dismantling of their agency in 1985, but many

---

[F] A number of people were convicted for conspiring to kill Camarena, including Rubén Zuno Arce a brother-in-law of the ex-President of Mexico Luis Echeverria.

of those DFS agents simply transitioned into full-time employment for various cartels.[51]

Several top DFS officials were on the CIA's payroll, including the DFS's Director Miguel Nazar Haro. He was considered crucial to their intelligence efforts and the CIA pressured the FBI in 1979 to drop a case against Nazar for "national security" reasons. Nazar was involved in a car theft ring that stole an estimated 4,000 cars from southern California and transported them across the Mexican border to the DFS office. Nazar received this kind of protection due to his gruesome anti-communism efforts. The DFS included a death squad, "the White Brigade," which targeted anyone with even the slightest connections to liberal activism.[52]

The official version of the story is that Kiki Camarena was murdered in retribution for his high-profile busts, but many people suspected that the CIA may have been behind the murder to cover up their illegal activities. After all, a CIA operative was in the room during Camarena's interrogation/torture and later provided an audio tape to DEA investigators. In 1990, a jury listened to the horrific audio of this torture. Several different voices questioned Camarena, including one person who he referred to as "commandante," likely a member of the DFS.[53]

Again, the CIA's potential link with this murder was merely speculation at that point. However, Charles Bowden published *Down by the River* in 2002 and his book unveiled new secrets regarding Camarena's murder. Bowden's book centered on a quest by Phil Jordan, the former head of the DEA's El Paso office, to properly investigate a separate cartel murder. However, his book also mentioned that Phil Jordan met with Kiki Camarena in Mexico shortly before his death. The two agents were trailed by the DFS the entire time. Camarena told Jordan about several of the connections between the CIA, DFS, and the Guadalajara cartel. In fact, Camarena had been in contact with one of Mexico's top investigative journalists, Manuel Buendía who was murdered shortly thereafter. DFS agents stormed Buendía's office and took all of his files.[54]

The few people in-the-know remained tight-lipped about Camarena's murder until 2013 when Rafael Caro Quintero was released by Mexican officials from prison. At that point, the DEA's

Phil Jordan and Hector Berrellez (the lead DEA investigator), along with the former SETCO pilot/whistleblower, Robert "Tosh" Plumlee, contacted the media. Plumlee told reporters that he used to transport shipments to Caro Quintero's ranch and Camarena was aware of these flights. Five months before Camarena's murder, Plumlee met with a group of narcotics agents, including Camarena. He explained to them that his cocaine trafficking with SETCO was sanctioned by the CIA, but Camarena was furious with that revelation.[55] "The CIA ordered Kiki Camarena's capture and torture, and when he was killed they made us believe that it was Caro Quintero (Guadalajara cartel) in order to cover up their illegal activities in Mexico," said Hector Berrellez during an interview for Spanish newspaper *El País*.[56]

This was another absolute bombshell of a report, but this story was censored by the U.S. media. However, in 2015 *LA Weekly* was the first to print the full extent of the accusations of Hector Berrellez. According to Berrellez, his sources explicitly named the infamous CIA agent who was photographed next to Che Guevara's dead body, Félix Rodríguez, as the man who ordered the murder.[57] If these findings are accurate, this unveils an extra level of the lawlessness by the agency. Then again, Berrellez had nothing to gain by coming forward with these accusations and risked his life to do so. Nevertheless, everyone responsible for Camarena's murder will likely never be brought to justice.

The CIA is responsible for toppling various democratically elected leaders and is complicit in the murder of thousands of foreign political activists. Likewise, the patterns of CIA complicity with drug trafficking are still visible with the war in Afghanistan. The patterns of blowback from supporting radical leaders have also led to dire consequences in our homeland. Many times the "freedom fighters" of today turn into the "terrorists" of tomorrow.

In the aftermath of the Soviet Union's invasion of Afghanistan, there was a civil war among tribal leaders for control of the government. This war was fueled by the profits from the opium supply. As mentioned earlier, Gulbuddin Hekmatyar is an openly radical, fundamentalist Muslim who advocated jihad against the West. This war criminal, "the butcher of Kabul," is even responsible for terrorist attacks that killed thousands of Afghan citizens. He was appointed as the Afghan Prime Minister in 1994 to stop the bombings. In turn, known terrorist leaders found safe haven in his country, including Osama Bin Laden.[G][58]

The Taliban eventually overthrew Hekmatyar and subsequently inflicted a reign that was even more brutal and fundamentalist. They were comprised of former Mujahideen fighters and a group of Pakistani educated extremists. Unlike Hekmatyar, the Taliban had a different view of opium. They stated that they opposed opium production for religious reasons, but they probably were more interested in suppressing the finances of rival warlords. The Taliban initially implemented an opium ban after gaining power, but that decision was quickly overturned because they feared a violent uprising by the masses.[59] After all, an Afghan farmer can make $10,000 a year with opium compared to about $400 a year with legal crops.

The Taliban eventually decided to reinstate the ban on opium in 2000 in hopes that their government would gain international recognition. Accordingly, the Taliban strictly enforced the new policy and opium production was reduced by 96% within a year![H] Consequently, the U.S. government rewarded the Taliban in May of 2001 with $43 million for their opium elimination efforts.[60]

After the Taliban's opium ban, 90% of the remaining supply was controlled in 2001 by a U.S. ally, the Northern Alliance.[61] Consequently, the supply of Afghan opium exploded in the aftermath of 9/11 because the White House decided to not repeat the wide-scale, conventional war plan of the Soviets. This was a war led by foreign intelligence assets, notably the Northern Alliance whose leader, Ahmad Shah Massoud, was murdered by Al Qaeda two days before 9/11.[62]

Massoud had been a paid operative of the U.S. intelligence community during the Clinton administration in hopes of capturing Bin Laden.[63] Also, the Northern Alliance's drug trafficking

---

[G] In September of 2016, Afghan President Ashraf Ghani signed a peace deal that absolved Hekmatyar and his followers of all past war crimes.

[H] According to the U.N. report, there were 3,276 tons of opium produced in 2000. That number shrank to 185 tons in 2001. The U.S. State Dept. estimated that 3,656 tons were produced in 2000 and it decreased to 74 tons in 2001. The CIA estimated there were 4,042 tons in 2000 and 81 tons in 2001.

proceeds weren't a secret at the highest levels of the U.S. government. Some officials, such as Richard Clark, disagreed with the decision to support the Northern Alliance. Clarke, the White House counterterrorism expert for both the Clinton and George W. Bush administrations, labeled them as "drug smugglers" and "human rights abusers."[64] However, that alliance lost nearly all of its controversy in the aftermath of 9/11.

The CIA gave millions of dollars to the Northern Alliance to help with the fight against the Taliban in the weeks following 9/11.[65] And, needless to say, the intelligence community wasn't concerned with minimizing their drug trafficking efforts. The U.S. State Department reported in March of 2002 that the Northern Alliance had done nothing to curb the production of opium. Hence, Afghanistan's opium production surged and returned to a similar level (3,400 tons) before the ban by the Taliban. Afghanistan quickly regained its monopoly on the world's opium supply, roughly 90% of the world's opium.[66]

Despite the facts at hand, most American media outlets have blamed the Taliban for the resurgence in Afghan opium production. In fact, a few post 9/11 public service announcements began to state irrefutably that drug users are supporting terrorism. That specific piece of propaganda is only partially accurate. Yes, U.N. officials estimate that the Taliban generates about $125 million a year from the opium trade, but they're actually a relatively small player in the Afghan opium market which generates roughly $3 billion a year.[67]

The Taliban does not make money directly from growing, processing, or transporting heroin. Instead, farmers are "taxed" and "protection fees" are taken from the couriers. "The Taliban definitely get income from opium cultivation...but the lion's share of the income still disappears here, into the hands of the big patrons of this country," says Jean-Luc Lemahieu, the U.N.'s top narcotics official in Afghanistan.[68] It goes without saying, the most powerful opium traffickers in Afghanistan are usually military allies of the U.S. In fact, some news outlets, such as *ABC* and *Fox News*, reported that U.S. troops were ordered to allow farmers to continue growing opium.[69] Why? The general narrative is that U.S. authorities will intercept the drugs domestically. Also, the Afghan citizens would likely turn on the soldiers if they eradicated the poppies.

The Pentagon has an official hit list of 50 of the country's top traffickers associated with the Taliban who can be "killed or captured." Conversely, many of Afghanistan's most powerful drug traffickers have gone unpunished as long as they remain a military ally.[70] The former Afghan President, Hamid Karzai, officially banned opium production in January of 2002, but the charade quickly became apparent.[71] He actually gave presidential pardons to five police officers who were arrested in possession of 124 kilos of heroin. Likewise, Karzai also interfered with a narcotics investigation to protect a wealthy businessman who had supported him financially.[72]

In June of 2005, British forces raided the office of the Governor of the Helmand Province, Sher Mohammad Akhundzada. They found nearly ten tons of opium! "We don't need an investigation on (him). We will remove him from his place and bring him to do some other government work," said Karzai. "Maybe he should become a Senator or something."[73] Karzai claimed that the raid was just a rumor, but the DEA's spokeswoman, Rogene Waite, confirmed the seizure.[74] Regardless, Karzai appointed that same disgraced Governor to the House of Elder, the Afghan version of the Senate. In a separate incident, Graeme Smith, an investigative journalist for Canada's *Globe and Mail,* reported in 2009 that Afghan authorities detained a man carrying 183 kilograms of pure heroin, but he was promptly released because he was carrying a signed letter of protection from Afghanistan's drug czar, General Mohammad Daud Daud.[75]

The New York Times and *Washington Post* have reported that most of Hamid Karzai's inner circle was clearly connected with opium trafficking. Meanwhile, his network had also been on the CIA's payroll for many years. The CIA gave top members of the Karzai administration millions of dollars in unreported payments, "ghost money," which were then routed to various Afghan warlords.[76] Karzai's top aide, Mohammed Zia Salehi, was arrested in 2010 in connection with this cash smuggling. However, he was quickly released by Karzai and the CIA reportedly helped to block any further charges against him. That's why Salehi described himself as "an enemy of the FBI and a hero to the CIA."[77]

Moreover, Hamid Karzai's half-brother, Ahmed Wali Karzai, who led a counterterrorism unit, Kandahar Strike Force, was also a known drug smuggler. Despite this notorious reputation, he had been on the CIA payroll for years before 9/11.[78] Another suspected opium trafficker, Ahmad Zia Massoud, was the first Vice President of the Karzai administration. Those suspicions came to fruition in 2009 when *WikiLeaks* released a document stating that he had traveled to Dubai with $52 million in cash.[179] Likewise, Massoud's successor as Vice President, Mohammad Qasim Fahim, was another former anti-Soviet warlord/opium trafficker on the CIA payroll.[J80]

With such flagrant corruption, the U.S. government needed some sacrificial lambs to reduce the appearance of supporting a "narco-state." It should be no surprise that the scapegoats have been the ones with the strongest ties to the Taliban. An Afghan warlord, Haji Bashir Noorzai, received a life sentence in 2009 on drug trafficking charges and his conviction is reminiscent of what happened to Manuel Noriega. Noorzai was closely aligned with the Taliban, but he also secretly supported both sides of the wars. He had for years provided U.S. authorities with intelligence information, some of which led to the capture of thousands of Taliban weapons. In return, Noorzai made millions of dollars in the opium trade without any interference.

With that in mind, U.S. officials convinced Noorzai to travel to New York City in 2005 for intelligence sharing purposes. However, on this occasion, he was arrested by DEA officials.[81] In a similar fashion, another double-dealing, Taliban-linked drug trafficker, Haji Juma Khan, was arrested in 2008. Khan had been captured in 2001 by U.S. troops and promptly released. The size of his drug trafficking operation increased after 9/11 and he served as a well-paid informant for the DEA and CIA. In fact, he was flown to Washington D.C. in 2006 for a number of secret meetings.[82]

To be brief, the links between the CIA and drug trafficking are extensive and this chapter hasn't detailed every instance of CIA complicity. There are several articles printed in the most reputable

---

[I] Massoud Ahmad Zia Massoud is the younger brother of the former Northern Alliance leader, Ahmad Shah Massoud.
[J] His reputation led Hillary Clinton to warn Karzai against having him as his running mate.

newspapers about drug traffickers with government connections. However, there is a reoccurring theme in which few journalists dare to connect the dots and point out that these cases aren't isolated incidents. One of those rare journalists is Jonathan Kwitny, from *The Wall Street Journal*, who wrote *The Crimes of Patriots: The True Tale of Dope, Dirty Money, and the CIA*. Kwitney detailed a particular Australian bank, Nugan Hand, which was entrenched with CIA interests and was a haven for Australia's most infamous drug dealers.

Because of the CIA's lack of transparency, providing the necessary proof is lengthy and complex. Several authors, notably Alfred McCoy, Alexander Cockburn, Jeffrey St. Clair, Peter Dale Scott, Jonathan Marshall, Dan Russell, Michael Levine, Douglas Valentine, among others, have written well-documented books specifically dedicated to this subject matter. In addition, Bill Conroy, an investigative journalist for *Narco News*, has produced some particularly astonishing work on this subject as well.

Various theories abound, but there's no evidence to a popular notion on the Internet that the CIA allies with organized criminals for some perverse conspiracy to poison and subjugate the population. Instead, their motives are simple; they want to bypass the democratic process and to maintain the American empire by any means necessary. With that said, it's not accurate to single out the CIA as a rogue agency. Several federal agencies have aided and abetted drug trafficking; the stand down orders come from above. Simply put, the CIA serves as the clandestine wing of a rogue *government*.

Government protected drug trafficking isn't even an original scheme; it isn't unique to U.S. intelligence officials. When the CIA first became involved in the Southeast Asia opium trade, they were merely following the lead of the French intelligence community in the same region from a few years earlier.[83] Moreover, remember that the British Empire even went to war with China in the infamous "Opium Wars." Considering the state of the U.S. military, this connection between wars and drugs likely won't go away. The U.S. is the world's unquestioned leader in weaponry, but it has struggled with enlisting new troops. That makes funding rebel groups through dirty money even more likely in the future. Foreign policy pundits can debate the merits of those missions, but what can't be denied is that the U.S. government's drug war is a failure and exceedingly disingenuous.

In conclusion, a very simple truth emerges. So many wrongs can be reversed by ending the drug war. Drug laws have damaged our society more than the actual harms associated with drug abuse. The drug war has wrecked lives, torn families apart, negated our civil liberties, indirectly supported domestic terrorism in foreign countries, propped up thuggish dictatorships, denied fantastic medical advancements, weakened our economy, denied vast entrepreneurial endeavors, unjustly flooded our prisons, perverted the criminal justice system, spawned government money grabs, rewarded the most corrupt bureaucracies, perpetuated racism, and damaged our reputation globally. Nonetheless, all of these inherent consequences would be less demoralizing if the government had tried in earnest but failed. Instead, it has all been based upon lies. The drug war truly is a trillion dollar con game.

Names and Organizations

(ACLU) The American Civil Liberties Union – The ACLU is one of the premier organizations defending civil liberties and Constitutional rights.

Anslinger, Harry – The first commissioner of the Federal Bureau of Narcotics. He crusaded for the criminalization of marijuana.

(AUC) (United Self-Defense Forces of Colombia) – A Colombia paramilitary organization that served as a proxy for the Colombian government. The AUC was an officially designated terrorist group by the U.S. government before it disbanded in 2006. The AUC had numerous links to drug trafficking.

Binney, Bill – NSA Whistleblower

Castillo, Celerino "Cele" – DEA whistleblower

(CCA) Corrections Corporation of America – CCA was the first for-profit prison corporation. This company is now called "CoreCivic."

(DOJ) Department of Justice

Drake, Thomas – NSA Whistleblower

(FARC) (Revolutionary Armed Forces of Colombia) A Colombian communist rebel organization with numerous links to drug trafficking. The FARC is an officially designated terrorist group that recently entered into a peace agreement with the government of Colombia after a 52-year civil war.

(GAO) Government Accountability Office

GEO Group – An influential for-profit prison contracting company that is headquartered in Boca Raton, FL.

Hearst, William Randolph – The most powerful newspaper magnate of the early 20th century.

Hekmatyar, Gulbuddin – Warlord and former Prime Minister of Afghanistan. The U.S. government supported this military leader and drug lord who fought against the invasion of the U.S.S.R.

Holder, Eric – Deputy Attorney General during the Clinton administration and U.S. Attorney General under Barack Obama. He is currently in private practice as a partner at Covington & Burling.

(KMT) (Kuomintang) - The Chinese Nationalist Party controlled the Chinese mainland from 1928 to 1949. The CIA supported the KMT, which had numerous links with drug traffickers.

(LEAP) Law Enforcement Action Partnership - This organization of current and former law enforcement officers was originally named Law Enforcement Against Prohibition and solely dedicated to opposing the war on drugs. LEAP is still committed to ending the drug war, but their group also raises awareness about a wider range of issues, including police/community relations, mass incarceration, harm reduction, and more.

Levine, Michael – DEA Whistleblower

Loomis, Ed – NSA Whistleblower

Matta Ballesteros, Juan – Honduran drug lord whose front company, SETCO, received a U.S. government contract to deliver "humanitarian aid" to the Contras.

(NORML) National Organization for the Reform of Marijuana Laws

(PDFA) The Partnership for a Drug-Free America

Purdue Pharma – The manufacturer of the prescription opioid, Oxycontin.

Plumlee, Robert "Tosh" – Whistleblower and former pilot for SETCO.

Reed, Terry – Whistleblower and former CIA operative

(SOA) School of the Americas – Counternarcotics training program in Fort Benning, GA. An untold number of human rights violations have been committed by graduates of this program. The name was changed eventually to Western Hemisphere Institute for Security Cooperation (WHINSEC).

Suarez Gomez, Roberto – Bolivian drug lord who was empowered by a military coup in 1980.

Weibe, Kirk – NSA Whistleblower

References and Notes

Chapter 1

[1] Scott Cohn. "Billions Behind Bars: Inside America's Prison Industry." *CNBC.*
[2] "DEA.gov / DEA Staffing & Budget." http://www.justice.gov/dea/about/history/staffing.shtml>.
[3] Roger Warner. *Invisible Hand: The Marijuana Business.* New York. Beech Tree Books, 1986. Print.
[4] Nick Wing. "Michele Leonhart, DEA Chief, Won't Say Whether Crack, Heroin Are Worse For Health Than Marijuana." *Huffington Post.*
[5] Jacob Sullum. "DEA Administrator Says Pot Prohibition Protects Dogs; Many Dead Dogs Would Disagree." *Reason.*
[6] "DEA.gov / Statistics & Facts." <http://www.justice.gov/dea/resource-center/statistics.shtml#seizures>.
[7] Radley Balko. "Driven By Drug War Incentives, Cops Target Pot Smokers, Brush Off Victims Of Violent Crime." *Huffington Post.*
[8] Tony Newman and Bill Piper. "Congress Includes Billions in Stimulus Package for Controversial Byrne Grant Program Linked to Racial Disparities, Police Corruption, and Civil Rights Abuses." *Drug Policy Alliance.*
[9] Randi Kaye. "Tonight on AC360: Rape evidence ignored for decades." *Anderson Cooper 360.*
[10] Laura Strickler. "Thousands of Rape Kits Wait to be Tested." *CBS News.*
[11] "8News Investigates: 400,000 Rape Kits in U.S. are Never Tested." *ABC 8 News.*
Gina Lazara of KEPR-TV in Washington found that crime laboratory scientists can simply test marijuana with hydrogen peroxide.
[12] "Is The War on Drugs 'All About the Money'?" *The Real News.*
[13] John F. Kelly and Phillip Wearne. *Tainting Evidence: Inside the Scandals at the FBI Crime Lab.* New York: Free Press, 1998. Print. P 15
[14] Ibid.
[15] Spenser S. Hsu. "Federal review stalled after finding forensic errors by FBI lab unit spanned two decades." *Washington Post.*
[16] Spencer S. Hsu. "FBI admits flaws in hair analysis over decades." *Washington Post.*
[17] O'Ryan Johnson. "Annie Dookhan's guilty plea puts focus on system." *Boston Herald.*

[18] Mark Hansen. "Crime labs under the microscope after a string of shoddy, suspect and fraudulent results." *ABA Journal*.

[19] Ross Tuttle. "AUDIO: New York's Police Union Worked With the NYPD to Set Arrest and Summons Quotas." *The Nation*.

[20] Ibid.

[21] Tracy Oppenheimer. "Cop Fired for Speaking Out Against Ticket and Arrest Quotas." *Reason*.

[22] Amanda Winkler. "Riverside Cop Tricks Autistic Teen into Buying Pot." *Reason*.

[23] Ross Tuttle. "AUDIO: New York's Police Union Worked With the NYPD to Set Arrest and Summons Quotas."

[24] Tracy Oppenheimer. "Cop Fired for Speaking Out Against Ticket and Arrest Quotas."

[25] Ibid.

[26] Peter Moskos. *Cop in the Hood: My Year Policing Baltimore's Eastern District*. Princeton: Princeton University Press, 2008. Print. P 121-124.

[27] Ross Tuttle. "AUDIO: New York's Police Union Worked With the NYPD to Set Arrest and Summons Quotas."

[28] Jeff Leen, Gail Epstein, and Lisa Getter. "Police cheating on overtime costs us millions." *Miami Herald*.

[29] Ibid.

[30] "Are $100,000 police officers racking up too much OT?" *FOX 12 Oregon*.
"Street cops making more than the mayor." *KRQE News 13*
David Chang. "City Controller: Police Overtime is Out of Control." *NBC 10 Philadelphia*.
Terri Langford. "HPD, HFD overtime cost $67 million last year." *Houston Chronicle*.

[31] Edward Jay Epstein. *Agency of Fear: Opiates and Political Power in America*. London: Verso, 1990. Print. P 67

[32] Don Thompson. "California Now Freeing Violent Inmates To Save Money." *Huffington Post*.

[33] Eric E. Sterling. "Drug Laws and Snitching: A Primer." *PBS Frontline*.

[34] Judge Mark W. Bennett. "How Mandatory Minimums Forced Me to Send More Than 1,000 Nonviolent Drug Offenders to Federal Prison." *The Nation*.

[35] "An Offer You Can't Refuse: How US Federal Prosecutors Force Drug Defendants to Plead Guilty." *Human Rights Watch*.

[36] Sarah Solon. "'You Have the Right to an Attorney...' We All Know the Hollywood Version, But What's the Real Story?" *ACLU*.

[37] FBI's Uniform Crime Reporting (UCR) Program. "Persons Arrested" report.

[38] Bureau of Justice Statistics. "Indigent Defense Systems." *Bureau of Justice Statistics*. <http://www.bjs.gov/index.cfm?ty=tp&tid=28>.

[39] Raymond L. Sanchez. "Hugh caseload for public defenders crushes help to clients Defense lawyers feeling pressure to plea-bargain." *Baltimore Sun.*
[40] Marcia Coyle. "New Report Confronts Lack of Lawyers at Bail Hearings." *Legal Times.*
[41] Spike Bradford. "For Better or For Profit: How the Bail Bonding Industry Stands in the Way of Fair and Effective Pretrial Justice." *Justice Policy Institute.*
[42] Richard M. Aborn and Ashley D. Cannon. "Prisons: In Jail, But Not Sentenced." *Americas Quarterly.*
[43] Pretrial Justice Institute.
[44] "The Price of Freedom." *Human Rights Watch.*
[45] Alice Brennan. "How long does it take for a criminal case to go to trial?" *New York Daily News.*
[46] Attorney General Eric Holder Speech at the National Symposium on Pretrial Justice. Washington, DC. June 1, 2011.
[47] William Glaberson. "In Misdemeanor Cases, Long Waits for Elusive Trials." *New York Times.*
[48] Joseph Shapiro. "Supreme Court Ruling Not Enough To Prevent Debtors Prisons." *NPR.*
[49] Valerie Strauss. "Mother of 7 in jail because her kids skipped school dies in cell." *Washington Post.*
[50] Steve Bogira. *Courtroom 302: A Year Behind the Scenes in an American Criminal Courthouse.* New York: A. Knopf, 2005. Print. P 41
[51] Steve Bogira. P 55
[52] Jessica Riordan and Andrew McDonald. "One in 31 U.S. Adults are Behind Bars, on Parole or Probation." *The Pew Charitable Trusts.*
[53] Ibid.
[54] "The Prison Crisis." *ACLU.*
[55] Noel Brinkerhoff. "Imprisoned U.S. Drug Offenders Skyrockets from 41,000 to 507,000 in 30 Years." *Blacklisted News.*
[56] Ibid.
[57] "The cost of a nation of incarceration." *CBS News.*
[58] *Not Here, Not Anywhere: The Private Prison Problem.* Narrated by Danny Glover. Produced by Tonyia Rawles and Natalie Bullock Brown. Grassroots Leadership, 2005. DVD.
[59] Tara Herivel and Paul Wright. *Prison Profiteers: Who Makes Money From Mass Incarceration.* New York: New Press: 2007. Print. P. 63
[60] Barbara Krauth, Karin Stayton, and Connie Clem. "Fees Paid by Jail Inmates: Fee Categories, Revenues, and Management Perspectives in a Sample of U.S. Jails." *U.S. Department of Justice National Institute of Corrections Information Center.*
[61] Daniel Wagner. "Prison banker cuts fees after Center report." *The Center for Public Integrity.*

Daniel Wagner. "Megabanks have prison financial services market locked up." *The Center for Public Integrity*.

[62] Nation Action. "Meet the Medical Company Making $1.4 Billion a Year Off Sick Prisoners." *The Nation*.

[63] Todd Shields. "Prison Phones Prove Captive Market for Private Equity." *Bloomberg*.

[64] Mike Elk and Bob Sloan. "The Hidden History of ALEC and Prison Labor." *The Nation*.

[65] Daniel Burton-Rose, Dan Pens, and Paul Wright. *The Celling of America: An Inside Look at the U.S. Prison Industry*. Monroe, ME: Common Courage Press, 1998. Print. P 103

[66] "Headlines for December 17, 2010." *Democracy Now!*

[67] Eve Goldberg and Linda Evans. "11. Private Prison Expansion Becomes Big Business - Top 25 of 1999."

[68] Tara Herivel and Paul Wright. P. 95

[69] Mike Elk and Bob Sloan. "The Hidden History of ALEC and Prison Labor."

[70] Rebecca Leber. "Lawmakers In 23 States Introduced Secret Lobbying Group ALEC's Anti-Immigrant Bill." *Think Progress*.

[71] "Vice." Season 3, Episode 7.

[72] Tara Herivel and Paul Wright. P. 95

[73] <http://www.unicor.gov/prodservices/prod_dir_schedule/>

[74] Keith Johnson. "The Prison Industry Stealing U.S. Jobs." *Blacklisted News*.

[75] Daniel Burton-Rose, Dan Pens, and Paul Wright. *The Celling of America: An Inside Look at the U.S. Prison Industry*. Monroe, ME: Common Courage Press, 1998. Print. P 16

Christian Henrichson and Ruth Delaney. "The Price of Prisons: What Incarceration Costs Taxpayers." *Vera Institute*.

[76] Eve Goldberg and Linda Evans. "11. Private Prison Expansion Becomes Big Business - Top 25 of 1999." *Project Censored*.

John Poirier. "American Express fined $65mln over money laundering." *Reuters*.

[77] <http://www.cornellcompanies.com/pages/acbfacilities.html>, <http://www.thegeogroupinc.com/locations_na.asp> <http://www.correctionscorp.com/facility-operations/>

[78] <http://www.thegeogroupinc.com/locations_na.asp>

[79] Tom D'Angelo. "Florida Atlantic back to square one for stadium naming rights after GEO Group backs out | FAU Focus." *Palm Beach Post*. <http://www.geogroup.com/george_c__zoley>

[80] Rebecca Boone. "CCA-run prison remains Idaho's most violent lockup." *Associated Press*.

[81] "ACLU Lawsuit Charges Idaho Prison Officials Promote Rampant Violence." *ACLU*.

[82] Nicole Flatow. "Private Prison Firm To Pay Idaho $1 Million For False Records That Left Key Security Posts Vacant." *Think Progress.*
[83] Office of the Inspector General. U.S. Department of Justice. "Review of the Federal Bureau of Prisons' Monitoring of Contract Prisons." August 2016.
[84] Matt Zapotosky and Chico Harlan. "Justice Department says it end use of private prisons." *Washington Post.*
[85] Paul Chassy and Scott H. Amey. "Bad Business: Billions of Taxpayer Dollars Wasted on Hiring Contractors." *Project on Government Oversight.*
[86] David Cay Johnston. "The U.S. Government Is Paying Through the Nose For Private Contractors." *Newsweek.*
[87] Craig Harris and Yvonne Wingett Sanchez. "Arizona private prisons may get extra $1 million." *AZ Central.*
[88] Tara Herivel and Paul Wright. P 11
[89] Dana Joel. "A Guide to Prison Privatization." *Heritage Foundation.*
[90] Tara Herivel and Paul Wright. P 11
[91] Rich Jinks. *From the Belly of the Beast: What Isn't Being Told About the U.S. Penal System.* Xlibris Corporation, 2011. Print. P 39
[92] Adam Peck. "As Private Prisons Enrich Lawmakers, Florida Legislature Pushes Massive Prison Privatization Plan." *Think Progress.*
[93] Pat Bealle. "Private prison firms give lavishly to legislators." *Palm Beach Post.* Tonya Alanez "Scott pushes for state prison privatization." *Orlando Sentinel.*
[94] Arturo Garcia. "Protesters converge on Florida Gov. Rick Scott's fundraiser with private prison CEO." *Raw Story.*
[95] Amanda McCorquodale. "Florida Bong Ban Approved By Rick Scott." *Huffington Post.*
Christina Silva. "Darryl Rouson: Anything but a typical politician." *Tampa Bay Times.*
[96] Nzong Xiong. "Private Prisons: A Question of Savings." *New York Times.*
[97] Marie Diamond. "Florida Republican Stripped Of Senate Chairmanship For Opposing Prison Privatization Scheme." *Think Progress.*
[98] Dara Kam. "Prison privatization critics say they'll kill the bill Tuesday." *Palm Beach Post.*
[99] "Gaming the System: How The Political Strategies Of Private Prison Companies Promote Ineffective Incarceration Policies." *Justice Policy Institute.*
[100] "CCA Letter." *Huffington Post.*
[101] Mike Elk and Bob Sloan. "The Hidden History of ALEC and Prison Labor."
[102] Tina Chen. "Texas Man Booked For Not Returning a Library Book." *ABC News.*
[103] Beau Hodai. "Corrections Corporation of America Used in Drug Sweeps of Public School Students." *PR Watch.*
[104] Thomas Frank. "Lock 'Em Up: Jailing kids is a proud American tradition." *Wall Street Journal.*

[105] Jacob Sullum. "Pennsylvania Railroad." *Reason.*
[106] United States of America v City of Meridian; County of Lauderdale; Judge Frank Coleman, in his official capacity; Judge Veldore Young, in her official capacity; State of Mississippi; Mississippi Department of Human Services; and Mississippi Division of Youth Services.
[107] Ibid.
[108] "Locked Up In America." *PBS Frontline.*
[109] John Burnett. "Miss. Prison Operator Out; Facility Called A 'Cesspool'." *NPR.*
[110] Ibid.
[111] Margaret Newkirk and William Selway. "Gangs Ruled Prison as For-Profit Model Put Blood on Floor." *Bloomberg.*
[112] Jeff Ostrowski. "102 best paid execs in PBC, TCoast for 2009." *Palm Beach Post.*
[113] Daniel Burton-Rose, Dan Pens, and Paul Wright. *The Celling of America: An Inside Look at the U.S. Prison Industry.* Monroe, ME: Common Courage Press, 1998. Print. P 160
[114] Barry Yeoman. "Steel Town Lockdown." *Mother Jones.*
[115] Lucas Anderson. "Kicking the Habit Arguments for Abolishing Private Prison Contracts." *Prison Legal News.*
[116] Richard A. Oppel Jr. "Private Prisons Found to Offer Little in Savings." *New York Times.*
[117] "The GEO Group Authorizes Special Dividend of $350 Million, Takes Critical Steps Toward 2013 REIT Conversion." *Business Wire.*
[118] Ibid.
[119] Nathaniel Popper. "Restyled as Real Estate Trusts, Varied Businesses Avoid Taxes." *New York Times.*
[120] "US: For-Profit Probation Tramples Rights of Poor." *Human Rights Watch.*
[121] "Geo Group to acquire Colorado's BI Inc." *South Florida Business Journal.*
[122] Michelle Alexander. *The New Jim Crow: Mass Incarceration in the Age of Colorblindness.* New York: New Press, 2010. Print. P 93
[123] Eric Blumenson and Eva Nilsen. "The Drug War's Hidden Economic Agenda." *The Nation.*
[124] Clarence Walker. "Caswell Motel Case Marks a Victory Against Federal Forfeiture Abuse." *Stop The Drug War.*
[125] Kyla Dunn "Reining In Forfeiture: Common Sense Reform in the War on Drugs." *PBS.*
Mike Riggs. "Michigan Cops Used Asset Forfeiture Funds to Buy Drugs, Prostitutes, and a Tanning Salon." *Reason.*
[126] Tom Feiling. *Cocaine Nation: How the White Trade Took Over the World.* New York: Pegasus Books, 2010. Print. P 74
[127] Scott Ehlers. "Policy Briefing: Asset Forfeiture." *Drug Policy Foundation.*
[128] Scott Bullock. "Foreword for Policing for Profit." *Institute for Justice.*

[129] Radley Balko. *Rise of the Warrior Cop: The Militarization of America's Police Forces*. New York: Public Affairs, 2013. Print. P 141
[130] Kyla Dunn "Reining In Forfeiture: Common Sense Reform in the War on Drugs."
[131] Marian R. Williams, Jefferson E. Holcomb, and Tomislav V. Kovandzic. "Policing For Profit." *The Institute for Justice*.
[132] Scott Ehlers. "Policy Briefing: Asset Forfeiture."
[133] Marian R. Williams, Jefferson E. Holcomb, and Tomislav V. Kovandzic. "Policing For Profit."
[134] "'Your property is guilty until you prove it innocent.'" *Washington Post*.
[135] Bobby G. Frederick. "Seizure of drug money or highway robbery." *Trial Theory*.
[136] Dick M. Carpenter II, Ph.D., Lisa Knepper, Angela C. Erickson, Jennifer McDonald, Wesley Hottot and Keith Diggs. "Policing for Profit: The Abuse of Civil Asset Forfeiture (2nd Edition)." *Institute For Justice*.
[137] "'Your property is guilty until you prove it innocent.'" *Washington Post*.
[138] Eric Blumenson and Eva Nilsen. "Policing For Profit: The Drug War's Hidden Economic Agenda."
[139] Phil Williams. "Middle Tennessee Police Profiting Off Drug Trade?" *News Channel 5*.
[140] Marian R. Williams, Jefferson E. Holcomb, and Tomislav V. Kovandzic. "Policing For Profit."
[141] Eric Blumenson and Eva Nilsen. "Policing For Profit: The Drug War's Hidden Economic Agenda."
[142] Ibid.
[143] Mireya Navarro. "When Drug Kingpins Fall, Illicit Assets Buy a Cushion." *New York Times*.
[144] Clarence Walker. "Caswell Motel Case Marks a Victory Against Federal Forfeiture Abuse."
[145] Shira Rawlinson. "Federal Lawsuit Challenges Philadelphia's Civil Forfeiture Machine." *Institute for Justice*.
[146] J. Justin Wilson. "Institute for Justice Calls on New Mexico to reform its Civil Forfeiture Laws." *Institute for Justice*.
[147] Lisa Fletcher and Bryan Myers. "How New Mexico is stopping cops from seizing money without a conviction." *Al Jazeera*.
[148] Scott Shackford. "Nebraska Ends 'Civil' Police Forfeiture Process, Will Require Convictions." *Reason*.

Chapter 2

[1] Edward Jay Epstein. *Agency of Fear: Opiates and Political Power in America*. New York: Putnam, 1977. Print. P 26

Dominic Streatfeild. *Cocaine: An Unauthorized Biography*. New York: Thomas Dunne, 2002. Print. P 126
[2] Dominic Streatfeild. P 60
[3] Ansley Hamid. *Drugs in America: Sociology, Economics, and Politics*. Gaithersburg, MD: Aspen Publishers, 1998. Print. P 18
[4] Gabriel G. Nahas and Helene Peters. *Cocaine: The Great White Plague*. Middlebury, VT: Paul S. Eriksson, 1989. Print. P 56, 57, 69
[5] Gabriel G. Nahas and Helene Peters. P 59
That statistic is based upon a population of 76, 212, 168.
[6] "DrugFacts: Nationwide Trends." *National Institute on Drug Abuse*.
Based upon a population of 308,745,538.
[7] Dale Gieringer. "The Opium Exclusion Act of 1909." *Counter Punch*.
[8] Cheryl Chambers. *Institutional Racism Is Law Used as a Tool to Perpetuate Racial Inequality?* 2008. Print. P 47
[9] "Hooked: Illegal Drugs & How They Got That Way." Episode Two. *History Channel*.
[10] Steven B. Duke and Albert C. Gross. *America's Longest War: Rethinking Our Tragic Crusade against Drugs*. New York: Jeremy P. Tarcher / Putnam Books, 1993. Print. P 83
[11] "Hooked: Illegal Drugs & How They Got That Way." Episode Three. *History Channel*.
[12] Theodore Roosevelt's speech at the Lincoln Club Dinner in New York City on February 13, 1905.
[13] Dale Gieringer. "The Opium Exclusion Act of 1909."
[14] Ibid.
[15] Kenneth Pletcher. "Opium Wars." *Encyclopedia Britannica*.
[16] "Importation and Use of Opium." Committee on Ways and Means. House of Representatives. December 14, 1910.
[17] "Hooked: Illegal Drugs & How They Got That Way." Episode Two. *History Channel*.
[18] Ansley Hamid. P 86
[19] Peter Andreas. *Smuggler Nation: How Illicit Trade Made America*. New York: Oxford University Press, 2013. Print. P 264
[20] Mike Gray. *Drug Crazy: How We Got into This Mess and How We Can Get Out*. New York: Random House, 1998. Print. P 46
[21] Karl Hart. "The Myth of the 'Negro Cocaine Fiend' Helped Shape American Drug Policy." *The Nation*.
[22] Paul M. Gahlinger. *Illegal Drugs: A Complete Guide to Their History, Chemistry, Use and Abuse*. New York: First Plume Printing, 2004. Print. P 42
[23] "Importation and Use of Opium." Committee on Ways and Means. House of Representatives. December 14, 1910.

[24] Charles Whitebread. "The Early State Marijuana Laws - History of the Non-Medical Use of Drugs."
[25] Ibid.
[26] Richard J. Bonnie and Charles H. Whitebread. *The Marijuana Conviction: A History of Marijuana Prohibition in the United States*. New York: Lindesmith Center, 1999. Print. P 95
[27] Charles Whitebread. "The Early State Marijuana Laws - History of the Non-Medical Use of Drugs."
[28] Steve Fox, Paul Armentano, and Mason Tvert. *Marijuana is Safer: So Why are We Driving People to Drink?* White River Junction, VT: Chelsea Green Publishing, 2009. Print. P 2
[29] Jack Herer. *The Emperor Wears No Clothes*. Van Nuys, CA: AH HA Publishing, 1998. Print. P 1
[30] Rowan Robinson. *The Great Book of Hemp: The Complete Guide to the Environmental, Commercial, and Medicinal Uses of the World's Most Extraordinary Plant*. Rochester, VT: Park Street Press, 1996. Print. P 132
[31] Chris Conrad. *Hemp: Lifeline to the Future: The Unexpected Answer for our Environmental and Economic Recovery*. Los Angeles: Creative Xpressions Publications, 1994. Print. P 28
[32] Jack Herer. P 2
[33] Rowan Robinson. P 129
[34] Robert Deitch. *Hemp: American History Revisited the Plant with a Divided History*. New York: Algora Publishing, 2003. Print. P 35
[35] Chris Conrad. P 29
[36] Eric Schlosser. *Reefer Madness: Sex, Drugs, and Cheap Labor in the American Black Market*. Boston: Houghton Mifflin, 2003. Print. P 19
[37] "Yellow Journalism." *PBS*.
[38] Ben Procter. *William Randolph Hearst the Later Years, 1911-1951*. Oxford: Oxford University Press, 2007. Print. P 106
[39] "The Battle Over Citizen Kane." *PBS*.
[40] Oliver Carlson and Ernest Sutherland Bates. *Hearst, Lord of San Simeon*. New York: The Viking Press, 1936. Print. P 260
[41] "The Battle Over Citizen Kane."
[42] Ibid.
[43] "MEXICO: End of An Empire." *Time*. September 7, 1953.
[44] Ben Procter. *William Randolph Hearst the Later Years, 1911-1951*. P 49
[45] Chris Conrad. P 42
[46] Ben Procter. *William Randolph Hearst: The Early Years, 1863-1910*. Oxford: Oxford University Press, 1998. Print. P 103
Ben Procter. *William Randolph Hearst the Later Years, 1911-1951*. P 49, 221
[47] Benjamin Runkle. *Wanted Dead or Alive: Manhunts From Geronimo to Bin Laden*. New York: Palgrave Macmillan, 2011. Print. P 83

[48] Ben Proctor. *William Randolph Hearst the Later Years, 1911-1951.* P 49
[49] Ibid.
[50] Jack Herer. P 10
[51] Jack Herer. P 15
[52] Martin Booth. P 185
[53] Douglas Valentine. *The Strength of the Wolf: The Secret History of America's War on Drugs.* London: Verso, 2004. Print. P 15
[54] Peter Andreas. P 266
[55] Ryan Grim. *This is Your Country on Drugs: The Secret History of Getting High in America.* Hoboken, NJ: John Wiley & Sons, 2009. Print. P 44
[56] Richard J. Bonnie and Charles H. Whitebread. P 59
[57] Richard J. Bonnie and Charles H. Whitebread. P 62
[58] David F. Musto. *The American Disease: Origins of Narcotic Control: Origins of Narcotic Control.* Oxford: Oxford University Press, 1999. Print. P 221
[59] Chris Conrad. P 45
[60] Richard J. Bonnie and Charles H. Whitebread. P 117
[61] Paul Guzzo. "Gruesome Ybor murder was backbone for anti-marijuana campaign." *Tampa Tribune.*
[62] Richard J. Bonnie and Charles H. Whitebread. P 177
[63] Douglas Valentine. *The Strength of the Wolf: The Secret History of America's War on Drugs.* London: Verso, 2004. Print.
[64] Alexander Cockburn and Jeffrey St. Clair. "The Bi-Partisan Origins of the Total War on Drugs." *Counter Punch.*
[65] Ibid.
[66] David E. Newton. *Marijuana: A Reference Handbook.* Santa Barbara, CA: ABC-CLIO, 2013. Print. P 163
[67] Steve Fox, Paul Armentano, and Mason Tvert. P 51
[68] Eric Schlosser. P 142
Johann Hari. *Chasing the Scream: The First and Last Days of the War on Drugs.* U.K.: Bloomsbury Press, 2015. Print.
[69] Martin A. Booth P 246
[70] David Patrick Keys and John F. Galliher. *Confronting the Drug Control Establishment Alfred Lindesmith as a Public Intellectual.* Albany, NY: State University of New York Press, 2000. Print. P 150
[71] "Clearing the Smoke: The Science of Cannabis." *PBS.*
[72] Richard J. Bonnie and Charles H. Whitebread. P 88
[73] Richard J. Bonnie and Charles H. Whitebread. P 4, 55
[74] Richard J. Bonnie and Charles H. Whitebread. P 124
[75] Jack Herer P 32
[76] Richard J. Bonnie and Charles H. Whitebread. P 165
[77] Jack Herer. P 187
[78] Jack Herer. P 191

[79] John Roulac. *Hemp Horizons: The Comeback of the World's Most Promising Plant*. White River Junction, VT: Chelsea Green Publishing, 1997. Print. P 49
[80] "Letter from Harry Anslinger - September 29, 1936." *Schaffer Library of Drug Policy*.
John Craig Lupien. *Unraveling an American Dilemma: The Demonization of Marihuana*. Malibu, CA: Pepperdine University, 1995. Print.
[81] H.T. Nugent. "Report of Survey Commercialized Hemp Crop (1934-35 Crop) in the State of Minnesota." *Schaffer Library of Drug Policy*.
[82] John Craig Lupien
[83] Martin A. Booth. P 221
[84] Richard J. Bonnie and Charles H. Whitebread. P 173-174
[85] Ibid.
[86] Jack Herer. P 32
[87] Jack Herer. P 194
[88] John Roulac. P 53
[89] John Craig Lupien.
[90] "Letter from H. W. Bellrose, October 12, 1937." *Schaffer Library of Drug Policy*.
[91] "New Billion-Dollar Crop." *Popular Mechanics Magazine*. Feb. 1938.
[92] Edwin Black. *Internal Combustion: How Corporations and Governments Addicted the World to Oil and Derailed the Alternatives*. New York: St. Martin's Press, 2006. Print. P 4
[93] Om V. Singh and Steven P. Harvey. *Sustainable Biotechnology Sources of Renewable Energy*. Dordrecht: Springer, 2009. Print. P 55
[94] Lynn Cooper. *Live Organic Brilliant Ideas to Purify Your Lifestyle and Feel Good About It*. Oxford: Infinite Ideas, 2008. Print. P 171
[95] Chris Conrad P 99
[96] William L. Stidger. "Henry Ford on Plastics." *The Rotarian Magazine*. Feb. 1943: 58. Print.
[97] Bonnie Zucker Goldsmith. *William Randolph Hearst: Newspaper Magnate*. Edina, MN: ABDO Publishing, 2010. Print. P 70, 99
[98] "The Battle Over Citizen Kane." *PBS*.
[99] David Nasaw. *The Chief: The Life of William Randolph Hearst*. Boston: Houghton Mifflin, 2000. Print.
[100] Jack Herer P 29
[101] David Cannadine. *Mellon: An American Life*. New York: Vintage, 2006. Print. P. 205, 272, 397
[102] David Cannadine. P 347, 450, 397
[103] Daniel Yergin. *The Prize: The Epic Quest for Oil, Money, and Power*. New York: Simon & Schuster, 1991. Print. P 295
[104] David Cannadine. P 451
[105] Jack Herer. P 26, 27

[106] John Craig Lupien.
[107] Jack Herer. P 26, 29
[108] Edwin Black P 98, 165
Vincent Curcio. *Chrysler: The Life and Times of an Automotive Genius*. New York: Oxford UP, 2000. Print. P 211
[109] <http://www2.dupont.com/Phoenix_Heritage/en_US/1939_b_detail.html> Edwin Black P 200-260
[110] Stephen H. Norwood. *Strikebreaking & Intimidation Mercenaries and Masculinity in Twentieth-Century America*. Chapel Hill: University of North Carolina Press, 2002. Print. P 196
[111] Jules Archer. *The Plot to Seize the White House*. New York: Hawthorn, 1973. Print. P 144
[112] Michael Donnelly. "Wall Street's Failed 1934 Coup." *Counter Punch*.
[113] Jules Archer. P 161
[114] "The Whitehouse Coup." *BBC*.
[115] <http://www.druglibrary.org/schaffer/Library/studies/lag/conc1.htm>
[116] Martin A. Lee. *Smoke Signals: A Social History of Marijuana: Medical, Recreational, and Scientific*. New York: Scribner, 2012. Print. P 61
[117] Martin A. Lee. P 62
[118] Martin A. Lee. P 62, 64, 118
[119] "Timeline: America's War on Drugs." *NPR*.
[120] Dan Baum. *Smoke and Mirrors: The War on Drugs and the Politics of Failure*. Boston: Little, Brown and Company, 1996. Print. P 54
[121] Robert Deitch. *Hemp: American History Revisited the Plant with a Divided History*. New York: Algora Publishing, 2003. Print. P 183
[122] Richard Nixon Oval Office meeting with H.R. Haldeman and John N. Mitchell at 4:18 pm – 6:13 pm on April 21, 1971.
[123] Report of the National Commission on Marihuana and Drug Abuse Commissioned by President Richard M. Nixon, March, 1972.
[124] Robert Deitch. P 183
[125] Edward Jay Epstein. P 10
[126] Edward Jay Epstein. P 241
[127] Robert Deitch. P 183
[128] Jimmy. Carter. "Call Off the Global Drug War." *New York Times*.
[129] David F. Musto and Pamela Korsmeyer. *The Quest for Drug Control: Politics and Federal Policy in a Period of Increasing Substance Abuse, 1963-1981*. New Haven and London: Yale University Press, 2002. Print. P 182
[130] "Interview Peter Bourne." *PBS Frontline*.
[131] Martin Booth. P 306
[132] Ronald Shaffer. "Cocaine – Sniffing Incident." *Washington Post*. July 21, 1978.

[133] Patrick Anderson. *High in America: The True Story Behind NORML and the Politics of Marijuana*. Garrett County Press Digital. 2015. Print.

Chapter 3

[1] *Back in Town*. Dir. George Carlin. Perf. George Carlin. Distributed by R & E Associates, 1996. VHS.
[2] Rajeev Syal. "Drug money saved banks in global crisis, claims UN advisor." *The Guardian*.
[3] Stephen Stead. "Anti money laundering - compliance vs. detection." *Credit Control Journal and Asset & Risk Review*.
[4] Eric Schlosser. "Book Discussion on *Reefer Madness: Sex, Drugs, and Cheap Labor*." *C-SPAN*.
[5] Dominic Streatfeild. *Cocaine: An Unauthorized Biography*. New York: Thomas Dunne Books, 2002. Print. P 238
[6] Guy Gugliotta and Jeff Leen. *Kings of Cocaine: Inside the Medellín Cartel, an Astonishing True Story of Murder, Money, and International Corruption*. New York: Simon and Schuster, 1989. Print.
[7] "Drug Wars: Interview with Mike McDonald." *PBS Frontline*.
[8] "Bank Secrecy Act and Anti-Money Laundering." *Federal Deposit Insurance Corporation*. <http://www.fdic.gov/regulations/examinations/bsa/bsa_3.html>.
[9] James R. Richards. *Transnational Criminal Organizations, Cybercrime, and Money Laundering: A Handbook for Law Enforcement Officers, Auditors, and Financial Investigators*. Boca Raton CRC Press, 1999. Print. P 212
[10] Joe Schneider. "FBI Says Cartel Used Bank of America to Launder Money." *Bloomberg*.
Michael Corkery and Jessica Silver-Greenberg. "Citigroup Affiliate's Troubles Multiply as Money-Laundering Subpoenas Follow Fraud." *New York Times*.
Julia Preston. "Ex-Broker Pleads Guilty To Moving Drug Money." *New York Times*.
[11] "Wells Fargo Skirts Money-Laundering Charges as Clients Probed." *Bloomberg*.
[12] Jay Weaver. "Spaniard López Tardón sent to prison for 150 years in Miami money-laundering case." *Miami Herald*.
[13] Catherine Upin. "Getting dirty money clean." *PBS*.
[14] Jeff Muskus. "Wachovia To Settle Money Laundering Case For $160 Million." *Huffington Post*.
[15] "USDOJ: HSBC Holdings Plc. and HSBC Bank USA N.A. Admit to Anti-Money Laundering and Sanctions Violations, Forfeit $1.256 Billion in Deferred Prosecution Agreement." *United States Department of Justice*. Dec. 11, 2012.

[16] Aruna Viswanatha and Brett Wolf. "HSBC to pay $1.9 billion U.S. fine in money-laundering case." *Reuters*.
Rob Davies and Tim Shipman. "HSBC let drug gangs launder millions: First Barclays, now Britain's biggest bank is shamed - and faces a £640million fine." *Daily Mail*.
[17] Aruna Viswanatha and Brett Wolf. "HSBC to pay $1.9 billion U.S. fine in money-laundering case."
[18] Ben Protess and Jessica Silver-Greenberg. "HSBC to Pay $1.92 Billion to Settle Charges of Money Laundering." *New York Times*.
[19] Aruna Viswanatha and Brett Wolf. "HSBC to pay $1.9 billion U.S. fine in money-laundering case."
[20] Ben Protess and Jessica Silver-Greenberg
[21] Phil Mattingly. "Too-Big-to-Fail Banks Limit Prosecutor Options, Holder Says." *Bloomberg*.
[22] Kevin McCoy. "Report: DOJ overruled recommendation to prosecute HSBC." *USA Today*.
[23] Peter Lilley. *Dirty Dealing: The Untold Truth about Global Money Laundering, International Crime and Terrorism*. London: Kogan Page, 2006. Print. P 195
[24] Robert Mazur. *The Infiltrator: My Secret Life Inside the Dirty Banks Behind Pablo Escobar's Medellin Cartel*. New York: Little, Brown, 2009. Print. P 165
[25] Mark Potts, Nick Kochan, and Robert Whittington. *Dirty Money: BCCI, the Inside Story of the World's Sleaziest Bank*. Washington, D.C.: National Press Books, 1992. Print. 172, 157, 32
[26] Robert Mazur. P 49
[27] Robert Mazur. P 340
[28] Ed Vulliamy. "Western banks 'reaping billions from Colombian cocaine trade.'" *The Guardian*.
[29] "Wells Fargo Fires Iowa Worker for Minor 1963 Crime." *Associated Press*.
[30] Moisés Naím. *Illicit: How Smugglers, Traffickers and Copycats are Hijacking the Global Economy*. New York: Doubleday, 2005. Print. P 144, 136
[31] "Media Censor CIA Ties With Medellin Drug Cartel." *Fairness & Accuracy in Reporting*.
[32] Alexander Cockburn and Jeffrey St. Clair. *Whiteout: The CIA, Drugs, and the Press*. London: Verso, 1998. Print. P 369
[33] Charles Bowden. *Down by the River: Drugs, Money, Murder, and Family*. New York: Simon & Schuster, 2002. Print. P 226
[34] Charles Bowden. P 239
[35] Alexander Cockburn and Jeffrey Clair. P 365, 366
[36] Charles Bowden. P 375
[37] Catherine Upin. "Getting dirty money clean."
[38] Ed Vulliamy. "The Wachovia Whistleblower." *The Nation*.

39 We Are Change. "HSBC Whistleblower Speaks, Uncovered Terrorist Financing." *YouTube.*

40 Matt Taibbi. "Gangster Bankers: Too Big to Jail." *Rolling Stone.*

41 We Are Change. "HSBC Whistleblower Speaks, Uncovered Terrorist Financing."

42 Matt Taibbi. "Gangster Bankers: Too Big to Jail."

43 Ann Woolner. "UBS Whistleblower Gets Rewarded With Prison Time: Ann Woolner." *Bloomberg.*

44 Peter Schweizer. *Extortion: How Politicians Extract Your Money, Buy Votes, and Line Their Own Pockets.* New York: Houghton Mifflin Harcourt Publishing, 2013. Print. P 47

45 Ann Woolner. "UBS Whistleblower Gets Rewarded With Prison Time: Ann Woolner."

46 "Banking: A Crack In The Swiss Vault." *60 Minutes.* Dec. 30, 2009.

47 Ann Woolner. "UBS Whistleblower Gets Rewarded With Prison Time: Ann Woolner."

48 "Banking: A Crack In The Swiss Vault." *60 Minutes.*

49 Ann Woolner. "UBS Whistleblower Gets Rewarded With Prison Time: Ann Woolner."

50 "UBS confirms fresh tax evasion probe in the US." *BBC News.*

51 "*UBS Whistleblower Bradley Birkenfeld Files Official Clemency Petition on Tax Day.*" *National Whistleblowers Center.*

52 Juan Gonzalez. "UBS whistleblower Bradley Birkenfeld deserves statue on Wall Street, not prison sentence." *NY Daily News.*

53 <http://www.opensecrets.org/pres08/contrib.php?cycle=2008&cid=n00009638>

Ron Suskind. *Confidence Men: Wall Street, Washington, and the Education of a President.* New York: Harper Collins, 2011. Print. P 25.

54 "Cause of Action Memos Impugn Obama Transparency Pledge." *Cause of Action.*

Ed O'Keefe. "Obama finally accepts his transparency award... behind closed doors." *Washington Post.*

55 John Kiriakou. "Obama's abuse of the Espionage Act is modern-day McCarthyism." *The Guardian.*

56 David Kocieniewski. "Whistle-Blower Awarded $104 Million by I.R.S." *New York Times.*

57 "Wealthy 'hiding' at least $21tn." *BBC News.*

58 Phil Mattingly. "Too-Big-to-Fail Banks Limit Prosecutor Options, Holder Says." *Bloomberg.*

59 "Will Justice Department's crackdown on Credit Suisse lead to more bank prosecutions?" *PBS Newshour.*

[60] Eric Tucker and Marcy Gordon. "Swiss bank Credit Suisse charged with conspiring to help tax evaders." *PBS*.
[61] Eric Tucker and Marcy Gordon. "DOJ: Credit Suisse guilty plea a warning to foreign banks that aid in U.S. tax evasion." *PBS*.
[62] "Will Justice Department's crackdown on Credit Suisse lead to more bank prosecutions?" *PBS Newshour*.
[63] "Too Big to Jail? Credit Suisse Bank Pleads Guilty to Decades of Tax Evasion, But Execs Avoid Prison." *Democracy Now!*
[64] Ibid.
[65] "5 Things You Need to Know about Credit Suisse's Criminal Charge." *The Real News*.
[66] "Too Big to Jail? Credit Suisse Bank Pleads Guilty to Decades of Tax Evasion, But Execs Avoid Prison." *Democracy Now!*
[67] Ryan Grim. *This is Your Country on Drugs: The Secret History of Getting High in America*. Hoboken, NJ: John Wiley & Sons, 2009. Print. P 82
[68] "Frequently Asked Questions." *FinCEN What We Do*. <http://www.fincen.gov/about_fincen/wwd/faqs.html>.
[69] "DEA Programs: Money Laundering." *Drug Enforcement Agency*. <http://www.justice.gov/dea/ops/money.shtml>.
[70] Elizabeth Nolan Brown. "DOJ's 'Operation Choke Point' May Be Root of Porn Star Bank Account Closings." *Reason*.
[71] Phillip Smith. "Feds Squeeze Banks in Bid to Freeze Out Medical Marijuana [FEATURE]." *Stop the Drug War*.
Peter Hecht. "Medical marijuana dispensary takes on IRS over what it calls 'punitive' taxes." *Washington Post*.
[72] Axel Gerdau and John Woo. "Guns, Drugs and Money." *New York Times*.
[73] Ibid.
[74] Lowell Bergman. "U.S. Companies Tangled in Web Of Drug Dollars." *New York Times*.
[75] *Now on PBS*. "Tobacco Traffic: Cigarette Smuggling."
[76] Ibid.
[77] Lowell Bergman. "U.S. Companies Tangled in Web Of Drug Dollars."
[78] Senate Caucus on International Narcotics Control, One Hundred Sixth Congress, first session, June 21, 1999.
[79] Oriana Zill and Lowell Bergman. "U.S. Business & Money Laundering." *PBS Frontline*.
[80] Lowell Bergman. "U.S. Companies Tangled in Web Of Drug Dollars."
[81] Mark Shapiro. "Big Tobacco: Uncovering the industry's multibillion-dollar global smuggling network." *The Nation*.
[82] Henry Weinstein. "Philip Morris Accused in Smuggling Scheme." *Los Angeles Times*.

[83] Erik J. Schelzig and Mary Beth Warner. "Tobacco firms used suspected drug traffickers, EU lawsuit claims." *International Consortium of Investigative Journalists*.
[84] George Parker and Neil Buckley. "Philip Morris pays $1.25 bn to settle EU smuggling case." *Financial Times*.
[85] Michael A. Hiltzik and Henry Weinstein. "Cigarettes Portrayed as Currency of Crime." *Los Angeles Times*.
[86] Lawrence Hurley. "Supreme Court rules for R.J. Reynolds in racketeering case." *Reuters*.

Chapter 4

[1] Bill Moyers. *PBS*. "American Dissenters."
[2] Gore Vidal. *Perpetual War for Perpetual Peace: How We Got to be so Hated*. New York: Thunder's Mouth Press/Nation Books, 2002. Print. P 140
[3] NORML "Marijuana Arrests For Year 2007: 872,721 Tops Record High -Five Percent Increase Over 2006."
[4] Michael A. Fletcher. "White House Had Drug Officials Appear With GOP Candidates." *Washington Post*.
[5] "Obama: Decriminalize pot." *Washington Times*.
[6] MJ Lee. "Marijuana legalization: 9 politicians puffing about pot." *Politico*.
[7] "Obama: Decriminalize pot." *Washington Times*.
[8] Mason-Dixon Research & Polling. "1 MARIJUANA POLICY PROJECT NATIONAL SURVEY QUESTION – MAY 2012." *Marijuana Policy Project*.
[9] Marijuana Policy Project. "Federal Enforcement Policy De - Prioritizing Medical Marijuana: Statements from Pres. Obama, his spokesman, and the Justice Department."
[10] Tim Dickinson. "Obama's War on Pot." *Rolling Stone*.
[11] Ibid.
[12] Gary Fields. "White House Czar Calls for End to 'War on Drugs' Kerlikowske Says Analogy Is Counterproductive; Shift Aligns With Administration Preference for Treatment Over Incarceration." *Wall Street Journal*.
[13] Ibid.
[14] "Q&A With the New Drug Czar." *Wall Street Journal*.
[15] Christopher Ingraham. "The DEA chief called medical marijuana 'a joke.' Now patients are calling for his resignation." *Washington Post*.
[16] John Hoeffel. "Holder vows fight over prop. 19." *Los Angeles Times*.
[17] Alex Dobuzinskis. "Ex-DEA heads urge Holder oppose marijuana ballots." *Reuters*.
[18] Ryan Reilly and Ryan Grim. "Eric Holder Says DOJ Will Let Washington, Colorado Marijuana Laws Go Into Effect." *Huffington Post*.
[19] Chris Isidore. "2 million jobs lost so far in '09." *CNN Money*.

[20] David Edwards and Ron Brynaert. "Obama fields 'marijuana as cash crop' question at town hall meeting." *Raw Story*.
[21] Jann S. Wenner. "The Day After: Obama on His Legacy, Trump's Win and the Path Forward." *Rolling Stone*.
[22] "President Obama speaks with VICE News." *Vice News*.
[23] Jeffrey M. Jones. "In U.S., Perceived Need for Third Party Reaches New High." *Gallup*.
[24] Jeffrey M. Jones. "In U.S., New Record 43% Are Political Independents." *Gallup*.
[25] Associated Press. "Corporations sponsor presidential debates."
[26] "Ending Federal Marijuana Prohibition Act of 2011 (2011H.R. 2306)." *GovTrack.us*.
[27] Matt Welch and Jim Epstein. "Video: Obama Wins and Nothing Changes; The Wildly Unpopular Status Quo Is Ratified!" *Reason*.
[28] James Hohmann. "Poll: Republicans embracing libertarian priorities - James Hohmann." *Politico*.
[29] Manuel Klausner. "Inside Ronald Reagan." *Reason.com*. July 1979 Issue.
[30] David Barsamian. "Gore Vidal Interview." *The Progressive*.
[31] "Dems Say No Nader at Convention." *FOX News*.
[32] *Spin*. Dir. Brian Springer. Perf. Bill Clinton. Video Data Bank, 1995. VHS.
[33] Associated Press. "Agran Arrested as Protester at Debate." *Los Angeles Times*.
[34] Rachel Weiner. "Green Party candidate arrested outside debate site." *Washington Post*.
[35] "Money Wins Presidency and 9 of 10 Congressional Races in Priciest U.S. Election Ever." *Center for Responsive Politics*.
[36] Simon Johnson and James Kwak. *13 Bankers: The Wall Street Takeover and the Next Financial Meltdown*. New York: Pantheon Books, 2010. Print. P 90 "Money Wins Presidency and 9 of 10 Congressional Races in Priciest U.S. Election Ever." *Center for Responsive Politics*.
[37] David Murdock. "Durbin: Time Spent Fundraising "Nothing Short of Amazing." *Huffington Post*.
[38] "The Inside Scoop On Life In Congress - Former GOP Rep Joe Walsh Interview w/ Cenk Uygur." *The Young Turks*.
[39] Dana Milbank. "As Voinovich leaves Senate, he sees a deficit of good sense." *Washington Post*.
[40] Charles Lewis. *The Buying of the Congress: How Special Interests Have Stolen Your Right to Life, Liberty, and the Pursuit of Happiness*. New York: Avon Books, 1998. Print. P 37
[41] Ryan Grim and Sabrina Siddiqui. "Call Time For Congress Shows How Fundraising Dominates Bleak Work Life." *Huffington Post*.

[42] Chuck Philips. "Rap's Bad Boy to Get Lunch With the Prez." *Los Angeles Times*.
[43] Elizabeth Flock. "196 People Control 80 Percent of Super PAC Money: Who Are They?" *U.S. News & World Report*.
[44] Michael Beckel. "Federal Lobbying Expenditures Plateau after Years of Rapid Growth." *Center for Responsive Politics*.
[45] Janie Lorber and Kate Ackley. "K Street Files: Tracking Lobbyists for Other Countries." *Roll Call*.
[46] T.W. Farnam. "Revolving door of employment between Congress, lobbying firms, study shows." *Washington Post*.
[47] Lesley Stahl. "Jack Abramoff: The lobbyist's playbook." *60 Minutes*.
[48] Robert G. Kaiser. *Act of Congress: How America's Essential Institution Works, And How It Doesn't*. New York City: Random House, 2013. Print. P 28
[49] Matthew Continetti. *The K Street Gang: The Rise and Fall of the Republican Machine*. New York: Doubleday, 2006. Print.
[50] Dan Friedman. "Former Congressmen make huge salaries as lobbyists while still collecting congressional pensions." *NY Daily News*.
[51] "Revolving Door." *Center for Responsive Politics*. <http://www.opensecrets.org/revolving/departing.php?cong=112>.
[52] Sharyl Attkisson. "The Revolving Door: Lawmaker To Lobbyist." *CBS News*.
[53] Ibid.
[54] Lester Grinspoon and James B. Bakalar. "Common Medical Uses." *Marihuana: the Forbidden Medicine*. New Haven: Yale University Press, 1997. Print. P XI
[55] Lester Grinspoon and James B. Bakalar. P 26
[56] Lester Grinspoon and James B. Bakalar. P XI
[57] Ibid.
[58] Fred Backus and Stephanie Condon. "Poll: Nearly half support legalization of marijuana." *CBS News*.
"State Medical Marijuana Laws." *National Conference of State Legislatures*.
[59] Testimony of Dr. David Murray
Chief Scientist, Office of National Drug Control Policy Before the Judiciary Subcommittee on Crime, Terrorism, and Homeland Security "Hearing on the Drug Enforcement Administration's Regulation of Medicine" July 12, 2007.
[60] Rob Reuteman. "The Marijuana Lobby: All Grown Up" *CNBC*.
[61]
<http://www.opensecrets.org/orgs/summary.php?id=D000027913&cycle=A>
< http://www.opensecrets.org/orgs/summary.php?id=D000027382&cycle=A>
<http://www.opensecrets.org/orgs/summary.php?id=D000033289&cycle=A>
[62] Lee Fang. "The Top Five Special Interest Groups Lobbying to Keep Marijuana Illegal." *Truthout*.
[63] <http://www.opensecrets.org/pacs/industry.php?txt=H04&cycle=2012>

< http://www.opensecrets.org/pacs/superpacs.php?cycle=2012>
[64] < http://www.mpp.org/jobs/>
[65] <http://www.opensecrets.org/lobby/indusclient.php?id=H04&year=2012>
[66] < http://www.opensecrets.org/lobby/indusclient.php?id=N02&year=2012>
[67] < http://www.opensecrets.org/lobby/indusclient.php?id=K01&year=2012>
< http://www.opensecrets.org/lobby/indusclient.php?id=F03&year=2012>
[68] "Legal Issues." *NORML.*
<http://norml.org/legal/medical-marijuana-2>
[69] Nicole Perlroth. "Pharma Oversold?" *Forbes.*
[70] "World Press Freedom Index 2014." *Reporters Without Borders.*
[71] Nick Gillespie and Amanda Winkler. "Former CBS Reporter Sharyl Attkisson on Benghazi Emails." *Reason.*
[72] Peter Phillips. "Big Media Interlocks With Corporate America." *Project Censored.*
[73] Craig Reinarman and Harry Gene Levine. *Crack in America: Demon Drugs and Social Justice.* Berkeley: University of California Press, 1997. Print. P 20
Steven B. Duke and Albert C. Gross. *America's Longest War: Rethinking Our Tragic Crusade against Drugs.* New York: Jeremy P. Tarcher / Putnam Book, 1993. Print. P 101
[74] Dan Baum. *Smoke and Mirrors: The War on Drugs and the Politics of Failure.* Boston: Little, Brown and Company, 1996. Print. P 226
[75] Craig Reinarman and Harry Gene Levine. P 28
[76] Doris Marie Previne. *The Many Colors of Crime: Inequalities of Race, Ethnicity, and Crime in America.* Ed. Ruth D. Peterson, Lauren Joy Krivo, and John Hagan. New York: New York University Press, 2006. P 282
[77] Richard Lawrence Miller. *Drug Warriors and Their Prey: From Police Power to Police State.* Westport, CT: Praeger, 1996. Print. P 22
[78] Tom Leonard. "Day Elvis begged Nixon to let him be a secret FBI agent: Revealed in the King's own rambling words, the story behind a truly bizarre encounter." *Daily Mail.*
[79] Steve Fox, Paul Armentano, and Mason Tvert. *Marijuana is Safer: So Why are We Driving People to Drink?* White River Junction, VT: Chelsea Green Publishing Company, 2009. Print. P 88-89.
[80] Donna Leinwand. "Anti-drug advertising campaign a failure, GAO report says." *USA Today.*
[81] Mike Males. "Pot Boiler: Why Are Media Enlisting in the Government's Crusade Against Marijuana?" *Fairness & Accuracy in Reporting.*
Cynthia Cotts. "The Partnership: Hard Sell in the Drug War." *Schaffer Library of Drug Policy.*
[82] <http://www.drugfree.org/about/our-partners/>
AbbVie, Actavis, Chevron, CVS/Caremark Corporation, Endo Pharmaceuticals, HBO, IBM, Jazz Pharmaceuticals, Johnson & Johnson Health Care Systems,

Major League Baseball, Mallinckrodt Pharmaceuticals, Pfizer Consumer Healthcare, Pfizer Inc. Pura Vida Bracelets, Purdue Pharma, Teva Pharmaceuticals Industries, The Hershey Company

[83] Craig Hlavaty "Drug company cites abuse, pop culture hype in ending cough syrup production" *Houston Chronicle.*
[84] Jonah Engle. "Merchants of Meth." *The Investigative Fund.*
[85] Art Swift. "Support For Legal Marijuana Use Up to 60% in U.S." *Gallup.*
[86] Frank Newport. "Record-High 50% of Americans Favor Legalizing Marijuana Use." *Gallup.*
[87] Timothy Stenovec. "Legal Weed: Marijuana More Popular Than Barack Obama In Colorado." *Huffington Post.*
[88] Phillip Smith. "Colorado Marijuana Legalization Measure Polls 51%." *Stop The Drug War.*
[89] Christopher Ingraham. "Marijuana Wins Big on Election Night." *Washington Post.*

Chapter 5

[1] Ariel Nelson. "How Big Is The Marijuana Market?" *CNBC.*
Donna Leinwand Leger. "More Americans are using marijuana." *USA Today.*
[2] Ariel Nelson. "How Big Is The Marijuana Market?"
[3] Peter Moskos. *Cop in the Hood: My Year Policing Baltimore's Eastern District.* Princeton: Princeton University Press, 2008. Print. P 190
[4] "Colorado collects $44 million in recreational marijuana taxes for 2014, below projections." *Associated Press.*
[5] Art Way. "Colorado One Year Later: Thousands Not Arrested for Marijuana, Millions of Dollars Saved." *Drug Policy Alliance.*
[6] German Lopez. "Legal marijuana created thousands of jobs in Colorado." *Vox.*
[7] Carly Schwartz. "Marijuana Market Poised To Grow Faster Than Smartphones." *Huffington Post.*
[8] Debra Borchardt. "Marijuana Jobs Higher Than Estimated." *The Street.*
[9] "Employment in New York State." *State of New York Department of Labor.* April 2005.
[10] "SunTrust: Many higher income households living paycheck-to-paycheck." *Sun Trust Banks.* April 16, 2015.
[11] James Sunshine. "Denver Now Has More Marijuana Dispensaries Than It Does Starbucks." *Huffington Post.*
[12] Gary L. Fisher. *Rethinking our War on Drugs: Candid Talk about Controversial Issues.* Westport, CT: Praeger, 2006. Print. P 9
[13] "The Economic Costs of Drug Abuse in the United States: 1992-2002." *Office of National Drug Control Policy.*

[14] "FREQUENTLY ASKED QUESTIONS ABOUT MARIJUANA OFFENDERS." *FAMM (Families against Mandatory Minimums)*.
"States That Have Decriminalized" *NORML*.
[15] Phillip Smith. "Feature: The Conviction That Keeps On Hurting -- Drug Offenders and Federal Benefits." *Stop The Drug War*.
[16] Mark Karlin. "Michelle Alexander on the Irrational Race Bias of the Criminal Justice and Prison Systems." *Truthout*.
[17] "New Billion-Dollar Crop." *Popular Mechanics Magazine*. Feb. 1938. <https://www.votehemp.com/new_billion_dollar_crop.html>.
[18] Matt Ferner. "Bill Aims To End Federal Ban On U.S. Hemp Production." *Huffington Post*.
[19] Scott Morgan. "Mitt Romney Doesn't Know What Industrialized Hemp Is." *Stop The Drug War*.
[20] Chris Conrad. *Hemp: Lifeline to the Future: The Unexpected Answer for our Environmental and Economic Recovery*. Los Angeles: Creative Xpressions Publications, 1994. Print. P 165
[21] "Schwarzenegger Vetoes Calif. Hemp Bill." *Partnership for Drug-Free Kids*.
[22] Renée Johnson. "Hemp as an Agricultural Commodity." *Congressional Research Service*.
[23] <http://www.votehemp.com/state.html>
[24] Eric Steenstra. "Letter to the Senate Committee on the Judiciary on the Nomination of Michele Leonhart to be Administrator of DEA." *Vote Hemp*.
[25] <http://www.votehemp.com/legal_cases_ND.html>
[26] Phillip Smith. "DEA Backs Down; Kentucky Will Get Its Hemp Seeds." *Stop The Drug War*.
[27] DEA Press Release October 9, 2001. "DEA Clarifies Status of Hemp in the Federal Register."
[28] *Bringing it Home*. Producer/Director. Linda Booker. Brook Productions and Green Hope Productions. 2015. Film.
[29] Renée Johnson. "Hemp as an Agricultural Commodity."
[30] Olivia Carville. "Ontario man sets sights high with world's first hemp plane." *The Star*.
[31] May Jeong. "Canadian firm really goes green with hemp car." *Reuters*.
[32] Eric Steenstra. "Obama Campaign Raises Money With Hemp Products While Administration Is Banning Farmers From Growing Hemp." *Huffington Post*.
[33] James Morgan. "Hemp fibres 'better than graphene.'" *BBC*.
[34] *Bringing it Home*. Producer/Director. Linda Booker.
[35] Karen Wynne. "A house made of hemp." *CNN*.
[36] Ibid.
[37] Ibid.
[38] Ibid.
[39] "Vote Hemp 2012 Presidential Candidate Report Card." *Vote Hemp*.

[40] "State Letters to DOJ." *Vote Hemp*.
[41] "Lawmakers, Executives, Slam Obama for Boosting Brazil's Offshore Drilling." *FOX News*.
[42] Tom Curry. "Obama, Libya and the authorization conflict." *MSNBC*.
[43] Scott Baldauf. "Nigeria charges Dick Cheney in bribery case." *Christian Science Monitor*.
[44] David Smith and Reuters. "Dick Cheney to be charged in Nigeria corruption case." *The Guardian*.
[45] Mark Clayton. "Budget hawks: Does US need to give gas and oil companies $41 billion a year?" *Christian Science Monitor*.
[46] "Strategies to Fix America." *CNBC*.
[47] Edwin Black. *Internal Combustion: How Corporations and Governments Addicted the World to Oil and Derailed the Alternatives*. New York: St. Martin's Press, 2006. Print. P 267
[48] Julie Teel. "Bush Global Warming Proposal Weaker Than Existing Law." *Center for Biological Diversity*.
[49] "$5 billion-a-year ethanol subsidy nearing its end?" *MSNBC*.
[50] Edwin Black P 287-291
[51] Forrest Jehlik. "Five Ethanol Myths, Busted." *Wired*.
[52] Joel K. Bourne Jr. "Green Dreams." *National Geographic*. Oct. 2007.
[53] Carl Franzen. "2012 Renewable Fuel Standards Fall Far Short Of Non-Corn Ethanol Goal." *Talking Points Memo*.
[54] U.S Department of Energy. Alternative Fuels Data Center.
[55] Kimball Christensen and Andrew Smith. "The Case for Hemp as a Biofuel." *Vote Hemp*.
[56] Jason Mick. "Switchgrass's Dirty Secret May Make Seaweed Biofuel Crop Of Choice." *Daily Tech*.
[57] Carl Franzen. "2012 Renewable Fuel Standards Fall Far Short Of Non-Corn Ethanol Goal."
[58] "Deforestation and Its Extreme Effect on Global Warming." *Scientific American*.
[59] Bob Ivry and Christopher Donville. "Black Liquor Tax Boondoggle May Net Billions For Papermakers." *Bloomberg*.
[60] Brian Palmer. "High on Environmentalism." *Slate*.
[61] "Cotton and Pesticides." *Environmental Justice Foundation*.
[62] Michael Grunwald. "Why the U.S. Is Also Giving Brazilians Farm Subsidies." *Time*.
[63] *Addicted to Plastic*. Dir. Ian Connacher. Bullfrog Films, 2008. DVD.
[64] <http://www.epa.gov/osw/conserve/materials/plastics.htm>
[65] Addicted to Plastic
[66] Bryan Walsh. "The perils of Plastic." *Time*.

[67] Sabrina Tavernise. "F.D.A. Makes It Official: BPA Can't Be Used in Baby Bottles and Cups." *New York Times.*
[68] Dominique Browning. "Hitting the Bottle." *New York Times.*
[69] <http://www.epa.gov/osw/conserve/materials/plastics.htm>
[70] Daniel K. Benjamin. "Eight Great Myths of Recycling." *Property and Environment Research Center.*
[71] Jack Herer. P 52
[72] "Do fish oil (omega-3 fatty acid) supplements contain mercury?" *Pharmacology Weekly.*
[73] Kayla Morgan. *Legalizing Marijuana.* North Mankato, MN: ABDO Publishing Company, 2011. Print. P 37

Chapter 6

[1] "Marijuana for life courtesy of the federal government." *Washington Post.*
[2] Julie Holland. *The Pot Book: A Complete Guide to Cannabis: Its Role in Medicine, Politics, Science, and Culture.* Rochester, VT: Park Street Press, 2010. Print. P 243
[3] "Marijuana for life courtesy of the federal government." *Washington Post.*
[4] Ibid.
[5] Lester Grinspoon. "Marijuana as wonder drug." *Boston Globe.*
[6] Mitch Earleywine. *Understanding Marijuana: A New Look at the Scientific Evidence.* Oxford: Oxford University Press, 2002. Print P 26
[7] Laura M. Borgelt, Kari L. Franson, Abraham M. Nussbaum, and George S. Wang. "The Pharmacologic and Clinical Effects of Medical Cannabis." *Pharmacotherapy.* Vol. 33, Number 2, 2013.
[8] Tony Newman and Michael Collins. "Senate Approves Funding Bill That Allows Veterans to Access Medical Marijuana." *Drug Policy Alliance.*
[9] Tashkin DP, Shapiro BJ, Lee YE, and Harper CE. "Effects of smoked marijuana in experimentally induced asthma." *National Center for Biotechnology Information.*
[10] Mitch Earleywine. *Understanding Marijuana: A New Look at the Scientific Evidence.* Oxford: Oxford University Press, 2002. Print.
Prakash Nagarkatti, Rupal Pandey, Sadiye Amcaoglu Rieder, Venkatesh L Hegde, and Mitzi Nagarkatti. "Cannabinoids as novel anti-inflammatory drugs." *National Center for Biotechnology Information.*
"60 Peer-Reviewed Studies on Medical Marijuana-Medical Studies Involving Cannabis and Cannabis Extracts (1990 - 2014)" *ProCon.org.*
"Summary of Systematic Review for Clinicians Efficacy and Safety of the Therapeutic use of Medical Marijuana (Cannabis) in Selected Neurological Disorders." *American Academy of Neurology.*
[11] Ibid.

[12] Elaine Minamide. *Medical Marijuana*. Detroit: Greenhaven Press, 2007. Print. P 12

[13] Elaine Minamide. P 21

[14] Dave Pate. "Interview: Dr. Mahmoud A. ElSohly." *Journal of the International Hemp Association*.

[15] "Clearing the Smoke: The Science of Cannabis." *PBS*.

[16] Rudolph Joseph Gerber. *Legalizing Marijuana: Drug Policy Reform and Prohibition Politics*. Westport, CT: Praeger, 2004. Print. P 97

[17] Steve Fox and Paul Armentano. *Marijuana is Safer: So Why are We Driving People to Drink?* White River Junction, VT: Chelsea Green Publishing Company, 2009. Print. P 85

[18] Rudolph Joseph Gerber. P 137

[19] Stephanie Condon. "AMA Calls for Feds to Review Marijuana Restrictions." *CBS News*.

[20] "The DEA: Four Decades of Impeding and Rejecting Science." *Drug Policy Alliance*.

[21] Dan Russell. *Drug War: Covert Money, Power & Policy*. Camden, NY: Kalyx.com, 2000. Print. P 578

[22] "NORML Policy on Medical Use." *NORML*.

[23] "DEA Administrative Law Judge Rules Against US Government's Monopoly On Pot Production." *NORML*.

[24] Testimony of Dr. David Murray, Chief Scientist of the Office of National Drug Control Policy, before the Judiciary Subcommittee on Crime, Terrorism, and Homeland Security. "Hearing on the Drug Enforcement Administration's Regulation of Medicine." July 12, 2007

[25] "Letter to President Obama from the FDA on April 2, 2009."

[26] Ibid.

[27] Ellen Nakashima and Lisa Rein. "FDA staffers sue over surveillance of personal e-mail." *Washington Post*.

[28] Marcia Angell. "Taking back the FDA." *Boston Globe*.

[29] "Pfizer sued by retailers for generic Lipitor delay." *Reuters*.

[30] Marcia Angell. "Taking back the FDA."

[31] Peter Whorinskey. "Pharmaceutical firms paid to attend meetings of panel that advises FDA, e-mails show." *Washington Post*.

[32] Talea Miller. "'Explosive' Growth in Foreign Drug Testing Raising Ethical Questions." *PBS NewsHour*.
Duff Wilson. "6,485 overseas Clinical Trials and Counting." *New York Times*.

[33] Ibid.

[34] "Federal Obstruction of Medical Marijuana Research." *Marijuana Policy Project*.

[35] Sandra Young. "Medical marijuana research stalls after Arizona professor is let go." *CNN*.

36 "UA drops researcher studying medical marijuana for vets." *AZCentral.com*.
37 Ibid.
38 Elaine Minamide. P 31
39 "Low or No THC, High CBD Medical Marijuana Bills: Leaving Most Patients Behind." *Marijuana Policy Project*.
40 "Clearing the Smoke: The Science of Cannabis." *PBS*.
41 "Medical Marijuana: The Hot Debate, Pt 2." *Dr. Oz Show*. March 28, 2011.
42 *What if Cannabis Cured Cancer?* Dir. Len Richmond. Len Richmond Films, 2010. DVD.
43 Steven Nelson. "Study: Cannabis Compounds Can Kill Cancer Cells." *U.S. News & World Report*.
44 Ibid.
45 "Doctors, Patients Assess Effectiveness of Medical Marijuana." *PBS NewsHour*.
46 Ibid.
47 Hampton Sides. "High Science" National Geographic. June 2015.
48 Raymond Cushing. "Pot shrinks Tumors; Government Knew in '74." *Project Censored*.
49 Ibid.
50 Ibid.
51 "Doctors, Patients Assess Effectiveness of Medical Marijuana." *PBS NewsHour*.
52 Hampton Sides. "High Science."
53 "Doctors, Patients Assess Effectiveness of Medical Marijuana." *PBS NewsHour*.
54 Brinna Nanda. "The Significance of US Govt Cannabinoid Patent 6,630,507." *Stop The Drug War*.
55 Jack Herer. *The Emperor Wears No Clothes*. Van Nuys, CA: AH HA Publishing, 1998. Print. P 106, 107
56 Mitch Earleywine. *Understanding Marijuana: A New Look at the Scientific Evidence*.
57 Jason Bellini. "Marijuana: Heavy Users Risk Changes to Brain." *Wall Street Journal*.
58 Mitch Earleywine. *Understanding Marijuana: A New Look at the Scientific Evidence*.
Eric Schlosser. *Reefer Madness: Sex, Drugs, and Cheap Labor in the American Black Market*. New York: Houghton Mifflin Company, 2003. P 17
Paul Armentano. "Cannabis and the Brain: A User's Guide." *NORML*.
59 "Marijuana use may lead to heart complications, death, study says." *FOX News*.

[60] Chris Conrad. *Hemp: Lifeline to the Future: The Unexpected Answer for our Environmental and Economic Recovery*. Los Angeles: Creative Xpressions Publications, 1994. Print. P 151
[61] Marc Kaufman. "Study Find No Cancer-Marijuana Connection." *Washington Post*.
[62] Maia Szalavitz. "Study: Smoking Marijuana Not Linked with Lung Damage." *Time*.
[63] Mitch Earlywine P 198-209
[64] "Study: Longtime Marijuana Smokers Lack Motivation, Reward-Seeking Behavior." *CBS*.
[65] "Treatment Episode Data Set (TEDS) 1998-2008.: National Admissions To Substance Abuse Treatment Services." *Substance Abuse and Mental Health Services Administration*.
[66] Dan Baum. *Smoke and Mirrors: The War on Drugs and the Politics of Failure*. Boston: Little, Brown and Company, 1996. Print. P 238
[67] Paul Joseph Gerber. P 142
[68] "Marijuana Not A Gateway To Hard Drug Use, Rand Study Says Conclusions Raise Serious Doubts Regarding The Legitimacy Of U.S. Drug Policy." *NORML*.
[69] Steve Fox, Paul Armentano, and Mason Twert. *Marijuana is Safer: So Why are We Driving People to Drink?* White River Junction, VT: Chelsea Green Publishing Company, 2009. Print. P 60
[70] David Bienenstock. "Nope, Still No Such Thing as a Fatal Marijuana Overdose." *Vice*.
[71] "Marijuana Myths and Facts: The Truth Behind 10 Popular Misconceptions." *Office of National Drug Control Policy*.
[72] "Clearing The Smoke: The Science Of Cannabis." *PBS*
[73] Aaron E. Carroll. "Alcohol or Marijuana? A Pediatrician Faces the Question." *New York Times*.
[74] Tom Angell. "One Marijuana Arrest Every 42 Seconds in U.S." *Law Enforcement Against Prohibition*.
[75] Ibid.
[76] Lynn Zimmer and John P. Morgan. *Marijuana Myths: Marijuana Facts*. New York: Lindesmith Center, 2009. Print. P 127
[77] Abby Haglage. "The Truth About Driving While Stoned." *Daily Beast*.
[78] "Marijuana and Actual Driving Performance: November 1993." *U.S. Department of Transportation National Highway Traffic Safety Administration*.
[79] "Medical Marijuana Laws Reduce Traffic Deaths." *NORML*.

Chapter 7

[1] Daniel Okrent. *Last Call: The Rise and Fall of Prohibition*. New York: Scribner, 2010. Print. P 113

[2] John Kobler. *Ardent Spirits: The Rise and Fall of Prohibition*. New York: G.P. Putnam's Sons, 1973. Print. P 190, 191
[3] Daniel Okrent. P 21
[4] Ibid.
[5] John Kobler. *Ardent Spirits: The Rise and Fall of Prohibition*. P 183
[6] *Prohibition*. Dir. Ken Burns and Lynn Novack. Narrated by Peter Coyote. PBS Home Video, 2011. DVD.
[7] Dan Russell. *Drug War: Covert Money, Power & Policy*. Camden, NY: Kalyx.com, 2000. Print. P 117
[8] Ibid.
[9] Dan Russell. P 113-117
[10] Michael A. Lerner. *Dry Manhattan: Prohibition in New York City*. Cambridge, MA: Harvard University Press, 2008. Print. P 97
[11] Ibid.
[12] Michael A. Lerner. P 31
[13] Edward Behr. *Prohibition: Thirteen Years That Changed America*. New York: Arcade Publishing: 1996. Print. P 69
[14] Michael A. Lerner. P 124
[15] Henry Ford. *Moving For War*. Garden City, NY: Doubleday, Doran & Co, 1930. Print. P 280
[16] Edward Behr. P 59
[17] Radley Balko. *Rise of the Warrior Cop: The Militarization of America's Police Forces*. New York: Public Affairs, 2013. Print. P 141
[18] Linda Jacobs Altman. *The Decade that Roared: America during Prohibition*. Brookfield, CT: Twenty-First Century Books, 1997. Print. P 17
[19] Daniel Okrent. P 375
[20] Michael A. Lerner. P 138
[21] Karen Blumenthal and Jay Colvin. *Bootleg: Murder, Moonshine, and the Lawless Years of Prohibition*. New York: Roaring Brook, 2011. Print.
[22] Frederick Lewis Allen. *The 1920s*. Ed. John F. Wukowits. San Diego: Greenhaven Press, 2000. Print. P 142
[23] J. Anne Funderburg. *Bootleggers and Beer Barons of the Prohibition Era*. McFarland Books, 2014. Print. P 14
[24] Herbert Asbury. *The 1920s*. Ed. John F. Wukowits. San Diego: Greenhaven Press, 2000. Print. P 139
[25] Edward Behr. P 221
[26] Deborah Blum. "The Chemists' War: The Little-told story of how the U.S. poisoned alcohol during Prohibition with deadly consequences." *Slate*.
[27] Ibid.
[28] Michael A. Lerner. P 261
[29] "Rumrunners, Moonshiners, & Bootleggers." *History Channel*.
[30] John Kobler. *Ardent Spirits: The Rise and Fall of Prohibition*. P 257

[31] Daniel Okrent. P 161-163
[32] Martin Gitlin. *The Prohibition Era*. Edina, MN: ABDO Publishing, 2011. Print. P 12
[33] John Kobler. *Ardent Spirits: The Rise and Fall of Prohibition*. P 242
[34] Edward Behr. 164
[35] Thomas M. Coffey. *The Long Thirst: Prohibition in America: 1920-1933*. New York: W.W. Norton, 1975. Print. P 97
[36] "The Man in the Green Hat: February 18, 1930." U.S. Senate History. <http://www.senate.gov/artandhistory/history/minute/The_Man_in_the_Green_Hat.htm>
[37] Ibid.
[38] Ibid.
[39] "The Man in the Green Hat: February 18, 1930."
[40] *Prohibition*. Dir. Ken Burns and Lynn Novack
The court's ruling in Van Oster v Kansas defended the state's right to confiscate property used for bootlegging.
[41] "Olmstead v. United States: The Constitutional Challenges of Prohibition Enforcement — Historical Background and Documents." *Federal Judicial Center*.
[42] John Kobler. *Ardent Spirits: The Rise and Fall of Prohibition*. P 223
[43] Steven B. Duke and Albert C. Gross. *America's Longest War: Rethinking Our Tragic Crusade against Drugs*. New York: Jeremy P. Tarcher / Putnam Book, 1993. Print. P 87
Thomas Reppetto. *American Mafia: A History of Its Rise to Power*. New York: Henry Holt and Company, 2004. Print. P 93
[44] "Olmstead v. United States: The Constitutional Challenges of Prohibition Enforcement — Historical Background and Documents." *Federal Judicial Center*.
[45] *Prohibition*. Dir. Ken Burns and Lynn Novack
[46] John Kobler. *Ardent Spirits: The Rise and Fall of Prohibition*. P 315-319
[47] John Kobler. *Capone: The Life and World of Al Capone*. New York: Putnam, 1971. Print. P 69
[48] Edward Behr. P 189
[49] "Prohibition: Big Bill Thompson." *PBS*. <http://www.pbs.org/kenburns/prohibition/media_detail/S0987/>
[50] Luciano J. Iorizzo. *Al Capone: A Biography*. Westport, CT: Greenwood Press, 2003. Print. P 79
[51] Laurence Bergreen. *Capone: The Man and the Era*. New York: Simon & Shuster, 1994. Print. P 367
[52] "History of Alcohol Prohibition." *National Commission on Marihuana and Drug Abuse*.
[53] Michael A. Lerner. P 231
[54] Daniel Okrent. P 333

[55] "History of Alcohol Prohibition." *National Commission on Marihuana and Drug Abuse.*
[56] Michael A. Lerner. P 294
[57] Dan Russell. P 598
[58] Tom Feiling. *The Candy Machine: How Cocaine Took Over the World.* New York: Viking Penguin, 2010. Print. P 282
[59] "AP IMPACT: After 40 years, $1 trillion, US War on Drugs has failed to meet any of its goals." *Associated Press.*
[60] Paul Armentano. "Over 100 Million Americans Have Smoked Marijuana –And It's Still Illegal?" *Alternet.*
[61] "Drug War Statistics." *Drug Policy Alliance.*
[62] Peter Moskos. *Cop in the Hood: My Year Policing Baltimore's Eastern District.* Princeton: Princeton University Press, 2008. Print. P 171
[63] Mark Thornton. "Alcohol Prohibition Was A Failure." *Cato Institute.*
[64] <http://www.bop.gov/about/statistics/statistics_inmate_offenses.jsp>
[65] John Kobler. *Ardent Spirits: The Rise and Fall of Prohibition.* P 275
[66] Ashley Fantz. "The Mexico drug war: Bodies for billions." *CNN.*
[67] Bernard B. Kerik. *The Lost Son: A Life in Pursuit of Justice.* New York: Reagan Books, 2001. Print. P 7
[68] Nick Gillespie and Amanda Winkler. "Former NYPD Chief Bernard Kerik Discusses Ferguson, Police Militarization, and Clemency." *Reason.*
[69] Niki D'Andrea. "High Science: Synthetic Marijuana is Legal, and It Might Get You High – But Is It Safe?" *Phoenix New Times.*
[70] David Zucchino. "Scientist's research produces a dangerous high." *Los Angeles Times.*
[71] "The War On Drugs At A Glance." *Law Enforcement Against Prohibition.*
[72] Connie Fletcher. *What Cops Know: Cops Talk about What They Do, How They Do It, and What It Does to Them.* New York: Villard Books, 1991. Print. P 28
[73] John Kobler. *Ardent Spirits: The Rise and Fall of Prohibition.* P 272
[74] Marc Lacey. "Police Officers Find That Dissent on Drug Laws May Come With a Price." *New York Times.*
[75] LEAP co-founder, Peter Christ, appearance on WGRZ-TV in Buffalo, NY
[76] Ibid.
[77] Steve Fox, Paul Armentano, and Mason Tvert. *Marijuana is Safer: So Why are We Driving People to Drink?* White River Junction, VT: Chelsea Green Publishing, 2009. Print. P 115
[78] "2008 Crime In The United States." FBI's Uniform Crime Reporting Program. <https://www2.fbi.gov/ucr/cius2008/offenses/violent_crime/index.html>
[79] Ali Akbar Dareini. "Drug abuse in Iran rising despite executions, police raids." *Associated Press.*
[80] Bruce K. Alexander. *The Globalisation of Addiction: A Study in Poverty of the Spirit.* Oxford: Oxford University Press, 2008. Print. P 195

[81] Steven B. Duke and Albert C. Gross. P 181
[82] Mary Carmichael. "The Case for Treating Drug Addicts in Prison." *Newsweek.*
[83] Ibid.
[84] "Drugs, Crime, and the Justice System." U.S. Department of Justice, Bureau of Justice Statistics. P 109
[85] "Tulia Texas." *PBS.*
< http://www.pbs.org/independentlens/tuliatexas/warondrugs.html>
[86] Azmat Khan. "Despite Show of Support, Federal Funding Ban on Needle Exchange Unlikely to Be Lifted Anytime Soon." *PBS.*
[87] "Needle Exchange: A Primer." *PBS.*
[88] Azmet Khan. "Despite Show of Support, Federal Funding Ban on Needle Exchange Unlikely to Be Lifted Anytime Soon."
[89] "Congress Ends Ban On Federal Funding For Needle Exchange Programs." *NPR.*
[90] "Needle Exchange: A Primer." *PBS.*
[91] National Institutes of Health: Interventions to Prevent HIV Risk Behaviors. 1997 February 11-13;15(2):1-41.
[92] "Lifting The Federal Ban On Syringe Exchange Funding." *Harm Reduction Coalition.*
[93] Janelle Brown. "Your glow stick could land you in jail." *Salon.*
[94] "Hooked: Illegal Drugs & How They Got That Way." Episode Four. *History Channel.*
[95] "U.S. Will Ban 'Ecstasy,' a Hallucinogenic Drug." *Associated Press.*
[96] Clayton J. Mosher and Scott Akins. *Drugs and Drug Policy: The Control of Consciousness Alteration.* Thousand Oaks, CA: Sage, 2007. Print. 467
Janelle Brown. "Your glow stick could land you in jail."
[97] Dan Baum. *Smoke and Mirrors: The War on Drugs and the Politics of Failure.* Boston: Little, Brown and Company, 1996. Print. P 248
[98] "Drug Overdose Immunity "Good Samaritan" Laws." *National Conference of State Legislatures.*
[99] "Naloxone for San Francisco Police Department!" *Harm Reduction Coalition.*
[100] "Naloxone Overdose Prevention Laws Map." *LawAtlas.org.*
[101] Stephanie Hegarty. "Can a hallucinogen from Africa cure addiction?" *BBC.*
[102] VICE on HBO. Season One Episode Seven. May 17, 2013.
[103] Stephanie Hegarty. "Can a hallucinogen from Africa cure addiction?"
[104] Sydney P. Freedberg. "Drug Users Turn Death Dealers as Methadone From Bain Hits Street." *Bloomberg.*
[105] Ibid.
[106] Ibid.
[107] Elizabeth Lopatto. "Heroin Better Than Methadone for Treating Addiction, Study Says." *Bloomberg.*
[108] Ibid.

[109] Jesse Singal. "Heroin Works Better Than Methadone, So Why Won't Politicians Allow It?" *Daily Beast*.
[110] Richard Nixon's Address to the Congress on Drug Abuse Prevention and Control. June 17, 1971.
[111] Phillip Smith. "Feature: Effort to Bring Safe Injection Facility to New York City Getting Underway." *Stop The Drug War*.
[112] Ethan Nadelmann. "Switzerland's Heroin Experiment." *National Review*. July 10, 1995.
[113] Ibid.
[114] "Alternatives to Public Injection." *Harm Reduction Coalition*.
[115] Roger Cohen. "Amid Growing Crime, Zurich Closes A Park It Reserved for Drug Addicts." *New York Times*.
[116] Robert J. MacCoun, and Peter Reuter. *Drug War Heresies: Learning from Other Vices, Times, and Places*. Cambridge: Cambridge University Press, 2001. Print. P 285
[117] Jennifer Warner. "U.S. Leads the World in Illegal Drug Use." *CBS News*.
[118] Lynn Zimmer and John P. Morgan. *Marijuana Myths: Marijuana Facts*. New York: Lindesmith Center, 2009. Print. P 49
[119] Clayton J. Mosher and Scott Akins. P 382
[120] David Downs. "Report: Dutch Lessons For U.S. Marijuana Policy." *San Francisco Chronicle*.
[121] "Libertarians assert powerful case for ending War on Drugs." *Libertarian Party of Minnesota*.
[122] Clayton J. Mosher and Scott Akins. P 382
[123] Gary L. Fisher. *Rethinking our War on Drugs: Candid Talk About Controversial Issues*. Westport, CN: Praeger, 2006. Print. P 20
[124] "Netherlands to close prisons for lack of criminals." <http://vorige.nrc.nl/international/article2246821.ece/Netherlands_to_close_prisons_for_lack_of_criminals>
[125] Glenn Greenwald. "Drug Decriminalization In Portugal: Lessons For Creating Fair And Successful Drug Policies." *Cato Institute*.
[126] Erik Kain. "Ten Years After Decriminalization, Drug Abuse Down by Half in Portugal." *Forbes*.
[127] Ibid.
[128] "Drug decriminalization in Portugal: setting the record straight." *TRANSFORM: Getting drugs under control*.
[129] Ibid.

Chapter 8

[1] (All statistics were derived from 2008 except for "deaths from lack of health insurance" which was based upon the year 2000.)

"Slightly Lower Adult Smoking Rates: Press Release: Nov. 13, 2008." *Centers for Disease Control and Prevention.*
"Fact Sheets- Alcohol Use and Health." *Centers for Disease Control and Prevention.*
Margaret Warner, Li Hui Chen, Diane M. Makuc, Arialdi M. Miniño, and Robert N. Anderson. "NHCS Data Brief: No. 81: December 2011: Drug Poisoning Deaths in the United States, 1980-2008." *National Center for Health Statistics.*
"Vital Signs: Overdoses of Prescription Opioid Pain Relievers --- United States, 1999—2008." *Centers for Disease Control and Prevention.*
"Crime in the United States: 2009." Federal Bureau of Investigation's Uniform Crime Reporting Program

[2] *Victory Begins at Home*. Dir. John Moffitt. Perf. Bill Maher. HBO Films, 2003. DVD.

[3] "High Risk List: 2013." *U.S. Government Accountability Office.*

[4] "Keeping Watch Over Direct-to-Consumer Ads." *Food and Drug Administration.*

[5] C. Lee Ventola. "Direct-to-Consumer Pharmaceutical Advertising-Therapeutic or Toxic?" *National Center for Biotechnology Information.*

[6] Beth Snyder Bulik. "Ad Spending: 15 Years of DTC." Ad Age Whitepaper. Jason Millman. "It's true: Drug companies are bombarding your TV with more ads than ever." *Washington Post.*

[7] "Global pharmaceutical sales from 2012 to 2014, by region (in billion U.S. dollars)*" *Statista.com.*

[8] Joseph Nordqvist. "Up to 60 percent of drug ads on TV are misleading." *Market Business News.*

[9] Jessica Firger. "Very Public Enemies: The Battle Between the FDA and Kim Kardashian." *Newsweek.*

[10] "Letter to FDA from Mark Gold: January 12, 2002: Evidence File #7: Aspartame History."
< http://www.fda.gov/ohrms/dockets/dailys/03/Jan03/012203/02P-0317_emc-000202.txt>

[11] Ibid.

[12] Ibid.

[13] David Burnham. *Above the Law: Secret Deals, Political Fixes, and Other Misadventures of the U.S. Department of Justice.* New York: Scribner Publishing, 1996. Print. P 230

[14] *Sweet Misery: A Poisoned World*. Dir. Cori Brackett. Perf. Cori Brackett. Cinema Libre Distribution, 2004. DVD.

[15] *Sweet Misery: A Poisoned World.*

[16] "Letter to FDA from Mark Gold: January 12, 2002: Evidence File #4: Reported Aspartame Toxicity Effects."

<http://www.fda.gov/ohrms/dockets/dailys/03/jan03/012203/02p-0317_emc-000199.txt>
[17] *Generation Rx.* Dir. Kevin P. Miller. Passion River Films, 2009. DVD.
[18] Ibid.
[19] "ADHD Misdiagnosed In Nearly 1 million U.S. Kids Say Researchers." *PreventDisease.Com.*
[20] Makiko Kitamura. "American Adults Surpass Children in Taking Drugs to Stay Focused." *Bloomberg.*
[21] Chelsey Dulaney. "Shire to Pay $56.5 Million to Settle False Marketing Claims." *Wall Street Journal.*
[22] Clyde Haberman. "Selling Prozac as the Life-Enhancing Cure for Mental Woes." *New York Times.*
[23] "Report: 1 in 5 of U.S. adults on behavioral meds." *Associated Press.*
[24] Rebecca White. "Pets on Prozac." *New York Post.*
[25] *Generation Rx*
[26] Christopher Bryson. *The Fluoride Deception.* New York: Seven Stories Press, 2004. Print.
[27] Dr. Peter Breggin testimony before the Veterans' Affairs Committee of the U.S. House of Representatives on February 24, 2010.
[28] Shankar Vendantam. "FDA Told Its Analyst to Censor Data on Antidepressants." *Washington Post.*
[29] Ray Moynihan and Allen Cassels. *Selling Sickness: How The World's Biggest Pharmaceutical Companies Are Turning Us All Into Patients.* New York: Nation Books, 2005. Print. P 34
[30] "Foster care kids put on too many psych drugs, report says." *CBS News.*
[31] David G. Savage. "Court Says Inmates Can Be Forced to Take Drugs: Rights: Justices hold that prison officials have the final say on using mind-altering substances. The ruling does not apply to California institutions." *Los Angeles Times.*
[32] Michael LaForgia. "Dosed in juvie jail: Drug firms pay state-hired doctors." *Palm Beach Post.*
[33] Stephen Foley. "GlaxoSmithKline pays $3bn for illegally marketing depression drug." *The Independent.*
[34] Ibid.
[35] David Evans. "Pfizer Broke the Law by Promoting Drugs for Unapproved Uses." *Bloomberg.*
[36] Ford Vox. "How Dr. Drew Sold His Cred to Big Pharma." *The Atlantic.*
[37] Katie Thomas. "Glaxo Says It Will Stop Paying Doctors to Promote Drugs." *New York Times.*
[38] Alex Jones Radio Show with guest Blair Hamrick on July 17, 2012.
[39] <http://www.cms.gov/openpayments/>

[40] Charles Ornstein, Eric Sagara, and Ryann Grochowski Jones. "As Full Disclosure Nears, Doctors' Pay for Drug Talks Plummets." *ProPublica*.
[41] Caroline Chen and Zachary Tracer. "Doctors Got $6.5 Billion From Drug, Device Makers in U.S." *Bloomberg*.
[42] Joe Whittington and Andrew Harris. "Ex-KV Pharmaceutical CEO Hermelin Pleads Guilty to Drug Label Law Breach." *Bloomberg*.
[43] Katie Thomas and Michael S. Schmidt. "Glaxo Agrees to Pay $3 Billion in Fraud Settlement." *New York Times*.
[44] Gardiner Harris. "Pfizer Pays $2.3 Billion to Settle Marketing Case." *New York Times*.
[45] Aaron Smith. "Pfizer pulls Bextra off the market." *CNN Money*.
[46] Gardiner Harris. "Pfizer Pays $2.3 Billion to Settle Marketing Case."
Christie Smythe. "Pfizer Agrees to $325 Million Neurontin Marketing Accord." *Bloomberg*.
Jonathan Stempel. "Pfizer to pay $325 million in Neurontin settlement." *Reuters*.
[47] Margaret Cronin Fisk. "Pfizer Settles Whistle-Blower Suit Over Detrol Marketing." *Bloomberg*.
[48] Brady Dennis. "Why the FDA approved OxyContin for kids as young as 11." *Washington Post*.
[49] "Critics Question FDA's Approval Of Zohydro." *NPR*.
[50] "Limbaugh on Drugs-People like Limbaugh should go to jail, says Limbaugh." *FAIR*.
[51] Jacques Steinberg. "Limbaugh Signs On Again, Sharing Life's Tough Lessons." *New York Times*.
[52] Carol Marin. "Rush Limbaugh, an outed addict." *Chicago Tribune*.
[53] Donna Leinwand Leger. "Cardinal Health settles drug distribution case." *USA Today*.
[54] Bob LaMendola. "How the George brothers made millions with pill mills." *Sun Sentinel*.
"The Oxycontin Express." V*anguard. Season 3 Episode 1*.
[55] Barry Meier. *Pain Killer: A "Wonder" Drug's Trail of Addiction and Death*. New York: Rodale, 2003. Print. P 67, 99
[56] Sam Quinones. *Dreamland: The True Tale of America's Opiate Epidemic*. New York: Bloomsbury Press, 2015. Print. P 132
[57] American Society of Addictive Medicine. "Opioid Addiction: 2016 Facts & Figures."
[58] Government Accountability Office (GAO) report number GAO-04-110. "Prescription Drugs: OxyContin Abuse and Diversion and Efforts to Address the Problem." January 22, 2004.
[59] Scott Glover and Lisa Girion. "OxyContin maker closely guards its list of suspect doctors." *Los Angeles Times*.

[60] Ibid.
[61] Alex Morrell. "The OxyContin Clan: The $14 Billion Newcomer to Forbes 2015 List of Richest U.S. Families." *Forbes*.
[62] Sam Quinones. P 31
[63] Barry Meier. *Pain Killer: A "Wonder" Drug's Trail of Addiction and Death.* P 196
[64] Sam Quinones. P 125
[65] Sanjay Gupta. "Unintended consequences: Why painkiller addicts turn to heroin." *CNN*.
[66] Chris Hawley. "'An Epidemic': Pharmacy robberies sweeping US." *NBC News*.
[67] Patrick Oppmann. "Addicts putting pharmacies under siege." *CNN*.
[68] Barry Meier and Eric Lipton. "Under Attack, Drug Maker Turned to Giuliani for Help." *New York Times*.
[69] Jesse Singal. "Heroin Works Better Than Methadone, So Why Won't Politicians Allow It?" *Daily Beast*.
[70] "Join Together" Staff. "Giuliani Accused of Shielding Purdue Pharma in OxyContin Scandal." *Partnership for a Drug Free America*.
[71] Barry Meier and Eric Lipton. "Under Attack, Drug Maker Turned to Giuliani for Help."
[72] Marianne Skolek. "Eric Holder negotiated an OxyContin settlement in West Virginia - working for Purdue Pharma!" *Salem-News.com*.
[73] Barry Meier and Eric Lipton. "Under Attack, Drug Maker Turned to Giuliani for Help."
[74] Barry Meier. "U.S. maker of OxyContin painkiller to pay $600 million in guilty plea." *New York Times*.
[75] Ibid.
Katherine Eban. "OxyContin: Purdue Pharma's Painful Medicine." *Fortune Magazine*.
[76] Amy Goldstein and Carrie Johnson. "U.S. Attorney Became Target After Rebuffing Justice Dept." *Washington Post*.
[77] Eric Schlosser. P 51
[78] Bryce Covert & Josh Israel. "What 7 States Discovered After Spending More Than $1 Million Drug Testing Welfare Recipients." *Think Progress*.
[79] Eric W. Dolan. "Oklahoma legislators kill provision to drug test politicians." *Raw Story*.
[80] Jonathan Karl. "Obama and His Pot-Smoking 'Choom Gang'" *ABC News*.
[81] Jacob Sullum. "Mitch Daniel's Disappearing Felony." *Reason*.
[82] Ibid.
[83] Phillip Smith. "Conservatives Board Sentencing Reform Bandwagon." *Stop The Drug War*.
[84] Sonya Ross. "Clinton Pardons More Than 100." *Washington Post*.

[85] Eric Schlosser. *Reefer Madness: Sex, Drugs, and Cheap Labor in the American Black Market*. Boston: Houghton Mifflin, 2003. Print. P 52
[86] Rudolph Joseph Gerber. *Legalizing Marijuana: Drug Policy Reform and Prohibition Politics*. Westport, CT: Praeger, 2004. Print. P 93
[87] Eric Schlosser. P 48
[88] Steve Fox, Paul Armentano, and Mason Tvert. *Marijuana is Safer: So Why are We Driving People to Drink?* White River Junction, VT: Chelsea Green Publishing, 2009. Print. P 11
[89] Newt Gingrich's Letter to the Editor. March 19, 1982 issue of the Journal of the American Medical Association (JAMA).
[90] Dan Russell. *Drug War: Covert Money, Power & Policy*. Camden, NY: Kalyx.com, 2000. Print. P 574
[91] Eric Schlosser. P 52
[92] Evin Thomas. "Top Gun's Tailspin." *Newsweek*.
[93] Eric Schlosser. P 52-53
"Politicians' Children's Encounters with Marijuana Prohibition." *NORML*.
[94] "Book: Bush was arrested for cocaine in 1972." *Salon*.
[95] Scott McClellen. *What Happened: Inside the Bush White House and Washington's Culture of Deception*. New York: Public Affairs, 2008. Print. P 48
[96] Deborah Sharp. "Jeb Bush's daughter charged with prescription fraud." *USA Today*.
[97] Mark Potter. "Jeb Bush's daughter charged with prescription fraud." *CNN*.
[98] "Noelle Bush given 10 days in jail for contempt." *CNN*.
[99] Ibid.
[100] Kate Bradshaw. "Jeb Bush and Newt Gingrich Agree With ACLU on Something: Criminal Justice Needs a Tweak."
"The Kelly File." *Fox*. February 25, 2015.
[101] Richard Lawrence Miller. *Drug Warriors and Their Prey: From Police Power to Police State*. Westport, CT: Praeger, 1996. Print. P 82
[102] Daniel Forbes. "Ashcroft's nephew got probation after major pot bust." *Salon*.
[103] Clayton J. Mosher and Scott Akins. *Drugs and Drug Policy: The Control of Consciousness Alteration*. Thousand Oaks, CA: Sage, 2007. Print. 205
[104] "PBS Newshour August 13, 2003." *PBS*.
[105] James Bovard. *The Bush Betrayal*. New York: Palgrave MacMillan, 2004. Print. P 130
[106] "Tommy Chong Interview with The Young Turks: August 21, 2006."
[107] Terry Gross. "Chong's Prosecutor: Operation Pipe Dreams." *NPR*.
[108] Greg Beato. "Tommy Chong's Bongs." *Reason*.
[109] James Bovard. P 131
[110] Kimberly Kindy. "A Tangled Story of Addiction." *Washington Post*.

Chapter 9

[1] James B. Comey, Director of Federal Bureau of Investigation at Georgetown University. "Hard Truths: Law Enforcement and Race." Washington, D.C. February 12, 2015.

[2] Jen Christensen. "FBI tracked King's every move." *CNN*.

[3] Ward Churchill and Jim Wall. *The COINTELPRO Papers: Documents from the FBI's Secret Wars against Dissent in the United States*. 2nd ed. Cambridge, MA: South End Press, 2002. Print. P 97-102

[4] Dan Baum. *Smoke and Mirrors: The War on Drugs and the Politics of Failure*. Boston: Little, Brown and Company, 1996. Print. P 7

[5] Ronald J. Ostrow and Robert L. Jackson. "Haldeman's Diaries Show Nixon's Dark, Human Sides: History: Secret memoir tells of President's alternate glee and guilt at provoking antiwar demonstrators." *Los Angeles Times*.

[6] Dan Baum. "Legalize It All." *Harper's Magazine*. April 2016.

[7] "Study Finds Racial Disparities in Incarceration Drive Support for Harsh Criminal Justice Policies." *Equal Justice Initiative*.

[8] Tyjen Tsai and Paola Scommenga. "U.S. Has World's Highest Incarceration Rate." *Population Reference Bureau*.

[9] M. Mauer. "Americans Behind Bars: The International Use of Incarceration, 1992-1993." *National Institute of Justice*.

[10] Douglas A. Blackmon. *Slavery by Another Name: The Re-Enslavement of Black Americans From the Civil War to World War II*. New York: Doubleday, 2008. Print.

[11] Ibid.

[12] Michelle Alexander. *The New Jim Crow: Mass Incarceration in the Age of Colorblindness*. New York: New Press, 2010. Print. P 103

[13] Michelle Alexander. P 98

[14] Matt Apuzzo. "Ferguson Police Routinely Violate Rights of Blacks, Justice Dept. Finds." *New York Times*.

[15] Alexandra Natapoff. *Snitching: Criminal Informants and the Erosion of American Justice*. New York: New York University Press, 2009. Print. P 102.

[16] Douglas Valentine. *The Strength of the Wolf: The Secret History of America's War on Drugs*. London: Verso, 2004. Print.

[17] "They told this DEA agent not to enforce drug laws in white areas. Really." *Brave New Films*.

[18] Michelle Alexander. P 115.

[19] Geoff K. Ward. *The Many Colors of Crime: Inequalities of Race, Ethnicity, and Crime in America*. Ed. Ruth D. Peterson, Lauren Joy Krivo, and John Hagan. New York: New York University Press, 2006. Print. P 77

[20] Carl Hart. P 192

[21] "President Obama Signs Bill Reducing Cocaine Sentencing Disparity." *ACLU*.

[22] Peter Moskos. *Cop in the Hood: My Year Policing Baltimore's Eastern District.* Princeton: Princeton University Press, 2008. Print. P 30-31
[23] Michelle Alexander. P 65
[24] Michelle Alexander. P 131
[25] Adam Liptak. "No crime, but an arrest and Two Strip-Searches." *New York Times.*
[26] Norm Stamper. "Book Discussion on Breaking Rank: A Top Cop's Expose." *C-Span.*
[27] Julie K. Brown. "In Miami Gardens, store video catches cops in the act." *Miami Herald.*
[28] "Police Harassment of Black Employees and Patrons at Miami Store Results in Civil Rights Suit." *Equal Justice Initiative.*
[29] Julie K. Brown. "In Miami Gardens, store video catches cops in the act."
[30] Jaisal Noor. "Former Prosecutor Gets Arrested to See The Other Side of U.S. Criminal Justice System." *The Real News.*
[31] Ibid.
[32] Bobby Constantino. "I Got Myself Arrested So I Could Look Inside the Justice System*." The Atlantic.*
[33] Michelle Conlin. "Off Duty Black Officers In New York Say They Fear Fellow Cops." *Huffington Post.*
[34] "Stop-and-Frisk Data." *ACLU.*
[35] Bill Hutchinson. "Gov. Cuomo looks to decriminalize possession of small amounts of pot to cut down on stop-and-frisk arrests." *New York Daily News.*
[36] Judd Legum. "10 Facts Everyone Should Know About New York City's 'Stop-And-Frisk' Policy." *Think Progress.*
[37] Ross Tuttle and Erin Schneider. "Stopped-and-Frisked: 'For Being a F**king Mutt' [VIDEO]." *The Nation.*
[38] Judd Legum. "10 Facts Everyone Should Know About New York City's 'Stop-And-Frisk' Policy."
[39] "Stop And Frisk And The Urgent Need For Meaningful Reforms." Office of Bill DeBlasio, Public Advocate for the City Of New York.
[40] Erin Durkin and Dareh Gregorian. "Mayor Bloomberg stands by his white frisk comment as Rep. Hakeem Jeffries calls for federal NYPD monitor." *New York Daily News.*
[41] Joe Rogan Experience podcast #670. July 8, 2015.
[42] Joseph D. McNamara. "LAW ENFORCEMENT: Has the Drug War Created an Officer Liars' Club**?**" *Los Angeles Times.*
[43] John Marzulli. "Judge Jack Weinstein rips NYPD on false arrests as brothers sue for $10M over wrongful narcs bust." *New York Daily News.*
[44] John Marzulli. "We fabricated drug charges against innocent people to meet arrest quotas, former detective testifies." *New York Daily News.*

[45] John Marzulli. "Judge Jack Weinstein rips NYPD on false arrests as brothers sue for $10M over wrongful narcs bust."

[46] Martin Booth. *Cannabis: A History*. New York: Thomas Dunne Books/St. Martin's Press, 20042003. Print. P 353.

Irene Lacher. "The Way Patti Sees It: While Some Question Her Motives, Davis Says She Just Wants to Tell the Truth About the Reagans." *Los Angeles Times*.

[47] Ronald J. Ostrow. "Casual Drug Users Should Be Shot, Gates Says." *Los Angeles Times*.

[48] "COAST POLICE CHIEF ACCUSED OF RACISM." *New York Times*.

[49] Mandalit Del Barco. "SWAT History a Series of Highs, Lows in L.A." *NPR*.

[50] Joe Rogan Experience podcast #670. July 8, 2015.

[51] Dr. Peter Kraska lecture. "Militarized Policing and Public Protest: From the WTO Protests to Ferguson." Recorded December 2, 2014 at the Ethnic Cultural Center at the University of Washington.

[52] Brian Bennett. "Police employ Predator drone spy planes on home front." *Los Angeles Times*.

[53] Matt Apuzzo. "War Gear Flows to Police Departments." *New York Times*. Christopher Ingraham. "The Pentagon gave nearly half a billion dollars of military gear to local law enforcement last year." *Washington Post*.

[54] David Nakamura and Wesley Lowery. "Obama administration bans some military-style assault gear from local police departments." *Washington Post*.

[55] Radley Balko. "Too Many Cops Are Told They're Soldiers Fighting a War. How Did We Get Here?" *ACLU*.

[56] Dr. Peter Kraska lecture.

[57] Martin Kaste. "Why Utah Is The Only State Trying To Track And Limit SWAT-Style Tactics." *NPR*.

"2014 Law Enforcement Transparency Annual Report." *Utah Commission on Criminal and Juvenile Justice*.

[58] Radley Balko. "Overkill: The Rise of Paramilitary Police Raids in America." *Cato Institute*.

[59] "War Comes Home: The Excessive Militarization of American Policing." *American Civil Liberties Union*

[60] Radley Balko. *Rise of the Warrior Cop: The Militarization of America's Police Forces*. New York: Public Affairs, 2013. Print.

[61] Philip Warden. "Save No-Knock Rule, Mitchell Asks Unit." *Chicago Tribune*. July 21, 1970.

[62] Nate Carlisle. "Salt Lake City police discipline detective for raid on wrong house." *Salt Lake Tribune*.

[63] Brian Haynes. "Owner still mourning 2005 death of pit bull shot by police." *Las Vegas Review-Journal*.

[64] Katy Moeller. "Dog Shootings by Police Prompt Mandatory Training in Other States." *MagicValley.com*.

[65] "Cop cleared of wrongdoing after shooting kittens in front of screaming kids." *RT*.
[66] "Mayor wants federal probe after SWAT raids house, kills dogs." *CNN*.
[67] Aaron C. Davis. "Police Raid Berwyn Heights Mayor's Home, Kill His 2 Dogs." *Washington Post*.
[68] "Cheye Calvo explores the money behind SWAT raids." *Cato Institute*.
[69] "Amish farmer targeted by FDA raids shuts down raw milk business." *NBC News*.
[70] "Monks Arrested In SWAT Team Action." *KETV 7 ABC Omaha*.
[71] Ibid.
[72] "War Comes Home: The Excessive Militarization of American Policing." *American Civil Liberties Union*.
[73] Alexandra Natapoff. P 125
[74] "Snitch." *PBS Frontline*. Air Date: January 12, 1999.
[75] Alexandra Natapoff. P 54.
[76] Alexandra Natapoff. P 28
[77] "The Informers." *60 Minutes*. March 28, 1993.
[78] Rich Lord. "U.S. agencies work to hide every detail about thousands of informants." *Pittsburgh Post-Gazette*.
[79] Megan O'Matz and John Maines. "Cops. Cash. Cocaine. How Sunrise Police make millions selling drugs." *Sun Sentinel*.
[80] Mark Donald. "Dirty or Duped?" *Dallas Observer*.
 Skip Hollandsworth. "Snow Job." *Texas Monthly*.
[81] Ibid.
[82] Ibid.
[83] Ibid.
[84] Ibid.
[85] Ibid.
WFAA 8 in Dallas ABC. "Another reversal for former Dallas officer Delapaz in fake-drug trials."
[86] "Tulia Texas: A Story of Injustice, and Mass Incarceration." Wagner & Lynch Attorneys at Law.
[87] Nate Blakeslee. *Tulia: Race, Cocaine, and Corruption in a Small Texas Town*. New York: Public Affairs, 2005. Print.
[88] "Tulia, Texas." *60 Minutes*. September 28, 2003.
[89] Nate Blakeslee. *Tulia: Race, Cocaine, and Corruption in a Small Texas Town*.
[90] Nate Blakeslee. P 44, 134
[91] "Tulia Talks Back." *PBS*.
[92] Janelle Stecklein. "Tulia drug busts: 10 years later." *Amarillo Globe News*.
[93] Francie Grace. "38 Drug Cases Thrown Into Question." *CBS News*.
[94] Nate Blakeslee. P 101
[95] "Town on Trial." *ABC News' 20/20*. Aired December 4, 2000.

[96] Janelle Stecklein. "Tulia drug busts: 10 years later."
[97] Nate Blakeslee. *Tulia: Race, Cocaine, and Corruption in a Small Texas Town*.
[98] Nate Blakeslee. P 233, 330
[99] Nate Blakeslee. P 120, 296
[100] Nate Blakeslee. P 156
[101] Janelle Stecklein. "Tulia drug busts: 10 years later."
[102] Nate Blakeslee. P 206

Chapter 10

[1] Lynn Zimmer and John P. Morgan. *Marijuana Myths: Marijuana Facts*. New York: Lindesmith Center, 2009. Print. P 159
[2] Craig Reinarman and Harry Gene Levine. *Crack in America: Demon Drugs and Social Justice*. Berkeley: University of California Press, 1997. Print. P 40
[3] Kenneth D. Lehman. *Bolivia and the United States: A Limited Partnership*. Athens, GA: University of Georgia Press, 1999. Print. P 188.
[4] Dan Baum. *Smoke and Mirrors: The War on Drugs and the Politics of Failure*. Boston: Little, Brown and Company, 1996. Print. P 235
Pee-Wee, Sgt. John Brennan, Jason Cherkis, Kevin Diaz, Thomas Durham, Laura Lang, David C. Morrison, Michael Schaffer, Annys Shin and Elissa Silverman. "Happy Anniversary, Crack!" *Washington City Paper*.
[5] William L. Darcy. *The Politics of Cocaine: How U.S. Foreign Policy Has Created a Thriving Drug Industry in Central and South America*. Chicago: Lawrence Hill Books, 2010. Print. P 91.
[6] Martin Booth. *Cannabis: A History*. New York: Thomas Dunne Books/St. Martin's Press, 2004/2003. Print. P 352
[7] "SOA Manuals Index." *SOA Watch*.
[8] Lesley Gill. *School of the Americas: Military Training and Political Violence in the Americas*. Duke University Press, 2004, Print.
[9] "Honduran Death Squad Leader and SOA Graduate Found Responsible for Torture and Disappearance in U.S. Court." *SOA Watch*.
[10] "11 Latin American Dictators." *SOA Watch*.
[11] Ray Bourgeois and Margaret Knapke. "Shining A Light on the SOA – School of Coups." *SOA Watch*.
[12] Daniel Lansberg-Rodríguez. "Coup Fatigue in Caracas." *Foreign Policy Magazine*.
[13] Christopher Marquis. "U.S. Bankrolling Is Under Scrutiny for Ties to Chávez Ouster." *New York Times*.
[14] Simon Hooper. "Chavez used force of personality to win votes, influence leaders." *CNN*.
[15] "Venezuela: How long does it take to buy 8 basic goods? BBC News." *BBC News*.

[16] "Notorious Graduates from Venezuela." *SOA Watch*.
[17] "The Assassination of Hugo Chavez." Greg Palast.
[18] Juan Forero. "Documents Show CIA Knew of a Coup Plot in Venezuela." *New York Times*.
[19] Ibid.
[20] *The War on Democracy*. Directed by Christopher Martin and John Pilger. Perf. John Pilger. 2007. DVD.
[21] "Four of 6 Generals Tied to the 2009 Honduran Coup Were Trained at the SOA." *SOA Watch*.
[22] Ginger Thompson. "A Cold War Ghost Reappears in Honduras." *New York Times*.
[23] Alex Renderos and Tracy Wilkinson. "Protests mount in Honduras after military coup." *Los Angeles Times*.
[24] "Honduran Elections Marred by Police Violence, Censorship, International Non-Recognition, CEPR Co-Director Says." *Center for Economic and Policy Research*.
[25] Dana Frank. "Honduras: Which Side Is the US On?" *The Nation*.
[26] Frances Robles. "Honduras becomes murder capital of the world." *Miami Herald*.
Frances Robles and Michael D. Shear. "U.S. Considering Refugee Status for Hondurans." *New York Times*.
[27] Dana Frank. "Open Season on Teachers in Honduras." *The Nation*.
[28] "The Deadliest Place in the World for a Journalist." *The Real News*.
[29] Ibid.
[30] Lee Fang. "During Honduras Crisis, Clinton Suggested Back Channel With Lobbyist Lanny Davis." *The Intercept*.
[31] Dana Frank. "WikiLeaks Honduras: US Linked Brutal Businessman." *The Nation*.
[32] "The Deadliest Place in the World for a Journalist." *The Real News*.
[33] Frances Robles. "Honduras becomes murder capital of the world."
[34] Benjamin Weiser. "Honduras: Ex-President's Son Arrested." *New York Times*. Nate Raymond. "Son of ex-Honduran president pleads guilty to U.S. drug charge." *Reuters*.
[35] Tracy Wilkinson. "Miguel Facusse dies at 90; colorful, ruthless Honduran tycoon." *Los Angeles Times*.
[36] "DRUG PLANE BURNED ON PROMINENT HONDURAN'S PROPERTY." *WikiLeaks*.
[37] Dana Frank. "WikiLeaks Honduras: US Linked Brutal Businessman."
[38] Frances Robles. "Honduras becomes murder capital of the world."
[39] Elisabeth Malkin and Alberto Arce. "Files Suggest Honduran Police Leaders Ordered Killing of Antidrug Officials." *New York Times*.
[40] Alberto Arce. "Honduras-Death Squads story." *Associated Press*.

[41] Dana Frank. "Just Like Old Times in Central America." *Foreign Policy Magazine*.
"Thousands march in Honduras after election controversy." *The Guardian*.
[42] Alex Emmons. "Death Squads Are Back in Honduras, Activists Tell Congress." *The Intercept*.
[43] "U.S. military expands its drug war in Latin America." *Associated Press*.
[44] Sasha Chavkin, Ben Hallman, Michael Hudson, Cécile Schilis-Gallego and Shane Shifflett. "How The World Bank Broke Its Promise To Protect The Poor." *International Consortium of Investigative Journalists and Huffington Post*.
[45] "World Bank Group: Inadequate Response to Killings, Land Grabs." *Human Rights Watch*.
[46] Greg Palast. *Best Democracy Money Can Buy*. New York: Penguin Group, 2003. Print. P 55
[47] "Timeline: Cochabamba Water Revolt." *PBS Frontline*.
[48] Amy Goodman. *The Exception to the Rulers: Exposing America's War Profiteers, the Media that Love them and the Crackdown on our Rights*. North America: Hyperion, 2003. Print. P 62
[49] Ibid.
[50] Jamie Doward. "Bolivians demand the right to chew coca leaves." *The Guardian*.
Clifford D. May. "How Coca-Cola Obtains Its Coca." *New York Times*.
[51] "Notorious Graduates from Venezuela." *SOA Watch*.
[52] Phil Gunson. "Hugo Banzer: Obituary." *The Guardian*.
[53] William L. Darcy P 26
[54] "Billions More Wasted on Anti Drug Contracts in Latin America." *AllGov.com*.
[55] Pierre-Arnaud Chouvy. *Opium: Uncovering the Politics of the Poppy*. Cambridge, MA: Harvard University Press, 2010. Print. P 113
David Barstow. "One Man's Military-Industrial-Media Complex." *New York Times*.
[56] "Merida Initiative." U.S. Department of State. <http://www.state.gov/j/inl/merida/>
[57] John Burnett and Marisa Peñaloza. "Mexico's Drug War: A Rigged Fight?" *NPR*.
[58] Doris Gómora. "La guerra secreta de la DEA en Mexico." *El Universal*.
[59] Anabel Hernandez and Roberto Saviano. *Narcoland: The Mexican Drug Lords and Their Godfathers*. English-language ed. London: Verso, 2013. Print.
[60] "Mexican Military refused to arrest Joaquin 'El Chapo.'" *SanDiegoRed.com*.
[61] "Mexico drug war deaths over five years now total 47,515." *BBC*.
[62] "Faces of the Fallen." *Washington Post*.
[63] Ted Galen Carpenter. *The Fire Next Door: Mexico's Drug Violence and the Danger to America*. Washington, D.C.: Cato Institute, 2012. Print P 85

[64] "Mexico/US: Obama-Calderón Meeting Questions and Answers." *Human Right Watch.*
[65] O'Reilly Factor. March 25, 2011 with guest Joachim Bamrud.
[66] Anabel Hernández and Steve Fisher. "New Witness Account Undermines Mexican Government Narrative Of Missing Students." *Huffington Post.*
[67] Michael Evans. "US: Mexico Mass Graves Raise 'Alarming Questions' about Government 'Complicity' in September 2014 Cartel Killings." *National Security Archive.*
[68] Ryan Devereaux. "Ghosts of Iguala: Mexico: Case Unravels in Disappearance of 43 Students." *The Intercept.*
[69] Alexander Cockburn and Jeffrey St. Clair. *Whiteout: The CIA, Drugs, and the Press.* London: Verso, 1998. Print. P 377-379
[70] Chris Arsenault. "US-trained cartel terrorizes Mexico." *Al Jazeera.*
[71] Ted Galen Carpenter. P 37
[72] Priyanka Gupta. "Colombian refugees seek justice in peace deal." *Al Jazeera.*
[73] Nick Miroff. "The staggering toll of Colombia's war with FARC rebels, explained in numbers." *Washington Post.*
[74] Peter Dale Scott. *Drugs, Oil, and War.* Oxford: Rowan & Littlefield Publishers, 2003. Print. P 74
[75] José de Córdoba. "U.S. Sanctions Venezuela Officials, Citing Drug Ties." *Wall Street Journal.*
[76] John Mulholland and Ed Vulliamy. "Preparing for peace: Inside Farc's Colombian jungle base." *The Guardian.*
[77] Peter Dale Scott. P 39
[78] Peter Dale Scott. P 72
[79] William C. Rempel. *At the Devil's Table: The Untold Story of the Insider who Brought Down the Cali Cartel.* New York: Random House Publishing, 2011. Print. P 23
[80] William C. Rempel. P 111
[81] William C. Rempel. P 143
[82] Russell Crandall. *Driven by Drugs: U.S. Policy Towards Colombia.* Boulder, CO: Lynne Rienner Publishing, 2002. Print. P 90
[83] William Avilés. *Global Capitalism, Democracy, and Civil-Military Relations in Colombia.* Albany: State University of New York, 2006. Print. P 131
[84] Marc Pilisuk and Jennifer Achord Rountree. *Who Benefits From Global Violence and War Uncovering a Destructive System.* Westport, CT: Praeger Security International, 2008. Print. P 86
[85] "Colombia's Cano Limon oil pipeline halted by bomb attack." *Reuters.*
[86] Marc Pilisuk and Jennifer Achord Rountree. P 84
[87] "Gore Attacked Over Ties to Occidental Oil for Environmental and Human Rights Violations." *Democracy Now!*
[88] Bill Mesler. "Al Gore: The Other Oil Candidate." *CorpWatch.*

[89] Ibid.
"Gore Attacked Over Ties to Occidental Oil for Environmental and Human Rights Violations."
Alexander Cockburn and Jeffrey St. Clair. *Al Gore: A User's Manual.* New York: Verso 2000, 2000 Print. P 230
Michael Savage. *The Savage Nation: Saving America from the Liberal Assault on our Borders, Language, and Culture.* Nashville: Thomas Nelson Publishers, 2002. Print. P 196
[90] "Chiquita accused of funding Colombia terrorists." *Associated Press.*
[91] Ibid.
[92] Steven Cohen. "How Chiquita Bananas Undermined The Global War On Terror." *Think Progress.*
[93] "Chiquita accused of funding Colombia terrorists." *Associated Press.*
[94] Ibid.
[95] Department of Justice press release March 19, 2007. "Chiquita Brands International Pleads Guilty to Making Payments to a Designated Terrorist Organization And Agrees to Pay $25 Million Fine."
[96] Charlie Cray. "Banana Land and the Corporate Death Squad Scandals." *Huffington Post.*
[97] Michael Evans. "The Chiquita Papers." *National Security Archive.*
[98] Lawrence Hurley. "U.S. top court rejects Colombian Chiquita human rights suit." *Reuters.*
[99] Juan Forero. "Colombia May Seek Chiquita Extraditions." *Washington Post.*
[100] "Bananas." *Main Justice.*
Heidi White, Lisa Stewart, Dean Krehmeyer, and Thomas Donaldson. "Chiquita and the Department of Justice." *Institute for Corporate Ethics.*
[101] Mark Bowden. *Killing Pablo: The Hunt for the World's Greatest Outlaw.* New York: Atlantic Monthly Press, 2001. Print.
[102] "Narco of the Month: September 2000: Carlos Castaño-Gil." *Narco News.*
[103] Peter Dale Scott. P 72
[104] George W. Bush's "Declaration of War on terror." Address to Congress on September 20, 2001.
[105] Robin Kirk. *More Terrible than Death: Massacres, Drugs, and America's War in Colombia.* New York: Public Affairs, 2003. Print. P 150
[106] Charles Parkinson. "Colombian Judge Orders Investigation into Uribe's Paramilitary Ties." *InSight Crime.*
[107] Michael Norby and Brian Fitzpatrick. "The Horrific Costs of the US-Colombia Trade Agreement." *The Nation.*
[108] Nick Miroff. "Colombian army killed civilians to fake battlefield success, rights group says." *Washington Post.*
[109] Michael Evans. "'Body count mentalities' Colombia's 'False Positives' Scandal, Declassified." *National Security Archive.*

[110] Nick Miroff. "The staggering toll of Colombia's war with FARC rebels, explained in numbers."
[111] Chris Arsenault. "Colombia: Refugees in their own country." *Al Jazeera*.
[112] Marianne Moor and Joris van de Sandt. "The Dark Side of Coal: Paramilitary Violence in the Mining Region of Cesar, Colombia." *Pax for Peace*.
[113] Ignacio Gómez G. "Colombia's black-market coltan tied to drug traffickers, paramilitaries." *Center for Public Integrity*.
[114] Tom Feiling. *Cocaine Nation: How the White Trade Took Over the World*. New York: Pegasus Books, 2010. Print. P 192
[115] "The Crisis In Buenaventura: Disappearances, Dismemberments, and Displacement in Colombia's Main Pacific Port." *Human Rights Watch*.
[116] "Colombian Port City Faces Plague of Violence." *Wall Street Journal*.

Chapter 11

[1] Keila Szpaller. "Police to withdraw grant application citing Rainbows as 'hazard." *Missoulian*.
Andrew Becker and G.W. Schulz. "Local Cops Ready for War With Homeland Security-Funded Military Weapons." *Daily Beast*.
[2] David Burnham. *Above the Law: Secret Deals, Political Fixes, and Other Misadventures of the U.S. Department of Justice*. New York: Scribner Publishing, 1996. Print. P 167
[3] Brad Heath. "U.S. secretly tracked billions of calls for decades." *USA Today*.
[4] June 3, 2015 Amendment to the Commerce, Justice and Science (CJS) Appropriations bill.
[5] Brian Ross. "CIA Didn't Share Info About 9/11 Hijackers." *ABC News*.
[6] Jeff Stein. "The Inside Information That Could Have Stopped 9/11." *Newsweek*.
[7] "Investigative Report Criticizes Counterterrorism Reporting, Waste at State & Local Intelligence Fusion Centers." Homeland Security and Government Affairs Permanent Subcommittee On Investigations.
[8] Beau Hodai. "Dissent or Terror: How the Nation's Counter Terrorism Apparatus, in Partnership with Corporate America, Turned on Occupy Wall Street." *Center for Media and Democracy*.
[9] "Why Did FBI Monitor Occupy Houston, and Then Hide Sniper Plot Against Protest Leaders?" *Democracy Now!*
[10] Mara Verheyden-Hilliard. "Exposed: FBI Surveillance of School of the Americas Watch." *Partnership for Civil Justice Fund*.
[11] Ibid.
[12] Richard A. Serrano. "FBI improperly investigates activists, Justice Department review finds." *Los Angeles Times*.

[13] Will Potter. "The shocking move to criminalize nonviolent protest." *TED Talks.*

[14] "Exclusive: "Eco-Terrorist" Freed 10 Years Early After Feds Withhold Evidence on Informant's Role." *Democracy Now!*

[15] Michael Isikoff. "Unaware of Tsarnaev warnings, Boston counterterror unit tracked protestors." *NBC News.*
Ralph Ellis. "Lawyers say FBI tried to recruit brother of Boston Marathon bombing suspect." *CNN.*

[16] *Unconstitutional: The War on Our Civil Liberties*. Dir. Nonny de la Peña. Disinformation Co., 2004. DVD.

[17] Wiretap Report 2013. Administrative Office of the U.S. Courts.

[18] *Unconstitutional: The War on Our Civil Liberties.*

[19] "Report of the Director of the Administrative Office of the United States Courts on Applications for Delayed-Notice Search Warrants and Extentions." <http://big.assets.huffingtonpost.com/SneakAndPeakReport.pdf>

[20] *Unconstitutional: The War on Our Civil Liberties.*

[21] Rick Young. "What Happens in Vegas..." *PBS Frontline.*

[22] Timothy B. Lee. "The Switchboard: NSA discussed using porn habits to discredit Muslim radicals." *Washington Post.*
James Risen. "Ex-Spy Alleges Bush White House Sought to Discredit Critic." *New York Times.*

[23] John Shiffman and Kristina Cooke. "Exclusive: U.S. directs agents to cover up program used to investigate Americans." *Reuters.*

[24] Ibid.

[25] David Ingram and John Shiffman. "U.S. defense lawyers seek to access to DEA hidden intelligence evidence." *Reuters.*

[26] John Shiffman and Kristina Cooke. "Exclusive: U.S. directs agents to cover up program used to investigate Americans."

[27] Senate Floor Statement of Senator Barack Obama on December 15, 2005

[28] R. Jeffrey Smith. "FBI Violations May Number 3,000, Official Says." *Washington Post.*

[29] Pete Kasperowicz. "White House wants longer extension of Patriot Act than House Republicans." *The Hill.*
Steven Gray. "Taking Professor Obama's Class." *Time.*

[30] James Bamford. *The Shadow Factory: The Ultra-Secret NSA from 9/11 to the Eavesdropping on America*. New York: Random House, 2008. Print. P 319

[31] Jeff Stein. "Of 2,000 civil liberties complaints, Justice Dept. investigates one." *Washington Post.*

[32] Devlin Barrett. "U.S. Spies on Millions of Drivers." *Wall Street Journal.*

[33] Rockefeller Commission Report. Chapter 11. Special Operations Group – "Operation CHAOS"

[34] Tom Charles Huston testimony before the Senate Select Committee to Study Governmental Operations with Respect to Intelligence Activities. September 23, 1975.
[35] Kade Crockford. "Former CIA director: In order to spy on domestic dissidents, just call them terrorists." *ACLU*.
[36] Ed Pilkington. "Declassified NSA files show agency spied on Muhammad Ali and MLK." *The Guardian*.
[37] Ward Churchill and Jim Wall. *The COINTELPRO Papers: Documents From the FBI's Secret Wars Against Dissent in the United States*. 2nd ed. Cambridge, MA: South End Press, 2002. Print.
[38] "Bill Moyers Journal: The Church Committee and FISA." *PBS*.
[39] James Bamford. P 113.
[40] James Risen and Eric Lichtblau. "Bush Let U.S. Spy on Callers Without Courts." *New York Times*.
[41] James Bamford. P 115
[42] David G. Savage. "U.S. Supreme Court ends suit against telecom firms for aiding NSA." *Los Angeles Times*.
[43] Jake Tapper. "Obama's FISA Shift." *ABC News*.
[44] Ibid.
[45] "Press Release 2004-148: SEC Charges Qwest Communications International Inc. with Multi-Faceted Accounting and Reporting Fraud." *U.S. Securities and Exchange Commission*.
[46] James Bamford. P 173
[47] Ibid.
[48] Craig Timberg and Barton Gellman. "NSA paying U.S. companies for access to communications networks." *Washington Post*.
[49] Daniel Strauss. "NSA revelations only the 'tip of the iceberg,' says Dem lawmaker." *The Hill*.
[50] "NSA spied on 'World of Warcraft,' other online games, leaked documents show." *Fox News*.
[51] Real Time with Bill Maher: Ep 285 June 7, 2013.
[52] "Former NSA Head Hayden on Snowden's Impact: "This Is It?"" *Wall Street Journal*.
[53] Faith Braverman. "Former FBI Agent Mike German Talks About the NSA." *Daily Caller*.
[54] Eric Lichtblau. "Another F.B.I. Employee Blows Whistle on Agency." *New York Times*.
[55] Rachel Weiner. "Tom Ridge: I Was Pressured To Raise Terror Alert To Help Bush Win." *Huffington Post*.
[56] Trevor Aaronson. *The Terror Factory: Inside the FBI's Manufactured War on Terrorism*. IG Publishing, 2013. Print. P 15
[57] "The Detroit Sleeper Cell That Wasn't. Retro Report." *New York Times*.

[58] "Informants." *Al Jazeera*.
David Boeri. "At Hearing, Informant Under Fire In Ashland Terror Plot Case." *WBUR Boston*.
[59] Trevor Aaronson. *The Terror Factory: Inside the FBI's Manufactured War on Terrorism*.
[60] Bob Norman. "Liberty City Seven Trial Travesty." *Miami New Times*.
[61] Trevor Aaronson. P 85
[62] Scott Horton. *Lords of Secrecy*. New York: Nation Books, 2015. Print. P 135. "American Experience: The Presidents: Nixon." *PBS*. Video.
[63] John Kiriakou. "Obama's abuse of the Espionage Act is modern-day McCarthyism." *The Guardian*.
[64] "Why I Was Targeted by the CIA." *Real News Network*.
[65] Adam Goldman and Sari Horwitz. "Petraeus reaches deal to plead guilty to misdemeanor; likely won't face prison." *Washington Post*.
[66] Jason Leopold. "FBI continues to investigate Hastings for 'controversial reporting.'" *Al Jazeera*.
[67] "Interview with William Binney." *PBS Frontline*.
[68] Ibid.
[69] "The Espionage Act: Why Tom Drake Was Indicted." *CBS News*.
[70] "Interview with J. Kirk Weibe." *PBS Frontline*.
[71] "Interview with William Binney." *PBS Frontline*.
[72] "Part 2: Former NSA Employee Thomas Drake and Jesselyn Radack on Obama Admin. Whistleblower Crackdown." *Democracy Now!*
[73] "Interview with Edward Loomis." *PBS Frontline*.
[74] "NSA is 'bamboozling' lawmakers to gain access to Americans' private records – agency veteran." *RT.com*
[75] "United States of Secrets." *PBS*.
[76] Ibid.
[77] "The Espionage Act: Why Tom Drake Was Indicted." *CBS News*.
[78] David Welna. "Before Snowden: The Whistleblowers Who Tried To Lift The Veil." *NPR*.
[79] Adam Zagorin. "Top NSA Watchdog Who Insisted Snowden Should Have Come to Him Receives Termination Notice for Retaliating Against a Whistleblower." *Project on Government Oversight (POGO)*.
[80] "Why I Decided to Blow the Whistle on the NSA." *Real News*.
[81] Ibid.
[82] "NSA Blackmailing Obama? Interview with Russ Tice." *RT.com*.
[83] "Podcast # 112: NSA Whistleblower Goes on Record – Reveals New Information & Names Culprits!" *BoilingFrogsPost.com*.
[84] Matthew DeLuca. "Obama: 'Nobody is listening to your telephone calls." *NBC News*.
[85] Lee Ferran. "Ex-NSA Chief: 'We Kill People Based on Metadata." *ABC News*.

[86] "NSA Blackmailing Obama? Interview with Russ Tice." *RT.com*.
[87] HBO's Real Time with Bill Maher: Episode 300. November 8, 2013
[88] "Is the NSA's massive new spy center watching you?" *Fox News*.
[89] "NSA is 'bamboozling' lawmakers to gain access to Americans' private records – agency veteran." *RT.com*.
[90] "Feds end prosecution of Barry Bonds without conviction." *Associated Press*.
[91] "James Clapper: I Gave 'Least Untruthful' Answer Possible On NSA Surveillance (VIDEO)." *Huffington Post*.
[92] Shaun Waterman. "NSA chief's admission of misleading numbers adds to Obama administration blunders." *Washington Times*.
[93] Unopposed Motion of Senator Ron Wyden, Senator Mark Udall & Senator Martin Heinrich to file a brief amicus curiae in support of plaintiffs <https://www.eff.org/files/2013/11/18/senatorsamicibrief.pdf>
[94] "From 9/11 to Mass Surveillance, The Man Who Knew Too Much - Thomas Drake on RAI (2/5)." *The Real News*.
[95] Dana Priest and William M. Arkin. "A hidden world, growing beyond control." *Washington Post*.
[96] "Report: 4.2 million hold security clearances." *Associated Press*.
[97] "Ex-Snoop Confirms Echelon Network." *CBS News*.
[98] "Terror Watch Lister Counter: A Million Plus." *ACLU*. Matthew Barakat. "Terrorist Database Continues to Grow at Rapid Rate." *Associated Press*.
[99] "Formal calls for probe into reporter's name on no-fly list." *CNN*.
[100] "Spying on the Home Front." *PBS Frontline*.
[101] Harry Truman Address at the Direction of the New Washington Headquarters of the American Legion. August 14, 1951. *Truman Library*.

Chapter 12

[1] "'New York Times' Correspondent Stephen Kinzer." *NPR*. Fresh Air segment.
[2] Stephen Kinzer. *Overthrow: America's Century of Regime Change from Hawaii to Iraq*. New York: Henry Holt and Company, 2006. Print. P 124-127
[3] Stephen Kinzer. *All the Shah's Men: An American Coup and the Roots of Middle East Terror*. New York: John Wiley & Sons, 2008. Print. P 3
[4] "CIA-assisted coup overthrows government of Iran." *History.com*
[5] Frank Smith. "Colombia's Blowback." *Transnational Institute*.
[6] Peter Dale Scott. *Drugs, Oil, and War*. Oxford: Rowan & Littlefield Publishers, 2003. Print. P 186
[7] Douglas Valentine. *The Strength of the Wolf: The Secret History of America's War on Drugs*. London: Verso, 2004. Print.

[8] Jonathan Marshall. *Drug Control Policy: Essays in Historical and Comparative Perspective*. Ed. William O. Walker III. University Park, PA: Pennsylvania State University Press, 1992. Print. P 94

[9] "Chiang Kai-shek." *History.com*.

[10] Jonathan Marshall. *Drug Control Policy: Essays in Historical and Comparative Perspective*. Ed. William O. Walker III. P 94

[11] Douglas Valentine. *The Strength of the Wolf: The Secret History of America's War on Drugs*.

[12] Frank Dikötter. *Mao's Great Famine: The History of China's Most Devastating Catastrophe, 1958-1962*. New York: Walker & Co, 2010. Print.

[13] Tim Newark. *The Mafia at War: The Shocking True Story of America's Wartime Pact with Organized Crime*. New York: Skyhorse Publishing, 2012. Print. P 82

[14] Alexander Cockburn and Jeffrey St. Clair. *Whiteout: The CIA, Drugs, and the Press*. London: Verso, 1998. Print. P 120

[15] Rodney Campbell. *The Luciano Project: The Secret Wartime Collaboration of the Mafia and the U.S. Navy*. New York: McGraw-Hill, 1977. Print. P 80

[16] Alexander Cockburn and Jeffrey St. Clair. P 128
Rodney Campbell. P 132, 97, 175, 180
John Tagliabue. "Villalba Journal; How Don Calo (and Patton) Won the War in Sicily." *New York Times*.

[17] T.J. English. *Havana Nocturne: How the Mob Owned Cuba...And then Lost It to the Revolution*. United Kingdom: William Morrow, 2007. Print. P 5
Alexander Cockburn and Jeffrey St. Clair. P 133, 134

[18] Alexander Cockburn and Jeffrey St. Clair. P 130

[19] Selwyn Raab. *Five Families: The Rise, Decline, and Resurgence of America's Most Powerful Mafia Empires*. New York: St. Martin's Press, 2005. Print. P 81-82

[20] Alfred McCoy. *The Politics of Heroin in Southeast Asia*. New York: Harper & Row, 1972. Print. P 22

[21] Alfred McCoy. *The Politics of Heroin in Southeast Asia*. P 31

[22] Alexander Cockburn and Jeffrey St. Clair. P 140

[23] Alexander Cockburn and Jeffrey St. Clair. P 137

[24] David J. Krajicek. "Justice Story: How 'French Connection' heroin went missing from NYPD Property Clerk's Office." *New York Daily News*.

[25] Alfred McCoy. *The Politics of Heroin in Southeast Asia*. P 126

[26] Uli Schmetzer. "Drugs Drying Up In Thai Enclave." *Chicago Tribune*.

[27] Alfred McCoy. *The Politics of Heroin in Southeast Asia*. P 127

[28] "A Tangled Web: A History of CIA Complicity in Drug International Trafficking." *Institute for Policy Studies*. Intelligence Authorization Act for Fiscal Year 1999 (House of Representatives - May 07, 1998).

[29] Alfred McCoy. *The Politics of Heroin: CIA Complicity in the Global Drug Trade.* Chicago: Lawrence Hill Books, 2003. Print. P 162
[30] Alexander Cockburn and Jeffrey St. Clair. P 245
[31] "A Tangled Web: A History of CIA Complicity in Drug International Trafficking." *Institute for Policy Studies.* Intelligence Authorization Act for Fiscal Year 1999 (House of Representatives - May 07, 1998).
[32] Alexander Cockburn and Jeffrey St. Clair. P 245
[33] Alfred McCoy. *The Politics of Heroin in Southeast Asia.* P 350
[34] Joseph Westermeyer. *Poppies, Pipes, and People: Opium and Its Use in Laos.* Berkeley: University of California Press, 1983. Print. P 272
[35] Alexander Cockburn and Jeffrey St. Clair. P 246
[36] Dan Russell. *Drug War: Covert Money, Power & Policy.* Camden, NY: Kalyx.com, 2000. Print. P 342
[37] Ibid.
[38] Dan Russell. P 334
[39] Alfred McCoy. *The Politics of Heroin in Southeast Asia.* P 248
[40] Alexander Cockburn and Jeffrey St. Clair. P 238
[41] Ibid.
[42] Peter Brush. "Higher and Higher: American Drug Use in Vietnam." *Vietnam Magazine.* Vol.15, No. 4, December 2002.
[43] "America's Book of Secrets." Season 2 Episode 8. *History Channel.*
[44] Alfred McCoy. *The Politics of Heroin: CIA Complicity in the Global Drug Trade.* P 475
[45] Peter Dale Scott. P 27
[46] Alexander Cockburn and Jeffrey St. Clair. *Imperial Crusades: Iraq, Afghanistan, and Yugoslavia.* New York: Verso, 2004. Print. P 142
[47] Alexander Cockburn and Jeffrey St. Clair. P 260
[48] Alexander Cockburn and Jeffrey St. Clair. P 266
[49] Stephen Kinzer. P 267
[50] Russell S. Bowen. *Immaculate Deception: The Bush Crime Family Exposed.* Carson City, NV: America West Publishers, 1991. Print. P 109
[51] < http://www.jimmycarterlibrary.gov/library/oralhistory/clohproject/India.pdf>
[52] Ibid.
[53] Dr. Ahmad Shayeq Qassem. *Afghanistan's Political Stability: A Dream Unrealised.* Burlington, VT: Ashgate Publishing Company, 2009. Print. P 83
[54] Stephen Kinzer. P 267
[55] Russell S. Bowen. P 108
[56] William L. Darcy. *The Politics of Cocaine: How U.S. Foreign Policy Has Created a Thriving Drug Industry in Central and South America.* Chicago: Lawrence Hill Books, 2010. Print. P 7

[57] Dominic Streatfeild. *Cocaine: An Unauthorized Biography*. New York: Thomas Dunne, 2002. Print. 245
[58] "Notorious Graduates from Bolivia." *SOA Watch.*
"Roberto Suarez Gomez, Bolivia's King of Cocaine, died on July 20th, aged 68." *The Economist.*
[59] Michael Levine and Laura Kavanau-Levine. *The Big White Lie: The CIA and the Cocaine/Crack Epidemic: An Undercover Odyssey*. New York: Thunder's Mouth Press, 1993. Print. P 34
[60] William L. Darcy. P 76
[61] Michael Levine and Laura Kavanau-Levine. P 34
[62] Michael Levine and Laura Kavanau-Levine. P 88-176
[63] Alexander Cockburn and Jeffrey St. Clair. P 176
[64] Michael Levine and Laura Kavanau-Levine. P 60
[65] Allan A. Ryan Jr. "Klaus Barbie and the United States Government: A Report to the Attorney General of the United States." August 1983.
[66] Annie Jacobsen. *Operation Paperclip: The Secret Intelligence Program that Brought Nazi Scientists to America.*
[67] Dominic Streatfeild. P 387
[68] Alexander Cockburn and Jeffrey St. Clair. P 183
[69] William L. Darcy. P 27
[70] William L. Darcy. P 27
[71] Michael Levine and Laura Kavanau-Levine. P 458
[72] Stephen Kinzer. P 245
[73] Alexander Cockburn and Jeffrey St. Clair. P 289
[74] Drugs, Law Enforcement and Foreign Policy: December 1988 Report By the Subcommittee on Terrorism, Narcotics, and International Operations of the U.S. Senate Committee on Foreign Relations.
[75] Alexander Cockburn and Jeffrey St. Clair. P 286
[76] Seymour Hersh. "PANAMA STRONGMAN SAID TO TRADE IN DRUGS, ARMS, AND ILLICIT MONEY." *New York Times.*
[77] Stephen Kinzer. P 247
[78] "Oliver North e-mail to John Poindexter August 23, 1986." *National Security Archive.*
[79] "Oliver North's diary entry August 24, 1986." *National Security Archive.*
[80] Peter Dale Scott and Jonathan Marshall. *Cocaine Politics: Drugs, Armies, and the CIA in Central America*. Berkeley, CA: University of California Press, 1991. Print. P 70
[81] William L. Darcy. P 146
[82] Drugs, Law Enforcement and Foreign Policy: December 1988 Report By the Subcommittee on Terrorism, Narcotics, and International Operations of the U.S. Senate Committee on Foreign Relations.

⁸³ Benjamin Runkle. *Wanted Dead or Alive: Manhunts From Geronimo to Bin Laden.* New York: Palgrave Macmillan, 2011. Print. P 109
⁸⁴ Stephen Kinzer. P 245
⁸⁵ Manuel Noriega and Peter Eisner. *America's Prisoner: The Memoirs of Manuel Noriega.* New York: Random House, 1997. Print. P 115, 190
⁸⁶ William L. Darcy. P 150
⁸⁷ *The Panama Deception.* Dir. Barbara Trent. Writer. David Kasper. 1992. VHS. "Human Rights in Post-Invasion Panama: Justice Delayed is Justice Denied." *Human Rights Watch.*
⁸⁸ Jonathan Marshall. "Unjust Aftermath: Post-Noriega Panama." *Consortium News.*
⁸⁹ Stephen Labaton. "Panama Is Resisting U.S. Pressure Alter 'Inadequate' Banking Laws." *New York Times.*
⁹⁰ Ibid.
⁹¹ William L. Darcy. P 149
⁹² Drugs, Law Enforcement and Foreign Policy: December 1988 Report By the Subcommittee on Terrorism, Narcotics, and International Operations of the U.S. Senate Committee on Foreign Relations.
⁹³ Peter Kornbluh. "'Frogman Case' helped spark CIA cover-up Agency feared 'explosive' publicity." *Baltimore Sun.*
⁹⁴ Ibid.
⁹⁵ Robert Parry and Brian Berger. "Investigators: Rebels dealing drugs to finance war." *Associated Press.*
⁹⁶ Gary Webb. *Dark Alliance: The CIA, the Contras, and the Crack Cocaine Explosion.* New York: Seven Stories Press, 1998. Print. P 11, 210
⁹⁷ Alexander Cockburn and Jeffrey St. Clair. P 318-329
⁹⁸ William LeoGrande. *Our Own Backyard: The United States in Central America, 1977-1992.* Chapel Hill: University of North Carolina Press, 2000. Print. P 449
⁹⁹ Alexander Cockburn and Jeffrey St. Clair. P 318
¹⁰⁰ Dan Russell. P 413
¹⁰¹ Peter Dale Scott and Jonathan Marshall. P 99
¹⁰² Jon Roberts and Evan Wright. *American Desperado: My Life-from Mafia Soldier to Cocaine Cowboy to Secret Government Asset.* New York: Broadway Paperbacks, 2011. Print. P 498
¹⁰³ "Interview: Fernando Arenas." *PBS Frontline.*
¹⁰⁴ "Nicaragua's Drug Connection Exposed as Hoax." *Fairness & Accuracy in Reporting.*
¹⁰⁵ Jonathan Kwitney. "Dope Story: Doubts Rise on Report Reagan Cited in Tying Sandinistas to Cocaine." *Wall Street Journal.*
¹⁰⁶ Ibid.
¹⁰⁷ Robert Parry and Peter Kornbluh. "Reagan's Pro-Contra Propaganda Machine." *Washington Post.*

[108] Robert Parry. *Fooling America: How Washington Insiders Twist the Truth and Manufacture the Conventional Wisdom.* New York: William Morrow and Company, 1992. Print. P 211

[109] Robert Parry. *Fooling America: How Washington Insiders Twist the Truth and Manufacture the Conventional Wisdom.* P 94

[110] "The Contras, Cocaine, and Covert Operations." *National Security Archive.*

[111] Gary Webb. P 265

[112] Terry Reed and John Cummings. *Compromised: Clinton, Bush, and the CIA.* New York: S.P.I. Books, 1994. Print. P 168

[113] Jon Roberts and Evan Wright. P 508

[114] Gary Webb. P 11

[115] "Ollie North and Drugs." *Powderburns.*

[116] Peter Kornbluh. "The Oliver North File: His Diaries, E-Mail, and Memos on the Kerry Report, Contras and Drugs." *National Security Archive.*

[117] Ibid.

[118] William L. Darcy. P 126

[119] Peter Dale Scott and Jonathan Marshall. P 13

[120] Clara Nieto. *Masters of War: Latin America and U.S. Aggression From the Cuban Revolution Through the Clinton Years.* New York: Seven Stories Press, 2003. Print. P 317

[121] Drugs, Law Enforcement and Foreign Policy: December 1988 Report By the Subcommittee on Terrorism, Narcotics, and International Operations of the U.S. Senate Committee on Foreign Relations.

[122] "Censored News: Oliver North & Company Banned From Costa Rica." *Fairness & Accuracy in Reporting.*

[123] Robert Parry. "John Hull's Great Escape." *Consortium News.*

[124] "The Contras, Cocaine, and Covert Operations." *National Security Archive.*

[125] Drugs, Law Enforcement and Foreign Policy: December 1988 Report By the Subcommittee on Terrorism, Narcotics, and International Operations of the U.S. Senate Committee on Foreign Relations.

[126] Justine Gerety. "Accountant Sentenced For Money Laundering." *Sun Sentinel.*

[127] Andrew Cockburn and Leslie Cockburn. "Guns, Drugs, and the CIA." *PBS.*

[128] Drugs, Law Enforcement and Foreign Policy: December 1988 Report By the Subcommittee on Terrorism, Narcotics, and International Operations of the U.S. Senate Committee on Foreign Relations.

[129] Peter Kornbluh. "The Oliver North File: His Diaries, E-Mail, and Memos on the Kerry Report, Contras and Drugs." *National Security Archive.*

[130] Ibid.

[131] Steve Stecklow. "Pilot Held as Drug Suspect Got U.S. Contra-aid Contract." *Philadelphia Inquirer.*

[132] Drugs, Law Enforcement and Foreign Policy: December 1988 Report By the Subcommittee on Terrorism, Narcotics, and International Operations of the U.S. Senate Committee on Foreign Relations.
[133] Lorraine Adams. "North Didn't Relay Drug Tips: DEA Says It Finds No Evidence Reagan Aide Talked To Agency." *Washington Post.*
[134] Robert Parry. "Gary Webb's Enduring Legacy." *Consortium News.*
[135] Drugs, Law Enforcement and Foreign Policy: December 1988 Report By the Subcommittee on Terrorism, Narcotics, and International Operations of the U.S. Senate Committee on Foreign Relations.
[136] Steven Dudley and Michael Lohmuller. "Docs Reveal CIA-Guadalajara Link, Not Conspiracy." *InSight Crime.*
[137] Steven Dudley. "Honduras Elites and Organized Crime: Juan Ramón Matta Ballesteros." *InSight Crime.*
[138] Peter Dale Scott and Jonathan Marshall. P 54
[139] Ioan Grillo. *El Narco: Inside Mexico's Criminal Insurgency*. New York: Bloomsbury Press, 2011. Print. P 71
[140] John McPhaul. "Reagan administration, CIA complicit in DEA agent's murder, say former insiders." *Tico Times.*
[141] Michael Levine. *Abuse Your Illusions: The Disinformation Guide to Media Mirages and Establishment Lies*. Ed. Russ Kick. New York: The Disinformation Company, 2003. Print. P 31
[142] Bill Conroy. "Release of DEA Agent Kiki Camarena's 'Murderer' Is Game Changer for CIA." *Narco News.*
[143] William La Jeunesse and Lee Ross. "US intelligence assets in Mexico reportedly tied to murdered DEA agent." *FOX News.*
[144] Robert O'Dowd and Tim King. "Former CIA Pilot Tells of Guns and Drugs Shipments." *Salem News.*
[145] Nick Schou. "Cocaine Airways." *OC Weekly.*
[146] "Ollie North and Drugs." *Powderburns.*
[147] Ibid.
[148] Michael Ratner and Michael Steven Smith. *Who Killed Che?: How the CIA Got Away with Murder*. New York and London. OR Books, 2011. Print.
[149] Alexander Cockburn and Jeffrey St. Clair. P 294
[150] Peter Kornbluh. "Luis Posada Carriles: The Declassified Record." *National Security Archive.*
[151] Sarah Wagner. "Ex-Venezuela Soldier Says CIA Tried to Bribe Guards for Cuban Terrorist's Escape." *Venezuela Analysis.*
[152] Chris Arsenault. "Mexican official: CIA 'manages' drug trade." *Al Jazeera.*

[1] Terry Reed and John Cummings. *Compromised: Clinton, Bush, and the CIA.* New York: S.P.I. Books, 1994. Print.
[2] "The Mena Connection." Dir. Laura Phillips. Peoples Network. 1995. VHS.
[3] Rodney Stitch. *Drugging America: A Trojan Horse.* Alamo, CA: Silverpeak Enterprises, 2008. Print.
[4] *The Clinton Chronicle: An Investigation into the Alleged Criminal Activities of Bill Clinton.* Dir. Patrick Matrisciana. Citizen's Video Press, 1994. VHS.
[5] Rep. Dan Burton Calling for Expanded Congressional Hearings on June 30, 1994.
[6] Gary Webb. *Dark Alliance: The CIA, the Contras, and the Crack Cocaine Explosion.* P 118
[7] Rep. Dan Burton's Statement on Whitewater and Drug-Related Activities on June 9, 1994
[8] *The Clinton Chronicle: An Investigation into the Alleged Criminal Activities of Bill Clinton.*
[9] Testimony of William Duncan: Hearing before the Commerce, Consumer, and Monetary Affairs Subcommittee of the Committee on Government Operations, House of Representatives, One Hundred Second Congress, First Session, July 24, 1991.
[10] Rodney Stitch. *Defrauding America: 4th Ed. Vol. One: Encyclopedia of Secret Operations by the CIA, DEA, Other Government Offices, and White House Politicians.* Alamo, CA: Silverpeak Enterprises, 2008. Print. P 474-475
[11] Gary Webb. *Dark Alliance: The CIA, the Contras, and the Crack Cocaine Explosion.*
[12] "THE CIA-Contra-Crack Cocaine Controversy: A Review Of The Justice Department's Investigations And Prosecutions." Department of Justice Inspector General's Report.
[13] Gary Webb. "Cocaine pipeline financed rebels." *San Jose Mercury News.* Nick Schou. *Kill the Messenger: How the CIA's Crack-Cocaine Controversy Destroyed Journalist Gary Webb.* New York: Nation Books, 2006. Print P 99
[14] Alexander Cockburn and Jeffrey St. Clair. *Whiteout: The CIA, Drugs, and the Press.* London: Verso, 1998. Print. P 46
[15] Robert Parry. "The Warning in Gary Webb's Death." *Consortium News.*
[16] Ibid.
[17] "Investigative Reporter Gary Webb Who Linked CIA to Crack Sales Found Dead of Apparent Suicide." *Democracy Now!*
[18] Dylan Byers. "Newsweek's Tina Brown to Howard Kurtz: 'Didn't I fire you for serial inaccuracy?'" *Politico.*
[19] "Time Suppresses Contra Drug Story." *Fairness in Reporting & Accuracy.*
[20] <http://www.foia.cia.gov/sites/default/files/DOC_0001372115.pdf>
[21] Linda Steiner. *Encyclopedia of American Journalism.* Ed. Stephen L. Vaughn. New York: Taylor & Francis, 2008. Print. P 201

[22] Nick Schou. P 132
[23] Ryan Grim. *This is Your Country on Drugs: The Secret History of Getting High in America.* Hoboken, NJ: John Wiley & Sons, 2009. Print. P 187
[24] Carl Bernstein. "The CIA and the Media." *Rolling Stone.* Oct. 20, 1977.
[25] CIA memorandum for Director Robert Gates from the Task Force on Greater CIA Openness. December 20, 1991. PAO 91-0586.
[26] Ken Silverstein. "The CIA's Mop-Up Man: L.A. Times Reporter Cleared Stories With Agency Before Publication." *The Intercept.*
[27] Glenn Greenwald. "Correspondence and collusion between the New York Times and the CIA." *The Guardian.*
[28] Nick Schou. P 116
[29] "CIA Drug Trafficking Town Hall Meeting Nov. 15, 1996." *C-SPAN.*
[30] Report of Investigation Concerning Allegations of Connections Between CIA and The Contras in Cocaine Trafficking to the United States (96-0143-IG). Central Intelligence Agency Office of Inspector General Investigations Staff. "Overview: Report of Investigation."
[31] Michael C. Ruppert. *Crossing the Rubicon: The Decline of the American Empire at the End of the Age of Oil.* Canada: New Society Publishers, 2004. Print. P 66
[32] Robert Parry. "The Warning in Gary Webb's Death."
Nick Schou. P 221
[33] Robert Parry. "Contra Narco-Terrorists." *Consortium News.*
[34] Nick Schou. P 183
[35] "Interview Frederick Hitz." *PBS Frontline.*
Douglas Valentine. *The Strength of the Pack: The Personalities, Politics and Espionage Intrigues that Shaped the DEA.* Walterville, OR: Trine Day, 2009. Print. P 319
[36] Tim Weiner. "Venezuelan General Indicted in C.I.A. Scheme." *New York Times.*
[37] Ibid.
[38] "The CIA's Cocaine." *60 Minutes.*
Bill Orlove. "Accused Delray trafficker also an informant." *Palm Beach Post.*
ABC News – Primetime. July 8, 1998
[39] "The CIA's Cocaine." *60 Minutes.*
[40] Tim Weiner. "C.I.A. Formed Haitian Unit Later Tied To Narcotics Trade." *New York Times.*
[41] "Haiti and the School of the Assassins." *SOA Watch.*
[42] Kenneth Freed. "U.S., Haiti Keep Up Ties on Drug Flow: Caribbean: Junta officers have been accused of masterminding the island nation's drug trade. But embassy official says providing them with information is necessary to try to stop trafficking." *Los Angeles Times.*

[43] "A Leader of Former Haitian Junta Is Charged With Smuggling Tons of Drugs to U.S." *New York Times*.
[44] Tim Weiner. "Haitian Ex-Paramilitary Leader Confirms C.I.A. Relationship." *New York Times*.
[45] David Grann. "Giving "The Devil" His Due." *The Atlantic*.
[46] Scott Shifrel. "Haitian paramilitary leader Emmanuel Constant convicted of fraud." *New York Daily News*.
[47] William Yardley. "Rubén Zuno Arce, Guilty in Drug Killing, Dies at 82." *New York Times*.
[48] Peter Dale Scott and Jonathan Marshall. *Cocaine Politics: Drugs, Armies, and the CIA in Central America*. Berkeley, CA: University of California Press, 1991. Print. P 41
[49] Alexander Cockburn and Jeffrey St. Claire. P 349
[50] William La Jeunesse and Lee Ross. "US intelligence assets in Mexico reportedly tied to murdered DEA agent." *FOX News*.
[51] Kate Doyle and Jesse Franzblau. "Archival Evidence of Mexico's Human Rights Crimes: The Case of Aleida Gallangos." *National Security Archive*.
[52] Alexander Cockburn and Jeffrey St. Claire. P 354-356
[53] Henry Weinstein. "Jury Hears Camarena Interrogation Tape: Court: The Spanish-language recording conveys the desperation of the kidnaped and slain DEA agent. A 10-foot-high translation was beamed onto the courtroom wall." *Los Angeles Times*.
[54] Charles Bowden. *Down by the River: Drugs, Money, Murder, and Family*. New York: Simon & Schuster, 2002. Print. P 147-149
[55] John McPhaul. "Reagan administration, CIA complicit in DEA agent's murder, say former insiders."
[56] Luis A. Marentes. "Was the CIA Behind 'Kiki' Camarena's Murder? Investigative Journalists and Congress Must Follow Up." *Huffington Post*.
[57] Jason McGahan. "How a Dogged L.A. DEA Agent Unraveled the CIA's Alleged Role in the Murder of Kiki Camarena." *LA Weekly*.
[58] Peter L. Bergen. *Holy War Inc.: Inside the Secret World of Osama Bin Laden*. New York: Touchstone, 2001. Print. P 73-74
"Afghanistan: Ghani, Hekmatyar sign peace deal." *Al Jazeera*.
[59] Azmat Khan. "Why Eradication Won't Solve Afghanistan's Poppy Problem." *PBS*.
[60] Alfred McCoy. *The Politics of Heroin: CIA Complicity in the Global Drug Trade*. P 518
Peter Dale Scott. *Drugs, Oil, and War*. Oxford: Rowan & Littlefield Publishers, 2003. Print. P 44
[61] Peter Dale Scott. P 44

[62] Steve Coll. *Ghost Wars: The Secret History of the CIA, Afghanistan, and Bin Laden From the Soviet Invasion to September 10, 2001.* New York: Penguin Press, 2004. Print. P 575
[63] Bob Woodward. *Bush at War.* New York: Simon & Schuster, 2002. Print. P 40
[64] Steve Coll. P 516
[65] Bob Woodward. P 155
[66] Alfred McCoy. *The Politics of Heroin: CIA Complicity in the Global Drug Trade.* P 520-525
[67] Ryan Harvey. "How Afghan Poppy Eradication Efforts Are Helping the World's Largest Heroin Dealers." *TruthOut.*
[68] Emma Graham-Harrison. "Opium farming in Afghanistan rising again, bleak UN report admits." *The Guardian.*
[69] Nick Schifrin. *ABC News* on May 23, 2010.
Geraldo Rivera. *Fox News* on April 16, 2010.
[70] Patrick Gallahue. "A worrying front in the war on drugs." *The Guardian.*
[71] Antonio Maria Costa. "The thriving drug trade: Afghanistan's battle with the opium poppy." *New York Times.*
[72] "Leaked Docs: Karzai Freed Connected Drug Dealers." *CBS News.*
[73] Christopher M. Blanchard. "Afghanistan: Narcotics and U.S. Policy." *Congressional Research Service.*
[74] David E. Kaplan and Aamir Latif. "A Stash to Beat All." *US News and World Report.*
[75] Graeme Smith. "Afghan officials in drug trade cut deals across enemy lines." *Globe and Mail.*
[76] Matthew Rosenberg. "Afghan Leader Confirms Cash Deliveries by CIA." *New York Times.*
[77] Mark Mazzetti. "C.I.A. Delivers Cash to Afghan Leader's Office." *New York Times.*
[78] Taimoor Shah and Azam Ahmed. "Afghan Says Force Backed by the CIA Beat Him." *New York Times.*
Dexter Filkins, Mark Mazzetti, and James Risen. "Brother of Afghan Leader Said to be Paid by C.I.A." *New York Times.*
Jeff Stein. "CIA hired Karzai brother before 9/11, Woodward says." *Washington Post.*
[79] Jonathan Steele and Jon Boone. "Wikileaks: Afghan vice-president 'landed in Dubai with $52 m in cash.'" *The Guardian.*
[80] Matthew Rosenberg. "Afghan Leader Confirms Cash Deliveries by CIA."
James Risen and Mark Landler. "Accused of Drug Ties, Afghan Official Worries U.S." *New York Times.*
[81] Benjamin Weiser. "Afghan Linked to Taliban Sentenced to Life in Drug Trafficking Case." *New York Times.*

[82] James Risen. "Propping Up a Drug Lord, Then Arresting Him." *New York Times.*
[83] Alfred McCoy. *The Politics of Heroin: CIA Complicity in the Global Drug Trade.* P 133

www.ingramcontent.com/pod-product-compliance
Lightning Source LLC
LaVergne TN
LVHW040612250326
834688LV00035B/525